PROMISE AND DELIVERANCE

S. G. DE GRAAF

PROMISE AND DELIVERANCE

VOLUME II

THE FAILURE OF ISRAEL'S THEOCRACY

Translated by H. Evan Runner and
Elisabeth Wichers Runner

PAIDEIA PRESS
St. Catharines, Ontario, Canada

First published in Dutch
as *Verbondsgeschiedenis,*
© J. H. Kok of Kampen.

ISBN 0-88815-006-7
Printed in the United States of America.

Table of Contents

JUDGES

SAMUEL AND SAUL

SAUL AND DAVID

DAVID

SOLOMON

EPHRAIM AGAINST JUDAH

JUDAH

CAPTIVITY

AFTER THE EXILE

Judges

1: The Earth Is the Lord's

Judges 1-5

Israel had been called to wipe out the Canaanites. The Lord had given the land of Canaan to Israel so that He alone would be served there. Thus Canaan stands for the entire earth: the Lord alone is to be served on the earth. To achieve this goal, the Lord calls His people to engage in unceasing spiritual warfare against anything and everything that opposes the honor of His name. For us today it would be just as sinful and disobedient to enter into a spiritual agreement to live in peace with the forces of unbelief as it was for Israel to make an alliance with the Canaanites.

After Joshua's death, the desire to renew the battle with the Canaanites began to stir again. Judah, in particular, made some significant progress—assisted by Simeon. But the desire to fight soon wore off.

What the tribes dreaded especially was going to war against the inhabitants of the valleys, who had iron chariots. Sometimes they managed to subdue these Canaanites to the extent of making them pay tribute, but they did not wipe them out. Fear, always the opposite of faith, kept them from the conflict.

Because of this attitude, the battles against Sisera and his many chariots did not come until much later. The victory over Sisera was a sign that the Israelites did not have to be losers, even when they fought against the people with chariots. All they had to do was believe.

Now the Angel of the Lord, the Christ, pronounced a judgment against them: God would no longer drive the Canaanites out before them. We should be careful not to confuse this judgment with a divine ordinance in Joshua's time, when the Canaanites were not to be wiped out all at once. In Joshua's day, the reason for sparing the Canaanites was so that the land would not be surrendered to the forces of devastation as

11

long as the Israelites could not yet populate it completely.

Now, however, the sparing of the Canaanites was to be a judgment and a continual ordeal. Since the Canaanites would go on attacking the Israelites, the younger generation of Israelites, who had not experienced warfare under Joshua's leadership, would learn what the conflict was all about; that is to say, they would come to understand that the Canaanites and the other foreign peoples stood over against God's people as enemies. By means of this realization, the new generation would learn anew that Israel belonged to the Lord. Even in this judgment there would be a blessing.

The peoples that remained in Canaan would be a trial for Israel. Through that trial and through the chastisements resulting from Israel's unfaithfulness, God's people would be cleansed and sanctified.

Often the Israelites yielded completely to temptation. They made alliances with the Canaanites and intermarried with them. They also took over the worship of Baal and Astarte.* As the unfaithful Israelites saw it, there were many Baals. The Lord was reduced to one among them—albeit the mightiest one.

By this abomination they broke the covenant. But the Lord remained faithful. In spite of Israel's neglect of its duty, in the end He cleansed Canaan of its enemies and consecrated the land unto Himself.

During the time of the judges, the Israelites fell from the spiritual peak they had attained under Joshua. Now we find faith and unbelief, faithfulness and unfaithfulness struggling against each other in Israel. This lasted until the reformation under Samuel.

Main thought: *The Lord maintains His claim on the entire land of Canaan.*

Sinful negligence. In the years just prior to Joshua's death, the war against the Canaanites had come to a standstill. For some years Israel had enjoyed the land it was given. When Joshua died, the people understood that it was their duty to wipe out the remaining enemies. Therefore the elders of the people gathered together and asked the Lord which of the tribes should start the

---

Astarte is the Greek spelling. In some Bible translations, the Hebrew form *Asherah* (plural: *Asherim*) is used. The Hebrew form of this name can be misleading, since it is sometimes used to refer to cultic objects as well. The goddess Astarte is also referred to on occasion as *Ashtoreth* (plural: *Ashtaroth*). The RSV reports that Solomon worshiped *Ashtoreth*, while the Jerusalem Bible uses the name *Astarte* (I Kings 11).—TRANS.

battle and set an example for all the other tribes.

It should not surprise us that the Lord pointed to Judah to give leadership to the people. Judah was the royal tribe, the tribe from which the Christ would eventually be born. The tribe of Judah invited the tribe of Simeon to join in the battle, for Simeon's territory lay inside that of Judah. The tribe of Simeon agreed.

But before these two tribes could start conquering the land, one of the mightiest kings still remaining in Canaan attacked them—Adoni-bezek, the king of Bezek. The Lord delivered him into their hands, and they killed 10,000 men of his army.* They cut off Adoni-bezek's thumbs and big toes. He himself viewed this as retribution for what he had done to 70 Canaanite kings. Yet it was a cruel deed which the Lord had not commanded. A short time later Adoni-bezek died.

Judah and Simeon then proceeded to capture the city of Jerusalem, which was located on the border between the territories of Judah and Benjamin. They left it up to the tribe of Benjamin to rebuild Jerusalem and inhabit it. But the Benjaminites never got around to it, and soon the Canaanites took possession of the city and rebuilt it.

The tribes of Judah and Simeon conquered many other cities. But while they remained master of the situation in the hill country, this was not the case in the valleys, where their enemies fought with iron chariots. The Israelites simply did not believe that the Lord also intended to deliver these enemies into their hands. They were afraid. When we are afraid, we cannot have faith.

The other tribes fared no better. Ephraim and Manasseh succeeded in taking Bethel and some other towns, but because of their unbelief they could not drive out the Canaanites completely. The

---

*Throughout the book of Judges and elsewhere in the Old Testament, we come across these round numbers representing the number of soldiers in an army or the number of men killed in a certain battle. As we consider their meaning, we must remember that Old Testament Hebrew used words as numbers and never developed a system of symbols or characters to represent numerals. The Hebrew word for thousand (eleph) can also be used to refer to an army division or even a family. Gideon declared: "My clan (eleph) is the weakest in Manasseh" (Judges 6:15). Thus we cannot always be sure that these references to "thousands" are to be understood as numerical thousands.—TRANS.

only thing they could do was make them pay tribute.

The northern tribes (Zebulun, Asher and Naphtali) were no more successful. The tribe of Dan was even forced back into the hill country by the Amorites. Ephraim and Manasseh finally managed to put a halt to the victories of the Amorites.

Because of their unbelief, the Israelites left the land in the hands of the Canaanites. As a result, idol worship continued in the land and the Israelites lived in peace with the idol worshipers.

The Lord had decreed that He alone was to be served in Canaan. He claimed the entire land for Himself—just as He now claims the whole world for Himself. He does not want us to live in peace with an unbelief that rejects Him. After all, the Lord Jesus allowed His blood to be shed so that the whole world would be consecrated to the Lord. The cleansing of Canaan was to be a prefiguration of that total consecration.

Shouldn't the Lord Jesus have said something to the Israelites about leaving the land in the hands of God's enemies? That's exactly what He did. He appeared to them in the form in which He had already appeared a number of times—as the Angel of the Lord.

On a certain day the elders of the people gathered together, at Bochim. There the Angel of the Lord came to meet them. He came from the direction of Gilgal, the first campsite of the Israelites after they crossed the River Jordan on their way into Canaan. At Gilgal the covenant had been renewed, and it was there that the Angel of the Lord had promised to deliver Jericho (the key to the entire land of Canaan) into the hands of the Israelites. He had also promised that He and His angels would fight alongside Israel.

What intimate fellowship there had been between God and His people! But how Israel had departed from the Lord since then! In a spiritual sense, Bochim was a long way from Gilgal; That's why the Angel of the Lord approached from Gilgal; He wanted to remind the people of that former covenant intimacy.

At Bochim He reproached the people for their unfaithfulness in not consecrating the entire land. That was why the Lord was so angry with the Israelites. And now He announced the judgment: the Lord would no longer deliver their enemies into their hands. He would use their own sins to punish them. From then on, those enemies would be a constant trial to the Israelites and a continual temptation: the Canaanites would tempt the Israelites to join them in their way of life and their idol worship. Thus the Israelites would have to learn to be faithful in the midst of unfaithfulness.

When the people heard the Words of the Angel of the Lord, they wept and offered a sacrifice to the Lord as a token of their repentance. But the Lord did not reconsider His judgment. Now Israel would have to be sanctified through tribulation. Thus the judgment was a judgment of *mercy*, a judgment in favor of His people. Because the people wept, the place where they had gathered was called *Bochim,* which means *weeping.*

Sinful alliances. After Joshua and the entire older generation died, a new generation arose, a generation that had not experienced the wars of the Lord under Joshua. The Israelites of this generation no longer looked upon the Canaanites as enemies— because they no longer recognized that they were enemies of *the Lord.* As a result, they not only made a covenant with the Canaanites but even intermarried with them. Before long the Israelites began joining them in their idol worship.

The Canaanites' idols were the Baals and the Ashteroth.* Actually, these idols were nothing more than forces through which God worked in nature, but the Canaanites thought of them as gods and worshiped them. We are not so far removed from such idol worship ourselves if we assume that there are forces of nature existing by themselves apart from the Lord who governs all things.

The idol worship of the Canaanites was interwoven with their entire way of life—their home life, their agriculture, all their activities. When the Israelites looked for ways to associate with the Canaanites and get closer to them, they took over their idol worship. The Lord was still their God, of course, but He was one among the Baals, albeit the mightiest one. What an abomination! Thereby Israel broke the covenant in which the Lord alone is God. If the Lord had not remained faithful, what would have become of Israel? In His grace, which is obtained for us through the Christ, He is able to gain the victory over sin time and time again.

This the Lord demonstrated in the days of the judges. Because

---

*See the note on the name *Astarte* on p. 12.—TRANS.

of the sins of His people, He let them fall into the hands of their enemies. Even then His purpose was mercy: He did it to make them return to Him. When they cried out to Him, He sent them judges, by whom He gave the people deliverance from their enemies.

These judges were leaders who restored the Lord's claims on His people. They subjected Israel anew to those claims. They also maintained the Lord's justice over against the Canaanites. Out of hatred of the Lord, the Canaanites had attacked His people. It was the Lord's just demand that His people be free to serve Him—and not their enemies. After all, He had brought them into Canaan for that purpose.

But now, according to the Word of the Angel of the Lord at Bochim, these enemies were to remain in Canaan so that the new generation would learn a lesson from their attacks, namely, that the Canaanites were indeed enemies of the Israelites and of the Lord. Then the new generation would lose all desire to get involved with the Canaanites.

In this way the Lord maintained His claim on His people. Because of Israel's unfaithfulness, He left the enemies in the land for the time being. One day He would cleanse the land completely of these enemies.

He maintained His claim on the people and the land especially through the judges. The judges were only human beings, and the time of their judging did not last long. Therefore one judge followed upon another. But we have a Judge through whom the Lord never surrenders His claim on His people and the entire earth, namely, the Christ.

The first judges. The Lord allowed His people to fall into the hands of Cushan-rishathaim, the king of Mesopotamia, who had apparently subdued several nations and was the head of the world power of that time. This king oppressed Israel for eight years. Then the Israelites cried out to the Lord. After all, it was a reproach to *His* name that His people were not living in freedom. The Lord gave them a deliverer—Othniel, the younger brother of Caleb. (Othniel was the man who had earlier captured Debir.)

The Spirit of the Lord came over Othniel; that is to say, the Spirit of the God of the covenant opened his heart so that he would have faith in the Word of the Lord and in His covenant promise. By faith in that promise, Othniel could do anything. He defeated the foreign tyrant, and for 40 years Israel was at peace.

The faith generated by the Spirit of the Lord had won the victory. The Lord Jesus Christ, of whom Othniel was a type, also lived by faith through the Holy Spirit and became a victor. He wishes to give us faith through His Spirit, a faith by which we, too, can do all things.

As a result of the deliverance through Othniel, the land was at rest for 40 years. But there was no lasting return to the Lord, nor did the people put an end to all their connections with the Canaanites. Therefore the Lord, true to His Word, gave Eglon, the king of the Moabites, authority over the Israelites.

While the previous oppressor had come from the north, this one came from the east. He made an alliance with the Ammonites and Amalekites, subdued Transjordan, pressed far into the land across the Jordan, and took possession of Jericho, which had not yet been made into a fortress again. From there he dominated the central part of the land.

This oppression lasted for eighteen years. During that time the Israelites again learned to cry out to the Lord. They saw that the other peoples in the land were indeed God's enemies and theirs as well. Then the Lord raised up a deliverer—Ehud, a Benjaminite.

Ehud dealt with Eglon as an enemy and thereby broke all the connections between the Moabites and the Israelites. In the name of the Lord he again declared war. But not all means are permitted against an enemy—not even against an enemy of the Lord. This Ehud forgot.

The Israelites were subject to the Moabites at the time. They had been forced to accept a treaty arrangement through which they paid taxes to the Moabites. Ehud, with a delegation of the people, brought the tax money to Eglon in Jericho. There he assassinated Eglon and even managed to escape. He fled to Ephraim's territory and summoned the people with the trumpet. He declared that Israel and Moab had now become enemies, and that the Lord had delivered the Israelites' enemies into their hands just as he, Ehud, had been able to kill Eglon.

The Israelites seized the fords along the Jordan and killed

10,000 of the Moabites. In this way Israel regained its former authority over Moab. If only God's people have faith, they always have the strength they need. After that there was rest in the land for 80 years.

At the end of that 80-year period, the people were threatened by the Philistines to the west. Shamgar attacked the Philistines and killed 600 of them with an oxgoad. Apparently he grabbed the first weapon he could lay hands on. That was all he needed to deal with the Lord's enemies. By means of that weapon he expressed his contempt for them. Israel had become strong again—stronger than her enemies.

Like the rising sun. In the time after Ehud, the Israelites again did not recognize that they were the Lord's people, called and set apart. Neither did they understand the Lord's command not to tolerate the Canaanites. They quietly allowed them to rebuild the city of Hazor, which had been burned down by Joshua because Jabin, Hazor's king, had been the leader of the kings of the north who formed an alliance against Israel.

Yet, Canaan was the holy inheritance. Therefore the Lord chastised Israel by raising up another Jabin over Hazor. This new king oppressed the Israelites. They did not dare raise a finger against Jabin because Sisera, the commander of his army, had 900 chariots at his disposal. The Israelites were so afraid of Jabin that they did not dare go from town to town along the normal roads; they followed secret routes instead.

What was left of Israel's honor? The name and favor of the Lord, the Light upon Israel, was greatly obscured. Finally the people cried out to the Lord, who, they knew, had turned away from them.

This oppression took place in the north and involved especially the tribes of Zebulun and Naphtali. In the central part of the land lived a female judge, Deborah, who restored the law of the Lord to a place of honor among the people. The zeal of the men in Israel had flagged, and they sought to associate themselves with the Canaanites. Now the Lord put them to shame by having a *woman* judge Israel.

Deborah was also a prophetess. In the Lord's name she commanded Barak, a man of the oppressed tribe of Naphtali, to go with 10,000 men to Mount Tabor. There the Lord would deliver Sisera into his hand. But Barak thought of Sisera's iron chariots and was afraid to carry out that order unless Deborah went with him. It is understandable that he was very eager to have the prophetess with him—and thereby the Word of the Lord. But making her presence a condition for obeying was unbelief. Deborah did go along. It appeared that the woman was stronger in her faith than the man. This was also symbolized in the prophecy that Sisera was to be killed not by a man but by a woman.

According to the command, Barak summoned 10,000 men from Naphtali and Zebulun and went with them to Mount Tabor. This mountain lay all by itself in a wide plain—wonderful terrain for Sisera to utilize the power of his chariots. Sisera advanced. Once Barak came down from the mountain, he would be crushed to pieces.

What Sisera did not realize was that he was being drawn to the plain around Mount Tabor by the Lord Himself. At Deborah's command, Barak attacked Sisera from the mountain—as though he came from the very presence of God. The Lord shocked Sisera's army by extraordinary signs of nature. Thus the Israelites did not have to fight for victory; all they had to do was pursue the fleeing men.

At Barak's summons, other tribes had also joined the battle. Now the faithful from among all Israel pursued the enemy. What did those fearsome chariots mean to the Lord and to those who believed? In that pursuit, the Light, Israel's honor, went up again over Israel. In victory the Israelites recognized that they were indeed the people of the Lord's favor.

Sisera jumped from his chariot in an effort to make his escape easier. A man named Heber had pitched his tents in the area to which Sisera fled. Heber belonged to the Kenites and was thus a descendant of Hobab, Moses' brother-in-law. The Kenites actually lived in the south, but Heber had come up north to live. He lived in peace with Jabin, Israel's enemy, and was no stranger to Sisera. In his tent Sisera hoped to find refuge.

Heber, therefore, did not fully share Israel's lot. But his wife Jael belonged with all her heart to the God of Israel. While the battle was going on, she stood in the door of her tent. She burned with longing to hear some news of the victory of the Lord's people. Then she saw Sisera come running. She understood immediately that the Lord had delivered Sisera and his army into Israel's hands. She, too, suddenly felt a desire to fight for Israel's God.

She invited Sisera into her tent. When he asked for water, she gave him milk to drink and covered him with a blanket. At his request she stood at the door of the tent to say that there was no one inside. But when he fell asleep, she killed him by driving a tent peg into his temple. She was driven by zeal for Israel's God, even though the way she fought cannot be defended.

Barak, who was pursuing Sisera, found that his enemy had been killed by a woman's hand, just as Deborah had prophesied. The Israelites got the upper hand over Jabin more and more, until they wiped him out.

Deborah and Barak sang a song about this battle. Deborah praised the Lord, who had again come to Israel in His faithfulness, just as He had once come in glory to Mount Sinai. In this song she judged the tribes of Israel: she praised the faithful tribes of Naphtali, Zebulun and Issachar from the north and Ephraim, Manasseh and Benjamin from the middle of the land, and she reproached the unfaithful tribes. Reuben made a lot of plans beyond the Jordan, but he did nothing to carry them out; he loved his rest. Dan and Asher stayed close to the seashore. In the name of the Angel of the Lord, she cursed those who did not help pursue the enemy—not even when victory was sure. Then she described the consternation and confusion in the ranks of Israel's enemies.

Surely the light of God's name and favor had gone up again over Israel. Once more it became clear that the Israelites were the people among whom God dwelt in the Christ, that is, in the Angel of the Lord. Because the Christ is always Victor, those who believe in Him will someday be victorious for eternity. Thus Deborah ended her song with these words: "May those who love the Lord be like the sun as it rises in its might." Then there was peace in the land for 40 years.

2: The Reign of Grace

Judges 6-9

By the time of Gideon, the worship of Baal had apparently penetrated deeply into the lives of the Israelites. It is surprising that God still showed mercy or favor to the people who had broken so completely with His covenant. Yet, He did. The first thing Gideon discovered was that the Lord is peace.

The Lord did not wait for the people to confess their guilt. He took the initiative by sending a prophet, but we do not read that the people came to repentance through the words of the prophet. On the contrary, the idol worship in Ophrah continued. Nevertheless, the Lord is peace. He is the one who takes the initiative in the covenant, and He forgives.

How remarkable! That's why Gideon asked for a sign, more than once. He was not asking in unbelief. His attitude was: "I do believe, Lord. Help Thou my unbelief." In other words: "Help me fight against my unbelief."

Very significant is the request for a sign via the woolen fleece. Gideon's father had instructed him in the service of Baal, which is the worship of the forces of nature. Of course there are no forces simply inherent in nature. It is the Lord who rules over all things. Not Baal but *the Lord* is God. As the living God who does all things, the Lord proved Himself in the miracle of the woolen fleece. In such a case we should not speak of a supernatural force; all we need to say is that the One who ordinarily does things in the regular way was departing from the rules. He did so in answer to Gideon's prayer, as a way of revealing Himself to Gideon.

When we say that the Lord takes the initiative in the covenant, we are not saying that He does not intend to bring His people to a confession of guilt and a striving for righteousness. In this story He tried to elicit a confession from the people first of all by sending a prophet to preach

21

repentance. The same concern came out in Gideon's act of reformation—pulling down the altar of Baal. In that act Gideon was already a
judge. He was called *Jerubbaal*, that is, *Baal contended with him*. Later
this became a name of honor in the sense of *contender with Baal*.

Furthermore, through the victory of the 300, the Lord brought
Israel to a conversion from fear to faith. The punishment of Succoth and
Penuel, too, served to teach the people to fear the Lord, that is, to await
His mercy. Finally, the judgment upon Shechem and Abimelech (who
had set himself up as a king in the Canaanite manner) was meant to teach
Israel righteousness. But behind and in all of this, God's mercy in the
Christ reigned over His people.

Main thought: *The rule of God's mercy over His people is*
always victorious.

The Lord is peace. After the time of Deborah and Barak, the
Israelites continued to turn away from the Lord. Not only did they
call a halt to their war against the Canaanites, they associated with
them more and more. As a result, the worship of Baal penetrated
deeply into Israel's way of life. The Israelites worshiped the forces
of nature in the forms of Baal and Astarte—just as if there were
forces of nature apart from the Lord, who governs all things!
Surely the Israelites knew better. And if it was the Lord who
governed all things, they should have remembered that He was
motivated by His favor for His people. He wanted to glorify Himself in that favor.

But the Israelites forgot that favor and rejected it. Again the
Lord was true to His Word and caused the Midianites, the
Amalekites and the Arabians to attack them. These peoples were
nomads, shepherd folk on the move. Thus they were dependent on
other peoples for their produce. The easiest way for them to get
food was to steal it. Each year, toward harvest time, they invaded
Canaan. After crossing the Jordan, they took the very fertile plain
of Jezreel, and from there they pushed through to the plain on the
sea coast. They went all the way to Gaza, in the land of the
Philistines.

This went on for seven successive years. During these raids
they stole not only the harvest but also the cattle. The Israelites
became very poor and hid themselves and their possessions in

caves. What had become of the promised land flowing with milk and honey? God's people were not richly blessed, and they were not victorious in honor. In shame they were hidden and exhausted. Out of that situation the Israelites cried to the Lord for deliverance.

This is not to say that they repented and turned to the Lord by breaking their connections with the Canaanites and doing away with the idol worship in their midst. On the contrary, the idol worship continued everywhere. Yet, for Christ's sake, the Lord looked on His people with favor. Because of His faithfulness in His covenant, He forgave His people and wanted to lead them back to Himself again. Israel would be shown that mercy still held sway, that grace still ruled.

In response to this mercy, the people should have returned to the Lord. The Lord even sent them a prophet to remind them of the great deeds He had done when He delivered them out of Egypt and brought them into Canaan. In the Lord's name, the prophet reproached the people for their unfaithfulness.

But the Lord also showed His mercy in another way. One day Gideon, the son of Joash, who was head of the small town of Ophrah, was busy threshing wheat in the wine press. He did not go about his work in the normal way, by beating the wheat on the threshing floor; he did his work in secret, for fear of the Midianites. While he was busy, a man came up to him and said: "The LORD is with you, you mighty man of valor."

Gideon lived in an idolatrous environment. Baal was worshiped in his village and even in his father's house. Yet Gideon was deeply concerned about Israel's humiliation and often pondered the great deeds of the Lord in former days. Therefore, when the man spoke to him, he did not think in terms of himself but in terms of Israel. He answered that the Lord obviously was *not* with His people but had turned away from them. By faith, Gideon saw the situation in the proper light.

Yet, although the Lord was *against* His people in that plague, in Christ He was *for* them. In spite of everything, His mercy would prevail. That's exactly what the man promised Gideon: he was to proceed in the conviction that the Word of the Lord was with him, and that he would deliver Israel from the Midianites. "Have I not sent you?" the man said.

Gideon hesitated. It was not that he didn't believe the Word of the Lord, but he did feel impelled to point out that his clan was the poorest in Manasseh, and that he was the youngest in his father's house. Why would the Lord use such lowly means? Then the man answered that the outcome did not depend on the means but on the Lord, who would be with him.

During the conversation Gideon had noticed that he was dealing with an unusual person. Therefore he asked for a sign, so that he could be sure that it was the Lord who spoke through this man. He made this request not out of unbelief but to confirm his faith. Gideon left to prepare some food. That way the man would have to remain a while longer and would thus have a chance to perform a sign. Wasn't the faith awakened in Gideon's heart through the Word of the Lord already a sign that the Lord had not abandoned His people?

Gideon got his sign. When he came back with the prepared food, the man refused to eat it. Gideon was told to lay the food on a rock. Then the man made flames come out of the rock and consume the food as a sacrifice. With that He disappeared.

Now Gideon understood that it had been an angel, and he feared that he would die because he had seen the glory of the Lord. That fear had not yet been conquered by Gideon's faith. Then the Lord answered his fear, perhaps by an audible voice, or perhaps by a voice speaking in Gideon's heart: "Peace be to you; do not fear, you shall not die." To show that he believed, Gideon built an altar to the Lord and called it "The LORD is peace."

Gideon was right: that Man was a messenger of the Lord. In fact, He was the Angel of the Lord, the Lord Himself, the Christ. He had come to speak of mercy and of peace, to promise deliverance. Moreover, He did so even *before* Israel had confessed its sin. If the Lord did not take the initiative in turning to His people, they would never turn to Him. Even before Gideon understood what was really going on, he received the sign he had asked for.

Gideon's act of reformation. Gideon had built an altar of the Lord, as a sign. But next to it in Ophrah stood an altar of Baal, and beside it a pole portraying the goddess Astarte. One of the altars would have to go.

That same night the Lord ordered Gideon to pull down Baal's altar and cut down the pole next to it. Using the pole as wood, he was to burn his father's seven-year-old bull as a sacrifice on another altar which he was to build to the Lord. Here the Lord Himself commanded that a sacrifice be offered at a place other than Shiloh, and by someone who was not a priest. If the Lord Himself commanded it, it was all right.

Gideon was afraid the men of his town would not let him carry out this command in broad daylight. Therefore he went about his assignment by night, together with ten more men who were apparently opposed to the worship of Baal.

The next morning the men of the town discovered what Gideon had done. Immediately they wanted to kill him. Gideon must have been tense as he awaited the reaction of Joash, his father. But the Lord's grace also conquered Joash, who told the men of the town that Baal would just have to defend himself against Gideon. Joash added that anyone who dared lift up his hand against Gideon would be killed immediately. That's why Gideon was called *Jerubbaal*, that is, *let Baal contend* against him. Later on *Jerubbaal* became a name of honor, with the meaning reversed, namely, *contender with Baal*.

Now the Spirit of the Lord took possession of Gideon. He lived only by faith in the Word of the Lord and was capable of anything. He blew the trumpet to summon the people to battle. The first ones to join him were the men of his own tribe, who had wanted to kill him only a short time before. The Spirit of the Lord moved them too. Later many more came from the tribe of Manasseh, and also from the northern tribes of Asher, Zebulun and Naphtali.

Yet Gideon still had to wrestle constantly with his unbelief. His father had introduced him to the Baals as forces of nature. Let the Lord now prove that there are no forces of nature existing by themselves as gods to be worshiped. Let the Lord demonstrate that *He* does all things!

Gideon asked the Lord to prove this by way of a sheep's fleece. He wanted the Lord to make the fleece wet with dew at night while the land around it remained dry. Just to make sure it was the Lord's doing and not the wool attracting the water around it, Gideon wanted the situation reversed the next night. In granting

Gideon's request, the Lord demonstrated that He is indeed the One who does all things, that He is the living God. And Gideon believed.

Victory from the Lord. There were 32,000 men with Gideon. Such an army could hardly be compared to the Midianite army, but at least it meant something. At the command of the Lord, Gideon declared that anyone who dreaded the upcoming fight was free to return home. That was nothing unusual. However, the result in this case was unexpected: 22,000 men left, leaving him with only 10,000. That was the Lord's doing. He wanted to exclude the possibility that the victory might be attributed to Israel's bravery. The victory would have to be recognized as the fruit of the Lord's mercy and grace over Israel.

Therefore the Lord said that the 10,000 men were still too many. Gideon was to order all of them to drink. Those who quickly went down on their stomachs to drink were to be set apart. These proved to be 300 men, many of them Abiezrites, who came from Gideon's own part of the country. These 300 men were given the provisions and trumpets of the men who were sent home.

With this small army Gideon proceeded. That was a genuine act of faith on his part. He was to rely on the Lord alone. To strengthen him in his faith, the Lord had Gideon sneak into the camp of the Midianites at night. There, with his servant Purah, Gideon heard one soldier telling his comrade about a dream in which a tumbling cake of barley bread overturned the tent of the captain. The other soldier interpreted the dream to mean that Gideon would conquer them. This made it plain to Gideon that the fear of the Lord had already fallen upon the Midianites.

At the beginning of the second night watch, he divided his men into three groups. At a given signal, they were to blow their trumpets, break their jars, wave their torches, and shout: "For the LORD and for Gideon!" The shouting from all sides was intended to give the Midianites the impression that they were surrounded by a large army, and the breaking of the jars was intended to give them the idea that the destruction of the tents was already underway.

The work of the Lord was evident in the confusion that

followed, as the Midianites began killing each other. All the
Israelites had to do was pursue an already defeated enemy. The
victory was due to the Lord, who had mercy on His people in the
Christ.

Accepting the Lord's mercy. All the men who had gone home
were called back to take part in the pursuit. Gideon also had the
men of Ephraim called up to prevent the Midianites from crossing
the Jordan. When the fighting was done, 120,000 Midianite
soldiers were dead. The Ephraimites even captured and killed two
kings, namely, Oreb and Zeeb.

Did the Israelites now accept the victory as a gift of God's
mercy? It soon became evident that they did not. The Ephraimites
reproached Gideon for not having summoned them to battle at the
start. Now they did not get any credit for the victory. They seemed
to forget that they owed the victory to the mercy of God alone!
Gideon warded off the potential rebellion by saying that the
Ephraimites had done more than he and his men. Then they stopped
making trouble, but they did not submit in faith to the grace
of God.

Soon afterward the same attitude showed up again, only
stronger, when Gideon and his men crossed the Jordan to pursue
the enemy still farther. He asked the people of Succoth for bread
for his men, saying that he was pursuing the Midianite kings Zebah
and Zalmunna. But the officials of Succoth did not accept the
grace God had shown His people. They mocked Gideon for not
having captured those two kings yet. How unbelieving people can
be in the face of the Lord's mercy! They cannot and will not accept it. But such unbelief, such doubt, is sinful.

Gideon threatened to thresh the flesh of the men of Succoth
with the thorns and thistles of the wilderness as soon as God gave
him the last victory. And when the inhabitants of Penuel treated
him in the very same way as the men of Succoth, Gideon
threatened to destroy the tower of Penuel.

Zebah and Zalmunna still had 15,000 men left. That was
nothing compared with the original army of the Midianites, but
over against the 300 men under Gideon's command, it was still a
powerful force. The Midianite soldiers were at ease, however,

thinking that the pursuit was all over. When Gideon attacked, he defeated them easily. He captured both kings and took them back with him.

On his way home, he carried out his threats. He got the names of the elders of Succoth from a captured youth. He then flogged the elders with thorns and thistles. He destroyed the tower of Penuel and killed the officials. In the name of the Lord, contempt for the Lord's grace was punished.

Yet Gideon himself did not see matters clearly. He returned to his own land with the captured kings. There he reproached the two kings for killing his brothers and swore to them that if they had not done so, he would have spared their lives. Thus Gideon no longer saw the two kings as the Lord's enemies; he regarded them as his personal enemies. Because it was a case of blood revenge to him, he ordered his oldest son to kill the two kings. When his son did not dare do it, Gideon killed them himself and kept their treasures.

Even Gideon forgot that he was to be nothing more than a servant of the Lord's grace. Yet, he did make it apparent not long afterward that he was a servant: he refused the request of Israel's men that he become their king. He told them that the Lord would rule over them.

That request was not of the Lord. What those men wanted was a king such as the Canaanites had. Thus their request revealed their contempt for the reign of grace, which had just become so gloriously evident.

Gideon did refuse that request. But later he behaved more or less like an Eastern monarch. He took many wives, fathered 70 sons, and kept a concubine from Shechem, who bore him a son whom he named Abimelech. In these ways Gideon obstructed the revelation of the Lord's grace.

He did so as well in another way, a way that was even more offensive. He asked the men of Israel for a part of each man's spoil. From those spoils he had a splendid priestly robe made, and he established his own private cultic center in Ophrah, his hometown. Thus he wanted to have Ophrah compete with Shiloh. Like an Eastern monarch with power over the gods and the cults of the gods, he took the service of the Lord into his own hands.

What had happened to the simple faith with which he had accepted the promises of the Lord at the beginning? Success had become too much for him. Gideon did not live under the reign of grace anymore than the rest of Israel did. He did not leave room for the Christ—of whom he was supposed to be a type—to reign as King over Israel.

The rejection of the reign of grace. Gideon passed on the wrong spirit to his son Abimelech in particular. After the deliverance, all of Israel again forsook the Lord, but Abimelech was especially guilty of corrupting the life of the people. After his father's death, he said to the people of Shechem (his mother's hometown) that the 70 sons of Gideon would want to take control of Israel. Wouldn't it be better if Abimelech were recognized as the sole sovereign? The men of Shechem listened to him and gave him money from the house of Baal-berith. He used that money to hire some unscrupulous mercenaries. He then attacked his brothers, killing them all on one stone. Only Jotham, his youngest brother, escaped.

Thus, such heathen customs as fratricide and murder for political purposes were introduced into Israel. But what else could we expect in a time when even a Baal was venerated as Baal-berith, that is, the lord of the covenant? The honor of the covenant God was ascribed to a Baal!

From a hilltop opposite Shechem, Jotham called out to the citizens and told them a parable. He portrayed Abimelech as a bramble bush holding sway over the other trees as king. Even Jotham, in telling that parable, knew of no other reason for the Israelites not to have a king than that they were better off without one. And the acceptance of the kingship was merely a question of pride, as far as he was concerned. Thus it appears that the service of the Lord had disappeared from Israel completely. In that scornful speech Jotham already foretold that Abimelech would consume the citizens of Shechem and the house of Millo, which is the fortified summit of Shechem. He also declared that Shechem would devour Abimelech.

Jotham's prediction was fulfilled. In a later conflict Abimelech destroyed Shechem and killed its citizens. While conquering another city which had revolted against him along with

Shechem, his skull was crushed by a millstone which a woman
threw from the roof of the tower. He asked his armor-bearer to
pierce him with his sword, so that people would not be able to say
that a woman had killed him. All the same, his name went down in
shame.

God had judged the Canaanite form of kingship, which rejected the kingship of Christ. That way He avenged the rejection of
His reign of grace. How God will one day judge the world and all
who have not acknowledged the sovereignty of Christ!

3: Moved by Israel's Misery

Judges 10-12

The key to the stories to which we now turn our attention is Judges 10:16, where we read that the Lord "became indignant over the misery of Israel." Apparently the full revelation of God's grace in the deliverance through Gideon had not brought Israel back to the Lord. But now, under oppression by the Ammonites in the east and the Philistines in the west, the people cried to the Lord. Although they put away the foreign gods from among them and served the Lord, their conversion was not wholehearted. Consequently the Lord said that He would deliver them no longer. Let them cry instead to the gods they had chosen to worship.

This statement made by the Lord does not mean that He had withdrawn His eternal favor to His people in the Christ. All it means is that He did not want them to experience His favor at that time. He would not give them His full covenant communion. Instead He would keep His distance.

All the same, He did not wish to watch their suffering without doing anything about it. When enemies triumphed over the Israelites, the suffering of Israel saddened the Lord, for His name's sake. He was still bound to His people in grace, in the Christ. Yet He could not give Himself to them at that point. He held back, just as a father sometimes keeps his distance from his child, neither interfering nor punishing, in the hope that the child will eventually repent. And Israel did repent eventually, through the spiritual leadership and reformation of Samuel.

Because God did not give Himself to the people, they could not give themselves in faith to Him. Not even the judge Jephthah could do so. We do read that the Spirit of the Lord came upon Jephthah. The Spirit opened his heart in such a way that he saw what the Lord could be and wanted to be for His people (see Heb. 11:32-4).

What was missing in Jephthah—and in the rest of God's people as

31

well— was a continual, total surrender in faith to the mercy of the Lord. That's apparent from the vow Jephthah made.

A vow can be a sign of surrender in faith. By making the vow, one accepts the promises of the Lord in faith. It was in that spirit that Jacob once made a vow. But that was not how Jephthah viewed the vow he made. He regarded it instead as an achievement on his part, an achievement by which he would repay the Lord for His favor to him and to the people. Hence the absurd promise: "Whoever comes forth from the doors of my house to meet me when I return victorious I will sacrifice to You." It was not a matter of what the Lord would choose but of what chance would decide. Jephthah was not offering a sacrifice as a sign that he was consecrating his life completely to the Lord; he was expressing his willingness to undergo suffering provided that the Lord gave him the victory.

That this was indeed his attitude is evident from his grief when it came time to fulfill his vow by sacrificing his daughter. He was not filled with the joy of true sacrifice, a sacrifice in which he was really giving *himself*. No, he thought of the service of the Lord as requiring suffering and death. But this suffering struck him as being too severe, although he must have been aware from the very beginning that some human being might have to be sacrificed.

Jephthah clearly did not know what it means to rest in the grace of God, who, through Christ's sacrifice, can be everything to us. For Jephthah there had to be a certain amount of suffering offered to the Lord in return. We are reminded of Reuben's vow to Jacob: if Benjamin did not return from Egypt in safety, Jacob would be allowed to kill Reuben's two sons (Gen. 42:37).

Therefore Jephthah's sacrifice was futile, useless. As for the question what form the sacrifice took, I do not believe that Jephthah actually sacrificed his daughter on the altar or even set her apart for service in the sanctuary. Most likely she was sacrificed by being condemned to a lonely and barren existence without marriage or motherhood or communication with others.

For both Jephthah and his daughter, the sacrifice was useless. And Jephthah did not bother asking for the light of the Lord's Word by consulting the high priest.

This episode does not stand in the light of God's grace in Christ; it stands in the darkness of the shadow. When we tell this story to the children, then, we must not forget to remind them of Christ's sacrifice, as a contrast to the sacrifice made by Jephthah.

Throughout this chapter in Israel's history, the people displayed the same spiritual attitude as Jephthah. Indeed, they had called Jephthah in the first place because of his military prowess—not because he was designated by the Lord to be Israel's deliverer. Jephthah did not surrender unconditionally to the calling of the Lord; instead he made his service to

Israel conditional upon his appointment as head of his people. He wanted to be repaid for the scorn he had suffered earlier.

The civil war between Ephraim and the Israelites from Transjordan also shows how little the Lord was credited with the victory. Jephthah was not able to convince Ephraim on that point. Unlike Gideon, he could not find words to still the storm.

Main thought: *Even during a time of estrangement, the Lord is moved by the misery of His people.*

Turning away from His own people. After the time of Abimelech, two judges named Tola and Jair arose to keep Israel from falling apart and being destroyed. They are counted among those who judged Israel in the name of the Lord. Yet, we know nothing about their deeds.

More and more, the judges were eager for royal honors. Jair was no exception. He had 30 sons, who rode on the colts of donkeys. Jair let each of his sons have a city of his own.

After his death, the Israelites continued to turn away from the Lord and His covenant to worship the forces of nature. They wanted to honor the creature rather than the Creator. The Lord wished to give them His love and fellowship, but they rejected that fellowship. They learned the ways of the Canaanites and the other surrounding peoples, and they served the forces of nature, using the names given to them by those peoples. The Israelites had been given the opportunity of becoming more and more independent, as the people to whom the Lord had chosen to reveal Himself, but they lowered themselves to a state of utter dependence and slavish imitation of the heathen peoples around them.

Because the people became estranged from the Lord, He let them fall into the hands of the Ammonites in the east and the Philistines in the west. The Ammonites, in particular, pressed them hard. They conquered all of Transjordan and even crossed the Jordan River to oppress Ephraim and Benjamin and Judah.

Then the Israelites became terribly afraid. Their existence in Canaan was at stake. In this oppression, the Lord was demonstrating that He had not let go of His people: through the chastisement, He wanted to make them return to Him. Still, because they had abandoned the covenant, the Lord's face was turned away from Israel.

That did not change when the people cried out to Him in their distress. He reproached His people for their lack of faith after He had rescued them so many times, and He said that the Israelites should now seek help from the gods they had chosen to serve.

The Israelites confessed their sins and kept crying out to the Lord. They even put away the foreign gods from among them and restored the service of the Lord. Yet, because they had so persistently deserted the Lord in their hearts, they did not really return to Him, and the fellowship was not restored. The Lord was not willing to turn to His people with His full favor. All the same, He could not ignore their plight completely, for in the Christ they were still *His* people. Because their suffering and the triumphs of their enemies saddened Him, He wanted to give them some relief. Would the people learn righteousness if they lived in freedom once again? In the future He would send them a prophet to lead them in reformation.

Deliverance through divine compassion. The Ammonites gathered a large army to put even more pressure on Israel. The inhabitants of Gilead (in Transjordan) also gathered an army. They wanted to engage the Ammonites in a life-and-death struggle. That was an act of desperation on their part. Yet, it took place under the Lord's guidance. But who would be their commander in the fight?

In Gilead there was a man whose name was Gilead. In addition to his sons from his marriage, he also had a son by a sinful foreign woman. That son was named Jephthah. He was banished by his half brothers and fled to the northern borders of Gilead, where he became the leader of a gang. Men who for one reason or another were misfits in society collected around him. He became known as a mighty warrior.

The thoughts of the elders in Gilead turned to Jephthah, and they called for him, with the promise that he would be made their ruler if he should win the battle. Jephthah expressly made the elders of Gilead swear a vow to that effect. In the presence of the army at Mizpah, a solemn agreement was made before the face of the Lord. Jephthah wanted that honor so that the shame he had suffered at the hands of his half brothers would be wiped out.

Nowhere do we read that *the Lord* had appointed Jephthah to be the deliverer of the people. He was sought out because he was a mighty warrior. Jephthah himself did not interpret the people's request as the calling of the Lord, who demands unconditional surrender. All the same, Jephthah's appearance on the scene was the Lord's doing; it was *He* who had chosen Jephthah to be the deliverer of His people. The Lord often leads His people along the right path through their own unbelieving deliberations.

The other tribes refused to come to the rescue at Jephthah's call. Before he joined the men of Gilead in battle against the Ammonites, he tried to get the king of Ammon to withdraw. When the king refused, saying that the Israelites had originally taken the land away from the Moabites and the Ammonites, Jephthah answered that the land had belonged to the Amorites at the time, and that Israel had taken it from their hands. For that reason, neither Balak (Moab's king) nor his successors had ever disputed Israel's claim to the land. Reasoning further along this line, Jephthah said: "All that your God Chemosh has given you, you will possess, and all that the Lord our God has given us, we will keep. May the Lord, who is Judge, decide this day between the people of Israel and the people of Ammon."

When the Ammonites did not listen to him, the Spirit of the Lord came upon Jephthah. Through that power he could become Israel's deliverer. The Lord opened his heart so that he believed in the power of the Lord, which would deliver Israel.

It was by faith, then, that Jephthah was able to deliver Israel. Yet that faith did not set Jephthah free from all mistaken notions concerning the Lord and His service. He swore a vow to the Lord that the first one to come out of his house to meet him after the victory would be sacrificed to the Lord. What he meant was that the one to be sacrificed would be banished from society to live a life of solitude.

In spite of Jephthah's wrong ideas and the incompleteness of the people's repentance, the Lord gave Israel a complete victory by the faith His Spirit had aroused. As a result, Ammon was rendered powerless for many years. How true it is that the relief God grants His people often puts them to shame!

The useless sacrifice. As Jephthah approached his house, his daughter, his only child, came out to meet him, dancing and playing the tambourine. Remembering his vow, he immediately tore his clothes in mourning and lamented his promise and the welcome his daughter had given him. The joy of his victory was shattered completely. His daughter surrendered herself, saying that what her father had promised would have to take place.

What blindness in those two! Even the motive behind Jephthah's vow was wrong. He thought that he himself had to suffer a bit if the Lord gave the victory. This suffering, which he had taken on himself of his own free will, would serve as a kind of settlement of Israel's debt to the Lord—as if the Lord had not delivered His people out of free grace! Jephthah did not realize that the favor shown to Israel would be earned completely by the Christ, that we can never repay the least bit of our debt to the Lord. Moreover, what could such a sacrifice mean to the Lord? Would the sacrifice of Jephthah's daughter be pleasing to Him? Could it do anything to atone for the guilt of the people?

In their blindness Jephthah and his daughter carried out the vow. They did not ask the high priest about the Word of the Lord. But Jephthah's daughter did ask for a delay of two months; she wanted time to go to the mountains with her girlfriends and bemoan the fate awaiting her. Once the two months had passed, her father banished her from human society. Only four days per year were Israelite girls allowed to comfort her in her loneliness.

That was a senseless, aimless sacrifice. The Lord does not expect us to take suffering on ourselves to make ourselves pleasing to Him. The needed sacrifice was made by the Lord Jesus Christ. He made that sacrifice to atone completely for our sins. God will show us His full favor only because of that sacrifice.

Of that sacrifice we may boast. And we will never be able to repay even the tiniest bit of our immense debt to the Lord. We show our thankfulness by accepting and enjoying the life He bestows upon us for Christ's sake.

War between brothers. At the news of the victory, Ephraim's men gathered together. Their army crossed the Jordan, and they reproached Jephthah for not having called them to join in battle against Ammon. They, too, had wanted the honor of the victory. It did not occur to them that the honor was due only to the Lord. They even threatened to burn Jephthah and his house.

Unlike Gideon, Jephthah did not find words to ward off their anger. He blamed them for not coming when he summoned them to battle. He did say that it was the Lord who had delivered the Ammonites into his hand, but he did not find the strength to convince them in the name of the Lord.

The result was a civil war, a war between brothers. In the battle the men of Gilead prevailed. They took possession of the fords along the Jordan. Then, when fugitives came along, they made them say the word *Shibboleth*. The men of Ephraim could not pronounce this word properly; they said *Sibboleth* instead and thereby they betrayed their origin. Their failure in pronunciation cost them their lives. In all, 42,000 men of Ephraim fell.

Through this catastrophe, the Lord judged Ephraim for seeking its own honor. When will God's people learn not to seek their own glory but only to live with the Lord?

For six years Jephthah judged Israel. He was buried in Gilead and honored in the land of his fathers. Here we see God's favor resting upon Jephthah. The Lord does not deal with us according to our sins, nor does He requite us according to our iniquities (Ps. 103:10).

After Jephthah came three other judges, of whom we know little more than their names. Scripture tells us that they, too, showed a passion for surrounding themselves with royal honor and splendor. Men always grasp for something other than what God has given them. God has exalted our Mediator, who was the least of all. Our Mediator will exalt all who serve for God's sake.

4: The Mighty One of Israel

Judges 13-16

Samson judged Israel at about the same time as Jephthah. In the west Israel was being oppressed by the Philistines, and in the east by the Ammonites. The Philistine oppression of Israel lasted for 40 years; it ended with Israel's victory under Samuel. Samson only made a beginning in delivering Israel from the Philistines. His activities probably began at about the time the ark was carried away and Eli died suddenly. Thus Eli's activities preceded those of Samson. (The reason they are recorded in the book of Samuel rather than in Judges is because Samuel's work followed immediately upon Eli's priesthood.)

Samson, the mighty one of Israel, occupied a special place among the judges because he fought the Lord's enemies single-handedly. Especially in this respect, he was a type of the Christ. Because his personal life is brought to the fore so much, we are also told about the events surrounding his birth. In this respect, too, Samson is clearly a type of the Christ.

Although Samson fought the battle entirely alone, his actions revealed to all Israel that God's power would be manifested in Israel's weakness if Israel stayed close to the Lord. The Christ wants His Spirit to live in all of His people.

As the mighty one of Israel, Samson was not allowed to disappear into the mists of obscurity. His death was not just a restoration of his personal honor; it was also a restoration of honor for him as Israel's deliverer and as a type of Christ. His death was for *Israel's* sake. That's why we may not speak of it as sinful suicide. Instead we are to view it as a reminder of the self-sacrifice of Christ. Samson did pray for revenge for both his eyes, but he was really asking for revenge for the blinding of Israel's deliverer.

38

It is true that the Scriptures do not tell us anything about repentance on Samson's part for the sinful games he played with his special status as a Nazirite. Yet Samson knew that his life's goal was one with the Lord's cause, and that he personally could take refuge in the Lord, who would protect him for the sake of his calling. This we learn from Judges 15:18.

As a Nazirite Samson was a type of the Christ in a special sense. He had not become a Nazirite of his own free will; it had been determined even before his birth. His calling as a Nazirite even determined the manner of his mother's life before his birth.

A Nazirite was one who was set apart, consecrated to God's special service. Through the Nazirites, the people were to be shown that man does not owe his strength and influence to what is below, that is, to some imminent power, a power inherent in life itself. There is no such imminent power. Therefore the Nazirite was to abstain from everything that came from the vine and from the luxuries of the earth. In addition, he was to avoid touching anything unclean or dead. Death is the result of sin. The Nazirite, because he was consecrated to God, was to avoid all contact with sin. (However, in view of Samson's calling, the command to avoid all contact with the dead was not given in his case.) Finally, the Nazirite had to let his hair grow, as a sign of the unbroken strength of the one who was consecrated to the Lord, the one who had received His Spirit.

We are not to portray Samson's physical strength as an extraordinary strength that was naturally his. If we make this mistake, we can no longer tell the children about the Spirit of the Lord. It was the Spirit who drove Samson. If we focus on *Samson's* strength, the thought of mighty Samson carrying away the doors of Gaza's gate becomes the highlight of the story. In that case, the children will no longer be able to see that Israel's deliverer was *the Lord*. The Spirit of the Lord, that is, the Spirit of the faithful God of the covenant, gave Samson that extraordinary strength, which he then used to overcome the enemies of God's people. Therefore we are not to tell the children the story of Samson's life; we must focus on the deliverance of the people by the Lord.

On the other hand, we must not forget to point out Samson's sin. The Spirit of the Lord stirred continually in his innermost being, keeping his whole spirit in motion. The Spirit of the Lord, who took hold of him in such a mighty way, also stirred the sinfulness within Samson, with the result that sin often broke through unrestrained in his life.

There was no excuse for this unrestrained sin. Apparently Samson had not surrendered enough to the Spirit of the Lord in his heart and was not sufficiently governed by the Spirit. Because he was not fully in the grip of the Lord's Spirit, his daily life was not consecrated to the Lord as completely as it should have been. In that sinful unfolding of his life, he was also an antitype of the Christ—and thus a type of the people, with their sinful desires and their unfaithfulness to the Lord.

It is apparent from Samson's deeds that his conflicts with the Philistines were of a personal nature. The Israelites, who in those days had not yet received enough spiritual guidance, were spared. In that light it should be clear to us that Samson's search for a Philistine woman was indeed of the Lord (Judges 14:4). This is not to deny that Samson's desire for a Philistine wife was contrary to the covenant of the Lord and His revealed will. All the same, the Lord used this sin to bring Samson into conflict with the Philistines. Thus the Lord was carrying out His counsel to deliver Israel.

Main thought: *The mighty one of Israel appears to deliver his people.*

The miracle of grace in Samson's birth. After the deliverance under Barak and then under Gideon, the Israelites continued to turn away from the Lord. Again God let His people fall into the hands of their enemies, using the Ammonites in the east and the Philistines in the west. We have already seen how the Lord provided deliverance from the enemies in the east through Jephthah. In the west, too, God wanted to give relief.

In the southwest of Canaan, in the little town of Zorah, which really belonged to the territory of Judah but had been given to the tribe of Dan, there lived a man named Manoah. Manoah and his wife had no children. That must have been a cause of great sorrow to them. No doubt they prayed often for a child. When the Lord withheld that blessing from them, it seemed to them as if He had forsaken them. This must have made them sense that the Lord had forsaken the entire people of Israel in those days because of its unfaithfulness.

One day a man with something very distinct about his appearance came to Manoah's wife and told her that the Lord was going to give her a child. He would be a special child—a Nazirite, that is, one who is set apart for the special service of God. Moreover, he would be a Nazirite from birth. He would not be allowed to use anything that came from the vine, nor was he to drink strong drinks. It would have to be clearly visible that he did not receive his strength from anything of the earth, that it came solely from the Spirit of the Lord. Neither would he be allowed to shave off his hair. His enormous head of hair would be a sign of his unbroken strength as one who was consecrated to the Lord. Even his mother was not permitted any wine or strong drink or unclean food before he was born. In this way he was to be consecrated to the Lord, for he would begin to deliver Israel from the Philistines.

Manoah was not present when the man came to his wife. She thought the man was a prophet, although she did say to her husband that the man's face was like the countenance of God. And she had not even thought of asking his name. Manoah, to honor his position as her husband, asked the Lord in prayer to send the prophet to him too, so that he, as the head of the family, could share fully in the responsibility of training the child. Manoah and his wife lived by faith in the Word of the Lord. The Lord would bring about a change in their situation—and Israel's situation.

The Lord heard Manoah's prayer. When the prophet appeared to the woman again, she called Manoah, and he received the same promise and the same instructions. In grateful faith, Manoah invited the man to eat with them. He refused, but he did say that it would be all right for Manoah to bring the Lord a burnt offering. Normally that was allowed only on the altar at Shiloh. But the Word of the Lord had declared that it was all right to do it in Zorah on this occasion. This made Manoah a bit more aware that the man before him was no ordinary man. When he asked the man his name, he received no answer other than that his name was wonderful.

After Manoah sacrificed a young goat and laid it on a rock, he and his wife watched to see how the man was going to light the offering. The way he went about things was surprising: when the fire was lit, he ascended to heaven in the flame from the altar. This made Manoah and his wife realize that the man was an angel of the Lord, and they fell on their faces. In superstitious fear, Manoah said that now they would surely die, for they had seen the glory of the Lord.

This idea was widely prevalent. That's how estranged from God we have become! We forget that God's glory, through the Lord Jesus Christ, has become a glory that no longer strikes us dead but makes our lives wonderful. Manoah was set straight by his wife. "Why would the Lord want to kill us," she asked, "when He has given us such a marvelous promise?"

Manoah and his wife indeed saw many things in the proper light—but not everything. That man was not a mere angel; he was the Angel of the Lord, who had already appeared many times to His people. He was the Lord Jesus Christ. Didn't He say that His name was wonderful?

In God, in the Lord Jesus Christ, we see a miracle of grace. What we could never have suspected on our own is in Him. In Him there is grace for us, for sinners, for a wayward people!

God's grace in the Christ can overcome all sin. This was also shown in the birth of the child promised to Manoah and his wife. Therefore his birth was a prophecy pointing ahead to the Redeemer, who would deliver His people not just from the Philistines but from sin and all enemies. After His appearance in the flesh, He never again refused to eat bread with His people. He wished to live with them in full fellowship continually.

When the child was born, Manoah and his wife gave him the name *Samson*, which means *mighty one*. The choice of that name showed that they were being led by God: this child was to be a hero who would bring relief to Israel.

The deliverer revealed to Israel. The part of the tribe of Dan to which Samson belonged lived near the border of the Philistines' territory. When Samson became a man, the Spirit of the Lord began to stir in him. Restless among his own people, he visited the outposts of Dan and often came into contact with the Philistines.

One day, at Timnah, he saw a Philistine girl whom he wanted for his wife. Here Samson fell into the same sin as all the other Israelites, namely, seeking fellowship with the pagan people of Canaan. He talked it over with his parents, but they were against the marriage. Who could possibly have known that God would use this sin of disobedience to bring Samson into conflict with the Philistines and thereby reveal him as Israel's deliverer?

Finally his parents gave in and went with him to Timnah. On the way, Samson walked by himself for a while. Just then a roaring lion came at him. At that point the Spirit of the Lord came over him in a mighty way. The Spirit opened his heart in faith, so that he saw what he would be able to do in the Lord's strength. In that faith he tore the lion apart as though it were a mere goat. This showed him what he would be able to do against Israel's enemies in faith, relying on the strength of the Lord. Thus he saw his calling. However, he kept this extraordinary encounter with the lion a secret. He didn't even tell his parents about it.

Later, when he went with them to Timnah again to marry the girl, he took the same sideroad to see what had become of the lion's carcass. He was driven back to the place where his calling had been revealed to him. There he found that the body had not decayed; it had dried out in the sun, and a swarm of bees had made a nest in it and gathered honey. He took the honey and ate some of it. He also gave some to his parents, without telling them where he had found it. There would be abundance for him and his family if he was faithful to his calling.

The wedding feast began. It would go on for seven days. Thirty companions were provided for Samson, headed by the so-called friend of the bridegroom (our "best man"). Samson gave them a riddle to solve: "Out of the eater came something to eat; out of the strong came something sweet." In referring to his encounter with the lion, Samson was being reckless. He was playing with something God had given him, something he should have kept secret. He fell into the same sin several times later in his life.

But here he got his first lesson. The agreement was that his companions would give him 30 fine robes and 30 undergarments if they were not able to solve the riddle. On the other hand, Samson would give them the same if they did solve it. Toward the end of the seven-day period, the 30 Philistines threatened Samson's young wife. Out of fear she begged Samson to let her know the answer to the riddle. He refused, saying that he had not even told his father and mother. Finally, when she kept nagging him, saying that he did not love her, he told her his secret. At that point he gave away something very special in his life—to a heathen woman and, through her, to the Philistines. In the same way, the entire people of Israel played with its special calling by associating with the enemies of the Lord.

Because of this deceit on the part of the Philistines, Samson came to see how they stood over against him as his enemies. Then the Spirit of the Lord filled him in a mighty way. He went to

Ashkelon, killed 30 Philistines, and gave their garments to his companions. Angered by the deceit, he left his wife and returned to his father's house.

After a few days he felt sorry about leaving his wife. Here again he did not see her as a *Philistine* woman. His heart went out to her again. He took a little goat with him as a gift for her, to make up for the humiliation he had caused her. But when he arrived at her father's house, he found that his wife had been given to someone else, namely, the man who had been "best man" at his wedding. In his anger Samson punished the Philistines: he tied the tails of some foxes together, attached torches to them, and set them free in the Philistines' grainfields. The crop was quickly destroyed. The Philistines retaliated by burning Samson's wife and her father alive. Samson struck back by killing many of the Philistines. In his unsparing rage, he broke their arms and legs.

Despite all the things Samson did wrong, it was made clear to the Philistines that a deliverer had arisen in Israel, that there was someone in Israel who was stronger than all of them together, because the Lord was with him. If the Israelites would only believe, they would be mightier than all their enemies, for the true Deliverer lived in Israel, the One of whom Samson was only a type. Would the Israelites recognize Samson as a deliverer and receive him as a gift from the hand of the Lord? Events soon proved that they would not.

Israel's watchman. Samson withdrew and lived by himself in the heights of the rock at Etam. The Philistines were aware that Israel's protector lived there. If they did not overcome him, their power over Israel would be broken. Therefore they marched on Judah with an army.

In great fear, the men of Judah asked the Philistines why they had come up against them. They had already heard that it was on account of Samson. Did the men of Judah rejoice that the Lord had given Israel a deliverer? On the contrary, 3000 men from Judah went to see Samson and reproached him for embittering the Philistines. They said they had come to bind Samson and hand him over to the Philistines. The only thing Samson asked of them was that they themselves refrain from attacking him. When they agreed, he let himself be bound with two ropes, and he was led away to be delivered into the hands of the enemy.

Israel's deliverer was disowned by the Israelites themselves and handed over to the enemy! The Israelites did not want—or dare—to believe in the deliverance which the Lord wished to grant them.

At this point we cannot help but think of how the Redeemer Christ was rejected and delivered up by His own people. And aren't there many today who deny Him by their unbelief? Despite all the denial the Redeemer underwent that suffering in order to atone for the sin of His people. If only we would stop denying Him over and over again in gross ingratitude!

When the Philistines saw Samson bound at Lehi, they came shouting to meet him, thinking that their enemy was in their hands. But the Spirit of the Lord came upon Samson in a mighty way; he saw the favor of the Lord upon His people and received the strength to break the ropes. With a donkey's jawbone, which he found lying nearby, he killed a thousand men. Therefore he called that place *Ramath-lehi*, which means *jawbone hill*.

Tired from all the fighting, Samson looked for water but could not find any. He got very, very thirsty. The Lord used his thirst to humble him. Right after his victory he had boasted: "With a donkey's jawbone, one heap, two heaps; with a donkey's jawbone I have killed a thousand men." That was another example of his recklessness. But now he prayed: "You have given this wonderful deliverance by the hand of Your servant. Must I now die of thirst and fall into the hands of the uncircumcised?" Here he knew fellowship with his God. He recognized that it was the Lord who had given him the victory, and he realized his own dependence. His cause was God's cause. Here, in the most exalted sense, he was a type of the Lord Jesus Christ in His suffering.

Because of his fear of God,* Samson's prayer was heard. One day the Christ would fully bear the suffering. God then split open a hollow rock; water gushed out, and Samson drank. There he drank God's lovingkindness, which He pours out upon His people for Christ's sake.

---

*On the meaning of *"fear* of God," see the note on p. 54 of Volume I. — TRANS.

After this battle, Israel began to acknowledge Samson as a gift of God. In the Lord's name he judged Israel as its deliverer for 20 years.

Humbled and exalted. Samson was subject to the same weakness as the rest of the Israelites, namely, a desire to associate with the Canaanites. He often sought out Philistine women. Even though the Spirit of the Lord worked mightily in Samson, sin revealed its power in him.

One day he was with a sinful Philistine woman in Gaza. He stayed in the city past sundown. His enemies lay in wait for him all night. As usual, they had locked the city gates. Samson, they thought, would try to make his escape during the night, but with the gates locked he would have to wait until morning. Then they would capture him and kill him.

Samson did indeed want to get out of the city during the night. When he found the gates locked, he picked up the doors of the gates together with the two posts and carried them to a hilltop across from the Israelite city of Hebron, a distance of almost 60 kilometers.

In effect Samson was playing with God's grace. He had taken a sinful path. Yet, God did not want Israel's deliverer to perish at Gaza. Samson was allowed to see this again, in faith. And by that faith he received the strength to carry away the gate. Yet, how completely he had given himself up to sin!

All the same, the city gate, lying on the hilltop for all Israel to see, was a sign to Israel that all the Philistine cities lay open by the mercy of God. Nothing could withstand Israel's deliverer! This truth was not fully realized until the coming of the real Redeemer of God's people—the Christ.

Samson continued to give in to sin. After that episode he sought out another Philistine woman, namely, Delilah. She was a temptress who had made an agreement with the Philistine lords to try and find out the secret of Samson's strength. She would then sell his secret to the Philistines.

Twice Samson deceived her. The third time he began to play with the secret of his life, for he spoke of braiding his hair into a loom. The truth of the matter was that his hair was a sign of his calling as a Nazirite, of his devotion and consecration to the Lord as Israel's deliverer. The fourth time he betrayed the whole secret to his temptress. Thereby he not only delivered himself up to the enemy, he also spurned the mercy of the Lord, which was conferred upon the people through him. What would become of Israel now, when even its deliverer showed such contempt for God's favor? Fortunately, the Lord remained faithful.

Once Samson's head had been shaved, he was powerless. The Lord had left him, and he fell into the hands of his enemies. They gouged out his eyes, bound him with two bronze chains, and brought him to Gaza, where they made him grind grain in the prison.

It was not just a man named Samson who had been captured; *Israel's deliverer* was in the hands of the enemy. It appeared that God's people were conquered for good. Such a situation could not be allowed to continue indefinitely. For the sake of the only Redeemer Jesus Christ, Samson, too, would rise again.

The Philistines held a great feast for their god Dagon, a feast of thanksgiving for the victory over Samson. A great host of Philistines gathered in the idol's temple. Blind Samson was led inside by a boy, so that all the people assembled there could make fun of him.

During Samson's imprisonment, his hair had grown back. He also thought about his calling again. He asked the boy to bring him near the pillars on which the roof rested, so that he could lean against them. There he prayed to the Lord to repay the Philistines for what they had done to him, Israel's deliverer. Then, in the Spirit, he saw God's grace upon his people again, and he believed. In the strength of that faith, he took hold of the central pillars and pulled them away, so that the entire temple collapsed.

Samson died with the Philistines. He gave himself in death for the deliverance of his people. In his death he killed more enemies than during his lifetime. Israel's deliverer had proven to be stronger than Israel's enemies. What a comfort to Israel! In life and in death, Samson remained a deliverer—the mighty one of Israel, a type of the Redeemer who would one day deliver the entire people of God from all their enemies.

His whole family retrieved his body and buried him in the grave of his father Manoah. He was buried among his own people despite the fact that he had abandoned the path of obedience. He belonged to Israel. He was one of Israel's great sons, who brought deliverance through faith. He had judged Israel for 20 years.

5: Falling and Rising

Judges 17-21

Both of these stories (concerning Micah's priest and the Levite's concubine) took place near the beginning of the time of the judges. On the basis of Judges 18:11 and 25, we may conclude that the first story probably occurred before Israel was oppressed by the Philistines. The fact that Phinehas, Eleazar's son, appears as high priest in the second story also points to the beginning of the period of the judges.

These stories shed light on the deterioration of life in the covenant. Apparently that deterioration had set in at the very beginning, not long after the conquest of Canaan. The sin of Micah and of the Danites was a sin against the first table of the law (Judges 18:30), while the sin of the inhabitants of Gibeah was a violation of the second table (the seventh commandment). When we see the Danites worshiping idols and the sin of Sodom flourishing among the Benjaminites, we realize how much Israel had learned from the Canaanites.

In both stories a Levite plays a central role. In the first story we meet a Levite who was looking for work and a place to live (Judges 17:9). In the second story we meet a Levite who enjoyed the sinful luxury of a concubine.

The tribe of Levi, which was consecrated to the Lord, had become a stumbling block to Israel. This tribe became an unholy factor in the life of the people. The Christ, who had called the Levites as a tribe in order to use them to reveal His grace to Israel, made them stumble and fall when they left His service. Then the Levites were left with nothing to do, despite the fact that theirs was the highest calling of all. Through the tribe of Levi, the Christ made all of Israel stumble and fall.

The sin of idol worship as well as the sin of Sodom (unnatural forms of sexual activity, e.g. homosexuality) were both to be found in Israel.

49

But the broken covenant relationship drove the people to the most extreme forms of these sins.

In the family of Micah's mother, things were already amiss. Her superstition drove her to consecrate the recovered money to a self-willed form of divine worship. And when the Levite entered the picture, the sin became complete.

Apparently the sin of Sodom was already to be found in Benjamin's tribe. But the men of Gibeah knew that the stranger in their midst was a Levite. Because he served in the house of the Lord (probably a better translation than "I am going to the house of the Lord"), nobody wanted to take him into his house (Judges 19:18). But then, during the night, the men of Gibeah came up with a devilish idea: they would commit sodomy with the Levite. That would mean the worst conceivable desecration of something holy, something set apart. Thus the Christ was causing them to fall (see Luke 2:34).

The idol worship in Dan lasted "until the day of the captivity of the land" (Judges 18:30). This cannot be a reference to Israel's removal from Canaan by the Assyrians. It is unthinkable that such worship would have been allowed to continue undisturbed during the reformation under Samuel and the first kings. Neither do we read that when Jeroboam instituted the calf worship in Dan, he was building on something that was already there. On the contrary, he established something new. Therefore the words "until the day of the captivity of the land" must mean until the *honor* of the land was removed, that is, when the ark was carried off (see I Sam. 4:22).

Eventually the Christ exercised judgment upon the Danites for their sin. He also judged Benjamin through the other tribes, as well as the entire people of Israel through the initial defeats at the hands of Benjamin. By that judgment the Christ was once more causing Israel to rise.

More than once in these chapters we read: "In those days there was no king in Israel; every man did what was right in his own eyes." Through a centralized, kingly authority—if that authority were exercised in the name of the Lord—the public sin would have been rooted out. Since there was no king, the response to the sin depended on the spirit in the majority of the tribes and on the degree of community between the tribes. If there was indeed a sense of solidarity rooted in faith, then the fear of the Lord would be preserved through the joint action of the tribes. That sense of community was definitely evident in the action taken against the inhabitants of Gibeah. Yet, the exercise of justice degenerated into unrestrained retaliation. As a result, the tribe of Benjamin was almost completely wiped out. The people had already grown unaccustomed to the communion which they were privileged to share within the covenant. The calling of Israel's tribes to maintain justice together should say something to the (formerly) Christian nations of the Western world.

Main thought: *The Christ causes the falling and rising of many in Israel.*

Private, self-willed worship. During the first years of the judges, there was a man named Micah living in the hill country of Ephraim. One day his mother discovered that 1100 silver pieces were missing. Evidently they had been stolen from her. In her anger she cursed the thief, in the presence of her son. Shortly after that Micah came to her and confessed that he was the thief. Apparently his mother's curse had made him afraid.

Then his mother said: "May the Lord bless my son." Apparently she was happier about the recovery of the money than shocked about the misdeed of her son. In a family privileged to live in the covenant of the Lord, the situation had degenerated so far that a son stole from his mother and the mother, uttering a curse because of the loss of the money, was not disturbed because of the breach in the family! Without any ado, the breach was repaired when Micah returned the money. Covenant righteousness was not to be found in this family, and the blessing pronounced on Micah was unholy.

That soon became clear. Apparently Micah's mother had no lack of money, for she consecrated all that recovered money to the Lord. If her intention had been a holy one, she would have given it for the service of the Lord in the sanctuary at Shiloh. But now she ordered her son to have an image made of the money. He was to set up the image on a cast pedestal and establish a worship center for it in her own home.

What she had in mind was a worship center for the Lord, whom she could picture mentally as she looked at the idol. She wanted to worship the Lord in her *own* way, in the way *she* thought was best. For this she gave her money freely. In dedicating her money for such a purpose, she was really putting herself first, following her own desires. Thus, both she and her son were in conflict with the Lord's will.

Micah followed his mother's wishes. He took 200 pieces of silver to a silversmith to have them turned into an image on a pedestal. The remainder of the money he used to furnish a temple shrine with everything that was needed for worship, including a priestly ephod and teraphim. Here we see the triumph of pagan notions in Israel. This form of worship was produced by man, following the desires of his own heart without any recognition of God as the one and only, the one who has all authority in His covenant.

In those days there was no king in Israel. Had there been a king who reigned according to the covenant, he would not have tolerated this abomination. The tribes bore the responsibility for keeping an eye on each other. But they failed to carry out this responsibility. Consequently, Israel was in danger of sinking into the abyss of paganism.

At first Micah installed one of his sons as priest. But one day a young man arrived at his home, a Levite from Bethlehem. He was looking for work and a place to stay. Now, the tribe of Levi had been called to serve the Lord in the sanctuary. Therefore Micah installed this young man as priest in his temple. His worship center was complete! Thus, even the consecrated tribe was misused for sinful purposes and covenant breaking. And the Levite let himself be misused in this shameful way.

In his blindness Micah thought that the Lord would now make him prosper, for he had a Levite as priest. The consecrated tribe became a curse to Israel. The grace which God wishes to show us in the Christ can be a blessing to us, but unbelief turns it into a curse.

Self-willed worship in the tribe of Dan. In Joshua's days, the tribe of Dan had received an inheritance in the west, near the territory of Judah (Josh. 19:40ff). But because the Amorites had pressed the Danites back, they were in need of more land. They decided to look for room to expand elsewhere and sent out five men as spies.

In the course of their travels, the spies came to Micah's house. They noticed from the speech of the Levite that he came from their region. They became acquainted with him, and after they heard what he was doing there, they asked him for some divine light upon their path. The Levite told them that their mission would be successful. Here we have a classic example of people deceiving themselves and each other. They thought that the Lord would use such sinful worship to bestow His light and grace upon them!

After they left Micah's house, the spies found what they were looking for. In the north of the land, in the city of Laish, they came upon a people that lived a rather hidden existence, isolated from others and free from cares. Nobody disputed their claim to the land. It would be easy to attack them and take their territory away from them.

After the spies returned and reported to the tribe, 600 men, together with their families and possessions, made preparations to conquer this territory. When they passed the house of Micah on the way to Laish, the spies mentioned that there was a privately maintained worship center in that house. The Danites decided to transport that worship center to the territory they had set out to capture. The Levite was quickly won over when the Danites promised that he would become the priest of a whole tribe.

He went along with their wicked plan and let them steal all the contents of Micah's temple shrine. Then he escaped with them. The little army of Danites put the women and possessions in front, so that Micah would not dare attack them from the rear. When Micah did pursue them, they threatened to kill him and he turned back.

When the Danites arrived at Laish, they attacked the city and burned it, killing the inhabitants. They rebuilt the city and made it their home. They called it Dan and set up their self-willed worship center there.

Thus the Levite caused the people of an entire region to stumble and fall. It was clear that the Danites had not taken possession of that region in the north in the name of the Lord or with the purpose of serving Him there. This made the capture of Laish pure robbery; the Danites were not acting as agents of the Lord's judgment. More and more, the grace they rejected became a curse to them. The Danites went their own way in opposition to the Lord, the God of the covenant.

This worship center at Dan lasted until the Lord delivered Israel into the hands of the Philistines so completely that even the ark of the Lord was carried away. Then God exercised judgment upon all Israel for its apostasy—including the tribe of Dan.

Through that judgment, Israel was raised up to new faith. By way of judgment then, the Christ caused Israel to rise again. God remained faithful, even though the people were unfaithful. The people would be kept safe until the Redeemer came to save His people from their sin.

The abomination at Gibeah. In those same days, at the beginning of the period of the judges, there was a Levite living in the hill country of Ephraim. Although he had a wife, this Levite took another woman into his household, but without showing her sufficient respect to marry her. She was his concubine.

This woman became unfaithful to him and returned to her father's house in Bethlehem. After some months the Levite looked her up again to win her back. The two were reconciled, and her father received the Levite in his house. For three days they celebrated their renewed relationship together, flirting with sin in a carefree way. Acting as though there was nothing wrong with their relationship, they had a good time together. The woman's father enjoyed it so much that he insisted that they stay a fourth day also. Even on the fifth day, he did not let them go until late in the afternoon.

On their journey, darkness set in quickly as they neared Jerusalem. The Levite did not want to spend the night there because the Canaanites still inhabited that city. He went on to Gibeah instead, where the Benjaminites lived. The Levite thought he would find safety among his own people. But because he was a Levite, nobody took him in. That's how much the service of the Lord was already despised in Gibeah.

In the street, where the Levite expected to spend the night with his concubine and his boy, he met an old man who took him into his house. That night the men of Gibeah gathered around the house and demanded that the Levite be brought out to them so that they could commit sodomy with him. To honor his obligations as host, the old man refused. Instead he handed the Levite's concubine over to the men to do with as they pleased.

When the Levite left the house the next morning to continue his trip, he found his concubine lying dead on the doorstep. She had been raped by the men. The Levite was greatly upset. When he got home, he cut her body into pieces and sent the pieces throughout Israel. A cry of horror went up in all the land.

God's people had gone so far downhill that even the most horrible sins of heathendom were committed in their midst. Gibeah's inhabitants concentrated their sacrilege especially on the Levite—*because* he was a Levite. Everything holy had to be trampled underfoot. If God's grace does not take hold of us, we will come to hate it.

Judgment. All the tribes of Israel gathered before the Lord at Mizpah to avenge this abomination. After hearing the Levite out, they swore to destroy Gibeah, kill its inhabitants, and give the land to another tribe.

First they asked the tribe of Benjamin to hand over the men of Gibeah. But Benjamin refused and took up Gibeah's cause. Thus the curse of this sin came upon the entire tribe.

With an army of 400,000 men, Israel went to battle. Over against that army, Benjamin could come up with only 26,000 men. But among them were 700 carefully selected soldiers who could sling a stone at a hair without missing.

In the first battle Israel lost 22,000 men. This did not, however, bring the people to their senses. They did not ask themselves whether the Lord was perhaps against His people because of their sin. They did ask the Lord, by means of the high priest, if they should renew the battle against Benjamin. After receiving an affirmative command from the Lord, they attacked a second time—and lost 18,000 men.

Now the people came to themselves. Again they went back to Bethel, where the ark of the Lord had been brought from Shiloh. There they consulted Phinehas, the high priest. They fasted and confessed their sins. Then they renewed the covenant by bringing offerings. In the Lord's name Phinehas told them that Benjamin would be delivered into their hands the next day.

The people had gone out to war with a sinful sense of self-confidence, believing that in themselves they were better than the Benjaminites. The Lord had exercised judgment upon that sin via the two defeats. Now, in humble faith, they were to be nothing other than agents carrying out the Lord's judgment upon Benjamin. Nobody is any better in himself than the very worst of sinners.

The Israelites now defeated Benjamin through a trick, by setting up an ambush. They destroyed Gibeah and killed all its inhabitants. But the exercise of judgment deteriorated into unbridled revenge, with the result that the entire land of Benjamin was destroyed. Nothing was left of the tribe but 600 men, who hid themselves in the rock of Rimmon. Again the people had failed to exercise judgment in the name of the Lord. They had followed their own wishes instead.

Restored communion. After the war of extermination was over, the Israelites realized what they had done. One of the tribes was now missing from their assembly. That tribe was doomed to extinction, for the Israelites had sworn not to let their daughters marry Benjaminites.

In this difficult situation they did not seek the face of the Lord, asking Him to show them how to preserve the tribe of Benjamin. They tried to overcome the problem by themselves. They discovered that one city (Jabesh-gilead) had not participated in the war on Benjamin and decided to destroy that city. But when they did so, they spared the young women, whom they gave to the surviving Benjaminites as wives. When there were not enough wives to go around, they advised the Benjaminites to catch wives for themselves when the people gathered for the annual feast to the Lord at Shiloh. This the Benjaminites did.

By these actions the tribe of Benjamin was preserved. But the Israelites had tackled the problem in a cocky, conceited, highhanded way. How estranged from the Lord's service Israel had become! How little did it live by His light! It is a miracle that anything came of that people, that justice was practiced, that the fellowship of the tribes was preserved. There is no other explanation for this miracle than that God, in His grace in the Christ, wished to dwell in the midst of that people in spite of its sin.

What numerous and grievous sins the Christ would have to atone for one day! The Spirit of Christ was active among the people, repeatedly causing the people to fall, but also causing many to rise again in Israel.

6: The Redeemer

Ruth 1-4

The story of Ruth took place at the time "when the judges judged"—most likely during the days of the Midianite invasions. Until they were driven out by Gideon, the Midianites would invade Israel during the harvest season and occupy the Valley of Jezreel and the coastal plains. They also made regular raids in Judah. This oppression went on for seven years and probably explains the famine that caused Elimelech to leave the country.

Only after ten years had passed did Naomi hear that the Lord had visited His people and had given them bread. Most likely she waited to see if the plague was gone for good and if Israel would recover.

The history recorded in the book of Ruth is really the story of Boaz, the redeemer.* The line of Elimelech was in danger of dying out in Israel. If it did, his name would be wiped out from among his people. Furthermore, his inheritance in Israel was lost: Naomi was forced to sell her parcel of land after her return to Judah (Ruth 4:3). Thus Boaz was the redeemer in two senses. By way of the levirate marriage with Ruth, the name of Elimelech's line was preserved in Israel. The first-born son of Boaz and Ruth was counted as a son of Elimelech's line. In addition, Boaz redeemed the parcel of land sold by Naomi and restored it to Elimelech's line. In this twofold sense, Boaz was a type of the Christ.

---

*The Hebrew word for *redeemer* is *goel.* It means "one who acts as kinsman" or "one who performs the duty of the next of kin." This duty could be fulfilled by taking a kinsman's widow as wife in order to beget children for the departed through his widow, or by redeeming (buying back) a kinsman's field after he was forced to sell it to pay off a debt. The law of the *goel* was intended to prevent land from being lost to the family to which it was given and to keep families from dying out. The word *goel* is also used in connection with Israel's deliverance from exile in Egypt. The covenant God is spoken of as the *goel*.—TRANS.

Because of our sin, our name perishes with us. For Christ's sake, however, the Lord in His covenant preserved our name and the name of our family. Neither do we have any claim to a place on the earth. But the Christ gives us an inheritance among the saints on the new earth. The believer's earthly possession is a guarantee of his eternal inheritance as well as a prophecy pointing ahead to it.

The Christ is the true Redeemer. Boaz was both an ancestor and a type of the Christ.

Main thought: *The redeemer preserves the name of those who belong to his family and buys back their inheritance.*

A name and inheritance lost. Under Joshua's guidance, the land of Canaan had been divided among the twelve tribes. Every family had its own inheritance. That was Israel's pride and joy. Believers hoped that their families would continue to live on their own land until the coming of the Messiah. Then they would share with Him in the glory that was promised. Therefore no one was to give up his rights to his land. It was to be a guarantee of his share in the coming glory of the Christ.

Sometimes, when the faith of the Israelites grew weak, their link with the land was broken. That's what happened to a certain family in the time of the judges. There was a great famine in the land, perhaps as a result of the invasions by the Midianites. Elimelech, a man from the region of Bethlehem-Ephrath, grew weak in his faith and chose to sever his tie with the holy inheritance temporarily. Accompanied by his wife Naomi and his sons Mahlon and Chilion, he broke his ties with the land of Judah and went to live in the land of Moab. That was unbelief on his part, a lack of steadfastness, an unwillingness to bow under the judgment upon the land of his fathers and await the time of deliverance.

Elimelech died in Moab. His sons married Moabite women, Orpah and Ruth, and continued to live in Moab. Within ten years, both sons were dead and Naomi was left with her two daughters-in-law.

After those ten years, Naomi decided to return to Judah, for she heard that the Lord had granted deliverance and bread to His people. Her daughters-in-law accompanied her on the trip. As they were traveling, she urged them to turn back. Perhaps the Lord would yet give them a future with a family of their own among their own people.

At first neither of them would listen, for they both felt bound to Naomi and the family into which they had married. Then Naomi asked: "What expectation could you still have of this family? It is doomed to die out. That causes me even more bitterness than you. The hand of the Lord is against me."

These words persuaded Orpah to turn back. She did not see any future for herself in that family. But Ruth was bound not only to her husband's family but also to the nation from which that family had sprung—the people of Israel. And she was bound to Israel because she was bound to Israel's God. Her heart had been opened to the covenant in which the Lord wished to live with His people. That's why she said she wanted to live and die where Naomi lived and died, for Naomi's people were her people and Naomi's God was her God.

On they went together. When they got to Bethlehem, the whole town was moved and came out to meet them. The women exclaimed: "Is this Naomi?" Naomi told them to call her *Mara*, explaining that God had dealt bitterly with her. When she went away her family was blooming, but now she had nothing to look forward to. Her family had died out, and her husband's name would be wiped out from among the people. Moreover, she had to sell the field she still owned in Bethlehem because she was poor. She was left without land and without a name, a vagabond among her own people.

If the Lord had forsaken this family because of Elimelech's unbelief, it would have been wiped out. But the Lord, in His grace, wished to restore it, using the law of His covenant.

Because of our sin, the names of all of us should disappear forever, and we should lose our portion on this earth for all time. What if there were no mercy with God? Yet, in His covenant He wishes to restore the names of His people and give them a portion on the earth.

Finding a redeemer. It was the beginning of the barley harvest when Naomi returned. Ruth proposed to go to the fields of the wealthy and pick up the grain left behind by the reapers. That was God's way of taking care of the poor; there was a law in Israel providing for this (see Deut. 24:19). But not everyone adhered to that law. How would Ruth fare? Naomi agreed to her plan, and Ruth wound up in the fields of Boaz, a very wealthy man.

While Ruth was gathering heads of grain, Boaz himself came into the field. The master and his workers greeted each other in the Lord. The covenant of the Lord, which Boaz honored, also hallowed this relationship.

Boaz asked about the young woman who was busy gleaning ears of grain. He was told that it was Ruth, Naomi's daughter-in-law. Ruth's choice for the covenant of the Lord touched this man, who made a point of honoring the covenant himself. Hence he spoke to her and promised her freedom and protection in his fields. When Ruth showed surprise at such friendliness from a stranger, he told her that he was touched by her choice for the people of the Lord, with whom she had no future. He also invited her to come and eat with him at lunchtime and gave her some roasted grain, more than she could eat. He told his servants to let her glean among the sheaves as well and to drop some grain on purpose, so that she would have plenty.

That evening Ruth beat out what she had gleaned and came home with about a bushel of barley. She also brought Naomi what she had saved from her lunch. When Naomi expressed surprise, Ruth told her in whose field she had gathered the grain. She also talked about the friendliness she had encountered there. Then Naomi was even more surprised, for Boaz was one of her closest relatives—and therefore a potential redeemer. She began to see that it was the Lord who had led Ruth to Boaz's field. Within her rose the marvelous hope that God might yet provide a future for her family. Thus she had no objection when Ruth proposed to continue gleaning in Boaz's fields.

When she made the decision to return to Bethlehem, Naomi believed that all hope was cut off. Now the light began to dawn for her again, and she waited upon the Lord, who can always give new hope.

The redeemer's promise. Indeed, there was much that Naomi began to see. According to the decree of the covenant, the redeemer's duty would not be finished when he bought back the field she had been forced to sell. If he was to act in accordance with the law of the Lord, he would also have to take Ruth as his wife. Ruth's first-born son would then be counted as a son of Elimelech's line. In that way Elimelech's name would be preserved among his people. The family of Elimelech (including Naomi) would then have a future after all. Would the Lord be willing to grant that?

Naomi looked to the Lord in this matter. Yet she knew that she should not remain inactive. The redeemer would have to be asked to exercise his right of redemption. But that would have to be done with great tact. What would happen if, for one reason or another, he refused? That would mean disgrace for Ruth, and also for Boaz himself, whom she had learned to respect. The man had to be free in this decision, which would be of such crucial importance for Naomi's family.

When the harvest was over, Naomi told Ruth to go to the field in the evening. Boaz would be spending the night on the threshing floor because his men were going to winnow the reaped barley in the evening and morning breezes. Ruth should go there that night and put the question before Boaz. If he refused, nobody in Israel would know what had happened. And Boaz could then make up his mind in complete freedom.

Ruth went to the field in the evening and lay down at the feet of Boaz. When he woke up during the night and noticed Ruth, she asked him to become the redeemer of Elimelech's family by marrying her and buying back Elimelech's property for Naomi. Again Boaz was amazed and delighted at Ruth's faithfulness to Elimelech's family and to the laws of the Lord's covenant. He told her that he would be happy to perform the duty of the next of kin. But, as a man who was faithful to all decrees of the covenant, he also pointed out that there was another man in the picture, a man who had a prior claim to the right and duty of serving as the redeemer. That man would have to be consulted first. If he refused, Boaz would be the redeemer. To this Boaz swore an oath.

Ruth stayed on the threshing floor until it was almost morning. But Boaz sent her home before daybreak so that nobody would know what had happened. As a token of his vow, he gave her six measures of barley in her scarf.

Ruth went back to her mother-in-law, told her everything that had happened, and showed her the sign of Boaz's vow. Then Naomi believed the Lord, and together they waited to see what the other potential redeemer would do. Naomi saw the light breaking through upon her family again. She also saw how Boaz and Ruth, in their faithfulness to the Lord's covenant, had found each other.

Restoration. The next morning Boaz went and sat at the gate. He summoned the man who was first in line to serve as redeemer. He also called ten of the elders of the town to witness the negotiations. Then he asked the man if he was prepared to buy back Naomi's property for her. The man declared that he was willing to do so. He had it all figured out: although he was buying the field for Naomi, it would surely revert to him and his family when Naomi died. Boaz responded that the man would also have to take Ruth as his wife. This the man refused to do, for he realized that the field would then wind up in the hands of Elimelech's family, which would spring from the first son Ruth bore. If he married Ruth and she bore him a son, the parcel of land would be lost. For this potential redeemer, the question placed before him was simply a matter to be decided on the basis of financial considerations. Love for the covenant and the preservation of a family in that covenant played no role in his calculations.

Following the custom prevailing in Israel, Boaz then asked the man to take off his shoe, the shoe with which he would otherwise step onto the field to be redeemed. The removal of the shoe was a sign that he waived his right to the parcel of land and his right to serve as the redeemer (see Ps. 60:8). In the presence of the elders and the people standing at the gate, Boaz solemnly accepted the obligation to serve as the redeemer of Elimelech's family by marrying Ruth and returning the field to its original owners. The people and elders then called upon the Lord to bless Boaz and Ruth.

And the Lord did bless them for their faithfulness to His covenant. He gave them a son. Then, once again, the people of the town went to Naomi and gave expression to their great astonishment at the light which the Lord caused to rise over her family. This son would be considered a descendant of Elimelech, whose family would again have a name and place in Israel. The women of the neighborhood called the boy *Obed*, which means *servant*, for he served to save Elimelech's line.

Obed was one of the ancestors of David and therefore also of the Christ. Thus Boaz himself was one of the ancestors of Christ, of whom he was likewise a type. Just as the redeemer Boaz preserved the name and place of Elimelech in Israel, the Christ restores the names of His own for all time and gives them an eternal inheritance. The grace He shows them, together with all that they now receive on earth, is a guarantee of their eternal portion and a prophecy pointing ahead to it.

Samuel and Saul

7: The Forerunner of the King

I Samuel 1-4

The capture of the ark probably took place before Samson appeared on the scene as Israel's judge. If so, Samson's judgeship coincided with the first part of Samuel's career. In the period following the victory over the Philistines, God made Himself known in different ways as the God of the covenant with Israel.

It was during this period that the need for a king was keenly felt among the people. The Lord had indeed promised His people a king (see Deut. 17:14-20). What was sinful about their request for a king was their desire to put their trust in that king instead of in the Lord, who would give them a king in His own good time. In itself the desire to see the Lord's promise fulfilled was good. Such a desire was in the air in those days.

Mention is made of a king twice in these chapters. Hannah sings that the Lord will give strength to His king. And the prophet who announced the fall of Eli's house speaks of a faithful priest who will always walk before the face of God's "anointed."

In the final analysis, the promise of a king was a reference to the Christ. More immediately, however, such passages must be read as applying to the theocratic kings, such as David. But we must not forget about the Christ when we speak of the theocratic kings, for they were governed by the Christ.

Preparations had to be made for the coming of the king. It was for that purpose that Samuel was sent, just as John the Baptist was the forerunner of the Christ. The people had to be made ready to receive the king—by returning to God and also by turning the hearts of the children to their fathers again. Think of the relationship between Eli and his sons, and of the degeneration of Israel under the leadership of Eli's sons.

Samuel was the forerunner of the king because he was a judge. In him judgeship was combined with prophecy. In Eli we find the office of judge combined with the high priesthood.

This tie with the priesthood apparently promoted the growth of a sinful sense of familiarity with the holy, as we see from the conduct of Eli's sons. It also led to a vain trust in the sanctuary, as we see from the reckless decision to carry the ark into battle without repenting first.

The priesthood would be taken away from Eli's house, the prophet declared. Eli was of the line of Ithamar, the second of the remaining sons of Aaron. For some unknown reason, the high priesthood had shifted from Eleazar's line to that of Ithamar. In David's days, Abiathar, who was of Ithamar's line and was thus a descendant of Eli, and Zadok, who was of Eleazar's line, are mentioned together as high priests (II Sam. 15:24-9, 35; 19:11). When Solomon removed Abiathar as high priest, the high priesthood returned to Eleazar's line for good (I Kings 2:26-7).

Yet, in this later history we see only a partial fulfillment of the judgment upon Eli's house. Through the mouth of the prophet, the Lord said: " 'I had stated clearly that your house and the house of your father should go in and out before Me forever.' But now the Lord declares: 'Far be it from Me!' " Apparently the Lord was here referring to the promise made to Aaron.

In the sin of Eli's house, we are shown how the entire earthly priesthood of shadows was being destroyed by sin. That's why the rejection of that priesthood was announced. When the Christ came and the meaning of the priesthood of shadows was fulfilled in Him, He found the earthly priesthood in complete decay.

When Hannah sings her song of praise, she does not only sing about her own oppression by Peninnah. As a believer, she is one with the entire people of the Lord in her oppression. She sings of the Lord, who brings some people low and raises others up. Thus, when she sings about the people of the Lord, she cannot help but sing about their King. In her exaltation, she is given a revelation of how the Lord gives strength to His King. Her personal life, the life of the entire people of God, and the life of the Christ are all one in her song of praise. The dominant motif is the life of the Christ. The same can be said of the Psalms. Hannah's song can likewise be compared to Mary's song of praise (Luke 1:46-55), in which we find the same leading idea.

Main thought: *The Lord prepares the hearts of His people for the coming of the king.*

The birth of the forerunner. In the days of the judges, when Israel was oppressed by the Philistines, even before the Lord sent Samson, there was a Levite named Elkanah living in the hill country of Ephraim. Elkanah had two wives—Hannah and Penninah. That was not in accordance with the Lord's wishes. Misery is the inevitable result of taking more than one wife.

Thus misery descended on Elkanah's family. Penninah had children, but Hannah did not. Because Elkanah loved Hannah more, Penninah made use of every opportunity to oppose her. Driven by jealousy because of Elkanah's love for Hannah, Penninah tormented her. She would mock Hannah particularly when they went up to Shiloh for the great cultic feasts. It seemed as though the presence of the Lord brought out the sin in Penninah's heart in greater measure. And Elkanah made matters worse at the sacrificial meal by giving Hannah a larger portion after the thank offering than Penninah or her children. Satan did his best to spoil this family's appearance before the Lord in His sanctuary.

One day Elkanah's family was in Shiloh again to celebrate a certain cultic feast. The whole time they were there, Penninah scoffed at Hannah. Hannah wept. Her husband tried to comfort her by saying that his love should be more to her than ten sons, but Hannah would not be comforted. She knew that in her barrenness she was not helping to build the people of the Lord. There would be no descendant of hers on the earth when the Messiah finally came. Full of grief, she rose from the sacrificial meal and poured out her heart before the Lord in the sanctuary. That gave her relief.

Hannah prayed to the Lord for a son and vowed that if the Lord would grant her petition, she would consecrate the child to the Lord from his youth. He would be a Nazirite for life. While she was praying, Eli, the high priest, was sitting at the door of the tabernacle.

Hannah was praying quietly; only her lips moved. When Eli spotted her, he thought she was drunk and told her to go and sleep it off. That Eli assumed she was drunk shows how far things had gone downhill in Israel. It also shows that Eli lacked the ability to discern the working of the Spirit of the Lord. After Hannah gave Eli an account of her presence in the sanctuary, the spirit of prophecy awoke in him, and he prophesied that the Lord would give her what she had been praying for. Hannah believed, and she asked Eli to remember her in his prayers, for she knew that the prophecy would be fulfilled only through prayer. Then she stood up, a changed woman. Hannah lived by faith.

After praying in the presence of the Lord, Elkanah and his family went home. The Lord fulfilled His promise and gave Hannah a son, whom she called *Samuel,* that is, *heard of God.* Just as she had promised, she did not go up to Shiloh again until she could leave her son behind in the care of one of the women who served in the sanctuary. With a sacrifice and a present, Hannah and her husband brought the child to Eli, and Hannah let Eli know who she was. Eli glorified the Lord for revealing Himself so gloriously in Israel.

Driven by the Spirit, Hannah sang a song in which she spoke of her joy in the Lord, who glorifies Himself in His deeds and is a refuge for His own. The Lord had allowed her to triumph over her enemies, who were also enemies of God's grace. That's always the Lord's way. Those who do injustice and oppress others He will bring low, and those who are oppressed He will exalt. One day He will also exalt the King He has promised His people. Thus Hannah sang of the Christ, Israel's true King, with whom Israel and all God's people will be exalted. Hannah's own exaltation was a sample and proof of that exaltation.

Corruption in Israel. Although Hannah did not yet know it, her son would have a marvelous calling in Israel. He was to prepare the people to receive the king God was going to give them. The people would have to return to the Lord and receive their king from God's hand. Otherwise that king would not be a blessing to Israel.

The situation among the people of Israel had been degenerating for years. And the worst of it was that the corruption originated at the sanctuary. Eli's own sons, Hophni and Phinehas, profaned the holy services and stole from the Lord. They did not take from the offerings only what was rightfully theirs according to the law of Moses; when the sacrificial meals were being cooked, they took whatever they could get out of the pan with a fork. And they made matters even worse when they used force to steal from the people offering sacrifices: they took the fat and the best part of the meat, which was meant for the Lord on the altar. Willfully they provoked the Lord.

It was in such surroundings that Samuel grew up. Miraculously, he was kept from such sin. God's favor watched over him. That was an answer to his mother's prayer. Each year his mother made him a little robe, which he needed for his service in the sanctuary. Each time the new robe was a sign of her willingness to fulfill her vow. The making of the robe was accompanied by much prayer. Seeing such faith and obedience, Eli blessed Elkanah and Hannah and prayed for them, asking the Lord to give them more children. That prayer, too, was granted: the Lord gave them three more sons and two daughters.

Meanwhile, the ungodly conduct of Eli's sons continued. They committed adultery with women who came to the tabernacle and led Israel down the path of sin. Many of the people followed them by surrendering to sin. Of course, Eli heard complaints about his sons from some of the people. And he did warn them. If someone sins against a man, he told them, there will be judges who pass judgment on him, but there is always the possibility of praying to the Lord for forgiveness. Eli went on to point out that when a man interferes with the holy things of the Lord and hardens his heart against Him, then there is no room left for prayer.

Eli's sons did not listen to him. For them the time of mercy had passed. The Lord wished to put them to death, for their lives had been too deeply corrupted by sin. Eli was also to blame: although he warned his sons when he became an old man, he had not maintained strict discipline when they were growing up.

Finally a prophet came to Eli and announced in the name of the Lord that Eli's house was doomed to fall. God would remove the high priesthood from Eli's line and replace Eli with a faithful priest who would serve the Lord together with the king who was to come. The strength of Eli's house would be broken: no man of his house would grow old. Anyone in Eli's house who was still alive when the faithful priest took over would come to that priest begging for work and a piece of bread.

That judgment was later fulfilled when the Lord called someone from another family to the office of high priest. The new high priest served the Lord, together with the king. Finally, the promise implicit in that judgment was fulfilled in the Christ, who is both High Priest and King at the same time.

The judgment upon Eli's house was a judgment of God's

mercy upon His people. Because Eli's house led Israel to depart from the Lord, it would be punished severely. The honor of the Lord, that is, the honor of the mercy of the Lord upon His people, had been profaned by Eli's house. For that reason it would perish. The Lord is faithful to His covenant with His people.

The calling of the prophet. In those days the Lord rarely spoke to His people anymore. There was hardly a prophet left. There was no one who could speak in the Lord's name and make His Word known to the people. However, the Lord intended to call Samuel as a prophet. Through him, the Lord would speak to His people again. But Samuel had never heard the Lord speaking to him. The first time he was addressed by the Lord was a very strange experience for him.

One night, even before the candle which burned in the sanctuary at night had gone out, the Lord called Samuel. Samuel went directly to Eli's bedside, thinking that Eli, who had become blind and an invalid in his old age, had called him. This happened three times. Finally Eli realized that it was the Lord who was calling Samuel. The fourth time Samuel answered as Eli told him to: "Speak, Lord! Your servant is listening." Then Samuel heard God's first revelation to him—and a terrible revelation it was. The Lord said that the day would soon come when He would carry out His judgment upon Eli's house. It was already too late to do anything about it. The judgment would be so terrible that the ears of all who heard it would tingle.

Samuel would soon have to make this prophecy known to Eli. On this very first occasion, he already learned how difficult it can be to do what the Lord has commanded, and how much it can go against our flesh-and-blood inclinations. But if the Word of the Lord has really come to us and taken hold of us, we cannot break away from its influence. The first call from the Lord, therefore, was decisive for Samuel's entire life. Even though *we* do not hear God calling us in such a way and do not receive the particular calling to serve as God's prophet, the Lord does call us through His Word to serve Him in all of life.

In the morning Samuel took his time as he opened the doors of the forecourt. He did not relish the prospect of telling Eli what the Lord had revealed to him. Then Eli called Samuel. He noticed that Samuel was reluctant to give him the message, so he ordered him to tell everything he had heard from the Lord. And Samuel did. Then Eli bowed his head and said: "He is the Lord. Let Him do what seems good to Him." When we hear such words from one who had devoted his entire life to the Lord's service, we sense in them the victory of faith. The Christ, too, won the victory when He said: "Not My will but Yours be done." Could it be that Eli had not struggled enough in his life?

After that first occasion, the Lord continued to reveal Himself to Samuel. And He clearly fulfilled all that He had spoken to the people through Samuel. The entire people began to see that the Lord had given them a prophet, and Samuel began to lead the people back to the Lord, back to His covenant and His Word. Thereby he could begin preparing the people to receive the king whom the Lord would give them. In just such a way, John the Baptist made preparations for the coming of the Lord Jesus Christ. How will the Spirit of the Lord Jesus Christ come to His rule of grace in our hearts if not by His Word?

Ichabod. The fulfillment of the judgment upon Eli's house and upon Israel came about in a different manner and a good deal sooner than most people expected. In those days the Israelites were still oppressed by the Philistines. Perhaps the Israelites had become a bit more courageous because of Samson's deeds. In any case, they gathered an army together and marched out to do battle with the Philistines in the territory of Benjamin. But the Philistines defeated the Israelites; 4000 men were killed. Now the Israelites were faced with the prospect of complete subjection to the Philistines.

Returning to the camp, the elders asked each other why the Lord had abandoned Israel. They did not come up with the only true and obvious answer, namely, the abominations in Israel. As long as we can possibly cover up and seek the cause of our misfortune outside of ourselves, we will.

The elders considered bringing the ark into the battle. Then the Lord would be with them. What a sinful misconception! The ark was certainly the sign of the presence of the Lord, but the Lord revealed and gave Himself in that sign only to a people who looked to Him in faith. Repentance was required on Israel's part before the Lord would be with His people again.

The ark was brought to the battlefield accompanied by Hophni and Phinehas. How did these men, who had profaned the service of the Lord, dare do it? The Israelites had introduced an abominable sin into their camp. In effect they were begging the Lord to turn against them completely, as they soon discovered.

When the ark was brought inside the camp, the whole army shouted for joy. The Philistines heard the shouting. Once they learned the reason for the jubilation among the Israelites, they were afraid. But it was not the fear of the Lord that fell upon them, paralyzing them. On the contrary, they said to each other: "Be strong, and act like men!"

The battle ended in a great defeat for Israel. Thirty thousand men of the infantry fell, the ark was captured, and Hophni and Phinehas were killed. Catastrophe struck. The worst thing of all was that the ark was lost: it had fallen into the hands of the enemy. This had never happened before in Israel's history. When the Israelites lost possession of the ark, the Lord departed from His people. Israel's honor, its honor as the people of the covenant of His grace, was gone. What would come of the people now?

As a result of this catastrophe, the hope in Israel had to die. A Benjaminite ran to Shiloh to bring word of the disaster. When the people heard the news, the whole city cried out. Eli asked what the uproar was all about. How anxiously he had awaited the outcome of the battle! And now he heard that his people had been defeated, that his sons were dead, and that the ark had been captured by the Philistines. When he heard the worst news of all, he was so shocked that he fell from his chair and broke his neck.

The wife of Phinehas, who was expecting a baby, also heard the message. She, too, was shocked most of all at the capture of the ark. As she gave birth to a son, she died from the sheer horror of it all. The women looking after her still tried to awaken hope in her by telling her that she had given birth to a son. But hope could no longer live within her. As she died, she named her son *Ichabod*, that is, *the glory has departed*.

Total darkness descended on Israel. Hope had to die. Yet, both Eli and the wife of Phinehas were shocked most of all at the news that the ark had been captured by the enemy. This showed that true life and the fear of the Lord were still not entirely dead.

Eli was more beautiful in death than ever in life. And as the wife of Phinehas died, she earned undying glory. God would not forsake the work of His hands in Israel. From this death Israel would rise again, for the sake of the Christ, who was dead and is alive. One day, by the hand of Samuel, Israel would receive from the Lord a king for its deliverance.

8: The Return of the Lord

I Samuel 5-7

The fall of Dagon before the ark of the Lord does not show us first and foremost that God is mightier than heathen idols. We are to view it as a revelation of the God of the covenant. His grace is stronger than the idolatrous expectations of any man, stronger than any fabrication of the flesh. Dagon, together with everything else people use to hide from the Lord, will be conquered by the grace which is in Christ Jesus. Thus this episode is also a prophecy pointing ahead to the Christ, whose salvation is revealed to all peoples.

This revelation in Ashdod could not have taken place if the Lord in His mercy had not already returned to His people. Without His return, the ark would not have been a sign of His presence. We must remember that the ark was a sign of the covenant. Because the Lord had left His people, He was no longer connected with the sign (the ark), and He allowed it to fall into the hands of the Philistines. But the One who takes the initiative in the covenant returned to Israel and therefore joined His special presence to that sign again.

When the Philistines returned the ark on a cart drawn by two nursing cows, they were rightly conscious that God had not withdrawn Himself from this world but was directing it in His concern. That concern was a vehicle of His grace, which He had promised in His covenant.

The Philistines were risking something; they were taking a leap in the dark. By faith, in the covenant, we refuse to take such chances. In faith we confidently await the Lord's guidance. Today we enjoy that guidance not in some special sign but in the Word of the Lord.

In the story of the consecration of the golden mice, the Hebrew text (I Sam. 6:18) presents some difficulties. Instead of "even unto the great stone of Abel" (KJV), we should probably read: "The great stone is a witness" (RSV). A similar textual difficulty occurs in the very next verse.

In older translations we read that the Lord struck down the men of Beth-shemesh—"fifty thousand and threescore and ten men" (KJV). This reading should probably not be accepted. Beth-shemesh and surroundings did not have that many adult male inhabitants.

For 20 years the ark remained at Kiriath-jearim. During that time the Philistines oppressed Israel. Not until the end of this period did Samuel's work as a judge begin—with the gathering and subsequent victory at Mizpah, more than 20 years after Eli's death. In the meantime, God had revealed Himself through Samuel. But only then, for the first time, did Samuel act as judge and begin restoring Israel to a right relationship with God.

The return of the Lord was also a preparation for presenting His people with a king. They were to receive their king through Samuel.

Main thought: *After abandoning His people, the Lord returns to them so that they will fear Him.*

Commotion among the Philistines. The Philistines were able to capture the ark because the sins of Eli's house and of all Israel had caused God to turn away from His people. Once that happened, the ark was no longer a sign of His presence and could fall into the hands of the enemy.

The Philistines now thought they had permanent control over Israel, that is, over the grace God showed Israel. In that conviction they brought the ark to Ashdod and placed it in the house of their god Dagon. They believed they had cut off Israel's hopes for the future. God's grace would now be subject to the power of their gods.

But the Lord remembered His people. In His favor He returned to Israel. As the One who takes the initiative in the covenant, He could do so again and again, for Christ's sake—even before the people turned back to Him. Because He had returned to Israel, the ark again became a sign of His gracious presence. That grace reserved for Israel would now become evident in the land of the Philistines.

The Philistines had set the ark in the house of Dagon. The very next morning, the statue of Dagon was found on the floor, lying face down before the ark. The Philistines ascribed this to chance and set the statue up again. But the next morning they found its head and hands lying on the threshold as if they had been cut off; again the statue had fallen face down before the ark.

Here we have a clear revelation of God in His grace doing battle with the powers of heathendom. Just as the idol was without a head and hands, heathendom would become foolish and powerless before the grace of God, which was to be fully revealed in Christ Jesus. All power would worship *Him*.

In addition, the people in Ashdod began to suffer from boils. Their fields, like the fields throughout the entire land of the Philistines, were being eaten bare by mice. The grace God shows His people turns into judgment upon those who pay no attention to it.

There were also problems in Gath and Ekron. Finally the Philistines and their holy men gathered together to decide how to dispose of the ark. They had already decided to send it back to Israel; the question was how. On the advice of the priests and fortune-tellers, they put a certain box next to the ark, a box containing five golden boils and as many golden mice as there were Philistine cities and villages plagued by mice. By means of that gift, the Philistines hoped to reconcile the God of Israel—as if they could ever atone for an offense against His grace by means of such a gift!

Still, the Philistines were not mistaken by expecting deliverance from the plague once the ark was returned. Even though there was no eternal reconciliation for them, they were forced to stand in awe of the God of grace.

They were not entirely certain that the plagues were connected with the presence of the ark in their land. On the advice of the diviners, they put the ark on a new cart to which they hitched two nursing cows whose calves were returned to the stable. If the cows forgot about their calves and headed toward the land of Israel of their own accord, the Philistines could be sure that they were guided by the God of Israel. What an awareness of God's care they displayed! They sensed that God does not leave us in the dark but shows us the way! In their own heathen way, they took a chance on God's guidance, without prayer and outside the covenant of the Lord. People still do the same thing today when they attempt to learn God's instructions for them from a sign, apart from His Word. In those days God gave guidance in life by means of special signs. He still gives guidance today, but now he does so through His Word.

The cows, with the cart, went straight down the highway in the direction of Israel. The Philistine rulers followed them at a distance, going as far as Israel's borders. It was clear to the Philistines that God was again looking out for His people.

Learning to fear God. The cart stopped in Beth-shemesh. The people there were busy harvesting their wheat. When they saw the ark, they rejoiced. The return of the ark was indeed a miracle of grace; it was a sign that God had returned to His people!

The people of Beth-shemesh were delighted. They sacrificed the cows as a burnt offering to the Lord, using the wood of the cart and a great stone nearby. They were permitted to offer this sacrifice because the ark was no longer at Shiloh: they had the sign of God's presence right there in their midst. By means of this burnt offering, they renewed their dedication to the Lord. In addition, they offered peace offerings and held a sacrificial meal at which they enjoyed God's presence.

What a wonderful occasion! Still, the people of Beth-shemesh had apparently forgotten who the Lord really is and how much reverence is due His gracious presence. Without fear and reverence there can be no faith. However close the Lord comes to us in His covenant, He is not our equal. He is the Lord!

Unencumbered by a sense of modesty and reverence, some of the people of Beth-shemesh looked into the ark. The grace of the Lord is no object of curiosity which we may use to satisfy our inquisitive instincts! As a result, 70 of the inhabitants of Beth-shemesh died.

When that happened, the people of Beth-shemesh could endure the presence of the Lord no longer. But they did not dare send the ark on to Shiloh. Wasn't Shiloh thoroughly polluted by the sins of the house of Eli? Instead they sent messengers to a larger city nearby—Kiriath-jearim. The people of that city came for the ark and brought it to the house of Abinadab, whose son Eleazar was then specially appointed to have charge over it. There the Lord was shown the respect He demands. Thus the people had to learn to fear the Lord again.

The beginning of Samuel's judgeship. The return of the ark did not yet mean that Israel was reconciled with the Lord. Evidently the people did not have the slightest idea what to do with the ark. Although all of Israel must have heard about its return, the ark was left where it was. The people did not call a gathering of the elders to decide, in the presence of the Lord, what should be done.

This situation continued for 20 years. In the meantime, the Philistines continued to oppress the Israelites. Finally all Israel started complaining to the Lord. Now the time had come for Samuel, the forerunner of the king, to assume the office of judge in Israel. He sent a message throughout the land that the people should return to the Lord with all their hearts and put away the idols they were serving. If they would look to the Lord for help and serve Him only, He would deliver them from the Philistines.

When he saw that the people listened to him, Samuel decided that the time for the deliverance had come. Therefore he gathered the people together at Mizpah, where the reconciliation between God and the people was to take place. Samuel prayed for the people, and water was poured out before the face of the Lord. By this action the people indicated that their hearts and lives were melted under the just wrath of God. The people fasted as a sign that they had lost all claim to God's gifts, and they confessed their sins. Thus the people were restored to the right relationship with the Lord, and He forgave their sins.

When the Philistines heard that the people of Israel were gathered together at Mizpah, they marched out to do battle with them. The Israelites were afraid. They were too accustomed to being weaker than the Philistines. Therefore they asked Samuel not to be silent but to cry to the Lord on their behalf. How they needed a mediator! Samuel was only able to assume a mediator's role because of the one and only Mediator—Jesus Christ. When we appeal to Him, our appeal is never in vain.

Samuel sacrificed a newborn sucking lamb as a burnt offering to the Lord. That lamb, which he offered whole, was a sign of the newborn Israel. Israel would again be consecrated to the Lord as an undivided whole. Here we must not forget that Israel was only able to consecrate itself to the Lord because the Christ would consecrate Himself to God for Israel. Actually, the lamb pointed to the Christ.

While Samuel was offering the sacrifice, the Philistines drew near to attack. But the Lord responded immediately by frightening the Philistines with the thunder of His voice. Israel's God brought confusion over the Philistines, and they fled. All that the men of Israel had to do was pursue them.

Between Mizpah and Jeshanah, Samuel set up a stone and called it *Ebenezer*, which means *stone of help*. That stone was a sign of the beginning of God's help. The oppressed country was liberated, and Israel found relief.

From then on Samuel was judge. Every year he went through the land teaching the people the laws of the covenant. Then he returned to Ramah, where he had apparently taken up residence after the fall of Eli's house. From there he made the Word of the Lord known to all Israel. The Lord had turned to His people again. They had been restored to a right relationship with Him, and they had a judge again.

Yet, all of this was temporary. The people of the Lord must be led by Christ their King. Through Him they are kept in the right relationship with God. Before long Israel would receive a still better type of the Christ in the king whom Samuel was told to anoint.

9: Collision

I Samuel 8-12

As such there was nothing sinful about the Israelites' desire for a king; the Lord Himself had promised them one. Neither did the Israelites sin by declaring that they wanted a king "such as all the other nations had," for that was exactly what Moses had promised them (Deut. 17:14-20). Nor was there anything intrinsically wrong with the timing of their request: in those days the expectation of a king was in the air. Apparently the Lord Himself had aroused Israel's desire for a king. Samuel was getting very old, and his sons were not judging the people justly. In short, the people did have legitimate reasons for voicing their desire when they did.

The sin of the people lay in their conception of their king and in their motive for wanting just such a ruler. A king who would lead them in battle would make them more independent—and less dependent on the Word of the Lord than they were now, under the leadership of a judge-prophet. A king would be able to make his decisions more independently.

That this was indeed the sin of the Israelites is clear from their understanding of "the ways of the king who would rule over them." Samuel explained the inevitable deterioration that would result from the kind of kingship they wanted to see established. The people's understanding of the kingship was entirely different from the rights and duties of the king as Samuel wrote them down in a book which he "laid up before the LORD" (I Sam. 10:25).

By embracing the wrong understanding of the kingship, the people rejected not only the judge-prophet but also the Lord. Even so, the Lord gave them a king, for in His counsel the time for a king had come. Moreover, He Himself had aroused their desire for a king. Such a desire can be from God in principle even though it is corrupted by our ideas.

Thus, there was a conflict between the Lord's gracious intention and the ideas of the people. The intention of the Lord often collides with our wishes, just as His gift of the Christ clashes with our expectations.

Because this matter of the kingship had been raised in the wrong way from the people's side, both the king and the people would have to be tested. Immediately after Saul was anointed, Samuel warned him that he would be tried and tested (I Sam. 10:8). There would come a time when the army would be called up against the Philistines and would gather at Gilgal. It was a matter of course that the battle with this traditional enemy would be fought there. When that happened, Saul was to wait for Samuel—for as long as seven days, if need be. In this way the people would be tested in their relationship to their king. And the king would have to listen to Samuel, that is, to the Word of the Lord.

In that testing, the Lord gave the people and their king every advantage. Saul was an impressive figure with a noble character. And he was a pious man, as we see from the fact that he did not begin the battle before the sacrifice was offered. Moreover, the Holy Spirit came upon him and turned him into a new man. This was not rebirth or regeneration, nor was it repentance: the change in Saul was that he began to identify with the cause of God's people and with the honor of that cause. But Saul never saw God's greatness and the glory of his faithfulness in His covenant.

Saul took the defense of the people's cause upon himself. That could only mean that the people's cause would become Saul's cause and the people's honor Saul's honor. Later this led to his downfall. Yet Saul—and, in him, the people—had everything in his favor when that time of testing came. But flesh cannot stand when trials come. The fall of Saul should be a lesson to us showing us that no flesh may boast before God.

If we wish to draw a line from Saul to the Christ, we must point to Saul as an antitype of the Christ, as someone completely different from Him. In the Kingdom of grace, the Christ is the true theocratic King, ruling according to the Word of the Lord. Israel's hopes for Saul were not fulfilled. Saul's failure was intended to prepare the way for proper expectations of a future king, expectations that found their fulfillment in David, the theocratic king.

Main thought: *The Lord's counsel of grace collides with the expectatons of His people.*

Give us a king! Samuel judged Israel for many years. When he grew old, he appointed his two sons as helpers in the southern part of the land. His sons, however, did not walk in the way of their father; they accepted bribes. The elders of Israel came to Samuel about the problem. They pointed out that he was getting old and that his sons were not following in his footsteps. Therefore they asked him to appoint a king to succeed him as ruler.

The Israelites were not wrong in desiring a king. The Lord Himself had put that desire in their hearts. Moses had already promised them that they would have a king someday (Deut. 17:14-20). That king would be a revelation of God's rule of grace over His people—and therefore a type of the Christ, who is King over His people. In fact, the promised king would be an even more glorious type of Christ than Moses and the judges. By way of their king, the people should then be bound even more closely to the Lord and His Word.

But the people did not make their request with such considerations in mind. Through Samuel, the judge-prophet, they were already bound strongly to the Word of the Lord. Samuel made no decisions without seeking the direction of the Lord's Word. The people thought this was the reason why matters progressed so slowly for them, why they could not throw off the Philistine yoke. A king would decide things more independently. Thus the people did not see that the cause of their weakness lay in their sin. By means of the king they asked for, they hoped to become free of the Lord even more.

Their request to Samuel, then, was evil in his eyes. But because he was the mediator between God and the people, he passed the request on to the Lord. The Lord answered him that the people had not just rejected Samuel as judge-prophet; they had rejected the Lord Himself. All the same, Samuel was to give them a king. The Lord's counsel of grace was not to be blocked. But first Samuel was to warn the people and give them an idea of the tyranny which such a king as they had in mind could impose upon them.

Samuel did as the Lord commanded. He admonished the people about their sins and warned them of the power such a king could gather in his own hands. " And in that day you will cry out because of your king," he said, "but then the LORD will not answer you."

The people did not want to listen to Samuel. Thus the counsel of the Lord collided with the people's desire. What the Lord had meant for their well-being was immediately turned into something sinful by the people. We are like the Israelites in that respect: what we want from the Lord does not always coincide with what He chooses to give us. We even want a somewhat different King than the King whom God has given us, namely, the Lord Jesus Christ.

Anointed by Samuel. Samuel had sent the men of Israel home again. But the Lord did not forget His promise. In a strange manner, He let Samuel know which man he was to anoint as king over Israel.

In Gibeah, in the land of Benjamin, there lived a man named Saul who was still fairly young—about 40 years of age. One day Saul was out looking for the donkeys of his father, Kish. On that expedition he and his servant came to the vicinity of Zuph, where Samuel happened to be at the time. Samuel was there to bless the city's sacrifice and hold a sacrificial meal with the elders.

When Saul and his servant learned that Samuel was there, they decided to ask him about the donkeys. The day before, God had revealed to Samuel that he would soon meet the man whom God intended to make king over Israel. Samuel had therefore given orders that the best portion of the sacrificial meal be set aside. When Saul met Samuel at the gate as Samuel was on his way to the high place outside the city for the sacrificial meal, the Lord revealed to Samuel that this was the man who was to become king. Samuel invited Saul and his servant to take part in the meal with him. He promised to speak to Saul in the morning about what Saul had on his mind. Then he would show Saul that he, Samuel, was truly a prophet of the Lord. He also informed Saul that the donkeys had already been found. Finally, he made a puzzling remark: "And for whom is all that is desirable in Israel? Is it not for you and for all your father's house?" (I Sam. 9:20).

Saul was astonished and asked what Samuel meant. After all, wasn't he (Saul) from the smallest tribe in Israel? But he got no answer. Some preparation was necessary for what was about to happen. At the dinner Samuel gave Saul the choicest piece of meat that had been set aside.

That evening Samuel spoke with Saul for a long time on the housetop. He wanted to know what Saul was like, and he undoubtedly instructed him about Israel's spiritual and political condition. Because of this conversation, Samuel apparently felt quite close to Saul already. Saul was a noble man, and he had an eye for Israel's needs. Moreover, he was willing to learn.

Early the next morning, Samuel called Saul from the housetop where he had spent the night. When they went outside the city, Samuel told Saul to send his servant on ahead. Once they were alone, Samuel poured oil from a flask over Saul's head and so anointed him king over Israel. That oil was a symbol of the gift of the Holy Spirit, who would qualify Saul for office. Furthermore, Samuel promised Saul three signs to prove that he had truly acted in the name of the Lord.

Through these signs Saul would see that the people already honored him as king without knowing what they were doing: for example, they would give him some bread that was originally intended as part of an offering. The third sign was especially important. Saul would receive a share of the Spirit of a group of prophets. He would then prophesy among them and become a different man. He would see the need of the Lord's people clearly and give himself to their cause.

Because there was something basically wrong with the Israelites' desire for a king, their king would have to be tested. Would he rule the people according to the Word of the Lord alone? Or would he rule according to his own insight? Samuel warned Saul about the test: "You are called especially to deliver Israel from the yoke of the Philistines. When the armies meet, you will be in Gilgal with your army. But you may not undertake anything there until I have come to you and have made known the Word of the Lord to you. For seven days you must wait for me, no matter how tense the situation is."

How well God prepared Saul for this test! He was a noble man, he had received the gifts of the Holy Spirit, and he enjoyed the favor of the Lord's prophet. He had everything in his favor. The only remaining question was: Had Saul surrendered to the Lord in faith with all his heart? Could he thus be a leader of the people on the road of faith and a means of rectifying their mistaken expectations with regard to the office of king?

When Saul went home, all the signs which Samuel had foretold came to pass. The third sign made a deep impression on the people of Gibeah. Saul was taken up into a group of prophets.

The Spirit of the Lord came upon him, and he prophesied. The people were astonished at this. Some of them said that the gift of prophecy was not inherited and could be given to anyone God chose. Still, it remained a notable fact, and the saying "Is Saul also among the prophets?" became a proverb. Through that third sign, the people were given to understand that the Lord was close to them with His grace. God would carry out His intention, but this gracious intention would have to conquer the sinfulness in the people's desire for a king.

Appointed by lot. Samuel now called the representatives of the people together at Mizpah. Once again he admonished them because of their sin. Next they proceeded to cast lots. Saul, of the house of Kish, was chosen. But Saul could not be found. By means of the high priest, the Lord was asked if Saul would show up. The answer was that Saul was hidden among the baggage. Soon he was brought out before the people. There he stood, an impressive figure, a head taller than anyone else. Saul was a kingly figure, but a shy man too. Then all the people shouted: "Long live the king!"

Samuel spoke to the people about the rights and duties of the king and the people toward each other and the Lord. He laid down those rights and duties in accordance with the covenant of God, wrote them in a book, and kept that book in the sanctuary. The king would have to be a servant of the Lord, a type of the Christ, a man who thought not of himself but of the Lord's cause, a ruler who feared the Lord and thus led the people in the way of the covenant.

As the people departed to return to their homes, many of them honored the king with a present. Some of them, whose hearts God had touched, even accompanied Saul to his house. But others despised him out of anger and did not bring him a present. Saul pretended not to notice. In this way, too, he showed his noble character.

King Saul had everything in his favor. But if he was to stand up to the test and if the people were to be truly blessed through him, he would have to live by faith and trust the Lord in all things. His faith still had to be demonstrated. A noble disposition was not enough. Did Saul belong to the Christ? Did the Spirit of the Christ dwell in Saul and, through him, in the people as well?

Exaltation. God would soon reveal to Israel what a fine gift the new king was for His people. At the time they asked for a king, the Israelites were being oppressed by the Philistines in the west and by the Ammonites in the east. Under Jephthah Israel had decisively defeated the Ammonites, but now these enemies wanted revenge. They kept pushing forward in Transjordan until they threatened Jabesh in Gilead. Nahash, the leader of the Ammonites, was willing to spare the lives of the inhabitants of Jabesh, on the condition that they allow the Ammonites to gouge out their right eyes and thus bring disgrace upon Israel.

The people of Jabesh asked for seven days to send messengers throughout Israel so that the people would have an opportunity to respond to the challenge. If Israel was powerless or unwilling to do anything, the people of Jabesh would give themselves up to Nahash. Evidently Nahash had not yet heard that the Israelites had chosen a king. In any case, he was not afraid of Israel. Hence he agreed.

When the people of Gibeah got the message, they wept too. Saul was just returning from the field behind the oxen. When he heard the report, the Spirit of the Lord came upon him in a mighty way. He cut his oxen into pieces and sent the pieces throughout the land with the message that a similar fate would befall the oxen of any man who did not follow Saul and Samuel to battle. At that time, apparently, Saul was allying himself closely with Samuel. He also knew that this battle was the will of the Lord, who never forsakes His people.

All Israel came out—300,000 men, plus 30,000 from the southern tribes. Nahash was deceived by the inhabitants of Jabesh, so that Saul, who had divided his army into three companies, could make a surprise attack. The Ammonites were completely defeated and scattered; no two of them were left together.

After the victory, the Israelites wanted to take revenge on the people who despised Saul. But Saul rejected that course of action with the words: "Not a man shall be put to death this day, for today the LORD has wrought deliverance in Israel." Did the people truly accept their king as a gift from the Lord, or did they exalt him now because of his success? Did they recognize that this victory was a gift from the Lord's hand? In this battle, at any rate, Saul had led Israel along the right path.

Renewing the kingdom. Samuel saw that this victory had created a climate favorable to reformation. Perhaps he could now lead the people away from their mistaken expectations about their king and teach them to accept him in faith as a gift from the hand of the Lord. He called the people together in Gilgal to renew the kingdom. There Samuel solemnly made Saul the ruler over the people and laid down his office as judge, although he retained the office of prophet. God would continue to reveal Himself to the people through Samuel.

In Gilgal the people offered peace offerings, and Saul rejoiced with all the men of Israel. A new future seemed to be opening up for Israel, a future in the fear of the Lord.

When Samuel laid down his judgeship, he called all the people together. In the presence of God and His anointed king, to whom he now surrendered the leadership of the people, the people were to be his witnesses that he had always been fair in his judgments and had led them in righteousness.

Then Samuel gave an overview of Israel's history. He pointed out that the people had turned away from the Lord again and again, and that they had now left Him once more in their desire for a king of their own choosing. Yet the Lord had given them a king anyway. If they would now walk in the fear of the Lord, their king would be blessed, and they would be blessed in him. But if they forsook the Lord, His hand would be against them.

When Samuel prayed, the Lord sent thunder and rain. This was an unusual phenomenon, for it was the time of the wheat harvest (the dry season). The thunder and rain were signs of the Lord's anger at the new sin committed by His people. This made the people very afraid, and they confessed their sin. They asked for Samuel's intercession. He comforted them, saying that there was forgiveness with the Lord. Samuel promised not to stop praying for the people. The Lord, for His own name's sake, would not abandon His people. That was—and always would be—the basis of Samuel's prayer.

Yet, only time would tell how it would go with Israel. The sin had indeed been forgiven, but the time of testing was still to come. Would the king stand up under the test? Only if the Spirit of the Christ was in him would he be able to do so.

Only the Christ has stood up perfectly under the test, the great trial. Only He can give us the strength not to stumble and fall. We don't have to wait and see how our King will fare, for we know that He was faithful in all things. Under His guidance we are always safe.

10: Put to Shame

I Samuel 13-14

That Saul was a pious man is evident from the fact that he did not want to begin the war against the Philistines before the sacrifice was offered to the Lord. Also, when he heard the noise in the army of the Philistines, he first wanted to inquire about the Lord's will. When the noise increased, he interpreted the increase as a sufficient answer from the Lord.

Yet Saul was willful at times. He was not able to endure the test of waiting seven days for the arrival of Samuel. And his prohibition (under oath) that nobody was to eat before evening was willful. What is revealing in this episode is that he spoke of taking revenge not on the Lord's enemies but on *his own* enemies. Here we already see Saul's self-seeking attitude coming out.

It is in this light that we must view his sin at Gilgal. On the surface that sin does not seem serious enough to deserve the judgment Samuel pronounced on Saul. It is true that Saul was not told that the kingship would be taken away from him; what he was told was that his family would not inherit it, that the Lord had sought out someone else. The lesson was that he was to trust the Lord *in all things* and not fall back on his own resources—not even in the most dire emergency.

Saul had not given himself to the Lord without holding anything back. Only the Christ managed to do that perfectly. But through His Spirit, we are able to do it too.

Saul was very tense at that crucial moment. But exactly at that point he closed his heart to the Spirit of the Christ and preferred to go his own way. This still does not mean that Saul was not a believer. But it did become evident at Gilgal that his faith was not completely victorious. And because of him, his family was not in the grip of the covenant either.

As we tell such stories to the children, we must remind ourselves not to focus on the sin and failure of some human being as the central point. Instead we are to focus on the blessing given by God in spite of human sin and failure. In this story about Saul, God's blessing puts all the people to shame.

In Saul's kingship there are two motifs to be distinguished. On the one hand there is the kingship as God intended it for His people, and on the other hand there is the kingship that the people desired and Saul wrongly chose to exercise. Because of the former element, God still chose to bless the kingship in spite of Saul's sin. In Saul's kingship, especially at the beginning, we see something of the Christ—but also something of the antichrist.

Saul swore an oath by the Lord that nobody was to eat on the day of the victory. When Jonathan, unaware of his father's command, ate some honey, the name of the Lord was profaned. Consequently the Lord did not answer when called upon. Yet, the one who had sinned was not Jonathan but Saul, who had exposed the name of the Lord to dishonor by his willful oath. Therefore the people protested and rightly saved Jonathan from death. Shame came upon Saul through this episode. God protected Jonathan, who had been the real deliverer of Israel in this battle.

There is another reason why we must not talk only of Saul's sin: Saul was not the only one responsible for failing the test. The people who slipped away behind Saul's back made the test extremely difficult for him. We can look at this matter from two sides. The Spirit of the Lord did not come upon the Israelites in a mighty way in their battle against the power. This was to make the test harder for Saul, so that he would display the faith that conquers all things. On the other hand, by their lack of trust the people closed their hearts to the Spirit of the Lord. Therefore the victory put all Israel to shame. Despite the fact that the people failed to stand by their king, they were blessed under the leadership of Saul and his son.

Main thought: *The Lord puts His people to shame by giving them His blessing in spite of the sin of the king and the people.*

Failing the test. Shortly after becoming king, probably immediately after the gathering at Gilgal, Saul selected 3000 men to form a small standing army. Apparently he did not think that the Israelites were ready for the decisive battle with their traditional enemies, the Philistines. But he did want to prevent the enemy from pressing forward any farther. Therefore he placed a garrison of 1000 men under the command of his son Jonathan at Gibeah, his hometown. With the other 2000 men, Saul occupied Michmash, which was about an hour and a half from Gibeah.

The Philistines had pressed forward as far as Geba. Jonathan with his thousand men defeated the Philistine garrison there. This first deed of the Israelites after choosing a king caused unrest in the land of the Philistines. Saul saw it coming: the decisive battle with the Philistines might have to be fought quite soon after all. Therefore he had Jonathan's deed made known throughout the land, and he called Israel together.

While the Israelites were assembling, a huge army of Philistines came up and occupied Michmash. In response, Saul and all those who had responded to his call withdrew to Gilgal, near the Jordan. The people trembled as they followed him. The Spirit of the Lord did not come upon them in a mighty way. In distrust and fear, the people closed their hearts to God's Spirit, scattering and hiding themselves in the caves. Many of them even retreated beyond the Jordan. That's how deep-rooted the Israelites' fear of the Philistines was. Jonathan's victory did not become a sign by which their faith was lifted up.

When the people gave in to their fears, they made the test their king was undergoing much more severe. Here, indeed, the moment had come which Samuel had foretold when he anointed Saul. Saul was to wait for Samuel for seven days, no matter what happened. Now Saul would have to show whether he trusted in the Lord to save the day for Israel. It did not matter how critical the situation appeared to be—as long as the king obeyed uncon-ditionally. One who could not obey completely could not be used by the Lord to rule over His people. Only one who looked to the Lord even for the perseverance of his faith could rule as king, for it is the Lord who gives us faith for Christ's sake and sustains us. Only a man with the Spirit of the Christ within him would be able to trust completely. Was that Spirit in Saul?

Saul waited for seven days. Then the tension reached its peak because his whole army seemed to be scattering. On the seventh day Saul's patience was spent. With the eye of a general he sur-veyed the possibilities. If nothing happened now, the cause was lost. He had to act quickly and surprise the Philistines in one way or another to restore the courage of his people. But he could not do so unless the sacrifice was offered first. Finally he had someone bring him an offering, so that he could personally invoke the Lord's blessing on his undertaking. Evidently he placed more trust in his own insight than in the direction of the Lord, which he was to receive through Samuel.

The burnt offering had just been sacrificed, and Saul was about to set out for the battle. Then Samuel arrived. No excuse did Saul any good against Samuel's reproach that he had acted foolishly by wanting to trust his own insight. Samuel declared that the kingship would not be inherited by Saul's descendants. That privilege can only be given to someone who surrenders unconditionally to God, someone in whom the Spirit of the Christ prevails. The Christ remained faithful under the severest testing. He did it for those who belong to Him. And by His Spirit He will also uphold His own. Saul had not looked to that Spirit in his struggle to remain faithful. Therefore God found someone to take Saul's place.

King Saul had failed the test. When that happened, the kingship that the people had demanded out of a sinful desire stood condemned. Saul had been able to count on everything a man can have in his favor. Even so, he did not succeed.

The people, too, stood condemned in their king. They had been afraid; they had not been able to regard their king as a gift received from the hand of God. They did not see him as a sure sign of God's favor, which would give them the victory. We may look to our King in faith as the One given by God. He goes before us and leads us to victory.

Jonathan's act of faith. Although the people and the king had sinned, the Lord remembered that He had given the kingship to Israel as a blessing. Therefore He did not want to deliver the Israelites into the hands of their enemies; He wished to grant them deliverance by the hand of their king.

But the deliverance did not come through the king himself. Apparently Saul did not possess the kind of faith that can do all things, the faith that shows its greatest strength at the most difficult moments because it sees the Lord, the Deliverer in time of need. Such faith God had given to Saul's oldest son, Jonathan. By faith he saw the possibilities God offered.

After Samuel left, Saul and Jonathan and the men who were with them pressed on again to Geba, while the Philistines camped opposite them in Michmash. There were exactly 600 men with Saul and Jonathan. What could they do against the army of the Philistines?

Three companies of raiders came out of the Philistine camp and went off in three directions. The Israelites could not even defend themselves against these raiders, for the last time the Philistines had ruled over the Israelites, they had seized all the weapons they could find and killed the Israelite blacksmiths. They made sure that the Israelites would not be able to make any new weapons. Even the 600 men Saul had with him were not adequately armed.

But faith is not daunted by a lack of weapons! Directly opposite him Jonathan saw an advanced garrison of the Philistines encamped on a hill. A steep slope led up to the garrison. Jonathan viewed this as his opportunity. He would leave the outcome in the Lord's hands. Secretly he asked his armor-bearer to go with him. God was able to give deliverance by only a few as well as by many.

The two men proceeded without informing Saul, who would most likely have raised objections. On the way Jonathan and his armor-bearer agreed that they would show themselves to the Philistines at the foot of the slope. If the Philistines told them that they would come down and fight with them, they would stand still and see what happened. But if the Philistines taunted them and invited them to come up, they would draw the conclusion that the Philistines did not have the courage to start fighting with them and that God would deliver them into their hands.

Jonathan and the armor-bearer carried out their plan. When the Philistines shouted for them to come up, Jonathan took courage. He climbed up the slope on hands and knees, followed by his armor-bearer. Soon they reached the edge. The Philistines did not know that there were only two men attacking them. Fear made them weak, and Jonathan and his armor-bearer killed about 20 men.

Through this act of faith on the part of the king's son, the Lord showed that He was still with Israel. Is there anything we cannot do if only we proceed in faith? The Lord still performs miracles of His grace.

The victory. Those who fled informed the Philistine army that the Israelites had begun the attack. Their only thought was that their enemies were advancing in great numbers. As a result, a panic seized the entire army, all the outposts, and the bands of raiders. Confusion quickly developed in the ranks of the Philistines, and the soldiers began to flee. This confusion was caused by a fear which the Lord created in the ranks of the Philistines. The Lord blessed Israel with its king despite the king's sin. Israel had to realize that it would be blessed one day in its great King.

Saul and his men saw the confusion in the ranks of their enemies and did not understand the reason why. They asked if any of their own men were missing. It turned out that Jonathan and his armor-bearer were not present. Accompanying Saul's soldiers was the high priest, with the Urim and Thummim. Saul wanted to make use of them to find out what all of this meant and to ask the Lord whether he should proceed to attack. But while the high priest was seeking the Lord's counsel, the noise in the Philistine army became so loud that he decided he needed no further answer. He advanced. He noticed that the Philistines in their confusion were fighting each other. Moreover, Israelites who had once been subjugated by the Philistines and were in their service now took up the sword against their masters. All the Israelite soldiers who had hidden in caves came out. The result for Israel was one great victory. The Israelites pursued the Philistine army a long way.

Unfortunately, the king did not show the required wisdom here either. In his zeal he threatened to curse anyone who took time to eat before the evening. Because of this command, the pursuers grew faint. The king's self-seeking attitude had blinded him. The truth of the matter was that he uttered the curse so that he would be able to take full revenge on his enemies. He thought of the Philistines not as the Lord's enemies but as *his own* enemies. Here Saul already began to usurp the Lord's place.

Jonathan did not know about his father's oath binding all the soldiers. When the pursuers passed through a forest in which they found honey, he dipped his spear in the honey and ate some. One of the soldiers then told him about his father's prohibition. Immediately Jonathan saw how wrong the oath was, and he said so. But the soldiers kept their vow.

By evening the soldiers were exhausted and eagerly grabbed the spoil. Because they were famished, they slaughtered the cattle on the ground and wound up roasting the meat with the blood still in it. That was a sin against the law of the Lord. Therefore Saul ordered that the beasts be slaughtered in his presence, upon a stone. Here the king showed zeal for keeping the law of the Lord. However, he himself was partly to blame for the people's transgression because of the foolish oath he had sworn.

On that spot Saul built his first altar to the Lord, as a token of his thankfulness. Thus he wavered between acknowledging the Lord and glorifying himself.

The name of the Lord. After acknowledging the Lord via the altar, Saul wanted to pursue the Philistines farther and attack them during the night. The people agreed, but the high priest proposed to ask the Lord first. The Lord, however, did not answer. From this Saul understood that a certain sin separated the Lord from His people. The lot would be cast to show who had committed the sin. Saul vowed that the sinner would die, even if it turned out to be his own son Jonathan.

Sure enough, the lot pointed to Jonathan. When Jonathan confessed that he had eaten some honey, Saul wanted to kill him. But the people rushed to his defense, pointing out that it was through Jonathan that the Lord had delivered His people by means of this great victory. The Lord had been with Jonathan and would not want him killed for his unwitting transgression. Thus Saul was prevented from keeping his oath.

When Saul had pronounced his curse on anyone who ate before evening, he had called on the name of the Lord. When Jonathan ate, a sin was committed against that name. Yet, it was not Jonathan who had sinned but Saul: it was Saul's rash oath that had exposed the Lord's name to dishonor. Saul had wanted to take revenge on those he called his enemies. It was for this reason that he had misused the Lord's name. The Lord does not permit any man to use His name for his own purposes.

There the holiness of the Lord's name was revealed to Saul. Would Saul now come to his senses? In any case, he did not pursue Israel's enemies any farther. Perhaps this revelation led to some sanctification of Saul's reign, so that his own name was subordinated to the name of the Lord for a while.

Saul's reign. Now that he had attacked the traditional enemy and the Lord had given him the victory, Saul took the reigns of government in his own hands for good. He fought against the enemies of the Lord's people on all sides. He was courageous, and the Lord delivered Israel's enemies into his hand. Saul, his sons, his daughters, and his whole family were held in high esteem in Israel. In the constant battle with the Philistines, he gathered an army of brave men around him. Abner, Saul's uncle, became famous in Israel as the commander-in-chief of his army.

Thus the Lord in His goodness still honored Saul, and his kingship flourished. Through that kingship, the people were to develop an ever more powerful longing for the great King who would deliver the people of the Lord from all their enemies—especially sin, the evil one and death.

11: Divine Rejection

I Samuel 15

God's grace toward His people governs everything that happens in the story told in I Samuel 15.

Amalek had to be wiped out because it was the first of the heathen nations—the first to oppose Israel in the wilderness. Thus Amalek was a type of all the hostile powers opposing the Church. Amalek hated and rejected the grace God showed His people and the communion of the covenant. For that reason Amalek *had* to be destroyed.

Saul did not dedicate himself to the righteousness of grace. When he spared Amalek's best, he showed that the righteousness of grace was not everything to him. At that point he made it clear that he could no longer be God's servant. God could not use anyone who did not see the glory of that grace. God's mercy toward His people dominates the story of the rejection of Saul. From then on, Saul was especially an antitype of the Christ.

We must see to it that we have a proper understanding of the meaning of that rejection. God's judgment had already struck Saul for his disobedience at Gilgal before the battle against the Philistines: he was told that the kingship would not be inherited by his descendants. This time the judgment was that Saul himself was rejected as king. In other words, God's blessing would depart from Saul *as king*. It was only later that Saul was also rejected as a person.

Obeying is better than offering sacrifices, Samuel told Saul. But obedience is not to be contrasted with offering sacrifices as such. In fact, there can be no true sacrifice without obedience. When Samuel said that obeying is better than offering sacrifices, he was talking about sacrifices offered by someone who is not living by faith out of grace, someone who is not obedient to God's grace. This is confirmed by what he went on to say: "For rebellion is as the sin of divination, and stubbornness is as iniquity and idolatry." When we are rebellious, we insist on having our own way; *we* want to rule. Thereby we reject God just as the pagans do. Such a rejection goes hand in hand with a pretence of worship in which we subject the powers of the gods to our own will.

Main thought: *For the sake of His grace toward His people, the Lord rejects the one who rebels.*

Disobedience. One day Samuel came to Saul with an order from the Lord: Saul was to destroy the Amalekites utterly. The Amalekites had attacked the Israelites just after the Lord delivered them from Egypt. In Amalek there burned a hatred of the people to whom the Lord had bound Himself in a special way. Thus Amalek was a type of all the hostile powers that would rise up against the people of the Lord.

It is the Lord's desire that His grace be honored in the world and that we bow in faith before the glory of that grace. For blaspheming God's grace, Amalek had to be punished—with complete destruction. In the same way, God will destroy all those who do not honor His mercy by accepting it in faith.

Through Samuel, the Lord told Saul that he had been anointed king over Israel to serve the Lord in His grace toward His people. Therefore He ordered Saul to carry out this judgment on the Amalekites.

Saul mobilized the people—200,000 men from Israel and 10,000 from Judah. With this army he attacked the Amalekites. He told the Kenites, who were descendants of Moses' father-in-law, to separate themselves from the Amalekites. Saul wanted to spare them because they had once refrained from being hostile to Israel. Jethro had honored the God of Israel with sacrifices.

Up to this point, Saul seems to have been fully obedient. By a trick he conquered the Amalekites, and his soldiers pursued and killed them. But then disobedience set in. The Israelites captured Agag, the king of the Amalekites, and Saul did not put him to death. Also, at the insistence of his men, Saul allowed the finest of the Amalekites' cattle to be spared. Everything of Amalek was supposed to be subjected to the judgment of God's grace toward His people. But Saul, it now became clear, was not motivated by a zeal to have that grace revealed. That's why he could yield to the insistence of his men. He also wanted to glorify himself by having a defeated king as a captive at his royal court.

At that point Saul could no longer be the servant of the Lord in His grace toward His people. He could not be a type of the Lord Jesus Christ, who desired nothing but to serve God in His grace in His covenant.

Judgment. The Lord then said to Samuel that He was sorry He had made Saul king, since Saul had turned away from following Him. This does not mean that the Lord regretted ever having elevated Saul to the kingship. The Lord knew what he was doing all along; the anointing of Saul had its purpose. It would be revealed to Saul that only someone who surrendered fully to the grace of God could serve the Lord as king.

The Lord Jesus Christ did everything for the sake of the reign of God's favor. And we, in turn, can only serve Him in faithful submission. The Lord had turned away from Saul as king because it was clear that Saul did not honor His grace above everything else. God's blessing would no longer rest on Saul's kingship.

Then Samuel's anger was kindled against Saul's rejection of God's grace. As he thought about Saul's misdeed, he realized how it flew in the face of his love for Saul and his hopes for Israel under Saul's kingship. It even threatened his own life's work, which he had dedicated to the honor of God's grace in Israel. All night he wrestled with the problem in hopes that the course events were taking might somehow be reversed. If only Israel could escape being cursed because of Saul's kingship!

When the night was over, Samuel knew that the Lord's decision was irrevocable. God could not tolerate anyone trying to steal His people from Him. The faithfulness of the Lord to His people demanded the rejection of Saul as king. At that time Samuel did not know exactly how God would rescue the honor of the kingship through someone else, someone who would truly be a type of the Christ. But the Spirit of the Christ did live in Samuel, who freely devoted his life to the revelation of grace.

Samuel met Saul and his army in the Jordan Valley, at Gilgal.

With exaggerated cheerfulness, Saul came out to greet him. When Samuel reprimanded him, he answered that the cattle had been spared for an offering to the Lord. What nonsense! Nothing that was reserved for judgment and put under the ban could possibly be offered to the Lord. Didn't Saul understand anything about the Lord's righteousness anymore?

Samuel cut Saul short and told him the Lord's verdict. Saul still tried to excuse himself. Then Samuel replied: "To obey is better than sacrifice." Only in obedience will we be able to bring the Lord a true sacrifice. When we are rebellious, we make gods of ourselves and all service becomes mere pretence, like the vain worship of the pagans. Because Saul had rejected the demand of grace, he could not be king anymore.

Then Saul finally confessed his sins. Yet, his was no confession from the heart, for he still put the blame on the people. He had yielded, at the people's insistence. Because he did not confess from the heart, Samuel refused to worship with him and offer thanks for the victory.

When Samuel wanted to walk away, Saul grabbed him by the skirt of his robe and inadvertently tore it. This gave Samuel a prophetic glimpse of what was going to happen, and he prophesied: "The LORD has torn the kingdom of Israel from you this day, and has given it to a neighbor of yours, who is better than you." The Lord cannot use anyone for whom His grace is not the most important thing. Therefore this rejection was irrevocable. The unchangeable God of Israel does not lie. He does not forsake His people because of the injustice of some human being. When the sentence has been pronounced for the sake of the honor of His grace, He does not change it, for He is faithful to that grace.

Then Saul asked Samuel to honor him still before the elders of the people, by going with him for worship. Samuel did so—but mainly to carry out the judgment upon Agag. He killed Agag and cut him into pieces, not just because of the former sins of the Amalekites against the Israelites but also because of the cruelty toward Israel of which Agag himself was guilty. Agag would not live on to be used by Saul for self-glorification; he would die for the honor of the Lord's grace.

After this Samuel went back to Ramah. He never saw Saul again. The Lord's communion with Saul as king through the prophet Samuel was broken. Samuel grieved for Saul, for he had loved him. The Lord turned away from Saul and turned to another man, a man who would serve Him in His grace and be a type of the Christ.

Saul and David

12: Divine Election

I Samuel 16

The Lord chose David to replace Saul as king. When He did so, He considered what was in David's heart. It was not that David possessed any virtues in himself; whatever he could bring to the kingship was given to him by God. God considered what *He* had put in David from the beginning, to enable him to serve as king. David's birth was determined by his later calling to the office of king.

In no one—except the Christ—was it so obvious that God chose him in order to have His people wholly at His disposal. No one else went through such a period of waiting and humiliation after his election and calling. In this respect Joseph can be compared with David, although Joseph had nothing more than an indication of his future calling (in his dreams), while David received his calling unmistakably (by being anointed).

This chapter already tells us that David was called to the court to play for Saul. His task was to refresh the spirit of the one who had been rejected—the man he would succeed as king someday. Undoubtedly, it was an honor for David to come to Saul's court, and it was good training for his future task. But much more important was that he immediately began learning that he had to humble himself in God's way before His counsel.

It is touching to see how David, the chosen one, comforted and refreshed Saul, the rejected one. This was significant not only for Saul himself but for all Israel. Again and again satan was banished, so that Saul would not be completely in his power and Israel's affairs would not become totally chaotic before the successor was ready for the throne. This shows us that the Christ with His Church—and also the salvation which the Christ grants His Church—is highly significant for the unbelieving world. The "evil spirit from God," that is, the evil spirit sent by

107

God, is still being suppressed in the world by the grace in the Church and by the confession of that grace.

During this period, Saul was possessed by the evil spirit only occasionally. Later we do not read about the evil spirit anymore. The reason is that Saul's situation had become worse—not better. By that time he had consciously surrendered to this evil spirit of hate. Therefore it was no longer necessary for the evil spirit to attack him violently from time to time.

David is a type of the Christ in his election as well as in the path he followed to get to the throne.

> **Main thought:** *The Lord chooses a new king for His people and leads him toward the throne along His path.*

Anointed in the midst of his brothers. Samuel kept grieving over Saul, not only because he loved him but because of his high expectations of Saul's kingship. What was now to become of the king and of Israel? But the Lord in His counsel had long since decided on the way for Israel. One day, therefore, the Lord told Samuel to stop thinking about Saul and to go to Bethlehem. There he was to anoint one of Jesse's sons to be king.

Samuel objected, saying that Saul would kill him if he heard about it. Given the fits of bewilderment Saul was suffering, Samuel's fear was well-founded. Thus his response was not an expression of unwillingness on his part. He was simply putting the difficulties before the Lord, so that the Lord would solve them.

Samuel was told to go to Bethlehem and offer a sacrifice there. He was then to invite the family of Jesse to the sacrificial meal, which would be held in their home. There the anointing could take place privately. This course of action did not involve a white lie, for the sacrifice was indeed significant for Bethlehem.

When Samuel reached Bethlehem, the elders of the city came to meet him. Trembling, they asked whether he had come on a peaceful mission. This shows that Samuel went to Israel's cities now and then to uphold the righteousness of the Lord.

Samuel quietly put their minds at ease and ordered them to purify themselves by washing their clothes and confessing their sins. He had come to offer a sacrifice in Bethlehem. The central worship in the sanctuary still had not been re-established. That's why sacrifices were offered in different places throughout the land every now and then as the Lord commanded.

Samuel watched the purification of Jesse's household carefully, for it was with this family that he intended to eat the sacrificial meal. Before Jesse's sons sat down, he made them all pass before him. When the oldest one came along, Samuel thought he must be the one the Lord had chosen to be king, for he had a splendid build. But the Lord told Samuel in his heart that he was not the one; the Lord looks not at the outward appearance but at the heart.

What the Lord was particularly concerned about was what attitude the future king took toward Him. He was looking for an attitude of faith and submission, which He Himself had given to the future king. Saul's failure demonstrated that we cannot go by the outward appearances by which men judge.Saul had everything in his favor as far as people could tell. But he lacked humble faith, a faith for which the Lord is everything. The Lord was looking for that kind of faith, a faith which He Himself had given.

Seven sons of Jesse were presented to Samuel, but not one of them was the future king. Samuel asked Jesse whether these were all his sons. He was told that the youngest was still in the field, tending the sheep. Samuel insisted that they send for him. Until that was done, they could not sit down to eat the meal.

Finally David, the youngest son of Jesse, came in. He had reddish hair, which was considered very beautiful in the ancient Near East. Furthermore, he had animated eyes and a striking build. The Lord told Samuel to anoint him, for he was the one.

David was anointed in the presence of his brothers. The youngest son was chosen, the one whom the brothers would never even have considered as a possibility. The Lord's deeds and decisions often go counter to our expectations. From that day on, the Lord's Spirit worked in David in a mighty way. David began to see his calling on behalf of the people of the Lord, and he dedicated himself to it.

It must have felt strange to David to be called away from the sheep to be king over Israel. How would he come to the throne? It was still occupied by Saul and seemed destined to be inherited by the courageous Jonathan, Saul's oldest son.

Would David now desire that throne for himself, or would he want it only to serve the Lord? Was he willing to wait for it until it was the Lord's time? How sin threatened David from that time on! After all, he was nothing more than a sinful human being—in himself no better than Saul. The Lord would purify him by means of a long period of testing. In that way David was to learn to surrender to the Lord in faith more and more and to serve only Him.

When the Lord chose David, He intended to save His people through him. David would be a fuller and better type of the Christ than Saul had been. His would be a kingship which the Lord would use to bless His people. The people, in their unbelief, had not desired such a kingship, but the Lord would give it to them anyway as a blessing.

Likewise, He has given us the true King, the Lord Jesus Christ, who lived by faith alone and submitted to God in everything. He was led to His throne along a path of severe testing. Through Him David also received the strength to travel the road of suffering and waiting.

Believers, too, have been promised a throne. One day they will reign with the Christ. But that throne will only be reached via a road of suffering and waiting. On that road the Spirit of the Lord Jesus Christ will keep them safe.

Called to serve. Saul soon realized that the Lord had rejected him. The Spirit of the Lord had left him. He became blind to the cause of the Lord and His people. All he saw was his own cause; he was concerned only about his own name and future.

At times he even began to see that he was fighting a lost cause. Then satan could do with him what he pleased. At one time Saul had received a generous portion of the Lord's Spirit. Now that he had lost it, his mind was receptive to the evil doings of the devil. At times the devil governed him so completely that he was possessed.

The evil spirit was sent to him by God. Saul's life revealed what becomes of a person when he rises up against the Lord. Either we serve the Lord or we serve the evil one. And the yoke of the devil is heavy.

Saul's servants, moved by what he sometimes had to suffer,

advised him to look for someone who could play the harp for him. The music would make his mind less restless and less vulnerable to the influence of satan. When Saul agreed to this plan, one of his servants called his attention to a certain son of Jesse whom he knew as someone able to play the harp very well. Moreover, this young man was brave, prudent and handsome. Even though he was a country boy, he would fit in well at the court.

Saul had the young man summoned from his father's home. Soon David arrived at the court, with a present from Jesse. The Lord's leading had brought David to the court. There he could learn much that would benefit him in his future reign, and the people would gradually begin to notice him. Moreover, at the court David would learn especially to serve and wait upon the Lord in trusting faith.

Saul was very fond of David and asked his father if David could stay with him. He even made David his armor-bearer. There was David at Saul's court, playing his harp whenever the evil spirit came upon the king. The peace of David's trust in God was reflected in his music; it chased away the evil spirit and soothed Saul.

Thus David was a blessing to Saul and thereby also to Israel. Because of David's presence, Saul's mind was not immediately and wholly disabled, and Israel's affairs were not completely thrown into confusion.

Many thoughts must have crossed David's mind as he played for Saul. He was a blessing to the very man he would one day succeed! David gave himself willingly to this service, for the Lord's sake. Such service was already a preparation for the throne, for a king was not to be a man who used power for his own benefit. He was to use the throne to serve the Lord and to be a blessing to others. This applied especially to the king of the Lord's people.

In the same way, Christ on His throne serves the Father and is therefore a blessing to His people. He is even a blessing to those who do not fear God, preventing the world from collapsing in total disorder. Believers, too, are called to be a blessing to the entire world—even to the unbelievers among whom they continue to live.

13: The Deliverer Revealed to the People

I Samuel 17—18:13

The significance of this passage of Scripture is that David is revealed as Israel's deliverer. The condition of Saul's mind was already beginning to weigh heavily upon the people; they gradually realized that deliverance would not come from him. Now David became Israel's hope.

When David went out to fight Goliath, Saul asked Abner whose son David was. And after David's victory Saul asked David this question himself. Surely Saul knew that David was Jesse's son. Therefore the question must have been intended to get at something else. Saul was inquiring about the lineage and parentage of David, about the significance of his family in Israel. Had this heroic spirit ever appeared in David's family before? Saul was trying to explain David's courage of faith. It was not enough for him to acknowledge in faith the miracle of grace in David's deed. Saul, who knew that God had left him, could not and would not acknowledge that miracle.

Accordingly, David himself answered the question in a discussion with Saul. It was a fairly long discussion, as we see from the first words of I Samuel 18: "Now it came about when he had finished speaking to Saul . . . ." This conversation had brought to light something of David's simple faith, which had enabled him to perform this deed. That faith, and the deed itself, won Jonathan over to David. Jonathan had once known the same faith, as we see from his own courageous deeds. But much of the power welling up from Jonathan's faith had apparently been stifled by the atmosphere at Saul's court. Now Jonathan saw what David could do, and he listened carefully to him. David became the activator of his faith. Therefore Jonathan bound himself to David for good.

In his relationship to Jonathan, David is a type of the Christ. David is Jonathan's deliverer, and Jonathan, for David's sake, surrenders

112

everything—even his future claim to the throne. Jonathan could do so only in faith, a faith in David as the one chosen by God to be Israel's deliverer. Here, in Jonathan's life, we see a choice for the Redeemer.

David's action brought about a threefold reaction. First there was the response of faith in Jonathan. Then there was the reaction of the women, who saw nothing but the outward glory of David's deed. These women praised David instead of the Lord. Finally, there was Saul's reaction. Saul had previously known something of the Spirit now at work in David, but he had lost that Spirit and had grown to hate Him.

Main thought: *Israel's deliverer is revealed to the people.*

The decline of faith. During the time when the evil spirit repeatedly came upon Saul, the Philistines gathered for battle against Israel. The two armies camped on the slopes of two opposite mountains with a valley between them.

A champion fighter advanced from the Philistine camp—a giant named Goliath. He wore heavy armor, and his copper helmet glittered in the sun. Here was a man who could not be defeated!

In those days dueling was very popular among the Philistines. They heaped great honors on anyone who demonstrated his prowess in dueling. The fact that some of the babies born to the Philistines grew up to be giants may have had something to do with the popularity of dueling.

Standing there in the valley so that both armies could get a good look at him, the giant taunted Israel's army and asked for a man to step forth and fight with him. The outcome of the duel between the representatives of the two armies would then decide the outcome of the war between the Israelites and the Philistines.

The Israelites were terrified, and the battle line of their army fell back. Nobody dared take on the giant. Who could possibly survive such an encounter? Day after day Goliath sneered at the battle line of Israel, which was really the battle line of the living God. All Saul did in response was promise that the man who killed Goliath would become his son-in-law, and that his family would be exempt from all service, that is, be elevated to the nobility. Even this did not help.

Was there no faith left in Israel? Did the people no longer

support the army with their prayers? And where was Jonathan's faith? Wasn't Jonathan the man who had once dared to attack a whole garrison with only his armor-bearer? Was all of that gone?

No, faith was not gone, but its effects were stifled by Saul's self-seeking spirit and by the Lord's anger at Israel because of Saul. The people were being punished on account of their king.

Victory through faith. At this point David came to visit the army. Evidently he had gone home when the war began. His three oldest brothers were serving in the army. Now he was sent by his father to see how his brothers were doing. He brought with him a present for the commanding officer.

Just as David arrived, Goliath advanced again, and a current of fear swept through the army. David left the things he had brought with him in the hands of the baggage keeper. He wanted to greet his brothers and get a better look at the Philistine.

David, too, was overcome with emotion when he heard the giant sneer at the battle line of the living God and scorn the name of the Lord. But the prevailing emotion for him was anger rather than fear. Did this go on every day? Was there nobody to challenge the giant? Had the king promised to reward the man who killed Goliath? Why, then, was this uncircumcised Philistine allowed to go on blaspheming the name of the Lord?

A small group of soldiers quickly formed around David, for they could see that something had begun to stir in him. His oldest brother was among them. He told David that he could better have stayed with the sheep since he had come to the camp only out of curiosity. But David paid no attention to him. Overcome by emotion, he continued to ask questions and express his faith that the Philistine could be defeated.

Soon word reached the king, and he called for David. Right then and there David volunteered to go and fight the Philistine. Compassionately Saul pointed out to David that he was young and inexperienced. Then David testified about his faith. He had killed a lion and a bear who wanted to rob the flock. The Lord, who had given him the strength to overcome the lion and the bear, would also help him slay the Philistine, for the Philistine had blasphemed the Lord. With that Saul gave in. He said: "Go, and the LORD be with you!" These words had no deep meaning for Saul, but for David they were full of meaning. Saul wanted to dress David in his own armor, but David was not able to move freely in it. Hence he set out with only his shepherd's staff, his sling, and five smooth stones in his bag.

When the Philistine saw David coming, he sneered: "Am I a dog, that you come to me with sticks?" He cursed David by his gods and said that he would give his flesh to the birds to eat. David's response was: "You have come against me with sword and spear, but I have come in the name of the LORD, whom you have blasphemed." The Lord, he said, would deliver His enemy into his hand, and then all the people would know that there was a God in Israel. Later, when David was king, he had trained soldiers at his command. In the service of the Lord, we, too, must look for the appropriate tools. Yet, David knew that if the tools were not available, a sling and a stone would do just as well. As long as the Lord is with us, we can be sure of success.

Then David slung a stone. It hit the Philistine in the temple, and he fell to the ground. Using Goliath's own sword, David cut off the giant's head. The Philistines fled in panic. They had seen in Israel a power they could not match. The Israelites pursued the Philistines.

The Philistines were right: there was in Israel a power they could not match—the power of the Spirit of the Christ. By that Spirit, David had seen and taken hold of the power of the Lord's grace toward Israel. *That* was what made him the victor—and not first of all his skill with the sling.

The Spirit of the Christ had been revealed to Israel again. And David was revealed as the man in whom this Spirit was active. It turned out that Israel was no longer blessed in Saul. No doubt the faithful believers in Israel must soon have started asking themselves whether the Lord was now going to provide deliverance through David.

After the battle David headed for home, carrying the head of Goliath with him. He left it behind in Jerusalem, which was already occupied by Israel, even though its stronghold had not yet been conquered. Goliath's armor he took home with him. Later the sword was placed in the tabernacle.

A threefold reaction. Before David headed for home, he was called into Saul's tent. Saul had asked Abner whose son David was when David went out to face Goliath. Of course Saul knew that he was Jesse's son; what he meant to find out was whether a similar courage born of faith had ever manifested itself before in David's family. Under oath Abner testified that he did not know. Neither of these two men knew the Spirit of the Lord, nor did either one believe the miracle that was revealed in David. Saul was trying to explain the miracle wrought by the Spirit.

After Goliath was killed, Saul himself questioned David. Again David testified to the power of the Lord's grace toward Israel and talked of his faith in that power. How simply he must have expressed his faith!

Jonathan was also present at this meeting. Formerly Jonathan himself had been in the grip of this faith by which we can do all things. But such faith found no response at Saul's court and was in danger of being stifled by the spirit there. Seeing what David had done and hearing him witness about it now had a liberating effect on Jonathan. He made a covenant of friendship with David, for in his heart he was bound to him forever. As a sign of this covenant, Jonathan gave David his clothes and his weapons.

This gesture was a token of the greatest trust. Most likely Jonathan already sensed something of the role David would play in Israel. But this did not prevent him from honoring David as he did. Here Jonathan, the son of the king, was the lesser over against David. This deed on his part was an act of faith. Only faith makes us willing to be the lesser. Faith causes us to surrender the rights we pretend to have over against the Christ, who is truly Israel's King.

When Saul, David and the army returned from battle, the women met them, singing: "Saul has slain his thousands, and David his tens of thousands." This was not a song of faith. If those women had looked in faith at what had happened, they would have sung praises to the Lord. Now they sang of Saul and David. That's the way the Philistine women would have sung of Goliath if he had been victorious. In addition, because they lacked the vision of faith, these women stirred up Saul's envy with their thoughtless song. How little the people lived by faith those days!

Saul's jealousy was indeed provoked by this song. At that point Saul already suspected the truth. (Later his suspicion turned out to be well-founded.) He knew that he had been rejected as king, and he recognized that David was his rival and eventual successor. This suspicion was strengthened when he noticed how David was blessed in all the expeditions he carried out for the king and saw how David grew in favor among the people.

Saul knew the secret of David's courage and prudence. He knew that the faith revealing itself in David's actions and words was the work of the Spirit. In earlier days, Saul, too, had received the gifts of that Spirit. He knew something of the glory of a life ruled by the Spirit. Now that he had lost those gifts of the Spirit, he hated them when he saw them in David. There is no greater hatred in the world than hatred toward God's Spirit. That's why Saul wanted to kill David.

Not long afterward, David played the harp for Saul again. The evil spirit came over him, and he hurled his spear at David. Twice this happened, and twice David dodged the attack. Saul could not stand David any longer, for David's life had become a continuous finger of accusation pointing at his life. Therefore Saul removed David from his court by making him a commander over a thousand soldiers.

Through the victory over Goliath, the Lord had revealed Himself to Israel. But how differently this revelation was received by various people! Jonathan, the women, and Saul all responded in different ways. When the grace of the Lord Jesus Christ is made visible in the world, it still meets with varying responses.

14: Crisis

David had been revealed to the people as the one blessed by the Lord. Saul already had a strong suspicion that David would be his successor. What was required of Saul, then, was that he resign himself to this decision of the Lord and acknowledge David's calling. But that was impossible for Saul because of his unbelief. Saul had reached a crisis in his life.

The relationship between Saul and David became very close: David married Saul's daughter and became his son-in-law. This course of events and the blessing upon the military operations undertaken by David were tests of the Lord to bring Saul to submission in faith. But Saul rebelled against the decision of the Lord and rejected David. At that point Jonathan reconciled the two parties. Here again Saul faced the demand of the Lord to submit in faith. But even then Saul could not submit.

David's next move was to escape to Samuel, seeking the protection of the Word of the Lord. Saul sent messengers to Naioth and then went there himself, rebelling against the protection which the Word and Spirit of the Lord offered David.

When Saul arrived in the vicinity of Naioth, the Spirit of prophecy overpowered him; he was in the grip of the Spirit of the Lord even though he rejected that Spirit. This reminds us of the sin against the Holy Spirit. At that point the decisive choice in Saul's life was made.

This was the third stage in his rejection. First Saul lost the kingship for his posterity. Then he was rejected himself as king. Now he was finally rejected as a human being. After that point, Jonathan's attempts to reconcile Saul and David could not possibly succeed.

God did not take pleasure in Saul. Yet, Saul was seriously confronted with the covenant calling to bow before the rule of God's grace over

118

His people. Saul loved himself more than God's grace as that grace was revealed in the calling of David; he loved himself more than the Christ.

At the same time, David's life also reached a crisis. What would he do? Would he break his ties with Saul and rebel against him? No, he did not lift up his hand against the Lord's anointed. In this period David learned patience; he learned the patience of faith in his calling. Jonathan's attitude was a source of great comfort to him; he saw it as a sign of God's favor upon him. In this crisis David was able to carry on only because of God's grace.

What happened at the court in those days remained largely hidden from the people. Only later, when Saul pursued David, did they see the decadence in Saul's life. Yet the grace of God toward the people in the future kingship of David had already brought about the turning point.

Main thought: *In His covenant, God brings events to a crisis.*

Father-in-law and son-in-law. David was careful as he undertook the military operations ordered by Saul, and the Lord was with him. Saul's suspicion that David was destined by the Lord to be his successor developed into a certainty. Saul should have bowed before the Lord's decision and subjected himself in faith to the grace God showed His people by calling David to be their king. But sinful Saul loved himself too much to be able to do that. He continued to reject David in his heart, thereby rejecting the grace of God and even the Christ Himself. Yet, he observed the Lord's blessing on David and His sovereign good pleasure in him. This filled him with a haunting fear. The favor David won among the people was also evidence of the Lord's good pleasure in him.

Therefore Saul planned to lure David into a trap. The promise that the man who killed Goliath would become the king's son-in-law still had not been fulfilled. Saul considered giving David his oldest daughter, Merab, on the condition that he win another victory over the Philistines. Perhaps he would then be killed in battle. Saul was plotting in his heart against the good pleasure of the Lord. Didn't he realize that it is useless for man to fight against the Lord? How blinded we are by sin!

This plan did not materialize. Apparently Merab did not love David. In any case, she became the wife of another man. But Saul did not give up on his plan. His daughter Michal did love David.

When Saul found out, he put his plan into operation again and made a proposal to David. Apparently David's modesty kept him from accepting this proposal immediately. He waited for the king to make his will known more clearly. Saul, on the other hand, did not quite dare come forward with his conditions. The truth of the matter was that he had no right to set conditions; he was bound by the promise he had made before Goliath was killed.

Once more Saul communicated his wishes to David, this time through his servants. Eagerly he waited for a response. David's answer was exactly what Saul wanted to hear: he pointed out that he, David, could not provide a marriage present. At that point Saul informed David that he would settle for proof that David had killed 100 Philistines. David gladly accepted this condition. With his men he killed not just 100 Philistines but 200. He brought the proof to the king, and Michal became his wife.

How closely related Saul and David were now! Yet, Saul's hatred of David and his fear of him as the one blessed by the Lord still stood between them. When Saul saw that his plan had failed and that David was being blessed in his marriage because Michal loved him, his fear increased even more. How the Lord was testing him in all these events! The Lord was trying to get Saul to surrender to the counsel of His grace toward His people. On the other hand, the marriage to Saul's daughter constituted a severe trial for David. Would he conform to the spirit of Saul's court, or would he keep his simple faith in the calling of the Lord?

Saul did not surrender. On the contrary, even after it became obvious to him that the Lord's blessing rested on David's new military operations, he stated openly to Jonathan and his servants that he wanted to kill David. By rejecting David, he was actually rejecting God's grace toward His people. He did not want to give up his self-seeking ways. How often the Lord Jesus Christ also stands in our way! We refuse to give up our sovereignty and acknowledge Him alone as King, as the One called by God to be our King.

A new call to surrender. Jonathan had given his heart to David. Therefore he warned David about Saul's threats and promised to intercede with him on David's behalf. Shortly afterward he found himself alone with his father in the field. He used the opportunity to direct his words to Saul's heart: "David has been good to you, and the Lord has delivered Israel through him. You were happy about that yourself. Why, then, do you now wish to sin against David?" Saul's heart was touched at these words. He swore by the Lord that David would not be killed. How close Saul was at that moment to the Kingdom of God! How the Lord, using the words of Jonathan, urged Saul to surrender!

David was greatly comforted by Jonathan's friendship and his own restoration to honor. In all of this the Lord was with him. Again he fought the enemies of the Lord and defeated the Philistines in a mighty battle. He also played the harp for Saul again.

But Saul's change of heart was short-lived. He did not break with his sins radically. How close Saul had been to the Kingdom of God in former days, when the Spirit of the Lord came upon him! But he had repeatedly turned away. Now, too, he turned away.

Maddened by jealousy, he threw his spear at David, but David escaped and fled to his own home. However, Saul had his house surrounded. At first David's wife Michal outwitted Saul's messengers by telling them that David was sick. In the meantime she helped him escape through a window. When the servants of Saul returned to bring David to Saul on his bed, if necessary, all they found in his bed was a dummy—an image.* By means of Michal's love, the Lord had saved David.

When Saul called Michal to account for her deception, she lied and said that David had threatened to kill her. Undoubtedly Saul understood that this was a lie. How it must have pained his conscience that even his daughter took sides against him and chose for David! This was another call from the Lord. God does not let go easily of someone he has called in His covenant.

The decision. David fled to Samuel in Ramah. Where was he to unburden his heart if not before Samuel, the man who had anointed him king in the name of the Lord? And where would he

---

*Here the Hebrew text uses the word *teraphim*, which refers to the household gods originally taken along from Mesopotamia.—TRANS.

find protection except under the wing of the Word and Spirit of the Lord, which lived in Samuel?

Together David and Samuel went to the schools of the prophets in Naioth, close to Ramah. Surely Saul would not dare take David by force from these buildings; there David would be in the Lord's keeping. How mistaken Samuel and David were! The Lord had purposely let events take this course.

The hour of decision had come for Saul. Would he rebel openly against the Spirit of the Lord? But what can stop a man once he had surrendered his heart to the power of the evil one?

When Saul learned where David was, he sent messengers to get him. When the messengers came to the vicinity of Naioth, they met a group of prophets prophesying through the Spirit of the Lord. God's Spirit came upon Saul's messengers, and they prophesied too. The same thing happened to a second group of messengers, and a third. This should have been sufficient warning to Saul that the Spirit of the Lord was protecting David.

Despite the warning, Saul was daring enough to go to Naioth himself. Then the Spirit of the Lord came over Saul, and he prophesied as he continued on his way. In ecstasy he took off his tunic and lay on the ground for a whole day and night, overpowered by the Spirit. What a horrible night that was! There he saw and spoke of heavenly matters, while his heart burned with hatred of the Lord's Spirit. Unwillingly he spoke God's praises.

At that point the final decision about Saul as a person was made. He was rejected by God. And the saying "Is Saul also among the prophets?" took on a new and terrible meaning. David, meanwhile, was safe under the shield of the Spirit of prophecy. One day the point of separation will be reached between the Christ and all those who persecute Him by seeking their own glory over against His.

Steering an evil course. Then David looked Jonathan up and complained to him: "What wrong have I done?" Jonathan could not believe that his father's attitude toward David was as bad as David made out. Even though Jonathan was a believer who had surrendered in faith to David's calling, he did not want to face the extent and depth of the corruption in his father's heart.

They agreed that in the coming days, when the feast of the new moon was celebrated at Saul's court, it would become clear once and for all what Saul's attitude to David really was. David would be absent, and Jonathan would make some excuse for him by telling a white lie. Then Jonathan would have an opportunity to fathom his father's mood and convey to David by way of a signal what he had learned.

They both realized that a decisive moment had arrived in their friendship. Would they ever see each other again? At Jonathan's request, David swore that when the Lord restored him to honor, he would deal kindly with Jonathan and his family. This shows how completely Jonathan surrendered in faith to David's calling! Here Jonathan stands in direct contrast to Saul, as we are shown what the Spirit of the Lord can do in the heart of man. How precious the gift of faith was in Jonathan! We see just how marvelous the grace of Christ is: by means of that grace, Jonathan was able to win a great victory over himself.

Saul's mood soon became clear: he accused Jonathan of having chosen for David despite the fact that he would never become king himself as long as David was alive. Saul declared that Jonathan had disgraced himself and his mother as well. To the unbeliever, surrendering to the grace of God is a disgrace. Saul even threw his spear at his own son. Then Jonathan realized that Saul had fully decided to steer an evil course.

Jonathan rose from the table in fierce anger against his father. This was a case of lawful anger. He thundered against his father's rejection of grace in the person of David. He was deeply concerned about David and resented his father's unfounded accusations about him. He loved David as the one blessed by the Lord.

By means of the signal agreed upon, Jonathan informed David about the outcome. They had just a brief moment to take leave of each other. Both of them sensed that this was most likely a farewell for good. In any case, from that point on they went their separate ways. David was branded an outlaw and was no longer protected, while Jonathan had to stay at the court, which was pervaded with hatred of the Lord's grace.

David and Jonathan could hardly let go of each other. Deeply moved, David bowed three times before Jonathan as the one he still considered his superior. There was no desire whatever in

David's heart to push Jonathan from his place as Saul's successor. Jonathan did not harbor any such suspicion, and he let David go in peace after the two renewed their oath of faithfulness to each other.

The counsel of the Lord separated them, but they remained united in faithful submission to the rule of that counsel over Israel and over both their lives. Shouldn't we surrender willingly to the Lord's grace toward His people, a grace already decided on in His counsel and revealed to us in His Word?

15: No Place To Lay His Head

I Samuel 21-23

During his time of persecution by Saul, David is particularly a type of the Christ in His humiliation. Remember what the Christ said: "Foxes have holes, and birds of the air have nests; but the Son of man has nowhere to lay his head" (Matt. 8:20).

But this does not mean that David's conduct during this period was beyond reproach. He was not a type of the Christ in everything he did. He went wrong in particular by wanting to seek refuge outside Israel's borders. There was to be no place for him among the enemies of the Lord. Every effort to seek protection there meant a certain unfaithfulness toward the Lord and His people. David was supposed to surrender to the guidance of the Lord within the borders of the holy land.

In those days Saul turned into an utter tyrant. This became obvious especially when he wiped out the people of Nob, the city of priests. Acting as though the Lord's cause were somehow at stake, he put the entire city under the ban, even going so far as to kill all the cattle. He dared to identify himself, as the anointed one, with the righteousness of the Lord—while committing an arbitrary, highhanded sin!

What the people were supposed to learn during this period was that they would have to let go of Saul and choose for David. But the people were not at all ready to do so. They were not about to give up the mistaken expectations with which they had greeted Saul's kingship. Moreover, a tyrannical ruler like Saul was much more in tune with their carnal thoughts than a man like David, who knew that he had to go where God led him. Finally, the fear of Saul often led the people to betray David.

The attitude of the people strengthened Saul in his sinful ways. Therefore the people shared the responsibility with their king. David suffered the affliction of the rejected redeemer. And he had to learn to wait for the people to choose him. Through this waiting, he was being sanctified and prepared to become Israel's true king.

Main thought: *The anointed one has no place to lay his head.*

Not to the Philistines. After saying good-by to Jonathan, David fled from the vicinity of Saul's court. Where was he to go? The thought must already have come to him then that there was no place in his own country where he would be safe from Saul. The only thing left to do was to flee across the border. Wouldn't the enemies of Israel and of Saul gladly take him in when they saw that Saul was pursuing him as his adversary?

David was a clever man, full of cunning calculations. Sometimes these calculations clouded his childlike faith. Could he ever be justified in looking for protection among the enemies of Saul? After all, they were also the enemies of the Lord's people and of the Lord Himself. Could he be faithful to the Lord's cause while living among the Lord's enemies? The Lord would have to guide him in this matter.

From Gibeah he fled to Nob, which was then the seat of the tabernacle and the high priest, Ahimelech. Apparently David had been there many times carrying out Saul's orders. On such occasions he would inquire about the Lord's will through the high priest. This time he came to Ahimelech all by himself. Ahimelech trembled as he met David, for he was afraid he might become involved in some secret matter or other. And what David told him was that he was indeed on a secret mission for the king and had left his army behind so that he could be alone with the high priest and ask about the Lord's will. He asked whether the Lord would be with him if he continued to pursue the course he had started out on. He received a positive answer. Still, David had told the high priest a lie. In the tight corner in which he found himself, he saw no other way out than to lie.

In addition, he asked the high priest for bread. However, there was nothing available except the showbread or consecrated bread, which was just being replaced. Only the priests were allowed to eat the showbread, but in this case of extreme urgency, the high priest did not object to giving the showbread to David and his men. The law of the Lord is not to be used against the life which the Lord Himself has given.

David also asked for a spear or a sword. Evidently he had fled without any weapons. There was no other weapon there than the sword of Goliath, which was kept in the sanctuary. At David's request, the high priest gave it to him. Doeg, an Edomite who had an important position under Saul, happened to be in the tabernacle at the time, apparently for the purpose of becoming an Israelite. He saw everything. Through this man, the consequences of David's lie would make themselves felt.

From Nob David fled directly to the land of the Philistines. He hoped he would not be recognized as the one who had killed Goliath. And where would he be able to find better protection than among these archenemies of Saul?

But how could he ever justify seeking protection there? Weren't the Philistines the traditional enemies of Israel and the Lord? How would he be able to remain faithful to the Lord's cause while living among the Philistines? Was his fear of Saul stronger than his abhorrence of the enemies of the Lord? Even if he intended to deceive those enemies, was he at liberty to pretend to make common cause with them?

The Lord made David's calculations turn out wrong. Immediately he was recognized by the servants of Achish, the king of Gath, as the man who had killed Goliath. He was a prince in Israel, one in whom the people had placed their hope.

When David heard that he had been recognized, he was plunged into a state of extreme anxiety. He then thought that the only way he could save himself was to act like a madman. By this strategy he escaped from the hands of Achish. But Israel's future king and deliverer had escaped in a very unworthy manner. David's reliance on his own cunning had clouded his eye of faith.

Not to the Moabites. From there David fled and hid in the cave of Adullam. His father's whole family joined him—his father and mother and brothers. They did not feel safe under Saul anymore. In addition, many outcasts from society came to him.

The result was that a small army of 400 men gathered around him. Later this band swelled to 600 men.

On the one hand, this must have been a comfort to David in his loneliness. On the other hand, it created the impression that he was a gang leader in rebellion against his king. But he could not change the circumstances. Here, in the cave of Adullam, he knew the comfort of fellowship with his own people, of being surrounded by men who depended on him in their troubles. In this he experienced the comfort of the Lord.

The presence of all these followers made hiding more difficult for David. He did not feel safe in the cave any longer. Now he thought of seeking refuge among the Moabites. They were not such traditional enemies of the Israelites as the Philistines were. There were even ties of kinship between Israel and Moab. (The Moabites were descendants of Lot, Abraham's nephew.) Yet, Israel's future king should not be obligated in any way to any of the surrounding peoples, for the nations around Israel rose up time and again as enemies of the Lord and His people.

In Moab he did find shelter and protection, especially for his father and mother, for whom he specifically asked protection of the king. Yet the Lord did not leave him there in peace for very long. The prophet Gad, who was apparently with David, told him in the name of the Lord that he had to return to the land of Judah. He obeyed and went to the forest of Hereth. The Lord was leading him into a dangerous situation. It was time for David to be tested.

The tyrant's curse. Saul learned that his men knew where David was but had not told him. He viewed this as unfaithfulness. At a council meeting held in the open, he aired his bitterness about this matter. His servants were almost all men from his own tribe, the tribe of Benjamin. He had placed them in their high positions. "Will David, who is from the tribe of Judah, give you the same honor? Even my own son supports David!" he complained.

Then Doeg, the Edomite, revealed what he had witnessed in Nob. Saul quickly summoned the high priest Ahimelech and his whole family and all the priests who were in Nob. He accused Ahimelech of treason. But Ahimelech was completely innocent; he did not know of the conflict between Saul and David. Moreover, he testified: "David is the most faithful of your servants, and he is your son-in-law. It was certainly not the first time that I consulted the Lord for him. I have done so a number of times when he was carrying out one of your assignments."

Saul could not be convinced, so he ordered his servants to kill the Lord's priests. When his men refused, Doeg did it at Saul's command. The king was still not satisfied; he went on to have all the inhabitants of Nob killed, including the babies. Even the cattle were destroyed. Saul dealt with the city of Nob as if the ban of the Lord had been pronounced over it. All this he did to take personal revenge. As a matter of fact, he had withdrawn himself from the Lord, and his own cause was no longer the cause of the Lord. Thus Saul became a curse to the people.

Only Abiathar, the son of Ahimelech, escaped. He fled to David with the Urim and Thummim. David received him gladly. He recognized that it was because of his lie that this calamity had befallen Ahimelech and his house. From then on, Abiathar's lot would be united with David's.

Betrayed by the people. The people still held on to Saul. David stayed mainly in Judah, with his own tribe, but even there it was not safe for him. How long would it take before the people would be willing to let go of Saul and choose for David, the one who had been chosen by the Lord to be Israel's deliverer?

David received a message that the Philistines were attacking Keilah and stealing from the threshing floors. Everything in David prompted him to deliver his people from the burden of these traditional enemies of Israel. His men objected because of the danger threatening them from Saul's side. But since Abiathar had joined David, the Lord could be consulted. At the Lord's direction, David marched out and liberated Keilah.

This action, however, did not win him the support of the people. What a bitter pill that was for David to swallow! Saul marched against Keilah. When David asked the Lord whether the people of Keilah would hand him over to Saul, the answer was a definite yes. Therefore David fled from Keilah, and Saul returned home.

David and his men hid in a forest in the Wilderness of Ziph. Here Jonathan came to visit him. Jonathan predicted that his father Saul would not be able to find David here and kill him, for David would most certainly become king, as Saul himself was well aware. Jonathan would then be second in David's kingdom. How completely Jonathan submitted to the Lord's decision, and how David must have been comforted by their covenant, which they renewed that day!

The Ziphites betrayed David's hiding place to Saul. In tragic self-pity, Saul praised them for showing him compassion. They were to keep a close watch on all David's movements. In the meantime, Saul came with an army. In the Wilderness of Moan, he surrounded David and his men. There was no way of escape left. But at that moment Saul received word that the Philistines had invaded the country. He had to leave in haste. In this manner the Lord delivered David from the hand of Saul.

But this persecution was dreadful for David. He did not have a place where he could lay his head and be sure he was safe. All of this happened in the land which he would one day rule as king. David traveled this road of suffering as the Lord's anointed. In that regard he resembled the Christ, who would one day cry that although the foxes have holes and the birds of the air have nests, He had no place to lay His head. He would raise this lament on the earth, which He would rule one day in glory as King!

The Christ had to come to the throne along the path of suffering. David, too, had to travel that road. Aren't all believers strangers on this earth, the earth that has been promised to them? Aren't they strangers because sin is still so powerful all around them and in them? The history of David teaches us that after the time of humiliation is over, the Lord will certainly exalt His own. He will exalt them because the Christ in His humiliation obtained this exaltation for them. For that reason, David, too, was exalted.

16: Vengeance Is Mine

I Samuel 24-26

The Lord's anointed was not permitted to seek self-vindication. He was to concern himself only with the Lord's rights and make God's cause his own cause. David was supposed to surrender to the Lord and His righteousness in all circumstances—in his dealings with Saul as well as his dealings with Nabal.

In all such relationships, David was to be a type of the One who did not threaten others when He suffered but submitted His cause to God, the righteous Judge. By following that path, the Christ became the Savior of His people. And if David was to become the deliverer of Israel, he would have to follow a similar path. The Spirit of the Christ would truly have to dwell in him.

In his final conversation with Saul, David proceeded from the assumption that it might well be the Lord who was stirring Saul up and driving him to persecute David. The Lord sometimes punishes sin with sin. If it was indeed the Lord who was driving Saul on, Saul should offer the Lord a sweet-smelling sacrifice. What David had in mind was a sacrifice of true submission to the Lord. For Saul, however, the time for such a sacrifice was past.

Main thought: *The Lord's anointed is willing to submit his cause to the One who judges in righteousness.*

Let the Lord be my judge! The Lord's deliverance did not free David from Saul for good. Before long, David fled to the caves of the Wilderness of Engedi, near the Dead Sea. As soon as Saul

131

returned from his expedition against the Philistines, he resumed his pursuit of David.

When Saul reached the Wilderness of Engedi, he withdrew for a moment into a cave, leaving behind the 3000 men who were with him. It happened to be the very same cave in which David was hidden, but Saul, of course, did not know that. David's men declared that the Lord had delivered David's enemy into his hand. Now David could free himself from his enemy for good by killing him.

But David crept toward Saul with no such intention. All he did was cut off the bottom part of Saul's robe, which Saul had apparently taken off. Even this act bothered his conscience. Was he at liberty to do such a thing? In any case, he refused to lift his hand against the Lord's anointed. The Lord Himself would have to judge between Saul and David. After all, what really mattered was the Lord's cause. Therefore David kept his men from attacking Saul.

Here we observe in David the Spirit of the Christ, who did not insist that His own rights be upheld but willingly left His cause in the hands of the Father. And the Christ became the Preserver of His people. David, likewise, could be king only in God's name.

When Saul left the cave, David called out after him and showed him the hem of his robe as proof that he did not want to harm Saul. He was willing to submit his cause to the Lord, he told Saul. He asked the king why he continued trying to hunt him down. Had he, David, done anything wrong? Why didn't the king pursue the Lord's enemies instead?

Saul was deeply touched by David's words and his refusal to take his king's life. For a moment he saw the unfathomable depth of the unjust hatred in his own heart. The man who thought only of himself and pitied himself was deeply moved by David's noble conduct.

Saul even went so far as to admit to David something that he already recognized in his own heart, namely, that David would be king someday. All he asked of David was that he swear an oath not to wipe out his family after him. David swore to this, and the two went their separate ways.

Had Saul, then, submitted to the Lord's election of David? It looked that way, and yet it was not really so. Sentiment had moved Saul to speak as he did—and not a surrender to the Lord in faith. Therefore the change in Saul was short-lived.

Let not my hand avenge me! It was during this troubled period that Samuel died, leaving great confusion behind him in Israel. Saul was persecuting the man whom God had called to be a deliverer of Israel. And the people did not know whose side to take. Undoubtedly Samuel commended Israel's cause into the Lord's hands. The people honored him as a prophet of the Lord through their deep mourning at his funeral in Ramah.

Samuel's death led more Israelites to begin looking to David, whom the Lord was obviously favoring. Fortunately, Jonathan was not the only one who was willing to acknowledge David's calling. This soon became evident—through the action of a woman.

In those days David sent messengers to Nabal, a man of the family of Caleb, of the tribe of Judah. *Nabal* must have been a nickname, for the word means *foolishness.* He was a man who lacked discernment, common sense.

Nabal was very rich: he had 3000 sheep and 1000 goats. It was the time of the sheep shearing. When this work was completed, a great banquet would be held. David decided that he had a right to some reward from Nabal, for he and his men had never taken any animals from Nabal's flocks and had protected his herdsmen and flocks from the roving Bedouins.

This rich man refused David's request—and in a haughty way at that. He insulted David by calling him a rebel, that is, someone who had revolted against his lord. This fool's unwillingness made him think and say things that were clearly mistaken.

David was deeply offended by this indignant treatment and vowed that he would kill Nabal and all the males of his house. Off he marched with 400 men, leaving 200 with the baggage. He was indeed deeply offended, but would he now become his own judge? Was his anointing a private matter, a mere personal honor?

Wasn't the Lord Himself offended far more than David? Would David then dishonor his future kingship by seeking such self-willed revenge? But David did not see any of these things. He suffered from narrow-mindedness and could not see past his own burning desire for revenge. God's people can only rise above such passions by recognizing that it is not their cause but God's cause that is at stake.

If the Lord had allowed David to go on, his cause would have been stained for good. Fortunately, God preserved David's status as the anointed one and thereby also protected His people, to whom He intended to give David as king. He accomplished this through Nabal's wife Abigail, a beautiful and intelligent woman.

One of Nabal's servants informed Abigail what had happened and warned her that David might well seek revenge. He confirmed that David and his men had indeed protected Nabal's herdsmen. Abigail realized what could happen. What worried her most was not that Nabal's house might be wiped out but that David's calling was in jeopardy. In faith she had grasped David's calling as Israel's future king and deliverer. For the sake of the people and for the sake of the Lord's covenant, her heart was with David. That's why she was afraid.

Immediately she prepared a large present for David—200 loaves of bread, two skins of wine, five dressed sheep, five measures of roasted grain, 100 clusters of raisins, 200 fig cakes. She had all this food loaded onto donkeys. With this generous present, which was meant to honor David, she sent her young men ahead. She herself also went to meet him, without telling her husband what she had done.

When she met David, she bowed low before him and pleaded the cause that concerned her so deeply. "Blame me for Nabal's crime," she said, "and listen to what I have to say. Nabal acted foolishly, and I knew nothing of it. However, the Lord sent me to you so that you will not take the law into your own hands and stain your calling by shedding Nabal's blood. Look at this present I prepared for your followers—a token of my respect for you. I know that the Lord has destined you to be a leader in Israel. He will establish your house forever, for you walk in the ways of the Lord and fight against the Lord's enemies for His sake. The blessing of the Lord rests upon you. He will protect you in the midst of all danger, but your enemies He will throw out like stones from a sling. If the Lord has done these great things for you, see to it that there is no innocent blood on your conscience. Turn back, and one day you will remember me, your handmaid."

How could this woman speak such words? She had a glorious vision of David's calling for God's people, and she struggled with her whole heart to keep that calling pure. It was a comfort to

David that there was someone who could see things, in faith, as they truly were. Abigail's words were in harmony with his own faith in the calling of the Lord.

How great the danger that the sanctity of this calling would be lost through a lack of appreciation on the part of Nabal and others! Now David saw his calling again in all its splendor. Abigail's words were oil upon the waves of his anger. He praised the Lord, who had kept him from taking the law into his own hands, and he praised Abigail for her wise counsel. He let her go back after accepting her gift. By the grace of God, the Spirit of the Lord Jesus Christ had triumphed in David.

When Abigail got home, she told Nabal nothing of what she had done, for he was drunk. Not until he was sober again did she tell him. Nabal was so shocked by this news that he had a stroke. What upset him was not so much fright at the danger that had threatened him but bitterness and anger at the fact that David had emerged the winner after all. Ten days later he died.

When David received word of Nabal's death, he praised the Lord, for the Lord had judged righteously and had kept David from seeking vengeance himself. Then David asked Abigail to marry him, and she consented. She counted it an honor to serve the one the Lord had called. In this confession of faith, David must have received new strength to continue in the Lord's calling. Undoubtedly Abigail, acting as his conscience, reminded him of his calling in later years too.

David was also married to Ahinoam. Because of this, his relationship to Abigail was not what it should have been. David did not live out of faith in all things. He took both women as wives in place of Michal, who had been given by Saul to someone else.

Let the Lord reward the righteous! Again the men of Ziph told Saul that David was hiding in their neighborhood, this time on Hachilah Hill. From his spies David learned that Saul was pursuing him once more. With two of his captains, David found Saul's camp. He proposed to sneak into the camp with one of the captains. Abishai was willing to go with him.

Because all the soldiers in the camp were asleep, David and Abishai could penetrate right to where Saul lay sleeping. Again

Saul was in David's hand, and Abishai asked David's permission to kill him with his spear. But David wouldn't hear of it. He did not want to be guilty of taking the cause of the people into his own hands by killing the Lord's anointed and putting himself in his place. Either the Lord would slay Saul, or he would die in his bed, or he would be killed in battle. But however events might unfold, the Lord had the lives of Saul and David in His hand. Thus, all David did was take along Saul's spear and his jug of water.

When they were a safe distance from the camp, David cried out to Abner, Saul's general, and accused him of failing to guard the king's life. Saul recognized David's voice. Apparently it was not light yet, and Saul could not see David.

Again David asked Saul why he pursued him. Evidently there was something driving Saul to continue this pursuit. If it was the Lord who was stirring Saul up, punishing sin with sin, then Saul really ought to return to the Lord in repentance by submitting to Him and offering a sacrifice. But if Saul was being driven on by some person or other, let that person be cursed.

David's early morning lament was very moving. He complained that he was compelled to leave the holy ground, the land in which the Lord chose to dwell among His people, and go to the nations that served other gods. Shouldn't it be beneath Saul to chase David?

Again Saul confessed that he was in the wrong, but he was less moved than the first time. He was just ashamed. At David's request, someone came to get Saul's spear. David's last remark was that the Lord would reward each one according to his works. The Lord would spare David's life, just as He had spared Saul's.

All there was left for Saul to do was to bless David for his conduct and to confess that David would prevail. Then they parted, never to see each other again. Saul's last words were an acknowledgment of the victory of the one who fought only for the Lord's rights, the one who submitted to the Lord. Indeed, the victory is Christ's.

17: Forsaken and Sought Out

In these stories, too, we must pay careful attention to the position in which the people of Israel found themselves. We are not just dealing with Saul and David. The people themselves were passing through especially dark days at that time.

As the Philistines were marching against the Israelites, their future king was in the camp of their enemies and the king who was still ruling had snuck off to a medium or fortune-teller. At that point the Israelites were supported neither by the one who was anointed in the past nor by the one who was anointed for the future. They were truly forsaken; in the unfaithfulness of both Saul and David, the Lord was forsaking His people.

The people were being forsaken so that the Lord could reveal how He would remember them again in David out of free grace. David's kingship and the deliverance by his hand were rooted not in his own excellence but in God's favor. Many times David was an antitype of the Christ. Whatever he might become to the people he would become only through the Christ.

What happened in Endor can be completely explained in what the spiritists call "animistic" terms. The figure of Samuel lived on in the strong impression it had made on Saul's mind. By the way of telepathy, Saul transmitted that image to the mind of the medium. Saul himself did not see Samuel come up out of the ground; the medium did. She gave form to what Saul had transmitted to her mind. It is also noteworthy that as soon as she "saw Samuel," she recognized Saul. At that moment she had contact with Saul's mind—also in his self-consciousness over against "Samuel."

Given this framework, the conversation between Saul and "Samuel" must be understood as a conversation Saul had with himself. Saul asked and answered his own questions in his mind; the figure of "Samuel" and the answers given by "Samuel" were creations of Saul's own mind, which were then channeled through the medium. Saul's awareness of the true state of affairs and of the fearful events ahead was an answer to his own questioning consciousness.

Sometimes we, too, create someone in our dreams, someone who answers our questions. Sometimes the answers we receive are amazingly true. The voice speaking to us on such occasions is the voice of our conscience.

Yet, we must assume here that God used this activity in Saul's mind to make His final pronouncement of judgment on Saul. The certainty with which "Samuel" supposedly answered must be attributed to Saul's own prophetic mind. The question raised by "Samuel" ("Why have you disturbed me by bringing me back?") is not in conflict with this interpretation. This self-accusation must have been present in Saul's own mind.

We may not assume that Saul or the fortune-teller or anyone else could disturb those who have died in Christ. An appeal to the appearance of Moses and Elijah on the Mount of Transfiguration is out of place, of course, for it was God Himself who revealed Moses and Elijah there. When the medium declares, "I see a god coming up out of the earth," we must interpret her as meaning that she sees a supernatural figure coming up.

We are told that when Saul inquired of the Lord, the Lord did not answer him by the Urim (I Sam. 28:6). This poses a problem: earlier we read that the high priest Abiathar fled to David's camp, taking the ephod and the Urim and Thummim with him. Hence it would seem that Saul could not have inquired of the Lord by means of the Urim. Now, this puzzling text could conceivably be interpreted to mean that the Lord did not answer Saul in any way whatever. Yet, the words of the text seem to point in another direction.

After the murder of the priests in Nob and Abiathar's flight, the service in the sanctuary was apparently restored. If so, a high priest must have been appointed again. Abiathar was of the family of Eli and thus a descendant of Ithamar, the second of the remaining sons of Aaron. Could it be that Saul appointed as high priest a man of the family of Eleazar? And could this be the reason why we later find Zadok and Abiathar mentioned as high priests alongside each other? (II Sam. 15:24-9, 35; 19:11). This seems to be the most likely solution to the puzzle about the whereabouts of the Urim.

Main thought: *The people are forsaken by the Lord and then sought out again in the anointed one.*

David's denial of the Lord's people. Time and again the Lord had delivered David from the hand of Saul in a marvelous manner. Yet, David began to doubt whether he could long survive that way. Saul's arm reached to all corners of that rather small land of Canaan. Surely he would capture David one day.

In these deliberations David forgot that the hand of the Lord reached farther than the hand of Saul, and that the Lord could always rescue him from Saul's clutches. At these times David's faith was pushed back by his fear and by his desire to save himself through his own cleverness.

David decided to seek refuge with Achish of Gath again. By this time the Philistines must have heard enough about Saul's persecution of David to be convinced that David would be their ally. This plan worked out just the way David hoped. Achish received David in a friendly way and allowed him and his men and their possessions to stay in Gath. But David asked Achish if he would let them have Ziklag instead. Originally Ziklag had belonged to the Israelites, but it had apparently been captured by the Philistines and was still uninhabited. Achish agreed. (After that time, this city remained the property of David's family.)

David and his men lived in Ziklag for a year and four months. Time and again they attacked enemies living and roaming along the southern borders of Canaan, such as the Amalekites. When they triumphed over these enemies, they took no prisoners. They killed everyone in sight so that no one would be able to tell the Philistines just what they were up to.

David himself told Achish that he was fighting against Judah. Achish must have been pleased to hear that David had turned into a permanent enemy of his own people. David's destruction of the Amalekites was not an unjustifiable cruelty, for the Lord had already ordered Saul to wipe them out.

It is true that David was denying his own people—if not by his deeds, at least by his words. In the process he was also denying the God of his people. He declared himself an enemy of the people God had chosen. How could he ever deny them before the enemies of the Lord? The Lord Jesus Christ never denied His people, either in words or in deeds: in both His words and His deeds He confessed that they were His people and God's people.

For Christ's sake, the Lord was merciful to David and rescued

him from the difficulties in which he got entangled. David, as the
deliverer of his people, was not forsaken by God, even though he
had denied God in a shameful way. Like Peter, who denied the
Savior through his words, David was restored to his office.

Saul in the power of satan. In those days the Philistines went
to war against Israel. They made their camp at Shunem. Saul
mobilized his army and camped at Gilboa, facing the enemy. From
Gilboa Saul could see the Philistine army.

Rarely had Saul been truly frightened, but this time he was
frantic with fear. He had been forsaken by God. The terror of the
Lord, which fell on his enemies in times past, now fell on him.
Then he remembered how he used to consult the Lord before battle. He wanted to do so before this battle too. He forgot that he
had broken completely with the Lord—and the Lord with him.

The Lord did not answer—neither through dreams nor by the
prophets nor by the Urim. For Saul, this proof that he had been
forsaken was sheer agony. There was no turning back for him; it
was too late. He had degenerated too far in his sinful desires.

In the old days, Saul's desire to inquire of the Lord rose from
a longing to hear the voice of the Lord, a longing to have the Lord
lead him by the hand. Now Saul's only desire was to know the
future, the outcome. Such a desire by itself is always deeply sinful.
It is the exact opposite of submitting to the Lord in faith.

This sinful desire led Saul to a medium. He learned from his
servants that there was still one around, at Endor, not too far from
the camp. In earlier days, when Saul defended the honor of the
Lord's Word, he had ordered all the mediums expelled or
destroyed. Now he looked for one himself.

The Lord had refused to answer Israel's king. Samuel was
dead. David was living among Israel's enemies. It appeared that
the Word of the Lord was closed to Israel.

The woman sought out by Saul feared that the men at her
door had come to spy on her and have her killed. Saul took a
solemn oath that no harm would come to her—an oath he swore
by the Lord! How could he do such a thing?

The woman did not recognize Saul. He asked her to bring
back Samuel. Soon she claimed to see Samuel in her mind. At that

same moment she had such close contact with Saul's mind that she recognized him. She screamed with fear. Again Saul reassured her. He asked her what she saw. She said that she saw a supernatural figure coming up out of the ground. From her description, Saul thought that he recognized Samuel. Then he heard "Samuel" complaining about being disturbed by Saul. Saul admitted that he was afraid and that God had forsaken him. "Samuel" then wanted to know why he had been summoned if the Lord had turned away from Saul.

There Saul was confronted with the apostasy of his life. He was told that the Lord would deliver the Israelites and their king into the hands of the Philistines, and that he and his sons would be among the dead the next day. Because of Saul's sin, Israel, too, would be delivered into the enemy's hands. Here Saul was a perfect antitype of the Christ, for whose sake the people would be saved.

When Saul heard these words he collapsed—in part because he was weak from fasting. Only at the repeated urging of the medium and his servants did he eat what she prepared for him. Then he went away in utter despair, a man rejected. Israel's king was under sentence of death. That sentence was not only a judgment on Saul's sin but also on the sins of the people themselves, for the people had often walked in their king's footsteps.

David's restoration. David's tricks and disavowals got him entangled in greater and greater difficulties. When the Philistines went to war against Israel, he was forced to join Achish's forces. When Achish told David of the forthcoming campaign, David gave him an ambiguous answer: now Achish would find out what David could do.

David was a master of pretense. Yet, he found himself in a horrible spot. There he was, marching with his men in the army of the Philistines. Already they were going through the holy land. David could see for himself how the Philistines plundered and burned cities and villages in Israel. The one who had been called to be Israel's deliverer refrained from attacking Israel's enemies; he left his sword in its sheath. That by itself was a repudiation of his people! And soon he would be compelled to take up arms against the people of the Lord! What anxiety David must have felt!

The Lord Himself rescued David from his predicament. The leaders of the Philistines did not trust David, and Achish was forced to send him back. Achish apologized to him for this affront. David acted offended, but there must have been a song in his heart!

When he returned home with his men, he found that Ziklag had been plundered and burned by the Amalekites. Their wives and children had been kidnaped. Apparently the Amalekites had taken revenge for David's raids against them.

Beside themselves with grief, David's men threatened to stone him. They had probably been raising objections for a long time about living among the Philistines. That idle tramping along behind the Philistine army must have pricked their consciences too. They had lost everything on account of David's accursed cleverness. The Lord had apparently forsaken them. David felt forsaken by everything and everybody—including the Lord.

But in these threatening circumstances it was revealed what grace can do. Through the Spirit of the Lord, David was allowed to take hold of the Lord in faith. With the speed of lightning, the thought must have passed through his mind that he had been on the wrong path and that he was now faced with the results of his action. However, he sensed that God, in the faithfulness of His grace, forgives and overcomes sin. Thus he found new strength in the Lord his God.

Being strong in the Lord, he was also able to regain control over his men. Through the high priest, he asked the Lord whether he should pursue the Amalekite robbers and whether the Lord would deliver them into his hand. After receiving a favorable reply, he went after the Amalekites. But 200 of his men were too exhausted to even begin the pursuit. They stayed behind.

On the way David's company came across a slave whom the Amalekites had left to die. The slave's strength soon returned when David's men took care of him, and he directed them to the camp of the Amalekites. The Amalekites were careless after their victory—scattered about, eating, drinking, dancing. They were easy prey for David, and he defeated them. All the loot taken at Ziklag fell into his hands. Not one of the women or children was missing. In addition, David and his men took possession of all that belonged to those Amalekites. After their return to Ziklag, David commanded that the loot be shared equally with the 200 men who had stayed behind. From that time on, the law in Israel required that the booty taken in war be shared in such a way.

David was not only restored to his possessions and the command of his men, he also found the favor and fellowship of his God again. After the dark days in which Israel had been forsaken by Saul as well as by David, there was new hope for the people in this glorious restoration of David. The mercy of God for Christ's sake did not depart from His people—and therefore not from David either.

David sent part of the loot to the cities of Judah with the message: "Here is a present for you from the spoil taken from the Lord's enemies." He did this to win the favor of his tribe. For the men of Judah and for Israel, it was a sign that David had not forgotten them. There was still hope for Israel.

The death of Saul. Israel could certainly use such light, for the battle between the Israelites and the Philistines on the mountain of Gilboa had ended in complete defeat for Israel. Saul's sons were killed—even Jonathan, upon whom Israel's hopes had been fixed.

During the battle, Saul became separated from his men. The Philistines, especially the archers, kept after him. When Saul saw that escape was impossible, he asked his armor-bearer to kill him so that he would not be captured alive and mocked by the Philistines. When the armor-bearer refused, Saul fell upon his own sword. His armor-bearer died next to him, in the same manner.

That was the end of Saul, the man of whom there had been such great expectations. How close he had come to the Kingdom of God! The Lord had drawn near to him, but he had not surrendered to His grace in faith; instead he had glorified himself over against that grace.

After that things went from bad to worse. Saul's sin became a curse to all Israel, for the victorious Philistines pursued the Israelites, occupied a large part of their territory, and lived in their cities. What was left of Israel's power? The name of Israel would be wiped out unless the Lord intervened.

The day after the attack, some looting Philistines found the corpses of Saul and his three sons on the battlefield. They cut off their heads and sent them throughout the Philistine cities, together with their weapons, as a sign of victory. Saul, the man they had once feared so much, was defeated. Finally they placed the weapons in the temple of their gods as a votive offering. These gods seemed mightier than the grace of God toward Israel.

The Philistines fastened the corpses of Saul and his sons to the wall of Beth-shan, a city that was located in the heart of Israel but was now occupied by the enemy. Would the Lord let this pass without taking revenge? Israel's hopes were now fixed on David.

The people of Jabesh in Gilead heard what the Philistines had done to Saul. They had not forgotten the deliverance the Lord had given them through Saul. Under cover of darkness, their warriors took the corpses of Saul and his sons from the wall of Beth-shan. They burned the corpses in Jabesh and buried the bones beneath the trees there. They mourned Saul's death and fasted for seven days.

There was still some pity left for Saul and his house. Yet, judgment had come upon him, the leader of the people who had turned away from God. That judgment was a judgment of God's grace upon Israel. Because the Lord remained faithful to His people, Saul was removed.

David

18: The People's Submission to Their King

II Samuel 1-5

During this period, David's attitude was one of total dependence upon the Lord. He went up to Hebron only when the Lord told him to. He made no independent effort to get the people to submit to him as king.

Of course David's own judgment played a role in these matters. His praise for the inhabitants of Gilead was at the same time an invitation to submit to him as king. And his capture of Jerusalem was a deed of great statesmanship. After all, Jerusalem was centrally located, and it was close to the border between Judah and Benjamin. By making Jerusalem his capital, David could reconcile the tribe of Benjamin (Saul's tribe) to his rule without rebuffing his own tribe (Judah). The capture of the old citadel of the Jebusites immediately added luster to his name.

Yet, David's actions in this period are not to be explained primarily as clever political moves. They bear the stamp of God's grace, which caused him to put his hope in the Lord. David rejected all injustice; he was driven on by the awareness that Zion was to be delivered by justice. In all of this, David was a type of the Christ, who knows that His own have been given to Him by the Father. In David, the Christ pressed on to reveal Himself and the people recognized the true King.

Only in the case of his sister Zeruiah's sons (Joab and Abishai) was David powerless to execute justice—not because they were his nephews but because they were the leaders of his troops. His followers would not have permitted him to punish them. All he did was curse Joab's family. Later he instructed Solomon to make sure that justice was done.

Certain passages in these chapters are difficult to translate. The words in the middle of II Samuel 1:9 can be translated: ". . . for I am overcome by deathly cramps." Verse 18 of the same chapter should be read: "And he told them to teach Judah's children 'The Bow.'" It may

147

be that "The Bow" is the title of the lamentation David composed. He probably gave it such a title because it was a battle song.

II Samuel 5:8 should be translated: "Whoever would smite the Jebusites, let him cast the lame and the blind, who are hated by David's soul, into the cascade" (i.e. the abyss). The soldiers stationed inside the citadel in Jerusalem are here referred to as "the lame and the blind," a name taken from their own proud boast that even the lame and the blind could defend the city. From that time on, "the lame and the blind" became an expression for hated persons. One might say: "The blind and the lame shall not enter the house."

We read that Ish-bosheth ruled in Mahanaim for two years, and that David became ruler over all the tribes shortly after his death. By then David had already ruled over Judah in Hebron for seven years. These facts warrant the conclusion that Abner had not made Ish-bosheth king immediately after Saul's death. He must have done so about five years later, when he finally recaptured an important portion of the lost territory from the Philistines.

Main thought: *The Lord subjects the people to their king.*

The honor of the Lord's anointed. Two days after David returned to Ziklag, a man arrived with his clothes rent and earth upon his head—obviously a messenger with bad news. He informed David of the defeat of Israel's army and the death of Saul and Jonathan. When David asked him how he knew all this, he said that he had been in the battle and had come upon the king leaning on his spear, overcome by a deathly cramp, with the Philistines closing in on him. He went on to say that he then proceeded to kill Saul, at the king's own urging. He showed David the king's crown and arm bracelets as evidence that his story was true. (Apparently this man had been on the battlefield and had taken away the king's jewels, but the rest of his story was a lie.)

When David and his men heard this news, they tore their clothes and lamented the death of Saul and Jonathan, and also the defeat of the Lord's people, their own brothers. Even though they were on Philistine soil, where they had found refuge and disowned the Lord's people with their mouths, in their hearts they were still bound to the Lord's people with its destiny and king.

David must have become especially angry when he learned

that the messenger was an Amalekite living among the Israelites. The messenger seemed to be convinced that his claim that he had killed King Saul personally would be received by David as good news, and that he would receive a messenger's reward. His claim was that he had raised his hand against Saul, *the Lord's anointed*. The Lord had indeed forsaken Saul, but the execution of judgment upon him belonged to the Lord or whomever the Lord called for that purpose—and not the Amalekite. What business did this stranger have striking down the Lord's anointed? Surely his brazen deed was a disgrace to Israel and Israel's God! Was anyone permitted to deal with Israel and her king as he saw fit?

David must also have suspected that the messenger was lying. Yet, the man had condemned himself by admitting a crime. He would be judged by the words of his own mouth. David therefore commanded one of his men to put the messenger to death. Thus the Amalekite was killed.

The future king of Israel was not self-seeking, and he had no personal desire for revenge against Saul. He was not going to ascend to the throne by way of injustice and bloodshed. The entire people would be shown that David had not been self-seeking and had not given his blessing to an act of injustice. In this way David was a type of Israel's eternal King, the Lord Jesus Christ.

Then David composed a song of lamentation about Saul and Jonathan and ordered that it be taught to Judah's children. "How are the mighty fallen!" he lamented. "Those who were Israel's glory have fallen. Do not tell the Philistines, lest they rejoice in Saul's downfall! May the hills of Gilboa be cursed, for it was there that Israel's shield fell. The Lord's anointing should have protected Saul from the hands of the enemy. What heroes both Saul and Jonathan were! They remained faithful to each other in spite of Saul's sin. Jonathan remained faithful to his father; together they entered death. Weep, daughters of Israel, for Saul brought prosperity to Israel." Then David repeated: "How are the mighty fallen!" Thinking especially of Jonathan, he went on: "I am in distress for your sake, my brother Jonathan. Your love I valued most highly." Once more he repeated: "How are the mighty fallen!"

David was able to overcome his sinful, self-seeking desires because he was dedicated to the Lord's cause with all his heart.

That's why he could love Saul, who had treated him like an enemy, and appreciate what Saul had meant for God's people.

We overcome our sins by faith in the rule of the Lord's grace. The Lord Jesus Christ overcame all temptations by faith. By His Spirit, He was victorious in David. And by His Spirit He will also be victorious in us today.

King in Hebron. Now that Saul was dead, it was again safe for David in Israel. And after all he had experienced in the land of the Philistines, he longed to go back. He realized, however, that the time had finally come for God to exalt him by placing him on the throne. Especially at this point, he did not want to do anything without first acknowledging the Lord. He asked the Lord whether he should return and where he should go. The Lord told him to go to Hebron. Thus David and his men went to Hebron with their wives and possessions and took up residence there.

It was not long before the men of his tribe came to him and anointed him king over Judah. Here David experienced the initial fulfillment of the Lord's promise. He was allowed to tend to the needs of the Lord's people as their king. He must have desired this all the more strongly because of Israel's confused state under Saul. Would the Lord allow him to re-establish Israel after its disgrace? After all, he was only *Judah's* king; he would have to wait until the Lord gave him control over the rest of Israel.

David sent messengers to Jabesh in Gilead to express his appreciation for what the people of that town had done for Saul. "May the Lord reward you for what you have done," he declared, "and I will not forget you either!" He wanted to make it clear to all Israel that he had never wanted to obtain the throne by force, and that he had not forgotten the blessings the Lord had once given through Saul.

Waiting became more of a burden for David when Abner, Saul's commander-in-chief, began to deliver Israel from the domination of the Philistines. And when Abner was partly successful, he made Saul's son, Ish-bosheth, king in Mahanaim (in Transjordan). For David this meant a new obstacle on his way to the throne of all Israel. The Lord was teaching him to wait.

Civil war. A war broke out between the rest of the tribes and Judah. Abner gathered an army together and marched against Judah. David sent out Joab with the men of Judah. It had never been David's intention that there be a war between the tribes of Israel over his claim to the throne. Such a battle would be dreadful for anyone who hated the Lord's enemies and loved the entire people of Israel.

However, David was not allowed to turn his back on the calling the Lord had given him. Abner and his men were in rebellion against the Lord's calling of David. There would have to be a battle about the Lord's blessing as given in David.

Abner proposed that twelve soldiers from each side engage in man-to-man combat. There is no fighting fiercer than fighting between brothers. Without regard for their own welfare or safety, these 24 fighters battled so fiercely that all of them were dead by the time it was over. Then the two armies engaged each other in battle. Abner and his men were defeated.

As Joab's men pursued Abner's men, Abner killed Joab's brother Asahel, who was chasing him. Abner had warned Asahel beforehand; he did not want to kill him, for then the breach between Abner and Joab could never be healed. Thus the fighters sensed that their civil war was an abomination.

On the evening of that day, Abner gathered his men for further resistance. He also called out to Joab: "Shall the sword devour forever?" He pointed to the bitterness that would necessarily result from more fighting. Joab blew the trumpet and ordered his men to stop. That night they returned to Hebron.

That particular battle had ended, but the civil war continued. The war could not end until all Israel submitted to the Lord, who had chosen David to be Israel's shepherd. How could Israel be willfully blind for so long? In this struggle David grew stronger and stronger, while Saul's house became weaker and weaker. The Lord also blessed David with sons during this time in Hebron.

Negotiations. What Abner apparently had in mind was to become Israel's ruler himself. He had taken Saul's wife Rizpah as his wife. This amounted to a declaration that he wanted to assume the rights of his master. When Ish-bosheth reproached him for this, Abner responded by saying angrily that he would bring all of Israel under David's scepter, for it was obvious that the Lord had chosen David to reign. Unwillingly Abner had to acknowledge and submit to David's election. Ish-bosheth was not powerful enough to do anything about Abner's bold affront.

Abner began carrying out his intentions by sending messengers to David to discuss peace terms. David made it a condition that Saul's daughter Michal, who had once been his wife but had been given to someone else, be returned to him first. Did David still love Michal? Or did he want to remove the disgrace he had suffered when his wife was given to someone else? Or did he want to strengthen his position by having Saul's daughter for a wife again? Various motives must have driven David to make this demand.

In the meantime, Abner had talked with the elders in Israel, particularly the elders of Benjamin, Saul's tribe. He argued that the Lord had indicated clearly that David was to be Israel's deliverer. All Israel seemed willing to acknowledge David as king, for the Lord inclined the hearts of the people to David. The elevation of Ish-bosheth to the throne had been an act of pure arbitrariness. The only one permitted to rule as king over the Lord's people was the one the Lord Himself chose.

Abner had Michal taken away from her husband, and he shamefully chased him away when he tried to follow her. Here we see how much pain people sometimes inflict on each other by their highhandedness—even the Lord's people.

With twenty men Abner came to David in Hebron. David received him as a friend, and Abner promised that he would unite all Israel in the covenant with David.

However, David's accession to the throne was not to be achieved by this path of human calculation. The Lord always follows His own ways, even if those ways sometimes use the sins of men as a channel.

Joab was not in Hebron when Abner made his appearance there. When he returned from a campaign, he learned what had happened during his absence. He reproached David for letting Abner depart in peace, arguing that he had come to Hebron as a spy. Without David's knowledge, Joab used a false pretense to draw Abner back and then assassinated him at the city gate to avenge the death of Asahel.

When David heard what had happened, he declared that he was innocent of Joab's crime. But he was not in a position to allow justice to run its course concerning Joab; his own men would have rebelled against it. He did, however, curse Joab's house: it would always be plagued by disease and want. He saw to it that Abner was buried with honors in Hebron. He ordered Joab and the people to march in front of the bier with clothes rent, while he himself followed behind. Weeping, the procession proceeded to the graveside. David himself composed a song of lamentation about Abner. He fasted all day long and lamented his powerlessness to avenge this crime. All the people acknowledged that David was innocent of Abner's blood, and they saw all the more clearly that he had no desire to come to power over all Israel by way of unrighteousness and crime.

Thus the people were now bound to the Lord through their king. For the Lord's sake, they had to regard the king as the head of the people.

King over all Israel. Abner's death had made a deep impression on the people. Everyone sensed that Saul's house was now a lost cause. In his own home Ish-bosheth was assassinated by the leaders of two raiding bands. He did not have a successor; Jonathan's son Mephibosheth, who would have been next in line, was crippled in both feet as a result of an accident.

Ish-bosheth's murderers brought the dead king's head to David, thinking that their deed would please him. But David also rejected any involvement with this new crime. He had the two men killed and ordered that their hands and feet be cut off and their bodies hanged. Ish-bosheth's head was buried in Abner's grave.

Then the elders of all the tribes came to David and acknowledged his calling as Israel's shepherd. All Israel finally submitted to God's choice of David. The Lord Himself subjected the people to their king. After seven years of waiting in Hebron, the goal was reached. In the name of the Lord, David was privileged to be Israel's king and deliverer. And all the people were convinced that David understood that Israel could be saved only by justice. The people were permitted to see in David a type of the Messiah. Today, too, the Lord Himself subjects the people to the Christ, their King.

Jerusalem chosen. One of David's first official acts as king of all of Israel was his military expedition against the citadel of the Jebusites. Although Jerusalem was already in Israel's hands, the Jebusites still occupied the stronghold of the city. David had chosen Jerusalem as the capital of his kingdom. This city was centrally located—on the border between Judah and Benjamin. Besides, the continued occupation of the citadel by the Jebusites was a disgrace to Israel.

The garrison inside the citadel scoffed that "the blind and the lame" would be all they needed to defend it. That's how impregnable the stronghold appeared to be. But the Spirit of the Lord was working in David and his men so that their anger was kindled against those who mocked the God of Israel. The Scriptures hardly mention a battle for this citadel. It was just as though it lay open to David.

David made Jerusalem his capital. The Lord Himself had given him the city. Later the Lord declared that He had chosen Jerusalem in order to reveal His name there. David fortified the city wall and built a palace with wood sent to him by Hiram, the king of Tyre. David saw that *the Lord* had established his kingdom, and that He had done it because of His grace to His people.

When the Philistines heard that David had become king over all Israel, they marched up from the Philistine plain to establish their superiority. But the Lord granted David the victory. Then the enemy marched on Israel a second time. At the Lord's instruction, David went around behind the Philistines; at the sound of marching in the tops of the balsam trees, he attacked them from the rear and defeated them.

The Lord Himself had come to deliver Israel. And the people understood that David ruled Israel by the favor of the Lord and in fellowship with Him, bringing deliverance to God's people.

19: King of Israel

What we are told in II Samuel 7 is central to the four chapters to which we now turn our attention. David wanted to build a house for the Lord, but the Lord declared that *He* would build a house for David. Here again it becomes clear that the Lord's work precedes ours. Not until the Lord had begun to fulfill His promise to establish David's house (during the reign of Solomon) would He allow His own house to be built. Our actions are always a response to the Lord's deeds.

In I Chronicles 17 we read that David was not allowed to build the Lord's house because his hands had shed blood. We are not to conclude from this that there was something inherently sinful about David's military expeditions, for he was fighting *the Lord's* battles. The shed blood defiled him only in a ceremonial sense; it was a symbol of the sin still present in the world, the sin that was punished by death. Not until sin is completely conquered will the full indwelling of God be granted. Only then can God's temple be among His people.

The building of the temple was a prophecy pointing ahead to this complete indwelling. But we must not forget that the indwelling ultimately became real in the Christ event and the subsequent outpouring of the Holy Spirit in the Church in communion with the Christ.

The promise to David that his house would be established, that his son would reign forever, and that his son would build the Lord a house was only partially fulfilled in Solomon. That promise was fulfilled perfectly in the Christ. The fulfillment of God's covenant with David we find described in Luke 1:32-3. In that covenant God also promised to accept Solomon as His son. That promise, too, found its complete fulfillment in the Christ.

David brought the ark to Jerusalem, but we do not read that he set up the tabernacle there. This can perhaps be explained by the fact that there were two high priests (see Chapter 17 above). David wanted the ark, which represented God's throne, to be with him in Jerusalem. Its presence there would show that the Lord was the true King of Israel. It may have been at this time that David composed Psalm 24.

The stories in II Samuel 6-9 are not all recorded in chronological order. We may not assume that everything described in chapter 8 happened after the events of chapter 7. The battle against the Ammonites and the Syrians is described only briefly in chapter 8; in chapter 10 it is dealt with more extensively, where it is seen as the immediate cause of David's sin.

Main thought: *Israel's king will rule over God's people forever.*

That the King of glory may come in. Once the Lord had initially established David's kingdom, David remembered the ark, the symbol of God's presence in Israel. The ark was still in Abinadab's house. David wanted it in Jerusalem, the capital city of his kingdom. The presence of God's throne (the ark) in Jerusalem would show that not David but *the Lord* was the true King of Israel. David, as the people's king, could only be blessed if he lived close to the Lord and in communion with Him.

David summoned all the people's representatives to the place where the ark had been kept. The people agreed with the king's intention, and the ark was placed on a new cart. Ahio, one of Abinadab's sons, went before the ark, while another son, Uzzah, walked alongside. David and all Israel followed—dancing, singing, and playing all kinds of instruments before the Lord.

On the way to Jerusalem, the oxen stumbled near the threshing floor of Nacon and the cart threatened to topple over. With his hand Uzzah took hold of the ark to keep it from falling. The Lord immediately struck him dead. Despite his good intentions, Uzzah had lost sight of the Lord's holiness. In the covenant, the Lord indeed wishes to be our God, but He is a holy God. We are to serve Him only in accordance with His will.

Then David's anger flared up—not against the Lord or against Uzzah but against himself. He realized that there must be something wrong with the procession, although he did not know what. Otherwise the Lord would not have let this happen.

David was deeply shaken by the fact that sin had ruined the whole procession. Under such circumstances he did not dare bring the ark up to Jerusalem. The Lord's holiness made him afraid. He would have to find out what was sinful about the procession. The ark would go no farther; he had it brought to Obed-edom's house nearby.

After three months David was told that the Lord had blessed Obed-edom's household because of the ark. Then he realized even more clearly that the Lord's holiness is no cause for fright, provided that we live in the right relationship to the Lord in His covenant. During those months David had also come to see what the cause of the Lord's anger had been. The ark had been transported on a new cart. David had copied the Philistines and had not paid attention to the Lord's command that the ark be carried by the Levites.

Therefore David decided that the ark could safely be brought to Jerusalem. This time he made sure that the Levites carried it. There went the ark, carried up the ascent to Jerusalem. Now it went through the gate. David and the people sang and played and danced before the Lord. The Lord, as Israel's true King, would dwell in the midst of His people in Jerusalem. David's reign would derive its splendor from the presence of the ark.

David was dressed in a white linen ephod or robe with a cape, a garment that looked like a priestly robe. After all, he was king of a people of priests. At the beginning and end of the procession, sacrifices were offered to the Lord and David blessed the people. A large sacrificial meal was held, with David giving bread-cakes, meat and wine to the people. They ate in communion with the Lord, who was now dwelling in Jerusalem.

The ark and David belonged together. The ark was a sign of God's presence in the midst of His people through the Angel of the covenant. David's reign derived its splendor from this indwelling. Because of this tie with the ark, David was a type of the Lord Jesus Christ. The Christ is the Angel of the Lord, who has now become flesh so that He Himself could be King of His people.

In that procession David sang to Jerusalem's gates: "Lift up your heads, you everlasting doors, that the King of glory may come in!" In the same way, the Lord Jesus Christ was honored when He accepted His royal authority at the time of His ascension.

And one day He will be honored again when He reveals Himself in all His glory.

Not everyone was happy on this occasion. Saul's daughter Michal, who had been restored as David's wife, watched the procession from a window and noticed how the king rejoiced in the midst of his people. At that moment she despised David in her heart. She loved the famous hero in David—not the simple believer. No one in Saul's household had been concerned about the ark. To Michal it was a mystery how David and the people could be so happy about the arrival of the ark.

When David entered his home to bless it after he had blessed the people, Michal met him with sarcastic taunts. She scoffed that he had lowered himself to the level of his servants' maids. That was not Michal's idea of a king's behavior. David answered that he was praising the Lord, who had put him in Michal's father's place precisely because Saul had been concerned with his own honor instead of the Lord's honor. Michal's attitude was a perfect illustration of her father's sin. David went on to say that she would see how he would be held in honor by those maidservants.

Because Michal did not share David's faith, the Lord did not give her a child. Out of her David's house would not be built. David's own attitude toward the people was different from Michal's. When we fear the Lord, we are one with God's people.

The covenant with David. David had to fight many wars. When peace finally came and he could relax in his palace, he thought about the fact that he lived in a house while the ark of the Lord still stood in a tent. David could not get the ark off his mind. He wanted to be king only in the name of the Lord. And he wished to honor the Lord through the ark. Therefore he spoke with the prophet Nathan about his desire to build the Lord a house. Nathan's first reaction was to approve of the plan.

However, that same night the Lord told Nathan in a vision that David would not be allowed to build the house. Until now the Lord had used a tent as His dwelling place; He still had not given instructions that a house was to be built for Himself. The time had not yet come. First the Kingdom of God had to be fully established in Israel.

The Lord had indeed given David the victory over his enemies, but because of those wars, David's reign was filled with conflict. David's son would reap the fruits of the victories; he would be a king of peace. To him and his descendants the Lord would give sovereign power forever. The Lord would be a father to David's son, and he would be a son to the Lord. If he should sin, the Lord would not spare him but chastise him. Yet, the sovereign power would never depart from his descendants as the kingship had been taken away from Saul. Thus the Lord would build David's house forever, and David's son, in gratitude, would build a house for the Lord. The Lord's work of grace always precedes our work; the Lord is always the one who takes the initiative.

This was the Lord's covenant with David. The Lord gave David that great promise not because of any merit on David's part but out of free grace. The promise could not be completely fulfilled in David's son, who could never be an everlasting king. Thus it was really a promise that the Christ would be born of David. *He* was David's great Son. David's own son would build a temple in Jerusalem, but the Christ would build the real temple. God's dwelling among men did in fact become a reality in the Christ, who would make His people—and one day the entire earth— a house in which God would be pleased to dwell.

Nathan told David all that God had said. Deeply moved, David answered: "Who am I, Lord, that You grant me this? What shall I say to express my humble thanks? You have done this to glorify Your grace toward Your chosen people, who are already blessed beyond compare. In this You will make Your name great. Your name will be glorious because of Your grace, which You will grant in the Messiah." David concluded his prayer not by doubting whether all of this would come to pass but by accepting the promise in faith.

Didn't the Lord fulfill that promise in a marvelous way? The Christ, David's great Son, is now our eternal King. And He built His people as a temple when He poured out His Holy Spirit. When He returns, He will make the entire earth a house of God.

Justice and righteousness. When the Lord gave David power and honor, all of Israel's enemies turned on him. They were driven by enmity against the Lord's people and—in the final analysis—against the Lord Himself. But the Lord gave David the victory over all his enemies.

First he defeated the Philistines and subdued them. Then he defeated the Moabites. He executed two thirds of the prisoners, and the other third he pardoned. In earlier days, David himself had looked to the Moabites for protection for a brief period of time and had found safety in their land for his father and mother. Something horrible must have happened to make him punish the Moabites so severely. After that they were forced to pay tribute to him regularly.

He also subdued two Syrian kings, one from Zobah and the other from Damascus. He had the chariot horses hamstrung as a symbol that there is no strength over against the Lord's people. He took much gold and silver from Syria and devoted it to the Lord for the sanctuary that was to be built. The king of Hamath, who had fought a war with the Syrians, sent his son to David with royal presents. These gifts, too, David dedicated to the Lord.

Moreover, he defeated the Ammonites, the Edomites and the Amalekites. He put occupation troops in the defeated countries so that the conquered peoples would continue to pay taxes to him.

In all these wars, David had his failures and shortcomings; he was not a sinless man. Yet, more than once he exercised the Lord's judgment on Israel's neighbors because they had been hostile toward the Lord's people and toward the grace shown to them. Furthermore, in the subjection of the surrounding nations lay a promise that one day all peoples would submit to Christ's rule of grace—and also a warning that the Christ would execute judgment on all who opposed His grace.

Among his own people David carried out justice and righteousness. The Israelites were not in the hands of an arbitrary ruler; they could feel safe under the shield of their king. How safe the people of the Lord are under the shield of the Christ, of whom David was only a type!

David had many government officials under him. During his lifetime there were *two* high priests—Zadok and Abiathar (the only one to escape Saul's massacre of the priests at Nob). David had to wait upon the Lord, who Himself would remove this irregularity in Israel. The adult sons of the king were chief officials in the king's service.

The king's faithfulness. David also remembered Saul's house. He summoned Ziba, who had been a servant in Saul's house and was probably in possession of the fields of his master's house. From him he learned that Mephibosheth, the crippled son of Jonathan, was still alive. Someone in Israel had taken him into his home.

At David's command, Mephibosheth came to David's court, fearing that the king would kill him. But David spoke to him as a friend, for Jonathan's sake, and he gave him Saul's possessions, putting Ziba in charge of the land. He also declared that Mephibosheth was to eat at his own table.

Here we see the Lord's lovingkindness toward Saul's descendants. His family was not wiped out from among the people of Israel. Mephibosheth already had a little son whose name was Mica. The family's name and its inheritance in Israel were preserved.

Israel's king had shown his faithfulness to the covenant he had once made with his friend Jonathan. If a covenant between two *people* can be upheld, as we see from David's faithfulness to his covenant with Jonathan, how much more faithful will the Christ be to the covenant in which He lives with all who belong to Him!

20: The Lord's Beloved

II Samuel 10-12

The heart of these three chapters is the story of the birth of Solomon, the son of David and Bathsheba. In that birth David saw a confirmation of God's renewed favor. That's why he boasted of peace* when he gave this child a name.

The Lord called the child *Jedidiah*, that is, *beloved of the Lord*. This child, David's son, was the Lord's beloved. The Lord's mercy upon David's house and upon Israel was tied up with Solomon. When the Lord gave him the name *Jedidiah*, He was indicating that the promise made to David would find its initial fulfillment in Solomon.

Through this name, the Word of the Lord again pointed to the future. The name had special significance because of what had happened before Solomon was born. Shame had come over David publicly. The people were shown that their salvation was not in David. Their salvation lay in the future, in the Christ, of whose birth Solomon's birth was a prophecy. The Christ is the Lord's Beloved. For His sake Solomon was also beloved of the Lord. And for His sake there was grace for the house of David in Solomon's birth.

In the entire line of Christ's ancestors, sin is clearly visible. Only by being conceived by the Holy Spirit could the Christ come forth, the pure from the impure. In His life and death He atones for sin. In Him God's grace is revealed.

---

*The name *Solomon* in its Hebrew form is related to the word *shalom*, which means *peace*.—TRANS.

Main thought: *The Lord's grace for His people is in His beloved.*

Warfare. David's war with the Syrians and the Ammonites is related here in greater detail. His conduct during that war was the immediate occasion for his sin with Bathsheba.

When a new king was elevated to the throne in Ammon, David sent emissaries to him to express condolences at the death of his father. This was a friendly gesture on David's part; it was a response to the friendliness he had experienced from Ammon's deceased king. We do not know what the nature of that friendliness was.

At the instigation of his advisers, Ammon's new king treated David's delegation as a group of spies. He deeply offended the emissaries—and thereby David himself—by having half of their beards shaved off and the bottom part of their clothing cut off before sending them back.

David did not want to see this offense with his own eyes. Therefore he ordered the emissaries to remain in Jericho until their beards had grown back. The Ammonites understood that now there would surely be war with Israel. Hence they hired many auxiliary troops from the Syrians. Joab, whom David had sent out to make war on the Ammonites, wound up with his army between the Syrians, who were in the open field, and the Ammonites, who had lined up in front of their capital. Joab divided his army between his brother Abishai and himself, and they agreed that the one would come to the other's rescue in case of emergency. Joab himself faced the Syrians and defeated them. When the Ammonites realized this, they retreated into their city. With that the first campaign against the Ammonites ended. Joab and his army returned to Jerusalem. At that time, it seems, he did not dare lay siege to Ammon's capital.

A second campaign was necessary, for the Ammonites had not been defeated. Besides, the Syrians formed a new army; their king, Hadadezer, even had soldiers brought in from Mesopotamia. David gathered all Israel together and defeated the Syrians, rendering their chariots useless and executing the Syrian commander-in-chief. All of Hadadezer's vassal kings deserted him, made peace with Israel, and became subject to David.

David had settled accounts with the Syrians, but he had not been able to do anything against the Ammonites. In the meantime, the rainy season had set in. Therefore David had to wait. After the rains, he sent Joab with an army to besiege Rabbah, the capital of the Ammonites. That was the third campaign.

Thus Israel's king fought against enemies who had heaped shame upon him as the Lord's anointed—and therefore upon the name of the Lord as well. The honor of the Lord's grace toward His people demanded the execution of the sentence upon the Ammonites. Justice would have to be done—not for David's own sake but for the Lord's.

Undisciplined luxury. Shouldn't David himself have gone out to battle at the head of his army to carry out the sentence of the Ammonites? After all, the honor of the Lord's people and their king had been shamefully offended! But David remained in Jerusalem and sent Joab out with an army. Apparently he was content to "rest on his laurels." He thought that his throne was now definitely established and secure. And it was—but only because of the grace and faithfulness of the Lord, not because of David's own strength as king. David did not rest exclusively in the Lord's grace any longer; he looked to his own power. At such moments a certain feeling of self-satisfaction and of undisciplined luxury comes over us. Then we are far from the Lord. What big risks we take when that happens!

One day, after he had taken his afternoon nap, David was on the roof of his palace. From there he spotted a beautiful woman whom he immediately wanted as his wife. He made inquiries about her and learned that she was the wife of Uriah the Hittite, an officer in the army with Joab. When David found out she was married, he did not suppress his desire; desire overpowered him. He asked her to come to him anyway. Even though she was married, she consented and committed adultery with him. Afterward she returned to her own home again.

Apparently David wanted to rehabilitate the marriage between this woman, whose name was Bathsheba, and her husband

Uriah. Therefore he had Uriah called back from the army to Jerusalem. It would appear that Uriah had heard something about his wife's unfaithfulness and refused to return home. Even when the king urged him, he refused to spend the night with his wife.

Afraid that his sin would become public knowledge, David was driven to a second misdeed. He sent Uriah back to the army with a personal letter for Joab, instructing Joab to place Uriah in a dangerous spot so that he would be killed in battle. David would then be able to make Bathsheba his wife. After committing adultery, David was willing to commit no less a sin than murder.

Joab faithfully carried out the king's command. He was all too eager to become a partner in the king's crime, for this would weaken David's position over against him and make David unable to deal firmly with him for his crimes.

One day, when the Ammonites made an attack, Joab launched a counterattack in which he had Uriah come close to the city wall. From there he was hit by the sharpshooters. Several other soldiers were killed in this skirmish as well.

Joab sent news to David that many had been killed in action. He told the messenger that if the king became angry at Joab's recklessness and subsequent loss of life, he was to add that Uriah was among the dead. Thus Joab was playing with the king; David was in his hands.

David was calm as he received the messenger's news. Once the messenger told him everything, David saw to it that Joab's mind would be put at ease about the loss of life. By responding in this way, David lost his honor as the shepherd of the Lord's people.

After Bathsheba mourned for her husband for some days, David took her into his house as his wife. At that point David thought that the sin had been covered up. But it was a great evil in the eyes of the Lord, who did not intend to let this sin go unpunished.

The Lord did not confront David immediately. For months he let him live with his sin. A child was born of the sinful relationship between David and Bathsheba. All this time the sin weighed heavily upon David. Later, in some psalms he composed, he sang about how terrible that time had been for him. When he tried to pray and went to the ark of the Lord, he found that he could not pray a genuine prayer; there were unconfessed sins standing between the Lord and himself. In this misery the Lord was preparing him for the severing of ties which was to come.

The Lord's judgment. After three months, the prophet Nathan came to David and told him a fabricated story about a crime that had occurred in Israel. When David responded in anger and sentenced the criminal to death, Nathan said that the king himself was the guilty party. The Lord had given him all Israel, and He was willing to give him much more besides. But David had not accepted those gifts in true gratitude. Rather, in his greed, he had taken what was not his, namely, the wife of another man. Because he had used the sword unjustly to kill Uriah, the sword would never depart from his house. And because he had taken the wife of someone else, another man would take his wives someday and make them his own. What David had done in secret the Lord would do to him in the open for all to see, since David had sinned first of all against the Lord.

This judgment pronounced by the Lord was terrible. Yet, it contained an element of grace. In the judgment, it already became clear that David was not about to die. Not even his kingship would be taken.

David listened to the judgment, and he sensed the Lord's grace in it. The note of grace is what broke his heart. Immediately he bowed his head and confessed his sin. It must have been a relief for him to be able to confess what had been eating away at him for so long.

Then Nathan confirmed the Lord's grace: God had put away David's sin, and he was not about to die. But because the name of the Lord had been openly put to shame by this crime, the Lord would immediately reveal His judgment in the death of the child born to David and Bathsheba.

After Nathan departed, the child became severely ill. David humbled himself before the Lord. He prayed and fasted and lay all night upon the ground. He refused to eat, in spite of his servants' pleading. Now he wished that the child would yet be spared—not only because it was his own flesh and blood but also because he dreaded facing the depth of his sin as reflected in the death of the child! If the child were spared, David would have a sign that the Lord had put his sin behind Him.

For seven days David wrestled with the Lord. Then the child died. His servants did not dare tell him. What would the king do when he heard that the child was dead?

From their attitude David realized that the child was dead. Then he stood up, bathed, anointed himself, changed his clothes, and went to the ark of the Lord. There he bowed under the judgment of God, while laying hold of Him at the same time in His grace. After that he ate.

David's servants understood nothing of all this. They did not see that David had been struggling for the Lord's grace more than for the life of the child. He had struggled for that little life as a sign of God's grace. Now he intended to bow under the judgment. Nevertheless, in faith he would take hold of the Word of grace spoken to him by the prophet. He would not be able to bring the child back to life by fasting and praying. One day, like that child, he would die, but he wanted to live and die believing in the grace of the Lord.

The people heard all about this. They understood that David, too, was a sinful man. The people could not put their trust in him. They could only live by faith in the coming Redeemer. Because of that Savior, there was grace for David. If only the people saw that! And if only we would learn to see God's grace for His people because of the Christ!

Forgiveness. In those days the Lord was teaching David and the people of Israel to look ahead to that coming Savior. After the child's death, the Lord gave David and Bathsheba another child. David considered it a sign of God's forgiving grace that he was allowed to have another child by this woman with whom he had first lived in sin. This token of God's mercy set his heart completely free. That's why he gave his son the name *Solomon*: there was *peace* between God and himself.

That divine favor was soon revealed to him even more gloriously when the prophet Nathan came to him with a message. At the Lord's command, the child was given the name *Jedidiah*, that is, *beloved of the Lord*. The Lord especially loved this child.

Surely the thought arose in David's mind that the Redeemer might be born of this child. Through the name *Jedidiah*, David and Israel were being told to look ahead to the coming Savior, for that Savior is indeed the Beloved of the Lord.

Because of that Savior, there is also a love of God for His own, for David, for Israel. David was not to look to himself, and Israel was not to look to David. Together they were to look to the Christ. We, too, are to look away from ourselves in everything and look to the Christ.

Victory. While all of this was happening, the campaign against the Ammonites continued. Joab captured the lower town of Rabbah, Ammon's capital city. Then he sent a message to David that he should gather all Israel together and take the citadel of Rabbah himself. That way David—and not Joab—would have the honor of the victory in this campaign.

David did so: with the assembled army, he took the stronghold. The crown of Ammon's king was placed on David's head. This meant that Ammon's territory was incorporated into Israel. The army carried off a great amount of booty, and all the Ammonite people were assigned to hard labor for the benefit of Israel. This judgment on the Ammonites revealed God's everlasting judgment on the enemies of His grace.

21: Rejected and Restored

II Samuel 13-20

When we tell the story recorded in these chapters, we must be careful not to put all the emphasis on Absalom's shameful behavior. We could indeed do a lot of moralizing about the relationship between children and parents as we talk about that behavior, but then we would not be able to shed light on the principal issue and tell of the Lord in His covenant with His people.

David was the Lord's anointed. As king he was a type of the Christ. He was also Israel's head in the covenant. In His grace toward David, God was being gracious toward His people. David was Israel's deliverer—and was rejected as such.

He was rejected first by Absalom. Absalom must have despised his father's extravagant enthusiasm for the ark and the covenant and the Lord's rights. Absalom was more businesslike, more realistic in his approach to politics. What dominates here is not Absalom's revolt against his father but his rejection of the head of the covenant and of the covenant itself.

Later David was also rejected by Israel. Undoubtedly there were defects in David's conduct as king. Besides, he had lost much of his authority because of his sin with Bathsheba. The Lord's punishment of David and his house had become known to the people. Nevertheless, God had forgiven him his sin and had preserved him as Israel's king. It could not have been a secret from the people either that David had humbled himself before the Lord because of his guilt.

Shouldn't the people realize how much they had been blessed in David and were still being blessed? Yet the people rejected him and chose for flashy Absalom instead. After Absalom was defeated, the people accepted David again. Then, because of a quarrel with Judah, the ten tribes again forsook David and followed Sheba. Thus they trifled with the

Lord's anointed and with God's covenant. But in spite of them, God in His grace gave David back to Israel and thereby confirmed the promise made to David's house, the promise of the coming Redeemer.

There were moments when God's grace sparkled wondrously in David. David and his men were able to cry. That emotional response on their part was not merely a show of Eastern sensitivity—at least, not in David's own case. David wept because of sin; he saw sin as a rejection of the covenant. Anybody who suffers for this reason knows what grief is; indeed, he feels all sorrow twice as deeply. Without such a relationship to the Lord, all sorrow ultimately remains superficial.

David's true character was best revealed when he sent the ark of the Lord back to Jerusalem. Who could fail to be moved by what he said at that moment? (II Sam. 15:25-6). God's grace was also evident in him in the way he bowed under Shimei's curse.

What influenced David's attitude when he went wrong was his weakness towards his sons Amnon and Absalom. When Absalom was defeated and killed, David did not react first of all by submitting to God's judgment on this covenant breaker; his first response was to give in to his self-centered fatherly love for his son. For a long time he could not rise above that self-centered love, which perhaps explains the unjust and unreasonable measures he took upon his return.

The battle between the armies of David and Absalom is related in only a few words. It may be that the armies of Transjordan returned to the western side of the Jordan to do battle in Ephraim's territory.

Main thought: *The Lord preserves the place of the king among His people.*

The abomination in David's house. Once David's sons had grown up, sin began to rear its ugly head among them. In the misery that resulted from their sin, the judgment of the Lord on David's sin was carried out.

Amnon, one of David's sons, violated Tamar, who was his half sister and a full sister of Absalom. From then on Absalom brooded about revenge, although he did not let it show. Here David was already lax: we do not read that he disciplined Amnon. David was aware that he himself had forfeited any right to the throne and even to his life because of his sin, and he knew that God had been merciful to him. His awareness of his guilt made him weak in disciplining his sons.

For two long years Absalom concealed his hatred. Then he invited all his brothers to a feast at sheep-shearing time. He had asked David's permission for this. At the feast he had his servants kill Amnon. All the other princes fled back to Jerusalem. Before they arrived, a rumor circulated in Jerusalem that Absalom had killed all the king's sons. David and his men believed the rumor. That's how filled with fear they were because of the curse on David's house. In this way the Lord showed David what devastation could come over him because of his sin.

The rumor was not true, but what had actually happened was bad enough. First a shameful instance of rape, and then fratricide in David's house! Absalom fled to the king of Geshur, who was his mother's father, and stayed there for three years.

Reconciliation. During that time, David's heart longed for Absalom, whom he loved very much. His anger and grief over Amnon's death had been pushed into the background.

This was no sanctified love on David's part. Absalom had destroyed the unity in David's house; he had killed his brother and cast off the yoke of the Lord's covenant. Shouldn't the anger in David's heart because of this sin be stronger than his love for his son? And could there ever be any thought of reconciliation without true repentance? David himself had not been restored by God without true repentance.

When Joab noticed how much the king thought about Absalom, he hatched a plan. He sent a wise woman to David, a woman who pretended to be in misery. She told David that she was a widow and that one of her sons had killed her only other son in a quarrel. Now the relatives were demanding blood revenge against the surviving son. Soon she would be bereft of all her sons and her husband's line would be wiped out.

The parallel with David was not complete, for in the widow's story the one son had struck the other dead in a quarrel, whereas Absalom had deliberately murdered Amnon. That's why the widow was not content when David promised that no harm would come to her son. She made the king swear it. Only after he did so did she reveal her real intention: Would David be bereft forever of both his sons? The people would be destroyed by his decision, she declared, exaggerating. That could not possibly be God's will.

Now David realized that Joab was behind the whole thing. When the king asked her if this was so, she admitted it. Yet, David allowed himself to be persuaded by her and commanded Joab to bring Absalom back. Absalom was to return to Jerusalem, but he would not be allowed to see his father. Obviously David had not forgiven him.

To let Absalom return without showing any evidence of a change of heart was weakness on David's part. All too eagerly he had let the woman's reasoning convince him, since he longed for Absalom in his heart. An important factor in this decision was that Absalom, because of his good looks, was his father's pride and hope.

For two full years Absalom remained in Jerusalem separated from his father. Then he sent for Joab. He wanted to ask Joab to put in a good word for him and bring about a reconciliation with David. The position in which Absalom found himself did not offer him any opportunity to fulfill his ambitious plans.

But Joab did not come when Absalom summoned him, even though the summons was repeated. Finally Absalom forced Joab to come by burning his barley field. And Joab, at Absalom's urging, went to David to arrange a reconciliation. Once again David let himself be persuaded: he received Absalom and kissed him.

Thus a reconciliation was brought about, but not for the right reasons. Absalom's heart was not with his father because it was not with the Lord. Absalom did not share his father's faith. David was hopelessly weak with this son. The eyes of the believing king were blinded. He would soon find out that he was harboring a viper in his bosom.

The revolt. Now Absalom was in a position to carry out his plans. He stole the hearts of the people by his love of splendor. He rode about with much pomp and ceremony. And whenever anyone came to the king with a case to be judged, Absalom would tell him not to expect justice from the king—and he would declare the man's cause just, to win favor with him. He was condescending and friendly, and he would not let anyone bow down to him.

By these means he won the people over to his side. The people let this flatterer draw them away from the Lord's anointed, from their head and deliverer. How few of them had their eyes opened by faith and recognized Absalom's conduct for what it was!

As soon as Absalom was convinced that he had the majority of the people behind him, he asked his father's permission to go to Hebron—supposedly to fulfill a vow he had made to the Lord during his exile. He sent messengers throughout the land with instructions: upon receiving a certain signal, they were to cry out everywhere that Absalom was king in Hebron.

Absalom himself went to Hebron with 200 men who knew nothing of his intentions. Ahithophel, David's wise advisor, was apparently in on this plot with Absalom, for he was summoned to Hebron too. The revolt spread quickly and many followed Absalom.

Soon David was notified. Immediately he made plans to leave Jerusalem. He recognized that he would not be able to offer sufficient resistance to Absalom just then. Absalom would slaughter the people of Jerusalem if David stayed.

David left Jerusalem with his house, his bodyguard, and 600 faithful soldiers. He left only ten women behind to keep the palace in order. There he went through Jerusalem's gate. Keenly he felt God's judgment in this turn of events. As the Lord's anointed, he was rejected by the people. The grief this realization caused him broke his heart, but he was not filled with bitterness. Knowing his own sins, he was also able to forgive the people for what they did wrong. At bottom he was upset because it was the Lord who was being rejected by the people in their rejection of David as king.

Some distance outside the city gate, David had the people who were with him drawn up in order. He advised Ittai, a Philistine who had only recently entered his service, to go back, but the Philistine would not hear of it. He insisted on sharing the king's uncertain lot. By his faithfulness he put the faithfulness of the people to shame.

David and his company moved down the mountain and crossed the Kidron Brook. All the loyal Israelites who saw the procession wept aloud. Then David ordered the priests Zadok and

Abiathar to go back with the ark of the Lord. On this humiliating journey, in which he felt the Lord's judgment upon his sin, David did not dare take the ark with him. "If I find favor in the eyes of the Lord, He will bring me back and let me see both the ark and the tabernacle again. But if He says, 'I have no pleasure in you,' then let Him do to me what seems best to Him." Thus David bowed before God's good pleasure. Furthermore, the king agreed with both priests that they would keep him informed about events in Jerusalem by means of their sons, Ahimaaz and Jonathan, who would remain outside the city.

David walked up the road that led to the Mount of Olives, weeping as he went. He walked barefoot with his head covered. All who were with him wept as they walked. There went David down the road of suffering, the road of rejection. He was rejected by the people as the Lord's anointed. Centuries later David's great Son was to travel that same road. Completely innocent, He would bear the sins of His people and yet be rejected by His people.

On this road of suffering there was still comfort for David—but also much added bitterness. When he learned that Ahithophel was backing Absalom, he prayed that the Lord would turn Ahithophel's counsel into foolishness. But he was comforted somewhat when Hushai, his other advisor, came to meet him. He sent Hushai to Jerusalem. He was to pretend to join Absalom's party and then do his best to nullify Ahithophel's advice.

Ziba, who cultivated Mephibosheth's fields, brought David food and slandered his master, trying to create the impression that Mephibosheth hoped to get Saul's throne back again. Shimei, also a member of Saul's family, cursed David, shouting that this judgment was coming upon him because he had wiped out Saul's house.

Shimei threw stones and dust into the air, but David was silent. Abishai asked permission to kill Shimei, but David refused, saying that it was God who had sent Shimei to curse him. How submissive he was in these circumstances as the Lord chastised him! Shimei's words were slander, but David had to face up to what he heard in that slander, namely, God's punishment for his sins. Therefore he bowed under Shimei's tongue-lashing.

That evening David and his men were weary when they reached the field at the Jordan where they planned to stay for the night. How David longed for Jerusalem and for the ark of the Lord! But he was like one rejected. As such he was a type of the Lord Jesus Christ, who was rejected by His own people.

The counsel of the wicked nullified. Meanwhile, Absalom and his men had arrived in Jerusalem. Ahithophel declared that Absalom should make a show of taking the ten women whom David had left behind as his wives. In David's eyes that would be an abomination. Then all the people would know that a reconciliation between Absalom and David was out of the question, and they would definitely side with Absalom. In this crime of Absalom, the judgment which Nathan had pronounced on David's sin with Bathsheba was fulfilled.

Furthermore, Ahithophel advised that a force of 12,000 men be sent out to attack David at once. David was now beaten and tired, and the victory would be certain. That was clever advice on Ahithophel's part; humanly speaking, such an attack would be David's downfall.

But the Lord heard David's prayer and made Ahithophel's counsel of no effect. By then Hushai had joined Absalom's party. When he first arrived, Absalom was astonished and wanted to know how such a friend of David's could come over to him. Hushai had a crafty answer ready: he wanted to serve the one the Lord chose. With these words he hinted that in his opinion, Absalom's success showed that he had been chosen by the Lord. He added: "How can I serve the father better than by serving the son?" Absalom was totally blinded by these words and wanted to hear Hushai's advice before he made up his mind about Ahithophel's suggestion.

Hushai saw the danger in Ahithophel's advice. With great eloquence he tried to convince Absalom and his men that Ahithophel's suggestion was dangerous. Hushai himself advised that Absalom and his followers take the time to get all Israel reunited and then crush David. He understood that this would give David an opportunity to gather his followers together. Hushai realized that not all the Israelites would rally behind Absalom.

Hushai's great eloquence made a deep impression on Absalom and his men. Yet it was really the Lord who put these words in Hushai's mouth and caused Absalom and his men to be influenced by them. Ahithophel's advice was overridden and David was safe for the moment.

This was a surprising turn of events, for people often said that advice was like the very Word of God. Rarely had there been a man as gifted as Ahithophel. He had served David, but in serving him he had not served the head of the covenant; he had not served the Lord. Ahithophel was not of the Christ. He was David's right hand man only in an external way. God's calling for Ahithophel and His lovingkindness toward him had been focused on David: Ahithophel was to serve David. And he did serve, but he was never gripped by that calling. He trusted in himself and in his own wisdom.

Now the Lord nullified his advice, for Ahithophel had taken a definite stand over against the Lord's covenant. His rejection of the head of the covenant had made him twice as sly. But he was fighting against the Lord, who overcame him through Hushai. He saw that he had been defeated and that Absalom's cause was lost. He had come up against the grace of the Lord, who fights for His people. That's why he went home and hanged himself. Thus the man who had risen up in opposition to the Lord's grace and the head of the covenant perished.

The victory. Through the priests' sons, Hushai had sent word to David not to remain where he was that night but to cross the Jordan. These messengers were almost captured by Absalom's men, but a woman saved them by hiding them in a well. David received the message and moved on to Mahanaim, in Transjordan. There he gathered his men around him, and there Absalom sent his army against him.

Apparently the two armies stood over against each other in Transjordan. After that they may have crossed the Jordan River again to fight their battle near the forest of Ephraim. Absalom's army was defeated, and Absalom himself was killed by Joab and his men, even though David had given orders to Joab and the army to spare his life.

The soldiers piled up a heap of stones over Absalom's body as a sign of his shame. That heap of stones is not to be confused with the monument Absalom had earlier erected in his own honor. His sons had died at an early age; he had only a daughter left—Tamar. It was by this monument that he wanted to live on in Israel. That's how vain he was. But his name went down in shame, for he had rejected the head of the covenant and ultimately the Lord Himself.

Joab did not dare send Zadok's son Ahimaaz to David with news of what had happened, even though Ahimaaz eagerly requested permission to bring David the news of the victory over Absalom. Joab knew his master; he realized how David would respond to the message about Absalom's death. The friendly Ahimaaz would make him feel his bitter grief even more. Therefore Joab sent someone else. But later, after further pleading, he let Ahimaaz go anyway. Ahimaaz took a short cut across the Jordan Valley and got there before the other messenger. He wisely said nothing about Absalom's death. Immediately after him came the other messenger, who then informed David of Absalom's destruction.

David had been waiting for news between the inner and outer city gates. Now he went into his room over the gate and lamented: "Absalom, my son, my son! If only I could have died for you, Absalom, my son!" The entire army had returned to greet the king and accompany him victoriously back to Jerusalem. But now the soldiers had to creep through the gate in a stealthy manner.

Here we face David's real sin. Joab's deed was undoubtedly an act of disobedience. But David failed to see himself as the head of the covenant and Absalom as the covenant breaker. David let himself be governed by his self-centered love as a father for his son—a son with such handsome features! How little awareness of his calling David displayed in this situation! He was supposed to be a type of the Christ, but so often he fell short. The Christ is the only one for whom life was simply the pursuit of God's calling.

In a harsh and brazen way, Joab reproached the king for his attitude and even threatened to desert him and take the army along. Then the king controlled himself and sat at the city gates to greet the army.

The return to Jerusalem. Yet, David was not in full control of himself. His life was not governed completely by an awareness of his calling. This sometimes caused him not to see things clearly and to do unreasonable things.

After Absalom's death, the people came to themselves. They had been bewitched by that handsome flatterer. That was no excuse, of course. If, by faith, they had recognized David as the Lord's anointed and the head of the covenant, they would never have been infatuated by Absalom. Now, however, they remembered the deliverance the Lord had given them through David, and their hearts went out to him again. But what vacillation there still was! They were not united in returning to David and the Lord with a confession of guilt. Instead they debated the advantages and disadvantages of bringing David back as king. How shamefully the people acted toward their covenant obligations!

When David heard about this, he decided he would have to act. He did not inquire about the Lord's will, as he had done in the land of the Philistines before he became king, nor did he wait for the working of the Lord's Spirit. The effect of his hasty action was to ruin what was beginning to stir among the people. His appeal to Judah stimulated the feeling of tribalism among the people of his own tribe.

He also made a promise to Amasa, who had been Absalom's commander-in-chief and was distantly related to David, namely, that he would become commander-in-chief in place of Joab. That was an act of shameful unfaithfulness toward Joab, no matter what Joab had done wrong or how disobedient and insolent he had been. It would have been much better if David had disciplined Joab as soon as he committed his offenses instead of waiting to pay him back in this manner.

Then, as one man, Judah's tribe chose for David and asked him to return. Yet this development later became a source of misery.

Thus David began his return. At the Jordan Shimei met him, begging for forgiveness. He pointed out that he was the first one to come out and greet David—as if that were a guarantee of a change of heart! When Joab's brother Abishai urged David to have Shimei put to death, he rejected the suggestion out of a certain obstinacy over against his sister Zeruiah's sons and spared Shimei's life. Perhaps Abishai had a desire for personal revenge, but he did speak out about Shimei's offense against the Lord's anointed.

On David's part there was an unwillingness to act because of Absalom's death and his own weakness. He did say that it seemed as though he was now becoming Israel's king for the first time. But here he was being governed by his feelings rather than a consciousness of the Lord's calling. Shimei's wrong could not be allowed to go unpunished. David felt that too, and he instructed his successor to see to it that justice was done (I Kings 2:8-9).

Ziba, who had slandered his master Mephibosheth, also came to David at the Jordan, as did Mephibosheth himself. The whole time David was banned from Jerusalem, Mephibosheth had been living in mourning. This brought Ziba's deception to light. Nevertheless, Mephibosheth told David to deal with him as he saw fit. David did not want to hear any more about the matter and decided that Mephibosheth and Ziba would divide the land equally between them. This was not exercising justice. The king was shirking his responsibility in this matter.

Barzillai, who had helped support David's army in Transjordan, accompanied the king across the Jordan, but because of his old age, he refused to go to Jerusalem and stay there. His son Chimham went instead, and David honored him as he would have honored his father.

At Gilgal, on the other side of the Jordan, all the men of Israel came to David to take him back to Jerusalem again. They expressed their anger to the king over the fact that the men of Judah had gotten to him first. After all, every tribe shared in the king; David was not just king over Judah. The men of Judah answered that the king was their kinsman and that they had approached him on their own because they received special favors from the king.

Judah's men took a tough line in their replies. David did not know what to say to ward off the impending quarrel between brothers. He was aware that he himself had caused it.

A certain Benjaminite named Sheba then blew the trumpet and declared that the Israelites had no part in David and should return to their homes. The men of Israel withdrew and followed him, deserting the Lord's anointed again.

Thus the people committed sin upon sin. Yet the Lord did not desert them but wished to continue blessing them in David and in David's house. Therefore the Lord restored David to power in spite of the people's unfaithfulness.

David finally came back to Jerusalem. He had been restored by God Himself. Still, the people were not all behind him yet. Later the Israelites would have to learn just how much they had sinned against the Lord.

In Jerusalem David restored order. The women whom Absalom had taken as wives were not restored as David's wives. However, David did provide for their needs for the rest of their lives.

Complete restoration. The king ordered Amasa, Absalom's former commander-in-chief, to mobilize the men of Judah for battle against Sheba in order to bring all the people under the rule of their king again. By doing so, David was persisting in his unjust treatment of Joab. David could have punished Joab for his offenses, but shoving him aside the way he did was a shameful thing to do.

David did not succeed in this course of action toward Joab. Apparently the men of Judah did not quite trust Amasa. In any case, he could not get them together very quickly. David was afraid that this would give Sheba an opportunity to strengthen his position. Therefore he instructed Joab's brother Abishai to pursue Sheba with all the faithful soldiers.

Near Gibeon, Abishai and Joab (who had joined his brother) met Amasa. Under the pretense of wanting to kiss him, Joab went up to Amasa and killed him. He left his body lying on the road and stationed someone at that spot to tell the men of Judah to follow Joab and Abishai in the battle against Sheba. However, the men of Judah did not go past that spot. This assassination was too much for them to take. They knew that the king's cause would not be furthered by such means. Therefore the guard at the scene covered the body of Amasa and removed it from the road. Then the men of Judah followed Joab in pursuit of Sheba.

Sheba had strengthened his position in Abel of Beth-maacah. Joab pursued him there. However, the civil war was averted. A wise woman accused Joab of wanting to swallow up the heritage of the Lord. (Perhaps Joab had already asked the inhabitants of the city whether they really wanted to make common cause with

Sheba.) At Joab's demand, Sheba's head was thrown out to him over the wall. Then the army returned to Jerusalem, and Joab was given back his position as commander-in-chief of the army.

Peace had come to Israel again. Yet, there was no inner unity. The people had not confessed their sins before the Lord. The Lord would still have to confront the Israelites with their guilt.

22: Israel's Lamp

II Samuel 21-24

In his song of thanksgiving, David sang: "You are my lamp, O LORD." On the other hand, David's warriors declared that *David* was Israel's lamp. It was possible for David to be Israel's lamp because the Lord was *his* lamp. The real Lamp of Israel is the Christ, of whom David spoke in his last words.

That David is Israel's lamp comes to particular expression in these chapters of II Samuel, especially in the contrast between chapters 21 and 24. Long after Saul's death, the curse on his deeds threatened his line with extinction. The kingship, in any case, had been permanently removed from his line, which scarcely continued in Mephibosheth. David's sin and the ensuing plague led to the altar of reconciliation that was built on the threshing floor of Araunah. In David's line, the light continued to shine for Israel—especially in the Christ who came later.

Saul, showing tremendous zeal for his own glory rather than for the name of the Lord, had tried to wipe out the Gibeonites. Blood had spoken in his deeds—not the Lord's justice. Under Joshua's promise, the Gibeonites had a right to protection in Israel. Joshua had invoked the name of the Lord when he made that promise (Josh. 9). The issue in II Samuel 21, then, is not just blood revenge; the Lord's name had been desecrated, and therefore there was a curse on Saul's descendants. The hanging corpses were not taken down in the evening but remained hanging for the entire harvest time.

Because of the sin of the king, the whole country felt the effects of the Lord's curse. The famine was widespread and lasted for three years. Now, however, with the public exhibition of the corpses, all Israel could see that something was being done about Saul's sin. The corpses were not removed until the first drops of rain showed that the curse had been lifted (II Sam. 21:1).

182

Rizpah's deed is not to be viewed in the first place as an act of a mother's love; it was an act of devotion to Saul's house. (After all, she was also protecting the corpses of five descendants of Saul who were not her own sons.) David was moved by her deed and saw to it that the bones of Saul and Jonathan and the seven who were put to death were buried in their family grave. Thus the line of Saul finally found rest in Israel. Rizpah's blessed act had contributed to that.

The numbering of the people by David and the plague in Israel were a result of God's anger. Apparently there was another sin the people had committed, a sin for which the Lord had not yet chastised them and for which Israel had not yet humbled itself. We naturally think of the sin committed when the people rejected their king at the time of the rebellions of Absalom and Sheba. The guilt of that sin continued to make itself felt. God caused that sin to have certain consequences in the sin of David.

It is in this framework that we are to understand David's sin in the census, a sin to which he was incited by the Lord Himself. The taking of a census was not in itself a sin. In the law, provision had been made for numbering the people: certain sacrifices were required, for when men look to numbers they can easily withdraw from the Lord.

We do not read that David observed the regulations of the law when he numbered the people. That was already indicative of where he went wrong. This particular census was no covenant act on David's part. The essence of his sin is surely not to be found in a childlike joy and pride in numbers. Apparently he wanted to make Israel into a military state, a state strong in its army rather than in its covenant with the Lord. All of life would be dedicated to the greatness of the state. Thus David's sin was not much different from Saul's.

In the first half of his song of thanksgiving, David was thinking especially of the persecutions of Saul. In the second half he turned to wars with foreign enemies and the conflicts among his own people. In between he suggested the reason why the Lord delivered him. In the section that begins with II Samuel 22:21, we read: "The LORD rewarded me according to my righteousness."

David was not thinking of any righteousness of his own, of course; what he meant was that he was living in the right relation to God, that he was upright in the covenant with the Lord. It appears that David was well aware that the Lord comes first in this relationship and that it was the Lord who had chosen him for the position in which he found himself. This awareness comes through, for example, in David's recognition that the Lord is his lamp.

Main thought: *Through His anointed, the Lord is a lamp for His people.*

Saul's lamp extinguished. At one point during David's reign, a dry spell caused a famine which lasted three years. The king finally realized that the famine was not an accident but a sign of God's judgment. He inquired of the Lord and received an answer: a curse still rested on the people because of something that had happened during the time of Saul.

During his reign, Saul had tried to exterminate the Gibeonites and had killed many of them. He had been driven not by the honor of the Lord's name but by the glory of the name of Israel itself, the honor of Jewish blood. Joshua had invoked the name of the Lord when he promised security to the Gibeonites. Ever since then, they had found protection under that name. Now, because of Saul's attack, the name of the Lord had been desecrated. Thus the curse of Saul's reign continued to make itself felt long after his death. David was called to remove it.

David asked the Gibeonites how atonement could be made for the injustice, so that the curse could be removed from Israel. The Gibeonites replied that they were not interested in gold or silver, that the crime against them could not be expiated in that way. Nor did they have the right to take blood revenge on anyone in Israel. In their judgment, the curse would be lifted if seven descendants of Saul were surrendered publicly to the curse, that is, killed and then hanged.

David granted their request. He allowed seven males of Saul's line to be put to death. Their corpses were hanged at Gibeah, Saul's hometown. Jonathan's son Mephibosheth was spared, together with his line. The men killed were two sons of Rizpah, one of Saul's wives, and five sons of Saul's oldest daughter.

Their corpses remained hanging there day and night through the whole harvest time as a manifestation of the curse which weighed heavily on Israel. All Israel deserved such a curse—not only because of the sin of Saul, its king, but because of all the sin by which Israel desecrated the name of the Lord. We, too, deserve that curse and would have to be publicly displayed if the Lord Jesus Christ had not suffered that curse for us. In our place He was publicly displayed on the cross as the accursed One.

Were children to be punished for the misdeeds of their parents? In Israel, among the people of the covenant, children were not punished for the sins of their parents if the children broke with those sins and did not continue to walk in the ways of their parents. But here the Lord Himself let it be known by means of the famine that Saul's death had not removed the effects of his sin. Moreover, this was not just a sin of Saul's but of all the people in their king. Thus the seven men were killed for the sin of all the people. In this we see God's grace for all the people: the people were spared. That grace appeared much more gloriously in the death of the Christ, who died in the place of His people.

In this judgment on Saul's house, the kingship was forever removed from that house. Saul's descendants could not be a light for Israel. In that sense, Saul's lamp was extinguished. On the other hand, there was still mercy for his line. This became apparent first of all through a touching deed on the part of Rizpah, whose two sons were among the seven men put to death. During the whole harvest time, when the corpses were left hanging, she kept a vigil to prevent the birds and the beasts of the fields from mutilating the corpses. That was not just a mother's love for her sons; it was faithfulness to the house of Saul. Thus there was still some loyalty to that house! This by itself was honor and mercy. Not until the end of the harvest, when it began to rain, were the corpses removed. The falling rain was proof that the curse had been lifted.

David was told what Rizpah had done. Her loyalty to Saul's house touched him, and he decided to have the bones of Saul and Jonathan brought from Jabesh in Gilead to the family grave of Saul's father Kish, where they were buried along with the bones of the seven men whose corpses had been hanged. Thus Saul's line finally found rest in Israel. That, too, was mercy. The curse had come to an end, and Saul's line was not completely wiped out. His name did not cease to exist in Israel.

David and the Philistines. Throughout his entire reign, David had to fight against Israel's traditional enemies, the Philistines, and he grew weary of the struggle. But God had often been wonderfully near to him and his warriors. Through David, the Lord also delivered Israel from the giants among the Philistines.

Once David's life was in danger because a Philistine giant attacked him, but Abishai, the son of his sister Zeruiah, saved his life. Then his men pleaded with him not to go out to battle anymore, lest he quench the lamp of Israel which the Lord had given Israel in David and his house.

What bliss it must have been for David to be recognized by his men as the lamp of Israel! Israel's real Lamp was not David himself but someone who was to be born of his line according to the promise—the Christ. Through the Christ, David was a lamp to Israel in spite of his sins.

You are my Lamp, O Lord! During his lifetime David composed many psalms, both in the period of persecution by Saul and in the time of his reign. These psalms were sung by the Levites in the temple services. And they are still sung today by the church of the Lord. We can sing those psalms because David was not merely singing about his personal experiences. His experiences are the experiences of all the people of God. They are also the experiences of the head of that people—the Christ.

At the end of his life, David looked back on all the experiences the Lord had given him and sang a song of praise and thanksgiving. In that song he called the Lord his Rock, his Shield, his Refuge, his Redeemer. And he thanked the Lord for the many times He had delivered him during the days when Saul pursued him, during the battles against foreign enemies, and during the conflicts within the people of Israel. He sang that the Lord had been gracious toward him because he had lived uprightly with the Lord in the covenant.

David did not overlook his grave sins. The Lord led him to confess his guilt time and again and took that guilt away. In this song David did not boast of his own merits. On the contrary, he sang that the Lord was an enemy of the haughty. The Lord alone was his lamp; the Lord had changed the darkness in his heart and life into light. The Lord does indeed oppose those who revolt against Him. David could begin and end with praise and adoration to the Lord.

This song, too, finds its complete fulfillment in the Christ, who has been set over all His enemies in His resurrection and ascension. Only the Christ lived with God in the covenant in complete righteousness. Because Christ's Spirit lived in David, he, too, was made righteous before the Lord.

The prophecy of the righteous Ruler. There was still a very important experience in store for David: by the Spirit of the Lord, he became a prophet. Very clearly he saw and foretold the coming of his great Son, the one who would be a righteous Ruler. How David longed for the coming of that Ruler! Thereby he showed that he knew how full of defects and sin his reign had been.

Full of joy, he spoke of that Ruler, who would be like the morning light in glory. He confessed that he and his house were not worthy of the coming of that Ruler, who would be born of his descendants. But God had promised the coming of that Ruler and had made a covenant with David guaranteeing that promise. All of David's salvation and joy rested in that promise. Sinners who revolt against that glory will be thrown away like contemptible thistles.

David and his heroes. David gathered many heroes around him during various wars. He even divided them into three different groups. The spirit of faith that lived within David instilled courage and trust in his men. In that regard, too, the Lord had blessed David.

There was a spirit of trust and mutual appreciation between David and his men. One day this came out very clearly in a battle against the Philistines. The enemy had penetrated deep into the land, all the way to Bethlehem. David and his army camped opposite the Philistines. There was a shortage of water, and David longed for the cool water of a well near Bethlehem from which he had drunk so often in earlier days. Immediately three of his men forced their way through the bands of Philistines and brought David the water he wanted so badly. But David refused to drink the water they brought him, which they had obtained by risking their lives. To him that would have been like drinking their blood. He poured the water out before the Lord as an expression of thanks for the spirit which the Lord had put into his heroes and for the bond which existed between him and them. All this he considered a gift from the Lord.

The altar of reconciliation. At the end of his life, David committed a greater sin than any other he had ever committed. This sin was not committed apart from the Lord's control; there is not a single deed that occurs outside His governance.

David's sin led to an outbreak of pestilence among the people. The Lord brought this about because His anger was directed against the people on account of their misdeeds, for which they had not yet been punished. Hadn't the people rejected David for Absalom and then for Sheba? They had rejected the *head* of the covenant—and thereby the Lord's covenant itself. For this the Lord now intended to punish them.

The Lord caused an idea to arise in David's mind, an idea that immediately took a sinful twist: David would number the people. In itself a census was not forbidden, even though it would be easy to fall into a sin through pride when taking a census. During this period of his reign, David was occupied with the organization of the people; he reorganized the priesthood and the priestly service, for example. Now he wanted to number the people for military purposes, to make Israel a state that was strong in itself. In that way the trust of the people was diverted from the Lord and focused on the strength of the kingdom.

Joab, who was charged with carrying out the census, raised serious objections. He was afraid of opposition and restlessness among the people, who did not want to be numbered for military purposes. But the king persisted in his intention; David did not allow himself to be dissuaded, for he was in the power of sin again.

Joab set out to obey the king's orders, but he did not complete the census. With the tentative results in hand he came to David. Then the king's eyes were opened, and he saw what he was really doing and how he had cut himself adrift from the Lord. Because David was the head of the covenant, this was not just a personal sin; he had ruined things for all the people.

David's heart condemned him, and he confessed to the Lord and asked forgiveness. Then the prophet Gad came to him and said in the name of the Lord that he had not been rejected; the

Lord had forgiven him, but the rod of chastisement was to come over him and over Israel. David was to choose between three years of hunger, three months of flight before the enemy, and three days of pestilence. "I am in great distress," David replied. But when he saw that there was no escape, he chose the three days of pestilence. He did not wish to fall into the hands of men; he preferred to fall into the hands of the Lord, who always has mercy upon the sinner. How well he knew his God and confessed His grace, even when God's wrath was directed against him. That was a manifestation of faith on his part.

The plague broke out over all Israel, and the people were chastised for their sin. In the punishment of his people, David, too, was being punished. The Lord does indeed visit His people in His anger, even though He has graciously forgiven them for Christ's sake. Seventy thousand people died in all.

The plague still had not reached Jerusalem. Then David had a vision of the angel of destruction stretching forth his hand toward Jerusalem to strike it with the plague. He fell on his face and prayed: "It is I who have sinned; I am the one who acted wickedly. But these sheep—what have they done? Let Your hand, I pray You, be against me and against my father's house." Here David threw himself in the breach on behalf of his people and offered himself in their place, allowing God to see in him a reflection of the Mediator who would offer Himself on behalf of His people. For Christ's sake, the Lord decided to lift the plague before the appointed time.

Again the prophet Gad came to David. He ordered him to erect an altar on the threshing floor of Araunah where he had seen the angel of destruction standing. Araunah offered the king his threshing floor, his oxen, and his threshing sledges as wood for the sacrifice. But David did not wish to offer a sacrifice using another man's possessions. Therefore he *bought* the threshing floor and the oxen from Araunah, built an altar there, and offered burnt offerings and peace offerings. Then the plague was lifted.

David and the people had indeed been chastised, but there was forgiveness with the Lord. David and his house were not rejected; he was allowed to stay on as king and as the covenant head in whom the people were blessed. Saul's lamp had been extinguished, but David, because of the covenant the Lord had made with him, was permitted to remain the lamp of Israel.

Later the temple was built on the site of Araunah's threshing floor. For centuries the altar of atonement stood on the very spot where David had seen the angel of destruction. There sacrifices would be offered as a foreshadowing of the sacrifice of the Lord Jesus Christ, the great sacrifice by which atonement was made for the sin of the Lord's people. The Christ would be the Lamp of His people forever. By His sacrifice, atonement was made for David's sin and for Israel's as well.

Solomon

23: The Kingdom of Peace

I Kings 1-4

The Kingdom of God is foreshadowed as the Kingdom of peace especially in Solomon's kingdom. The blessing of Solomon's reign is described in I Kings 4:20 in these words: "Judah and Israel were as many as the sand by the sea; they ate and drank and were happy." And in verse 25 we read: "Judah and Israel dwelt in safety, from Dan even to Beer-sheba, every man under his vine and under his fig tree, all the days of Solomon." The various episodes in the history related in these chapters of I Kings are connected by this main thought.

The king in that kingdom is given by God. Not Adonijah but Solomon was God's choice as king. As the one chosen by God, Solomon was a type of the Christ.

There is no peace without justice. Solomon followed David's instructions and began his reign by exercising justice especially on those who were worthy of the judgment of death. In the judgment on Adonijah, in particular, we are to see Solomon as the Lord's anointed, the head of the covenant. Solomon was not merely eliminating a troublesome rival; he was executing someone who tried to seize the crown from the one to whom it belonged, namely, the head of the covenant.

Solomon's marriage to Pharaoh's daughter was not a forbidden marriage. Only marriage with the daughters of the Canaanites was forbidden. Of course Solomon was under an obligation to ensure that the women of other nations did not introduce their idolatry into Israel. Pharaoh's daughter is not mentioned among the women who later tempted Solomon.

In giving his daughter to Solomon, Pharaoh was honoring the king of the same people that the Egyptians had once despised. Someday all peoples will acknowledge the Christ.

193

Although Solomon brought Pharaoh's daughter into the city of David, he did not bring her into the house of David, for the places to which the ark of the Lord had come were holy to him (II Chron. 8:11). Apparently he still viewed her as a woman of a people that did not know the covenant of the Lord. Only later did he build a house for her.

When we tell these stories to the children, we are not to depict Solomon as a pious young man who chose for wisdom instead of riches and honor. If we make this mistake, Solomon's judgment in the case of the two mothers and the disputed baby becomes nothing more than an interesting story about a clever king. Scripture sums up the meaning of it all in I Kings 3:28: "And all Israel heard the judgment which the king had rendered; and they stood in awe of the king, because they perceived that the wisdom of God was in him, to render justice." The people saw that Solomon's extraordinary wisdom was a shield given to them by God, a shield under which they were safe.

The judgment of the two mothers shocked all the unrighteous. It seemed as if the king could see what was in their hearts. But the righteous got a feeling of security from Solomon's penetrating wisdom. Under the shield of the Christ there is safety for all who have faith.

Main thought: *The Lord establishes the Kingdom of peace.*

The king given by God. King David had become old. He was about 70. Perhaps that was not so old compared to some other people, but his strength was spent. Think of all that David had experienced during his lifetime! Because of his weakened condition, he could not pay careful attention to what was going on in his kingdom, as he had done in earlier days.

Adonijah seized on that weakness as his opportunity. He was a full brother to Absalom and had the same handsome build. David had a soft spot in his heart for Adonijah, just as he had had for Absalom. David never seriously scolded him.

His older brothers had died. Therefore Adonijah would have been his father's heir apparent if the Lord had not indicated that Solomon, the son of David and Bathsheba, was to be king. Adonijah must have known about this decree of the Lord, but he did not submit to it in his heart. Instead he plotted against Solomon. With David's infirmity, he saw his way clear to the throne.

Adonijah invited all his potential supporters to a sacrificial meal near Jerusalem. Among them were Joab, David's commander in chief, and Abiathar, one of the two high priests. But Zadok, the other high priest, Benaiah, the head of David's guards, the prophet Nathan, and David's men of valor were not on Adonijah's side. Therefore they were not invited to the sacrifice. Solomon was not invited either, although all the other sons of the king were present. At the end of the sacrificial meal, Adonijah would be acclaimed king.

However, the prophet Nathan found out what Adonijah was up to. Immediately he sent Bathsheba, Solomon's mother, to David. She was to tell him what was happening and remind him of the oath he had sworn to her that Solomon would be king over Israel in accordance with the Lord's instructions.

After Bathsheba talked to David, Nathan himself went to him and confirmed what she had said. David swore an oath that his earlier decision stood. Immediately he took action.

David ordered Zadok, Nathan and Benaiah to have Solomon ride on the king's mule and be anointed king near Jerusalem. They were to blow the trumpet and cry: "Long live King Solomon!" In a procession they were to return to Jerusalem. Then Solomon would sit on David's throne. David's servants blessed him for this decision.

Events unfolded just as David had ordered. The people in Jerusalem had a big celebration; they played music and shouted for joy. Before long Adonijah and his guests heard the noise.

Jonathan, the son of Abiathar, came to Adonijah's feast to notify him that Solomon had been elevated to the throne. He also told him how David's servants had congratulated him on the decision to make Solomon king, and that David had offered praise to the Lord after Solomon became king. This message shocked them all so much that they got up and went home.

Adonijah feared for his life and fled to the tent in which the ark of the Lord was kept. There he grabbed hold of the horns of the altar. In some cases, such as involuntary manslaughter, taking hold of those horns was a guarantee of protection. Adonijah hoped to find protection at the altar even though he had deliberately plotted revolution. Solomon heard what Adonijah had done and promised him protection, provided he would never again plot a revolt.

Thus Solomon became king over Israel. He had been chosen for the office by the Lord long before, and now he was elevated to the throne. The king, the leader of Israel, had to be given to the people by the Lord. His name was Solomon;* under him the kingdom of *peace* would flourish. Our King, the Christ, is also given to us by God. He establishes the Kingdom in which peace will reign forever. Solomon was only a type of that King.

The king's justice. There could be no peace in the kingdom if justice was not exercised, if crime was not punished. Any unavenged crime would become a curse in the kingdom. During David's reign, crimes had been committed which David was not able or willing to have punished. Therefore, before his death David ordered Solomon to make sure that the law took its course. He emphasized strongly that Solomon was to rule according to the Word of the Lord and walk in His ways. Then the Lord would confirm His promise that David's house would stand forever. After that David died.

Solomon acted on his father's advice and exercised judgment. At the very beginning of his reign he was forced to judge Adonijah. He became aware that Adonijah went on plotting against him. Therefore he had Adonijah put to death—not because Adonijah was a threat to him but because Adonijah did not subject himself to the one the Lord had chosen to be the covenant head. Adonijah was executed because he rejected God's covenant with Israel.

Abiathar, the high priest who had joined Adonijah's revolt, was banished by Solomon. He was to leave Jerusalem and go to his own estate. Solomon spared his life because he had shared in David's afflictions and had been high priest in good standing during David's reign. Yet Abiathar was removed from his office as high priest. With this step the judgment on Eli's house finally came to complete fulfillment. From then on only Zadok was high priest. Zadok was from another line, the line of Eleazar, the son and successor of Aaron.

---

*This name in its Hebrew form is related to the word *shalom*, meaning *peace* in the sense of wholeness, completeness, integrality.—TRANS.

When Joab heard what had happened to Adonijah and Abiathar, he realized that Solomon would execute judgment on him too. David had instructed Solomon to do so. Indeed, the king sent Benaiah to put Joab to death. But Joab fled to the tent of the ark and took hold of the horns of the altar. Joab was thinking only of the part he had played in Adonijah's revolt, not of his murder of Abner and Amasa. For the latter crimes there would be no protection for him at that altar.

Benaiah hesitated when he found Joab there. At the express command of Solomon, Joab was killed at the altar. Even so, Solomon arranged for his body to be buried. The king did not forget what Joab had done in his father's service. Because of that he was given a proper burial in his own grave.

At David's command, Solomon also judged Shimei. The judgment was very mild. Shimei was to live in Jerusalem and there witness the Lord's grace on the house of David, which he had cursed so terribly. But if he dared to leave Jerusalem even for the shortest time, he would surely die. Later on Shimei violated the condition: he went after runaway slaves. Therefore he was killed at Solomon's command. Solomon had rightly seen the Lord's guiding hand in this matter: the Lord did not want Shimei to die in peace.

On the other hand, the king dealt loyally with those who had blessed David. This, too, David had commanded. Barzillai's sons, for example, ate at the king's table.

There is no peace without justice. The Christ will be King forever in His Kingdom of peace, but He will judge His enemies, who did not want Him for their King.

Honored among the nations. At the beginning of his reign, Solomon married the daughter of Egypt's king. A marriage with an Egyptian woman was not forbidden in the law of the Lord. But such a wife was not to bring her idolatry into Israel. Apparently this Egyptian woman made no attempt to do so. Yet, Solomon did not bring her into the house of David, next to which David had erected a tent for the ark of the Lord. Because those places were holy to Solomon, he did not want to bring this foreign woman

near them. Here he showed that he respected his father's principles
and honored the covenant of the Lord.

It is certainly significant that the king of Egypt let his
daughter marry the king of the once despised and oppressed nation
of slaves. Israel had clearly assumed a place of honor among the
nations. This acknowledgment is to be read as a prophecy that
one day all the nations would honor the great King to come forth
out of Israel. In His name the nations will worship God.

Wisdom to govern the people justly. In those days there was
still no temple in Jerusalem. The tabernacle was in Gibeon, and the
ark was in a tent in the city of David. There was no central sanctuary to which all the people could come for worship. They still
sacrificed on the high places throughout Canaan and everywhere
in Gibeon.

At the beginning of his reign, Solomon wanted to seek the
Lord. Therefore he went to Gibeon and offered a thousand burnt
offerings. With this enormous sacrifice, he consecrated his entire
reign to the Lord.

The Spirit of the Lord Jesus Christ was in him. The Christ
gave Himself with His whole life to God. Thus it could be said of
Solomon that he loved the Lord.

At Gibeon the Lord appeared to Solomon in a dream. The
dream was a response to his consecration of his life to the Lord. In
the dream the Lord said to him: "Tell Me what you would like Me
to give you." Solomon replied that he knew that he had been given
to Israel in place of his father to be the nation's head and king, and
that he therefore bore a very heavy burden of responsibility. How
was he to govern the people in the spirit of his father David, the
man after God's own heart? He was still so young, so incapable of
carrying out his calling! Thus Solomon was thinking not about
himself but about his calling as head of the people. He wanted an
understanding heart to govern the people justly.

This choice was pleasing to the Lord. Because God saw in him
the Spirit of the Christ, the Head of the covenant, He gave him so
much wisdom that he could not be compared with anyone else. In
addition He gave him riches and honors beyond all the kings of his

time and promised him a long life as well, provided he continued to walk in the ways of the Lord.

When Solomon awoke, he realized that he had been dreaming. But he knew that the Lord had revealed Himself in that dream and that His Word would come true.

After that Solomon returned to Jerusalem and stood before the ark of the Lord. There he sacrificed burnt offerings and peace offerings because of what the Lord had promised and given to him. After he made the peace offerings, Solomon dined with all his officials at a great banquet. There they ate and drank in fellowship with the God of Israel so that they could lead the people in such fellowship.

The shield of the earth. Very quickly the people noticed what an extraordinary gift God had given them in their king. Two women came to the king. One declared that the other had taken her child because her own child was dead. The other woman protested and said that the living child was hers. They asked the king to settle their dispute. How would Solomon ever determine who was the real mother of the child?

The wisdom God had given him illumined his understanding. He said he would have the child killed and give a half to each of the women. Immediately the real mother spoke up; she wanted to spare the child even if it meant surrendering her own claim to it. Then it was clear to Solomon who the real mother was, and she got her child back.

All of Israel heard about that judgment of Solomon's. The people feared their king; they looked up with respect to the wisdom God had given him. The ungodly were horrified because they realized that they could not hide from such wisdom. The people who feared the Lord felt safe under this shield which the Lord had given them.

Never again has there been anyone with such wisdom as Solomon possessed. In that wisdom he was a type of the Lord Jesus Christ, who sees through the wicked and is a shield for all those who fear Him. How safe our lives are under that shield! He protects us forever. He does so also by the means He has provided in this life. Earthly government is one of those means. Government, too, has been given to us by Christ as a temporary shield. The shields of the earth are God's, Scripture says (Ps. 47:9). That's why we ask the Lord in prayer to give something of Christ's wisdom to these governments, in order that they may truly be a shield to us.

The glory of the king and the kingdom. In addition to the wisdom Solomon asked for, God gave him what he had not asked for—riches and honor. He had an enormous court with many servants. The daily necessities of the court were almost incalculable. The food did not come from Canaan only but also from the countries that had been subdued. Moreover, the subject nations paid taxes to Solomon. He reigned over a very wide area. He had a large army with chariots and cavalry. Because Solomon had everything so well organized, his army was well provided for.

Most glorious of all was the prosperity and peace Solomon brought to Israel. The people expanded in great numbers and rejoiced in the life God gave them. Everyone lived in the safety of his own vine and under his own fig tree.

This wonderful kingdom of peace was a foreshadowing of a still more glorious Kingdom of peace that Christ would establish one day. Through the remission of our sins, He gives us peace with God—and also peace with ourselves, peace with each other, peace with life itself. He gives us life and the possession of this earth. In this life His people receive all of this as a guarantee or pledge of what they will possess eternally. In that Kingdom the King is crowned with glory and honor.

The revelation of creation's meaning. Not only did Solomon have the wisdom to govern the people justly, in his wisdom he also saw much more of the meaning of life and creation than any other person—much more than all the wise men of his day and of all time. He made up 3000 proverbs in which he gave guidance for life, guidance for old and young, for rich and poor, for kings and subjects.

He also composed over a thousand songs. In these songs he sang of the glory of life when it is lived with the Lord in His covenant. In his wisdom he spoke about all the creatures, about plants and animals from the largest to the smallest. In all those creatures he discovered meaning—the Lord's intentions. Thus he opened the book of creation and of life for us. From all nations people came to hear his wisdom.

Solomon could do all this because the Spirit of the Christ was in him. God gave us the Christ to be our wisdom. He has uncovered the meaning of life for us. Now we do not have to go through life as though we were blind. Christ explains to us God's intentions for His creatures and for our lives. That's how marvelous God's Kingdom is. In that Kingdom there is wisdom for all the citizens. If we, by faith, live with the Lord in His covenant, we are citizens of that Kingdom. Then the world and all of life opens up to us.

24: The Palace of His Holiness

I Kings 5-9

It was time for the tabernacle to be replaced by the temple, God's "permanent dwelling place." The need for a temple was bound up with the change in Israel's situation. The kingdom was now firmly established in Israel. Particularly under Solomon, the kingdom was a foreshadowing of the Kingdom of God. In the glory of the temple, the palace of God's holiness, it was made clear that the Lord lived among His people as Israel's King.

Yet we must not forget that the peculiar character of God's Kingdom is that God rules over all things through a human being, just as He now reigns through the Christ. This, too, was foreshadowed in Israel. For this reason the construction of the temple is closely connected with the building of Solomon's palace. First we are told about the construction of the temple, then about the building of Solomon's palace, and finally about the provisions made for furnishing and equipping the temple. It took seven years to erect the temple and thirteen years for the royal palace. During those thirteen years, it appears, the furnishings and equipment for the temple were also made ready so that the temple could be dedicated once the 20 years were over.

The building of the temple and the palace are intimately connected. Therefore, if we are to bring out Scripture's intention as we tell this story, we must stress that while Solomon was building his magnificent palace, he was seeking not his personal honor but his honor as the king in God's Kingdom. His royal palace shared in the splendor of the palace of God's holiness.

On the meaning of the temple as a sign of God's presence among His people, see the Chapter on the establishment of the tabernacle (Vol. I, pp. 310-17). Bear in mind that God did not restrict His presence to the earthly temple, as Solomon pointed out in his prayer (I Kings 8:27); His presence filled all of heaven and earth. What the temple was intended to symbolize was not just God's presence but the presence of His *grace*; He used the temple to show that He was present among His people as the God of the covenant.

What Solomon asked for in his prayer was just such a revelation. The temple was a shadow of the presence of God's grace in the Christ and a prophecy pointing ahead to the day when the entire earth will be filled with God's grace.

Main thought: *The Lord establishes the palace of His holiness in Israel.*

Preparations for building. When Solomon became king, Hiram, the king of Tyre, who had been a close friend of David's, sent a delegation of emissaries to congratulate Solomon on his elevation to the throne. Solomon used that delegation to open negotiations with Hiram about the building of a temple in Jerusalem. Solomon wanted to make a trade agreement with Hiram. He reminded Hiram that David had already proposed to build the temple but that the Lord had said that the temple was to be built by David's son, to whom the Lord would give rest. Now Solomon proposed to bring that Word of God to fulfillment. He needed timber from the cedars of Lebanon growing in Hiram's kingdom. Solomon wanted to send his servants to Hiram so that they could begin cutting wood under the supervision of the men of Sidon.

Hiram rejoiced and praised the Lord once he saw that Solomon wanted to rule in the spirit of his father David. Hiram had seen some of the blessings of David's rule and had great respect for the God of Israel, even though he did not choose for Israel's God with his whole heart. He remained a heathen, but he appreciated the blessings which streamed forth from the kingdom which the Lord had established in Israel. Unbelieving people are often able to recognize something of the Lord's blessings.

An agreement was made: Hiram would make sure that timber arrived in one of Canaan's seaports. Solomon would in turn take care of providing food for Hiram's court.

When a beginning was made with the work, it became clear what great wisdom God had given Solomon. That wisdom guided him in the organization of this enormous task. He drafted 30,000 laborers from all over Israel and divided them into three groups of 10,000 men each. Each group worked for one month in Lebanon and then came home for two months. Solomon instituted forced labor for the Canaanites who still remained in Canaan. He made 70,000 of them work as load carriers. Another 80,000 served as stone cutters, since a great deal of stone would be needed in the building of the temple. The stone, too, came from Lebanon and was cut into blocks there.

The laborers were supervised by 3300 foremen. The work went smoothly, just the way Solomon had planned. In all these events, the Lord was working through the wisdom of Solomon; in fact, it was the Lord who originated everything and drove all the people to do the work. He Himself guided Solomon and his workmen in their preparations for the building of the temple, which was to be His dwelling place in Israel.

The building of the temple. The construction of the temple began in the fourth year of Solomon's reign, some 480 years after Israel's exodus from the land of Egypt. Now a new period set in for the people of Israel. The kingdom had been established among them in glory, and the Lord had shown that He was Israel's glorious King. Therefore it would be fitting for the Lord to live in the midst of His people in a glorious house. Besides, the Lord had made a covenant with David that a King who would rule over God's people forever would spring from David's seed. The Lord's kingship would come to expression in this kingship of David's house. Through the covenant with David, all of this was now firmly established. Hence the Lord could not go on living in a tent; He should have a temple as a permanent dwelling place.

Thus Solomon built a house for the Lord, using the tabernacle as a rough model. Like the tabernacle, the temple was divided into three areas—the Holy Place, the Most Holy Place (or Holy of Holies), and the outer court. The temple's Most Holy Place was cube-shaped, just as in the tabernacle. But in the case of the temple, all the measurements were doubled. Moreover, the front court of the temple was divided into several courts. And along the side walls Solomon made three floors of rooms for all kinds of services. The stone walls on the inside he covered with wood. Everything—the stones as well as the wood—had been cut in advance so that the temple could be assembled very quietly; the sound of the hammer, the ax and the saw was not heard. It was as though the Israelite workmen were deeply impressed with the holiness of the house they were building.

While the building was underway, the Word of the Lord came to Solomon with the promise that the Lord would live in the midst of Israel and would keep His Word concerning David's house. At the same time, this Word called Solomon to walk according to all the commandments and instructions of the Lord. This revelation gave Solomon new strength as the building progressed and made him understand anew the holiness of the Lord's covenant.

The walls of the Lord's house were overlaid with gold. In this gold the glory and holiness of the God of the covenant shone forth. The golden covering was decorated with carvings of rosebuds and open flowers, of cherubs (angels) and palm trees. The tabernacle in the desert could not be decorated with carvings of palm trees, but now Israel lived in the land of peace. In the Holy of Holies the king placed two statues of cherubs whose outstretched wings touched each other as well as the walls. These huge statues, too, were made of wood and were overlaid with gold.

It took seven years to build the temple, which was finished in the eleventh year of Solomon's reign. The temple represented the whole earth, which would one day be holy to the Lord.

The building of the royal palace. Immediately after the temple was completed, Solomon began with the building of a royal palace. That God was King over Israel was expressed in the fact that He had given Israel a king who ruled in His name. Therefore it was necessary for the royal palace to be closely related to the temple. The palace would have to share in the luster of the temple. It would have to be a glorious building too.

The palace consisted of different sections. In the front was the Hall of the Forest of Lebanon. This hall took its name from the lower floor, which consisted of a forest of 45 cedar pillars. This part of the palace served as the king's arsenal, a storage room for his weapons. Behind it was the entrance hall with the Hall of Justice. There the throne was placed, and there the king gave audiences and judged legal matters. Then came the living quarters of the king himself, behind which was a wing set aside for the queen, Pharaoh's daughter.

This palace, too, was a marvelous structure. In the splendor of Israel's king, the people were shown a reflection of the glory of God. Wasn't our King, the Lord Jesus Christ, also exalted in glory by God and made to dwell in heavenly places, so that we would see the glory of God in the splendor of our King?

The furnishings and equipment of the temple. It took thirteen years to build the king's palace. During those years the furnishings and equipment of the temple were made. Solomon did not want to put the tabernacle's altars, the candle holder, the table of showbread, and the copper basin and all that came with it in the temple. They would look far too small there. He had new furnishings and equipment made on a larger scale. The copper basin was replaced by the bronze "sea" (a huge, round tank) supported by twelve cast bronze oxen plus ten four-wheeled movable stands. Replacing the one candle holder were ten candelabra. But he did not have a new ark made. The special sign of God's presence remained the same as in the desert.

To take care of the finer work, Hiram, the king of Tyre, had sent Solomon a master craftsman whose name was also Hiram. This craftsman was especially gifted in the detailed work that needed doing.

He first turned his attention to the two pillars which were erected in the front court or porch of the temple. They were lofty pillars with beautifully decorated capitals. These two pillars were completely unique in one sense: they received individual names. One was called *Jachin* ("He confirms"), and the other was named *Boaz* ("In Him is strength"). Both names pointed to the fact that this royal rule was forever sure. Solomon could give the pillars these names on the basis of the promise in the covenant with David. It is true that the temple was later destroyed, but the sovereign rule of God over His people by a son out of David's house stands forever sure in the Christ.

It had been David's desire to build a house for the Lord. When he was not allowed to carry out his plan, he made many preparations by gathering materials that Solomon now used. David had saved up so many treasures for the temple's construction that Solomon could not use them all. The treasures that were left Solomon put away so that in time they could be used for the holy service.

The Lord's presence in the temple. Once everything was finished, Solomon gathered the representatives of the entire people to bring the ark of the covenant into the temple. In a stately procession, the priests carried the ark plus all the furnishings and equipment used in the tent erected by David for the ark. As this procession moved ahead, Solomon, together with the people, offered countless sacrifices.

Finally the priests put the ark in its place in the Holy of Holies or inner sanctuary, under the cherubs. In the ark were the stone tablets on which the law of the covenant had been engraved. As soon as the priests left the sanctuary, a cloud filled the temple, and the priests were not able to continue with the service. The glory of the Lord, that is, the glory of His grace, was revealed there. This house would be the proof that the Lord would dwell in the midst of Israel according to the grace of His covenant.

In this Israel was richly blessed. It is true that the temple has passed away, but today the indwelling of the Lord is far more glorious. The fullness of His grace was in the Christ and is still in the Christ. In His grace He came to live in His people when the Holy Spirit was poured out.

Now think for a moment of the shining gold of the temple. In it shone the holiness of the Lord. God wishes to sanctify His people in order that His holiness may be glorified in them. Today, too, the Lord is a glorious King among His people.

Overjoyed by this sign of God's indwelling, Solomon said: "The LORD has said that he would dwell in darkness." The Lord still chose to dwell in the dark inner sanctuary behind the curtains (the Holy of Holies), and He hid much of His glory in the cloud. Reconciliation through the cross of the Christ had not yet taken place. One day, because of the Christ, God's glory would be seen in all its splendor. Solomon was grateful that there was now a permanent place for God's house.

Then Solomon turned around with his face toward the people. The one who was Israel's king and head in the name of the Lord proceeded to bless the people in the name of the Lord. In blessing them, Solomon remembered the covenant made with David and praised the Lord for the fulfillment of the promise. The people stood as they received this blessing. And we, in faith, receive the blessing of our King in heaven.

The king's prayer. Then the king knelt in front of all the people and stretched out his hands toward heaven and prayed: "There is no God like You! You have fulfilled Your promise to David. Along with that promise You gave us the calling to walk before Your face. Fulfill Your promise now. It is true that You do not dwell in a temple made with hands, for You fill the heavens and the earth with Your presence. May the presence of Your forgiving grace be known here! Show us that Your eyes are over this house night and day by hearing the prayers which are sent up to You from this place! When people come here to seek justice from You, Lord, hear them. Curse the guilty and bless the righteous. When You visit Your people because of their sins or their enemies defeat them or You send them drought or a bad harvest and the people return to You confessing their sins, then hear and forgive and grant deliverance! If one of Your people standing here cries out to You confessing his sin, hear him and forgive him so that men may fear You all the days of their lives. Yes, even if a stranger of any nation of the world calls on You here, hear and answer him in order that all the peoples of the earth may know Your name! When Your people go out to battle and they pray to You here, give them victory over their enemies! Even when Your people have been led into captivity because of their sins and they cry out to You in a foreign land, remembering this city and this temple, hear and forgive them, O Lord, and bring Your people back!

Show in all this that You have chosen this people to be Your people!"

Then Solomon blessed the people again. He praised the Lord and pronounced a benediction: "May the Lord continuously incline our hearts to serve Him. Then Israel will live in honor, and all the nations will know that the Lord—and no one else—is God."

The dedication of the temple. After this benediction, Solomon and all Israel dedicated the temple by way of thousands of peace offerings. The king had to consecrate the middle section of the front court as an altar, for the altar designated for burnt offerings was too small to handle all the sacrifices.

In connection with the peace offerings, Solomon and the people celebrated a sacrificial meal. The king and the people were one in their fellowship with the Lord. For seven days they celebrated together. On the eighth day, Solomon sent the people home. The people blessed their king and went home full of joy on account of all the goodness the Lord had given Israel because of His covenant with David. The result was that life became a continuous feast for the Israelites.

The situation of God's people in our time is no different. They could well offer the Lord thousands of sacrifices, for every day they are privileged to give themselves and all they possess to God, for Christ's sake. In fellowship with their King, the Lord Jesus Christ, they enjoyed the Lord's goodness. For believers, then, life becomes one continuous feast. Especially in the church, God's people are strengthened continually in their fellowship with the Lord.

The Lord's answer to prayer. After the dedication ceremonies in the temple, the Lord appeared to Solomon in a dream, just as He had appeared to him in Gibeon at the beginning of his reign. The Lord told him that He had heard his prayer and had hallowed the house Solomon had built for Him. His eyes and His heart would always be there to show forth His grace. But the king would have to walk in the ways of the Lord: only then would the Lord fulfill His promise to David. Should Solomon and his house turn away from the Lord to serve other gods, the Lord would uproot Israel from the land. The temple, which would then be destroyed, would become a disgrace to Israel and a sign of the judgment which the Lord had brought upon His people.

However, the Lord would always be true to His promise to David; He would never break His Word. But if the king and the people became unfaithful, the fulfillment of the promise would come by way of shame and disgrace, by way of judgment.

The king and the people did indeed become unfaithful. Over against their unfaithfulness, the faithfulness of the Lord's grace in the eternal sovereign rule of the Christ shines all the more brilliantly.

The organization of the kingdom. Solomon completed many more building projects. He built cities and fortified them. Hiram, the king of Tyre, lent him money for these projects. Solomon did not want to use the treasures of the house of the Lord for this purpose.

Solomon thought he could repay Hiram by giving him 20 cities in the northern part of the land, cities which were still inhabited mainly by Canaanites. But Hiram would not accept those cities as repayment; he found them too insignificant. In all probability Solomon later paid the debt out of his own resources. Not one portion of Israel's inheritance was lost to Israel through this proposal on Solomon's part.

The king strengthened Jerusalem's walls. Everywhere in the land he built storage cities and cities to keep his chariots. He completely subdued the remaining Canaanites and put them to work for the public good. The Israelites themselves were free people.

The queen, Pharaoh's daughter, went to live in her palace. The worship service in the temple was regulated. The great feasts were now held in Jerusalem. It was forbidden to sacrifice to the Lord any longer on the high places throughout the land.

Together with Hiram, Solomon built a fleet of ships in a shipyard on the Red Sea. The fleet went back and forth to Ophir, bringing much gold into the king's treasury.

The kingdom was strong and well organized. Was there no danger that the king and the people would begin to trust in the strength of the kingdom instead of in the Lord's grace? If they made this mistake, the people together with their king would become estranged from the Lord. Then sin would be just around the corner. With all the blessings and all the strength the Lord gives us, we still have to remain humble before Him!

25: The Light of the World

I Kings 10-11

When the Lord pronounced judgment on Solomon's sin, He said He would give one tribe to his son, "for the sake of David my servant and for the sake of Jerusalem which I have chosen." Here Jerusalem is mentioned specifically as the city the Lord has chosen. Later, in I Kings 11:36, that statement is amplified: Jerusalem is "the city where I have chosen to put my name."

The Lord chose Jerusalem in order to reveal His name there. This revelation of grace was to be a light to the world. For the sake of the Christ, who would come from David's line, the Lord gave His revelation at Jerusalem. Because of His insistence on revealing Himself at Jerusalem, we can be sure that He will uphold David's house. The lamp of David will not be extinguished.

As long as Solomon lived by the light of the revelation of grace, he was truly enlightened; he was a light to this world. The queen of Sheba honored him accordingly. In I Kings 10:1 we read that she heard about the fame of Solomon "concerning the name of the LORD." It was known throughout the world that Solomon was indebted to the Lord's grace for his wisdom. Thus the queen of Sheba encountered the light of grace. That's why the Christ could point to the queen of Sheba's visit to Solomon when He talked about His rejection at the hands of the Jews (Luke 11:29-32).

This is not to say that the queen of Sheba became a true believer. She was amazed at the glory of this light and at the solution it offered for life's deepest questions. Yet her amazement is no proof that her heart learned to rest in the truth of God's grace in the Redeemer.

Solomon, however, became estranged from his dependence on God's revelation of grace. He came to trust in his own wisdom and insight. As a result he became the "enlightened monarch" of his time. Such

212

"enlightenment" always leads to too much tolerance—hence the altars dedicated to idols, right near Jerusalem, the place where God revealed Himself.

Ten tribes would be torn from David's house; only one tribe would remain. As far as numbers go, this statement is not exact. Judah remained in David's house together with a large part of the tribe of Benjamin as well as the tribe of Simeon, whose territory was enclosed by Judah's territory. The number ten is to be read as a symbol of fullness in this context. "Israel" according to the flesh falls away from David's house. But mercy overtakes judgment: one tribe remains. A remnant is saved. Here, in this grace in the midst of judgment, we have abiding enlightenment for the world.

I Kings 11:40 points back to verse 26: because Jeroboam lifted up his hand against the king, Solomon sought to kill him. Jeroboam probably stirred up that revolt among the tribes of Joseph during the building of the walls of Jerusalem, when he had authority over many men.

The incentive for the revolt was the promise the Lord had given him through the prophet Ahijah. That response on Jeroboam's part was certainly a misuse of this promise. David once received such a promise, but he did not lift up his hand against Saul. Jeroboam should have awaited the fulfillment of the promise from the hand of God.

There was a significant difference, however, between Jeroboam's situation and David's. Jeroboam must have known that Israel, according to the Lord's promise, was to be blessed forever in the house of David. When Ahijah announced the judgment on Solomon's house, Jeroboam should have sought to avert that judgment by prayer. Instead he accepted the promise all too eagerly, even though it contained judgment for him too. Because of this eagerness, his actions stand condemned from the beginning. Jeroboam did not know the holy fear of the Lord's grace.

Main thought: *The world's only enlightenment is the revelation of the Lord's grace in the Christ.*

The light of the world in Solomon's wisdom. The fame of Solomon's wisdom spread to all nations. It also reached the queen of Sheba. The people of her kingdom heard that Solomon was indebted for his wisdom to the revelation of the Lord's grace. Solomon gave all the honor to the God who had made a covenant with Israel.

The queen of Sheba herself traveled to Jerusalem to hear Solomon's wisdom and confront him with some of the most serious

questions that life poses. She arrived with an impressive retinue
and asked Solomon all the questions that were on her mind. There
was not a single question he could not answer. Not only was it impossible to trap him in his own words, time and again the light of
the highest wisdom illuminated the darkness of the queen's heathen
mind. Thus Solomon was a type of the Christ, who always gave
answers revealed by God in His covenantal grace. The solution to
all of the ultimate questions life poses is to be found in the grace of
the Lord.

When the queen of Sheba heard Solomon's wise words and
saw the splendor and riches of his court and the order of the
ceremonies, she could not contain her amazement and ecstasy. If a
type of the Christ made such an impression on her, think of the
impression the Christ Himself must make on everyone who knows
Him by faith!

The queen of Sheba confessed that she had not been told even
the half of what she now saw and heard. Initially she had refused
to believe everything she was told about Solomon, but now she
was convinced. Solomon's servants she considered fortunate. And
she praised the Lord, who looked on Solomon with pleasure and
set him on the throne of Israel. The Lord must indeed love the
Israelites to give them such a king. How much truth this heathen
queen saw! It was eternal love for Israel, for Christ's sake, that
moved the Lord to give Israel a type of the Christ in Solomon.

We do not know whether the queen of Sheba became a
believer and submitted in her heart to the Lord's grace. When she
praised the Lord, she could conceivably have regarded Him as one
of the gods alongside the gods of the other nations. In any case,
she came from afar ("from the ends of the earth," as the Lord
Jesus said) to hear the wisdom of Solomon, and she was enchan-
ted.

When the Lord Jesus was on earth and displayed a wisdom
far greater than Solomon's, the Jews remained indifferent. Today
we have His wisdom in His Word. We live very near it, but often
we are neither delighted nor amazed. Could it be that the queen of
Sheba will rise up against us on the day of judgment if our ecstasy
has not exceeded hers?

The queen of Sheba gave Solomon a great gift of gold and
precious gems. She also gave him a large quantity of spices from

her country—such an abundance of them as never again came to Jerusalem. This was in addition to the treasures of gold, jewels and precious wood which Solomon received from other nations. With that wood he continued to decorate the temple and the palace. The splendor in Jerusalem could never be great enough if it was to reflect something of the glory of the Christ.

Solomon also gave the queen of Sheba a gift that was worthy of his majesty. She returned to her own country enriched in spirit. Think of how much more the Christ gives us when we worship Him!

At the summit of culture. The value of the gold which Solomon received annually could hardly be measured anymore. The king had 200 large shields and 300 smaller ones made from it. On solemn occasions these shields were carried in front of the king. At the place where he gave addresses and judged legal matters, he erected a magnificent throne overlaid with gold and inlaid with ivory. On each side of the throne stood two lions, and there were two lions on each of the six steps that led up to the throne. The lion figures symbolized Solomon's royal sovereignty. The king's drinking vessels were of solid gold.

In those days the value of silver was roughly comparable to the value of building bricks, and the wood of the costly cedars was assigned about the same value as wild fig trees! A continuous supply of all these treasures peculiar to the various countries kept coming in—gold and silver, ivory and apes and peacocks. From Egypt came horses and chariots and the most expensive clothes.

From every part of the world people came to Solomon to hear the wisdom God had put in his heart. He was at the summit of the culture of his time. There was nothing the Lord would not give him, for Solomon was to be a type of the Christ, in whose hands are all the world's treasures. The Christ does not despise and reject those treasures; He takes possession of the earth with all that is in it and will one day make it all completely holy again. In other words, one day the Christ will give the entire earth to those who belong to Him, to use for God's honor. And He is already making the whole world holy: in this life He gives the world to those who belong to Him so that they will use it to honor

God. The entire world's development is for the Christ and His
people.

Yet such possession of the world's wealth also has its dangers.
The Christ possesses all that is properly His only to use it for God's
honor. Would Solomon be able to continue possessing all that
God had given him in that spirit? And will we be able to possess
what is properly ours (in the Christ) for God's honor alone? Only
if we remain close to Him and rely on the power of His Spirit will
we be able to use all that we possess for the Lord.

"Enlightened" tolerance. Solomon did not escape the danger.
How easy it was for him in his mind to detach his wisdom and
wealth from the Lord's grace! Besides, there was something else in
Solomon's life that made him stray from the proper path. He had
taken a great many wives. In this respect, too, he wanted to outdo
the other monarchs of his time. But heathen customs were introduced into his court through these wives.

Among the wives were many from the nations with which the
Israelites were forbidden to intermarry. These wives did not give
up their idol worship when they came to Jerusalem. In time
Solomon was led astray by them. They flattered him and told him
that he was the most enlightened ruler of his time. Thus they made
him feel proud of the wisdom which God had bestowed upon him.
Then he no longer saw this wisdom as a gift of the Lord's grace.

Solomon's wives went further with their flattery and lies:
shouldn't an enlightened ruler like Solomon have an appreciative
eye for the progress that was to be found among the other nations?
This progress, they declared, was certainly no gift from the Lord,
the God of Israel. It was the fruit of other powers, powers which
those nations venerated as gods. Surely Solomon had to
acknowledge the existence of those powers. As an enlightened
monarch, he could not be so narrow-minded as to recognize only
the service of the Lord and reject idol worship as a lie and an
abomination. Surely Solomon would permit his wives to continue
with their worship of their own idols, even though they admitted
that the Lord was Israel's God and that it was He who had made
Solomon great.

Thus Solomon was led astray by his wives. He allowed altars

for the idols to be erected near Jerusalem—on the holy ground which was to be cleansed of the Canaanites so that only the Lord would be served there. The idols were worshiped right in front of the Lord, who revealed the presence of His grace in the temple!

Solomon allowed this despite the fact that the Lord had already appeared to him twice in his dreams. How close he had been to the Lord! And how far he drifted away from Him! How could the Lord ever permit anything or anyone to be worshiped alongside Himself? If we do not live wholly by faith in the Lord's grace and live wholly *for* the Lord, we are not serving Him only.

Light in the judgment. For this sin the Lord was angry with Solomon, for he had now broken the Lord's covenant. For the sake of the Lord's grace over His people, Solomon and his house would have to be rejected, just as Saul had earlier been rejected.

The Lord told Solomon that He would tear the kingdom away from him and give it to his servant. The judgment seemed final. Yet the Lord remembered His eternal covenant with David. David was to have a son sitting on the throne forever. This promise would not be entirely obscured. The Lord would allow David's house to continue reigning over one tribe.

It seemed as though the great mass of the people was lost to the covenant with David; only a small remnant remained under the protection of the blessing on that house. The Lord did this because He had chosen Jerusalem for the revelation of His grace when He made His covenant with David. The light in Jerusalem was not to be obscured. Because the light of God's grace continued to shine from there to the peoples, there was constant hope for David's house.

Besides, the Lord promised that the division in Israel would not come during Solomon's lifetime. This, too, was because of the covenant with David. For the sake of that covenant, David's son, in all his wisdom and splendor, was a type of the Christ. This light could not just be permitted to disappear into the darkness. Thus God's grace toward Israel, given in the house of David, overcame the judgment after all.

The Lord raised up formidable enemies against Solomon's kingdom even during his lifetime. In the south Hadad threatened him. Hadad was an Edomite of royal blood who had somehow escaped when Joab carried out a series of executions in Edom. Hadad had fled to Egypt, but after David's death he returned to his country.

In the north Rezon rose to power. He gathered together a gang made up of men who belonged to his master Hadadezer, king of Syria, who had been defeated by David. This Rezon had been successful in conquering Damascus and establishing a kingdom there.

But the most dangerous opponent was Jeroboam, a man of Ephraim's tribe. When Solomon took measures to complete the building of Jerusalem's walls, a certain young man of great ability caught his eye. This young man, Jeroboam, was among the workmen involved in the project and was put in charge of all the work to be done by Ephraim and Manasseh.

One day Jeroboam met the prophet Ahijah outside the city. The prophet was wearing a new robe, which he proceeded to tear into twelve pieces. He gave ten pieces to Jeroboam, together with a message from the Lord. The Lord would tear the kingdom away from Solomon's house and give ten tribes to Jeroboam. Ahijah stressed that this would not happen during Solomon's lifetime and that David's house would be left with one tribe and Jerusalem. If Jeroboam would walk in the ways of the Lord, the Lord would build him a lasting house too. In this way the Lord would humble David's house. But this humbling would only be temporary. One day the full glory of that house would shine again—in the Christ.

Jeroboam did not sense the horror of these prophetic words, and he did not seek to avert the judgment on David's house by prayer. He certainly knew about the blessing which had been promised to Israel in that house. All too eagerly he accepted the promise for himself. He did not wait for the Lord to put him on the throne, as David had done. Contrary to the express Word of the Lord, he and his men revolted against Solomon. Therefore Solomon sought to kill him, and he had to flee to Egypt. The jealousy between the tribes of Ephraim and Judah, the two most important tribes, had been stirred up again by Jeroboam's revolt.

Solomon's death. Solomon reigned in Jerusalem for 40 years. Then he died. The kingdom was still one.

Solomon had sinned greatly. In that respect he differed from the Christ, who was to come after him. Yet, grace did not depart from David's house. And we continue to remember vividly the splendor of Solomon, which we recognize as a prophecy pointing ahead to the glory of the Christ.

Ephraim against Judah

26: David's House Humbled

I Kings 12:1-24

We read in I Kings 12:24 that the division in Israel was of the Lord. The Lord was following His own way in bringing His deliverance. He humbled David's house so that it would not autocratically cut itself adrift from Him, as Solomon had begun to do. If David's house were to rule in an autocratic manner, it would only be a curse to Israel and would lead all Israel to revolt against the Lord. Because of Christ's grace toward David's house, the Lord had to humble it.

As Scripture views it, "Israel" turns away from David's house. That is to say, the great mass of Israel turns away. This makes the destruction of unfaithful Israel a certainty. But first sin must run its full course in this Israel. Only then will it be ripe for judgment.

The one tribe that remains with David's house is not simply the tribe of Judah as such. In Judah, too, many were lost. The one tribe of which Scripture speaks represents the remnant which is saved by David's Son. Thus Israel's destruction by the Assyrians does not completely parallel the Babylonian destruction of Judah. For the remnant there is hope. The difference between the fate of the two nations also comes out in the fact that few of the ten tribes are restored to Canaan.

True, the division was of the Lord, but it came about through the sins of men. Ephraim's jealousy of Judah provoked this division. Abandoning David's house meant breaking the Lord's covenant, for all Israel knew about the promise given to that house. Willfully that Word of the Lord was rejected.

Even so, David's house was to blame for this sin. Solomon had set the example for this emancipation, this break with David's house, when he emancipated himself from the Word of the Lord. Solomon's "enlightenment" had also "enlightened" the people of Israel.

Main thought: *The Lord humbles David's house in order to be a blessing to His people through it.*

The revolt. After Solomon's death, all Israel gathered at Shechem, ostensibly to make Solomon's son Rehoboam king. But the people were having second thoughts. It was already significant that they had gathered at Shechem instead of Jerusalem, which would have been the proper place to meet. Shechem was located in the territory of Ephraim, a tribe that was already envious of the tribe of Judah. In addition, Jeroboam had been summoned from Egypt, and he presided over the gathering.

Rehoboam went to Shechem. That must have been humiliating for him. When he arrived there, he heard the people complaining about the yoke which his father Solomon had laid upon them. The people laid down a condition for recognizing Rehoboam as their king: he would have to lighten their yoke.

The complaint about Solomon's yoke was in large measure a pretext. Solomon had indeed demanded much from the people, but the way the people were now talking showed that they failed to appreciate the blessings they had enjoyed. To be sure, Solomon was partly to blame for this lack of appreciation. When he turned away from the Lord and his splendor no longer served to glorify the Lord's grace, his reign seemed highhanded and his splendor seemed robbery. But the fact remains that the people were ungrateful. They could have followed the path of consultation, but the attitude with which they approached Rehoboam and their insistence on imposing a condition meant that revolt was in the air. The people wanted to be free of the yoke of David's house.

Folly in David's house. Rehoboam asked for a three-day postponement to make his decision. He consulted with the old men who had been his father's counselors. They urged him to yield. If Rehoboam would be a servant to the people now, they would be his servants forever. But this advice did not satisfy Rehoboam. The young men with whom he had grown up advised him to treat the people harshly and tell them that he would make their yoke immeasurably heavier.

Rehoboam chose to act on the advice of the young men. He was already irritated at having to come to Shechem. Was he now to give in altogether and become a servant of the people? He did not want to humble himself any further.

This was not just a tactical mistake on Rehoboam's part. It is by no means certain that the people would have acknowledged him as king even if he had taken the advice of the older men. His refusal to humble himself in any way showed that he did not see the guilt that had come over his house because of his father's sin. He should have sought the face of the Lord and been prepared to humble himself for God's sake. In that case he would have been a king after God's own heart. Now, however, he spoke in an autocratic and tyrannical way. This foolishness was a judgment on Solomon's sin.

Rupture. Rehoboam's uncompromising response brought the revolt to a head. The people shouted: "What portion have we in David? We have no inheritance in the son of Jesse. To your tents, O Israel! Look now to your own house, O David!" Then the people forsook Rehoboam. They stoned the treasurer whom Rehoboam sent to try and persuade them to come back. The king himself had to mount his chariot in great haste and flee to Jerusalem.

Did the people know what they were saying and doing? They knew about the promise which had been given to David's house. Willfully they rejected that promise and—with it—the Lord's covenant.

Shouldn't the Lord have responded by rejecting Israel? The Lord refused to abandon Israel at that point. First sin would have to run its full course—until Israel was ripe for judgment. One day the judgment of rejection would strike, the judgment which the Lord had already threatened through Moses. But for a long time to come, the Lord would wrestle with the sin in His unfaithful people Israel.

Division by the Lord. In one way, especially, the Lord continued to show His steadfast love to Israel: not all the tribes forsook the house of David. It was mainly the tribe of Judah that remained faithful, together with a section of Benjamin and the tribe of Simeon, as well as many members of other tribes scattered throughout Judah's territory.

Undoubtedly there were many even in Judah who did not believe the Lord's promise with their hearts and were lost. This one faithful tribe was a sign that a remnant in Israel would be saved by the grace of the Lord.

The ten tribes made Jeroboam their king. As soon as Rehoboam reached Jerusalem, he mobilized an army of 180,000 men to subdue Jeroboam and Israel by force. Through the prophet Shemaiah, the Lord forbade Rehoboam to fight. "This division," the Lord declared, "is My doing." Rehoboam obeyed the Word of the Lord and returned to Jerusalem. This was indeed a deep humiliation for David's house. Gone was the splendor of the past.

The Lord did this to humble the house of David again. Israel would have come to a thoroughly bad end if it had continued to follow Solomon's sinful paths. But if David's house humbled itself, there would still be some hope for it. Then, through that house, there would also be hope for Israel, which had suffered an immense indignity as a result of the rupture. That hope for David's house would not vanish, for it was guaranteed by the promise given to David.

27: Unquenchable Fire

I Kings 12:25—14:20

The prophet from Judah was prophesying about Josiah: on the altar in Bethel, Josiah would burn the bones of all who worshiped idols there. The main emphasis of the prophecy is that Josiah is coming. This Josiah would be a member of the house of David, the house from which Jeroboam tried to separate Israel completely by instituting calf worship. The son born of David's house is coming! The further import of this prophecy is that *the Christ* is coming.

The talk about digging up graves and burning bones points ahead to Israel's complete destruction, that is, the time when the name of Israel would be wiped out. In the same way, the Christ will destroy the godless among His people. According to Ahijah's prophecy, the ten tribes in their entirety would be uprooted and removed from the land.

Here we have the same thought we encountered in the preceding chapter; the mass of Israel will be destroyed while a remnant will be saved. In this section the prophecy is about the Christ: "He will clear his threshing floor . . . and the chaff he will burn with unquenchable fire" (Matt. 3:12).

Main thought: *The Christ will clear His threshing floor and burn the chaff with unquenchable fire.*

Complete separation from the house of David. Because the Lord stopped Rehoboam from going to war against the disloyal tribes, Jeroboam could begin his reign over those tribes in peace. He made Shechem (in the territory of Ephraim) his residence and fortified it. Later he moved the seat of government to Tirzah. He also fortified Penuel (Peniel) on the eastern side of the Jordan to protect that part of his kingdom.

Jeroboam concluded that if the people went up to Jerusalem each year for the great feasts, they would retain a connection with the house of David. In that case they might return to David's house and kill their new king. Therefore he wanted to separate them completely from David's house.

Jeroboam's analysis was correct: Jerusalem and the services in the temple belonged with the house of David. The revelation of the Lord's grace in Jerusalem was bound up with the promise made to David's house. If Jeroboam succeeded in separating the people completely from the house of David, he would also separate them from the ongoing revelation of God's grace. That chance he was willing to take.

After discussing this matter with his advisors, Jeroboam got them to agree to the erection of one golden calf in the north (at Dan) and another in the south (at Bethel). He chose Dan and Bethel for reasons of tradition. In earlier years there had been a temple with an idol at Dan. At Bethel the Lord had appeared to Jacob.

Jeroboam deliberately changed the times of the festivals from the seventh month to the eighth month. Anyone who wanted to serve as priest was welcome to the job. The Levites and the true priests were driven out of Jeroboam's kingdom.

Jeroboam himself led the people in offering sacrifices at the festival. To the assembled crowd he said: "Behold your gods, O Israel, who brought you up out of the land of Egypt." Here Jeroboam was using historic words. Aaron had used those same words when he spoke to the people at the foot of Mount Sinai after erecting the golden calf. Jeroboam was deliberately pointing back to that occasion in Israel's past. At Mount Sinai Moses was rejected as Israel's shepherd, and the covenant which the Lord revealed through Moses was rejected at the same time. Now the people and their king were rejecting all ties to the Son of David as the future Leader. They were thereby rejecting the covenant itself, just as they had done at Mount Sinai.

Jeroboam emphasized to all who were present that the intent was not to have the people turn away from the Lord. All the same, the rights of the Lord were being violated. Jeroboam's deed of making a representation of the Lord in the form of a calf was an abomination, a conscious denigration of the majesty of the Lord, a manifestation of a desire to have power over the Lord. Despite Jeroboam's words, Israel and its king were detaching themselves from the Lord at that festival.

Although there were still some faithful people who continued to go to Jerusalem, the mass of the people could not stand the yoke of the Lord's rights any longer. They were fed up with the kingship of David's house, which was governed so completely by the Lord's covenant.

Shouldn't the Lord have rejected the people at that point? He kept wrestling with their sin. This went on for a long time. Only when they were ripe for judgment did He reject them. But that coming rejection was already announced.

The prophecy about David's son. While Jeroboam was busy offering the sacrifice at the festival, a prophet from Judah suddenly appeared. The prophet called out: "A son shall be born to the house of David. That son, Josiah by name, will burn upon this altar the priests who are serving here at the time. He will dig up the bones of those who have served here before his time and burn them on the altar. Nothing will be left of them. Their names will be wiped out from among the people. As a sign that these words are from the Lord, this altar will split apart and the ashes will spill to the ground. This altar and all who serve here will be utterly cursed."

This prophecy was later fulfilled to the letter by Josiah, king of Judah. But we also think immediately of David's great Son, the Christ, who will fulfill this prophecy in another sense. He will forever wipe out from among His people those who served the Lord in appearance only. Their names will be wiped out along with them.

Beside himself with rage, Jeroboam cried: "Arrest that man!" But the hand he used to point at the prophet instantly became stiff. God's judgment was being revealed to Jeroboam—a judgment of the grace by which He wanted to save His people. Moreover, the altar split and the ashes fell to the ground. Overcome, Jeroboam asked the prophet to pray for him. The prophet did so, and the king's hand was restored.

Then the king asked the prophet to eat and drink with him at his house, promising to honor him with a gift. In this way Jeroboam wanted to restore something of his shattered authority. For him there was no other way out. This attempt failed, for the prophet refused the king's invitation, saying that the Lord had forbidden him to do any such thing. He was not even allowed to return by the same way he had come. No one was to try and bring him back. He was to have no fellowship with anyone in that accursed place. Then the prophet went his way. The Lord had completely rejected Bethel.

The grave to be spared. Unfortunately, the prophet was not faithful to the end. In Bethel there lived an older prophet. He had kept silent about the abomination of the idol worship and had continued to live in Bethel. How could he stand the sight of it?

Now the prophet heard from his sons what had happened. His sons had seen which way the young prophet from Judah went. Immediately the older prophet had his donkey saddled and rode off in pursuit. When he caught up with him, he invited him to turn around and eat at his home. When the younger man refused, the older man declared that he was also a prophet and that an angel had commanded him to bring back the prophet from Judah. Convinced, the younger prophet went with him.

What could have moved this old man to take such action and even tell a lie? He knew that he had remained silent about the abomination in Bethel and that he was not justified in continuing to live there without protesting against it. The Lord had made this known all too clearly by means of the prohibition imposed on the young prophet. If he could now persuade the prophet from Judah to return with him, his own stay in Bethel and his silence about the abomination there would not seem as serious a sin. Therefore, everything depended on getting the young prophet to come back with him.

And what moved the young prophet to give in? He knew for a certainty that the Lord did not want him to have any kind of contact with Bethel and its inhabitants. But being the bearer of the Word of complete curse was too heavy a burden for him. If an older colleague lived in Bethel, then it might be true that the Lord was sending him another message through the angel, as the older prophet claimed.

In his mind the young prophet was toying with the Lord's wrath. He did not care to see it so absolute, so final. Such wrath was too much for him. Thus the two prophets helped each other down the wrong path. The Lord demands absolute submission to His Word in His covenant, even when that Word is a message of damnation.

When the two prophets were seated at the table in Bethel, the Spirit of the Lord suddenly came over the older prophet, who then pronounced judgment on his guest. The young prophet, he declared, would not be buried in his family's grave. That was a judgment: the story of his life would be told and retold in Israel. A testimony of the Lord would always go forth from his grave. Yet, even in that judgment there was a note of grace to be heard. The young prophet would not be wiped out from among his people, as the priests of Bethel would.

As the young prophet headed home, a lion killed him but did not tear him to pieces. It was a miracle that the lion did not devour him and also left his donkey's body alone. In that miracle the Lord was speaking.

The older prophet went to get the body and buried it in his own grave. He expressly commanded his sons to bury him in the same grave when he died, for the Word of the Lord would surely be fulfilled, just as it had always been fulfilled. Then, when the son from David's house came to dig up the bones, the grave shared by the two prophets would be spared because the younger man had been a prophet of the Lord in spite of his disobedience.

This prophecy was fulfilled literally: Josiah did spare that grave (II Kings 23:15-20). At the great judgment, the Christ, too, will know His own. Thus the grave of the prophet from Judah continued to serve as a witness, in accordance with the Word of the Lord. Fortunately, it spoke not only of judgment but also of grace.

A remnant. Jeroboam still did not repent after all that had happened. Consequently the Lord decided to announce the judgment that awaited Jeroboam's followers.

Jeroboam's son Abijah became desperately ill. Jeroboam told his wife to disguise herself and go to the prophet Ahijah, the one who had spoken to him in the Lord's name years before and told him that he would become king. To make the deceit perfect, she would bring the prophet a present while pretending to be a poor woman. Then the prophet would be sure to prophesy some good about the father of the sick boy. That prophecy would surely be fulfilled, and their son would get well again.

What foolishness! It was not the word of the prophet that had the power to heal but the Word of the Lord! Moreover, the Lord was capable of revealing all things to the prophet—including the identity of the woman who came to see him!

Before Jeroboam's wife got to the prophet, the Lord revealed everything to Ahijah, who could no longer see because of his advanced age. When she arrived, he reproached her in the name of the Lord for her deceit and told her that the Lord would destroy Jeroboam's house because Jeroboam had rejected His covenant. The names of all the men of the house of Jeroboam would be wiped out, like the names of all the priests of Bethel. Anyone belonging to Jeroboam who died in the city would be eaten by the dogs, and anyone who died in the open country would be eaten by the birds of the heavens. When she re-entered the city, she was told, her son would die. All Israel would bury him with honor and mourn over him, for in this son there was still something of the Lord's grace at work. The Lord would raise up someone to destroy all who remained of Jeroboam's house. This destroyer was already born. Eventually all of sinful Israel would be uprooted from the land and scattered to the other side of the Euphrates.

When Jeroboam's wife entered her house in Tirzah, the boy died. In accordance with the Word of the Lord, he had an honorable burial. By God's grace there is always some light in the darkness. All of sinful Israel and the entire house of Jeroboam would be destroyed, but the honorable burial of this boy, to whom God showed mercy, proclaimed that a remnant would be saved from among Israel.

After a reign of 22 years, Jeroboam died. His family was under the curse and would be destroyed as a sign that the Lord would eventually destroy all of Israel that turned away from Him in apostasy.

28: Estrangement in Judah

I Kings 14:21—15:24
II Chronicles 11:5—16:14

In the period immediately after the rupture between Israel and Judah, there was hostility between the two kingdoms. Not until the time of Jehoshaphat and Ahab did Israel and Judah become allies—and then for evil purposes!

Because of His covenant with David, the Lord did not have the same relationship to Israel as to Judah. His relationship to Judah comes to expression particularly in I Kings 14:22: "And they provoked him to jealousy." Because of Judah's sin, the Lord was provoked to jealousy—the jealousy of a loving husband who does not receive his wife's full love. It is clear from this expression how much the Lord's love went out to Judah and to the house of David.

Judah, however, did not give itself to the Lord in complete love. There was spiritual destitution—a loss of favor with God and communion with Him. This resulted in an impoverishment of life in all its relationships. Azariah the prophet spoke about this as recorded in II Chronicles 15:5-6. This impoverishment came to typical expression in the story of the bronze shields made at Rehoboam's command to replace the golden shields.

We should note that Judah went even farther down the path of sin than Israel during this period. In Israel the sin went no further than idol worship, but we already read about horrible abominations in Judah. Although the Lord sought Judah in His love, Judah could not lose itself in Him. The typical words for this period are: his heart was "not wholly true" to the Lord. The less the people offered the sacrifice of their heart's love in Jerusalem, the more they busied themselves with the cultic services on the high places. Their spiritual energy was not consumed in the worship and service of the Lord. That energy was released in other ways and came to expression in their cultic and sensual passions.

In I Kings 15:2 and 10, we encounter a textual difficulty: we read that Abijam's mother was Maacah, a daughter of Absalom, while the very same name is given to the "mother" of Asa, Abijam's son. The solution may be that in the latter instance we are to take *mother* to mean *grandmother*. In Asa's time Maacah still served as queen mother, perhaps because Asa's mother had died at a young age.

We read that Asa's heart was true to the Lord all his days. Yet, later we are told that he relied on the king of Syria and not on the Lord (II Chron. 16:7). Neither did he seek the Lord at the time of his illness. At the end of Asa's life, his faith was not steadfast. In spite of this, Scripture judges him in merciful love.

Main thought: *The people of Judah provoke the Lord to jealousy by withdrawing their hearts from Him.*

Destitution due to estrangement. For the first three years of his reign, Rehoboam served the Lord and strengthened his kingdom. The Lord's favor went out to him as David's son. He enjoyed the privilege of being allowed to reign in Jerusalem, "the city which the LORD had chosen out of all the tribes of Israel to put his name there." The Lord had indeed humbled the house of David. But how He continued to seek out that house in His love and reach out to Judah's kingdom for His covenant's sake! How wonderful life could have been there!

When Rehoboam felt that he was securely established in his kingdom, he no longer gave himself wholeheartedly to the Lord. Because of his earlier humiliation, he had felt small before the Lord, but now that he began feeling stronger, it appeared that love for the Lord was not the foremost motive in his heart. He was no longer zealous for the name of the Lord.

All of Judah broke away from the Lord too. The people could not give themselves to Him with undivided heart, and they did not enjoy His rich favor. As a result, life in all its relationships became impoverished.

Abominable sins were committed regularly in Judah. The less the people worshiped the Lord in Jerusalem with their whole hearts, the more involved they became with their own willful practices on the high places. Such practices had been forbidden, but they gave the people more self-satisfaction because they were suited to what the people themselves wanted.

Through this worship on the high places, the people made the Lord into a local deity on the same level as the Baals. More and more, they embraced idol worship. The Canaanites who still remained in the land came out into the open again with their abominations and seduced Judah.

All of this went on among the Lord's people, the people that belonged to Him in His love. When they held back their hearts from the Lord and gave themselves to other things, the Lord became jealous. In particular, He sought the love of David's son. Would the house of David put the great Son to shame, the Son who would one day be born of that house?

In His jealous love the Lord chastised Judah. Shishak, the king of Egypt, attacked the land with a huge army, took the fortified cities, and came up against Jerusalem. Then the prophet Shemaiah said to Rehoboam and to the princes of Judah that the Lord would allow Judah to fall into the hands of Shishak because the people had abandoned Him (see II Chron. 12:1-8).

It seemed as if the Lord was abandoning His people. Yet, precisely in this act of chastisement He was seeking them out. When the king and the princes of Judah heard what the prophet had to say, they humbled themselves before the Lord, saying: "The LORD is righteous." Thus the Lord had reached His goal: He had drawn the people closer to Himself.

The chastisement had to continue so that the people would clearly see the difference between their service of the Lord out of love and the service of idols on the part of other nations. For this reason the Lord caused Shishak to enter Jerusalem. He took the city and plundered it, but he did not destroy it. The fact that he plundered it was bad enough. Foreign eyes and foreign hands passed over the treasures which had been gathered in love by David and the people, the treasures which had glittered to the honor of the Lord's glory in Solomon's time. God's holy mountain was desecrated, and the hiddenness of His communion was profaned. Was it not safe, then, with the Lord?

Shishak also took away the golden shields which had been made at Solomon's command. After Shishak left Jerusalem and the kingdom was restored to order, Rehoboam replaced the golden shields with bronze ones, which were carried before him when he went up to the Lord's house. How superficial! Rehoboam hoped to keep up appearances by way of those bronze shields. It would have been better if he had not replaced them but admitted in humility before the Lord that the robbery was a result of his sins. Now the bronze shields were a manifestation of the destitution of life in the sphere of God's favor.

Rehoboam continued to turn away from the Lord; he was not rich in God. After a reign of seventeen years he died. During all this time the kingdoms of Judah and Israel had been on a war footing.

Inequality before the Lord. Rehoboam was succeeded by his son Abijam, which showed that the Lord was still being merciful toward David's house. The Lord fulfilled the promise He had made in His covenant with David. Yet, the heart of this son of David was not wholly true to the Lord, as the heart of David had been. Out of His sovereign grace and because of His covenant, the Lord still gave David a lamp in Jerusalem; the light of his house's rule was not extinguished in deep darkness.

Abijam marched with an army of 400,000 men against Jeroboam, who marshaled an army of 800,000 men against him. Before the battle started, Abijam told the soldiers of Israel that because they had rejected the house of David and the promise given to David, they were living in rebellion against the covenant of the Lord. In addition Abijam said: "You have departed from the Lord by serving idols, but here in Judah the Lord is honored in the temple according to His law."

Jeroboam sent a division of his army to attack Judah from the rear. When the soldiers of Judah saw that they were caught between two parts of Jeroboam's army, they called upon the Lord. Then the priests blew the trumpets so that the soldiers, in faith, would look to the Lord to come and assist them. And the Lord did give Judah the victory: 500,000 men of Israel fell, and Jeroboam's strength was broken for good. Abijam took several cities of Israel.

The Lord gave Judah the victory because Judah had called upon Him in its distress and trusted Him. The Lord chose *against* Israel and *for* Judah; He was on Abijam's side. But this was not to say that the Lord was close to Abijam or that Abijam was close to the Lord. The estrangement which had begun under Rehoboam continued. What would come of Judah if the people did not repent? Again and again, the covenant with David was the basis for new hope. Abijam, however, reigned for only three years. His light was soon extinguished.

A partial return to the Lord. A change for the better came during the time of Abijam's son Asa, who reigned for 41 years. For ten years the Lord gave Judah rest from its enemies. Clearly the Lord's favor rested upon the kingdom. Asa did indeed seek the Lord with his whole heart. The Spirit of the Christ was again present in him. For Christ's sake the Lord was gracious to Judah.

Asa wiped out the idol worship and strengthened the land. He urged the people to seek the Lord while they could still find Him. In His covenant the Lord is near His people with His favor and wishes to be found by them. This was also clear from the prosperity enjoyed by the kingdom of Judah in those days.

Asa mobilized a large army from Judah. But what good was such an army against the huge army of more than a million men with which the king of Ethiopia advanced on Judah at the end of the first decade of Asa's reign? Judah was overrun.

This must have been a strange affliction for Asa and his people, but even in this turn of events the Lord was tempting them to have faith. It worked: in the time of trial, that faith took on wings. Asa confessed that the Lord could help the weak as well as the strong. Thus he relied on the Lord, who then gave Judah a complete victory. The triumphant soldiers returned with much booty. The Lord is always working to draw out the faith of His people, to make that faith stronger and fuller in an effort to draw the people closer to Himself.

When Asa returned with the army, the prophet Azariah was led by God's Spirit to go out and meet them. He painted a picture of how impoverished life in Judah had become: people did not live close to the Lord, and therefore they were not close to each other either. This had been the cause of all the disturbance in the land. But now there had come a reversal. During the war, this reviving faith had continued to grow to maturity. Now the king and the people would have to be strong and persist in their faith. Then the Lord would show them His deliverance.

Encouraged by these words, Asa pressed on with the reformation. Drawn by the spirit of reform, many people from the other tribes came over to Judah, people who could no longer endure the apostasy of Israel's kingdom. This added to Judah's spiritual strength.

Asa held a mass meeting in Jerusalem. The people sacrificed to the Lord and renewed the covenant with Him. They swore an oath that anyone who did not seek the Lord would be put to death. And all Judah rejoiced at the oath, for the people had sworn with all their heart. The king's heart, too, was true to the Lord. He made this clear in how he dealt with his grandmother, who was still functioning as queen mother. Because she worshiped the image of a certain idol, the king removed her from her position and burned the image at the brook Kidron. He did not spare her feelings. The treasures of booty collected by Asa himself and by his father were consecrated and brought into the house of the Lord.

Thus Judah returned to the Lord again. Yet, Asa had not become so accustomed to the Lord that he sought Him in everything. After Asa reigned for 35 years, Baasha, the king of Israel, began to oppress Judah. It vexed Baasha that so many from his kingdom went up to Jerusalem to worship and even established residence in Judah. Therefore he pressed into Judah to a point near the city of Jerusalem. Ramah, which was a good two hours away from Jerusalem and commanded the road to the city, he turned into a strong fortress. At the time Asa was not able to offer resistance.

Shouldn't Asa have brought this matter before the Lord? He should have, but he committed an act of unbelief instead: he sent all the treasures from the Lord's house and from his palace to the king of Syria. In this way he persuaded Benhadad to break his alliance with Baasha and attack Israel's king in the northern part of his kingdom. This freed Asa from Baasha's pressure. He had the men of Judah take the stones and timber from Ramah and use them to build their own fortified cities. The way to Jerusalem was open again.

But the Lord's prophet Hanani reprimanded Asa for relying

on the king of Syria rather than on the Lord. The Lord would have been able to deliver both Baasha and the king of Syria into his hand. Hanani reminded Asa of the pronouncement of faith he had made in the battle against the Ethiopians. Whenever our hearts are true to Him, the Lord is present with His grace to deliver us. Apparently Asa withdrew his heart from the Lord and could not surrender to Him completely. From then on Asa would be involved in wars, for the Lord was withdrawing His favor from him and from Judah.

Because Asa had once lived by faith, it was hard for him to receive such admonition from the prophet. Clearly Asa did not escape the danger of regarding himself as a truly pious man and being proud as a result. He got angry at Hanani and put him in jail. Now he was in revolt against the Word of the Lord. The result was that the justice of his government also became corrupt; Asa oppressed some of the people (II Chron. 16:10). Bronze had again replaced gold in Judah.

In the thirty-ninth year of his reign, Asa's feet became diseased and his illness got worse. In this sickness he did not surrender to the Lord's mercy. Therefore he could not pray to the Lord in faith to be healed. In his sickness, too, there was estrangement between the Lord and him. Hence Asa sought deliverance only through physicians. The wisdom of the doctors and the power of medicine became his idols.

Asa was not steadfast in his faith, and Judah still had not returned fully to the Lord. History called for a better type of the Redeemer—and for the Redeemer Himself. After a reign of 41 years, Asa died.

29: Israel Forsaken

I Kings 15:25—16:34

In those days the Lord was provoked to jealousy by Judah, but Israel was abandoned by Him. This is apparent from the instability of the throne in Israel. The Lord had promised that He would build Jeroboam an enduring house if he would be faithful to Him (I Kings 11:38). Evidently the constancy of that house was linked to the kingship. Thus the people would be blessed through the house that governed them. But there was no longer any respect for the authority of the king in Israel. Every man set himself up as king, until finally the decisions were in the hands of the army.

This situation reveals the abandonment of Israel. Only under Christ's reign of grace and through the recognition of that reign does the earthly crown possess authority. In connection with this situation in Israel, we cannot help but think of the confusion in Europe in the twentieth century.

Omri's house had more authority, but that royal house strengthened itself *against* the Lord. Omri built the city of Samaria, where acts of apostasy were soon committed in the open. Samaria then came to stand over against Jerusalem, with idolatrous pretentions of its own.

It was the Lord who decreed this course of history. He forsook Israel on account of its sin in order to make it clear what would become of Israel if it was left to itself. Israel was in imminent danger of being absorbed in heathendom. At this point in its history, however, the Lord opened a new phase in the struggle via the person of Elijah.

Israel's basic sin was the rejection of David's house, that is, of the Christ. The split with Judah was indeed the Lord's doing. All the same, Israel should have continued to put its hope in deliverance through David's great Son. Now it had cut all ties with David and was at war with Judah.

241

Main thought: *The Lord forsakes Israel because of the split with the house of David in order to seek this nation later in His grace.*

The destruction of Jeroboam's house. Jeroboam wanted to separate Israel completely from the house of David and from the promise given to that house. This meant that he wanted to separate Israel from the Christ. That's why he established the idol worship in Israel. The Lord had declared that his house would be utterly wiped out because of this sin. The Lord's intention was to save Israel by this means.

Jeroboam was succeeded by his son Nadab, who walked in the ways of his father. During his reign, the judgment over his father's house was carried out. When Nadab was laying siege to Gibbethon, a city occupied by the Philistines, he was assassinated by Baasha. This Baasha, of the tribe of Issachar, had hatched a conspiracy. He had himself declared king and then wiped out the entire house of Jeroboam. Jeroboam's lamp was extinguished because he had rejected the Christ.

Increasing confusion. Because Israel rejected the promise to David's house, that is, the salvation which is in the Lord Jesus Christ, the kingdom fell apart at the seams. When we bow together before the sovereign rule of the Christ, we willingly subject ourselves to those whom He has placed in authority over us. If we are not subject to Him, we are putting ourselves first. Authority is a great responsibility for those who have received it, a responsibility to be born in the name of Christ. Everyone aspires to the glory of power. This is the situation in the world today, and it was not any different in the Israel of Baasha's days.

Baasha did not desire to be Israel's king in the name of the Lord, in order to lead the people back to Him. He had followed a treasonous path to gain the throne for himself, and he ruled in the spirit of Jeroboam. He continued to lead the people away from the Lord by means of the calf worship. For this reason the Lord brought the same judgment on his house as he himself had carried out on Jeroboam's house.

This judgment struck when Baasha's son Elah was king. During a banquet at which Elah became drunk, he was killed by Zimri, the commander of half his chariots. Then Zimri wiped out Baasha's entire family.

Zimri himself was only able to reign for seven days, because the army made Omri king in his place. As the confusion in Israel increased, the kingdom seemed to fall apart. The Lord had certainly forsaken Israel.

Consolidation against the Lord. Omri also had a rival, but he was able to overcome him. After a few years, he could consider himself assured of the throne. His power was confirmed.

However, Omri did not use his power to bring Israel back to the Lord. More than any of the kings before him, he led Israel down the path of idol worship and apostasy from the Lord. How could the Lord, incensed as He must have been, allow this to go on for so long? He let the people go their own way so that it would be clear what would come of the Israelites if they turned away from the Lord.

Omri bought a mountain in the middle of the land and built a fortified city on it, which he made the capital. He called the city *Samaria*, after the original owner of the mountain. Samaria was to compete with Jerusalem in strength and honor.

In Samaria the movement which set itself up in opposition to Jerusalem took shape. The city of Jerusalem with its temple was a witness to the service of the Lord according to His Word. Samaria would be a sign of life lived in freedom from the Lord.

Thus life in Israel strayed further and further away from the Lord. Such a process cannot be brought to a halt once it is in full swing. The end result had to be a complete break with the Lord. Yet, didn't the covenant hold for the kingdom of Israel too?

The worship of Baal. Omri was succeeded by his son Ahab. During his reign, Israel broke completely with the Lord. Ahab did more than just continue the worship of images. At first when the images were worshiped, the Lord was still worshiped in name. But Ahab pushed the name of the Lord aside completely and introduced the worship of the Baals. He did so under the influence of his wife Jezebel, a heathen, the daughter of Ethbaal, king of the Sidonians. In Samaria he built a temple for Baal, in which he erected an altar for Baal and a column for Astarte, his female counterpart.

When the pagans worshiped these Baals, they were worshiping the forces of nature. They thought of these forces as independent of God and regarded them as entities in themselves. Thus they had made gods of them.

Ahab's introduction of this service into Israel implied a complete rejection of the Lord. Aren't all the natural forces of the Lord? Because the Lord remembers His people in grace, these elements are a blessing for all mankind. God's Word of grace toward His people governs all things. If He holds that Word back, all of life is doomed to perish. Didn't Ahab and the people realize this? They rejected His Word of grace. That's how Israel's complete break with the Lord came about.

Resistance carried to the limit. In those days the people persevered in their resistance to the Lord and to the grace of His covenant. Joshua had once sworn that Jericho was never to become a fortress again. This was to show that Canaan was a safe country for Israel not because of its walls and fortified cities but because of the protection of God's favor. Joshua had said that whoever undertook to rebuild the walls of Jericho would experience the Lord's curse in the loss of all his sons.

In Ahab's time someone ventured to rebuild those walls. The ring of fortresses had to be closed. Israel's protection came not from the Lord but from its fortified cities!

How the Lord thundered against this misdeed, and how the curse uttered by Joshua struck! When Hiel began to rebuild Jericho's walls, his oldest son died. After that he lost all his sons. His youngest son died when he erected the gate. Resistance to the Lord's grace brought death: Hiel's entire family was wiped out.

The break with the Lord came to light in this resistance to the Word of the Lord and in the Baal worship. It appeared that Israel was becoming completely absorbed in heathendom. The people of Israel showed no desire to live different lives than the people in the kingdoms surrounding them. Yet the Lord did not let go of them. His covenant was unshakable. Therefore He would struggle for a remnant to be preserved. The Christ had indeed been rejected, but for the sake of the Christ there was still grace for the kingdom of Israel.

30: The Word of Grace Concealed

I Kings 17

Elijah appears on the scene with a prophecy to the effect that there will be no rain except at his word. From this we see that the king and the land are placed in Elijah's hands as the bearer of the Word of God. Here God's Word and Elijah are one. When Elijah is silent, God's Word is silent.

Because Elijah is identified with the Word of God, we are not told about his previous life history. What was at stake was not Elijah but the Word of God, of which he was the bearer. Because of this, the hiding of Elijah was for Israel the same thing as the concealment of God's Word.

That Word of God is the Word of His covenantal grace toward His people. In that Word of grace, all blessing for His people is contained, including the blessing upon the fields. God's favor toward His people in the Christ governs everything in the world.

Elijah's career is really a struggle against the worship of the Baals. The Baals are the forces of nature personified. It is from the Baals, according to the Canaanite religion, that blessing descends upon the fields.

These so-called forces of nature were first separated from God and from the Word of His grace; then they were personified and deified. Over against this outlook, the power of the Word of God's grace, the power of the Word which the Lord's prophet brings, would have to be made plain. Natural forces, too, are governed by that Word of grace.

Main thought: *The Lord conceals the Word of His grace to make it clear that this Word possesses sovereign authority.*

The hiding of Elijah at the brook Cherith. In those days Ahab had an unexpected encounter with a prophet. That prophet, Elijah by name, appeared before the king in Samaria. We know nothing about the prophet's former life—because we don't need to know. All we have to do is focus our attention on the word he spoke, for that word was the Word of the Lord. The Lord put His Word in Elijah's mouth and gave him authority over all things, even over the king and the kingdom.

There stood Elijah. He swore by the Lord, the God of Israel, whom he served as prophet, that there would be neither dew nor rain in Israel until he, Elijah, said so. The Lord had commanded him to bring this message to Ahab. Now it would be made clear that the blessing on the fields did not come from the forces of nature. The blessing came not from the Baals but from the Lord, from the Word of His grace.

At the Lord's command, Elijah then hid himself at the brook Cherith. Nobody could find him there; that is to say, nobody could find the Word of grace of which Elijah was the bearer, the Word he was commissioned to speak. That Word of grace was hidden from Israel; the way to that Word had been closed off.

By the brook Cherith Elijah himself experienced the power of the Word of grace in a wonderful way. He drank the water from the brook. Ravens, led by the Word of the Lord, brought him bread and meat morning and evening. How was that possible? The most ravenous of birds obediently placed bread and meat before Elijah! If those birds had behaved according to their nature, they would have devoured the food themselves. Through this miracle it was made perfectly clear to Elijah that the deciding factor in the struggle was not any so-called force of nature but the Word of grace, which governs all the elements.

How comforting this must have been for Elijah! Israel itself seemed to have the raven's nature, taking everything for itself and looking out only for itself. Would the Word of grace be able to overcome this wickedness in Israel's life, just as it compelled the ravens to serve the Lord? This thought strengthened Elijah greatly in his prophetic calling.

There was still hope for Israel. At the very time when there was such a terrible outbreak of sin in that kingdom, God was taking steps to rectify the situation. Right then, by means of the

Word of His grace, God was initiating the struggle. The concealment of Elijah was intended to make the people see that they were dependent upon this Word. God was not yet abandoning the kingdom of Israel. He would not permit Israel to lose all connection with Judah and the house of David.

The hiding of Elijah at Zarephath. Because of the drought, the brook Cherith eventually dried up. At the Lord's command, Elijah then crossed the border and went to Zarephath, where, as the Lord had said, a widow would provide for him. He was not to stay in Israel's territory, where he might be discovered. Undoubtedly there were believing widows in Israel too, but Elijah was not sent to one of them (see Luke 4:25-6). All of Israel lay under the Lord's wrath. That God directed His servant to find lodging with a heathen woman was later to be Israel's shame.

There went Elijah, across the border. How his heart must have ached as he left his people knowing that the Word of grace had been withdrawn from them! When he arrived at Zarephath, he saw a woman gathering sticks. Would this be the woman with whom he was to find lodging? He wanted to find out. He asked her for water, and as she went away to get it, he called after her to bring him some bread too. Elijah had noticed that drought and hunger were also afflicting this neighboring country.

What was this poor woman's situation? She turned around and said with an oath: "As the LORD your God lives, I have nothing baked, only a handful of meal in a jar, and a little oil in a cruse; and now, I am gathering a couple of sticks, that I may go in and prepare it for myself and my son, that we may eat it, and die." Obviously this woman was in dire need. But she had recognized Elijah as a Jew and had sworn by the Lord his God. Was it possible that she knew the Lord and served Him?

To test her, Elijah asked her to make a little cake for him first and to keep the rest of her provisions for herself and her son. He added the promise that neither the meal in the jar nor the oil in the bottle would be used up until the Lord gave rain. There he was speaking to her about the power of the Lord's grace over all things and referring to the calling and promise of the Lord. Would she believe?

The woman went and did as Elijah said. That was an act of faith on her part. How did she know that this stranger was speaking the truth? Would she sacrifice herself for him? How could she suppose that such a miracle would happen to her?

In Elijah's words she had heard the Word of the Lord. That Word enabled her to overcome all her doubts. She did as she was told, for she believed the promise. What she could see and touch she surrendered for what she did not yet see. That's how faith works (see Heb. 11:1).

From her response Elijah could tell that she was the woman the Lord had in mind. He stayed at her home for a long time. Together they lived from the miracle. Wasn't the Word of grace all-powerful?

Living daily with that miracle must have been a constant joy for his faith and hers. Do *we* live any differently? That there is still a Word of grace today, that there is grace in the Lord Jesus Christ, is a miracle. Yet, it is through this grace that we receive all things. Everything we receive is a revelation of the miracle of grace in the Christ. This realization is the key to a life full of joy.

Elijah must have hoped even more strongly that the miracle would be revealed once again to the Israelites whose eyes were now shut. God had opened this heathen woman's eyes to the miracle; she was a prophecy pointing ahead to all the pagans who would see the miracle someday. Couldn't the Lord also show the miracle to His own people again? And wouldn't those pagans eventually provoke Israel to jealousy?

The Word of the Lord is truth. While Elijah was staying with the widow, her son became severely ill and died. The woman felt bitter about this turn of events. She connected the death of her son with the stay of the Lord's prophet in her house. God had come to her in this man, and now He had put her sins in the light of His countenance. By her son's death, she was being punished for her sins.

How admirable that this woman connected everything with the Lord and with her relationship to Him! But in her consternation she forgot that with the Lord there is always grace for those who belong to Him, and that although He disciplines His own for their sins, He never punishes or rejects them. She could no longer cling to the Lord's grace, despite the fact that her heart cried out for it.

Elijah laid her dead son on the bed in the upstairs room and cried out to the Lord: "It can't be true that You reject this woman now that You have come to her through my lodging here. Show her Your grace again, if it be Your will, by restoring her son to her." By faith Elijah saw that God would do just that. In faith he clung to the Lord in His grace. Then he stretched himself upon the boy three times, covering him with his own life. Thus the Word of grace covered the dead child.

To be sure, the widow and her son deserved death and rejection, just like everyone else. But the Word of grace, that is, the Christ Himself, is the reconciliation that covers us and protects us from the wrath of God. That's why Elijah cried out in faith for the boy's life when he stretched himself upon the child.

The Lord heard Elijah's prayer. The boy got up. One day, through the Christ, those who belong to Him will be raised to eternal life.

Elijah brought the boy to his mother, who recognized in this unprecedented event the miracle of God's mercy. Now she fully acknowledged Elijah as the prophet of the Lord. And she confessed that she saw, even more clearly than in the beginning, that the Word of the Lord is truth. The Lord's Word is the sure foundation on which we may always rely.

What overwhelming comfort this event gave Elijah! Here was an instance of resurrection. Couldn't the Lord revive Israel, which was now spiritually dead, to a life of faith in covenant with Him?

31: The Word of Grace Revealed

I Kings 18

The Word of grace, in the person of Elijah, was hidden from Israel, but this concealment did not have the desired effect on Ahab. He did not admit that Israel would be fully blessed *only* if it depended on the Word of grace. On the contrary, he became embittered. He sent out his men to look everywhere for the one he considered Israel's troublemaker.

This hiding was only a preparation for a more glorious revelation of the Word of grace. This was to happen in the events of I Kings 18. Concealment and revelation, judgment and grace would together bring about faith and repentance.

Through the fire that consumed the sacrifice, God not only revealed Himself as the Almighty who can do all things but also showed once more that He was willing to accept Israel's offering. The people still had not been rejected. Here we have the revelation of grace in the covenant.

Although Elijah's energies were directed to the kingdom of the ten tribes, he erected an altar of twelve stones. In this context the name *Israel* is used in reference to Jacob. The kingdom of the ten tribes represents the mass of Israel, which will be lost; the remnant which will be saved is the true Israel from among all the twelve tribes. The altar of twelve stones was a symbolic call to return to the fellowship of the covenant.

The objection that it would have been impossible for Elijah to find water to pour over the altar since there had been a long period of drought need not detain us long. In that vicinity there was probably a well that had not dried up.

By the strength of the Spirit, Elijah ran ahead of Ahab's chariot to Jezreel. Here he showed that he was both the herald and the servant of the king. That was a revelation of grace to Ahab. The Word of the Lord had not yet rejected the king; Ahab was still allowed to be the people's head and leader. As such he was being supported by that Word.

There was something remarkable about the fact that Elijah prayed seven times with his face between his knees for the rain which he himself had just announced. This illustrates the true nature of prayer. Prayer does not serve to move God to do something; in prayer we are to receive from Him what He has ready for us. At the same time, we do so in a sincere wrestling with God, especially since we are not always ready to receive what He plans to give us. When Elijah prayed with his face between his knees, he was searching his own heart and humbling himself before God.

In I Kings 18:1, we read that the Word of the Lord came to Elijah "in the third year." We must read this as meaning the third year of Elijah's stay in Zarephath. This text does not conflict with what we read in Luke 4:25, namely, that the drought lasted three and a half years.

Main thought: *The Lord reveals His Word of grace so that Israel will return to Him in faith.*

The revelation in Elijah's reappearance. In the third year of Elijah's stay at Zarephath, the Lord commanded him to show himself to Ahab. Finally the Lord was ready to give Israel rain again.

Ahab's men had been looking for Elijah for a long time, but they were unable to find him. Ahab had made them look everywhere. It was not that he wanted to confess his sins to Elijah; all he wanted was to wring from Elijah the word that would end the drought. But Elijah had remained hidden, and in him the Word of grace was hidden from Israel. The Christ had turned away from His people—that's why there was a drought. Only in His own good time would the Lord cause the Word of grace to speak again—and not as a result of Ahab's sinful coercion. Now, after a chastisement lasting several years, the Lord wished to let the Word speak so that His people would believe in Him.

Ahab had sent his steward Obadiah in one direction to look for grass for the herds, while he himself went in another direction. It was so dry that the herds were in imminent danger of dying.

Obadiah, who feared the Lord, met Elijah on the road. The prophet commanded him to tell Ahab that he was back. Obadiah was afraid to carry out this command. As someone who served the Lord, he was already in a dangerous position at Ahab's court. In secret he had hidden 100 of the Lord's prophets in two caves; he provided food for them and saved them from Jezebel's persecution. If he were now to bring the message that Elijah had reappeared, Ahab could easily draw the conclusion that Elijah and Obadiah had been in contact with each other all along. Besides, the Spirit of the Lord might suddenly remove Elijah from the scene. Then Obadiah would stand before Ahab as a liar.

Elijah overcame all these objections by declaring that the Lord had instructed him to show himself to Ahab. Obadiah then submitted, acknowledging God's sovereign power to speak His Word of grace whenever He pleased.

When Ahab met Elijah, he addressed him as the one who was troubling Israel. To our sinful nature, it is God who is to blame when He withdraws His grace from us. As far as Ahab was concerned, the Lord's prophet was responsible for the evil that had befallen Israel.

Elijah threw Ahab's words right back at him and declared that he and his father's house had troubled Israel by their sins. Now the Lord intended to reveal Himself once more to Israel as the God of grace. Again the Lord wanted to be the one who takes the initiative. The people still were not crying out and humbling themselves before Him. And the king, the head of the people, was certainly not doing so either.

The revelation in the fire from heaven. Even before this, through the Spirit of the Lord, Elijah had longed for a new, wonderful revelation of God's mercy, a revelation that would make the people abandon the Baals, kneel before the Lord, and thus receive the rain as a gift of God's grace. For this reason he asked Ahab to summon all the people to Mount Carmel, together with the 450 prophets of Baal and the 400 prophets of Astarte.

At Ahab's command, all the people and the priests of Baal gathered at Mount Carmel. Elijah addressed them and pressed them to make a choice. The one who answers the prayers of his people is the true God in whom men can trust. Why were the people torn between two opinions? At these words of Elijah the people maintained complete silence. They were not about to give in before the trial.

Elijah allowed the priests of Baal to go first and choose a bull. When Baal did not answer them, despite all the prayers and the religious dances of the priests, Elijah mocked them. This saint of the Lord *mocked* the abomination of idol worship among God's people. After that the priests called out even louder to Baal. In their excitement they began to cut themselves with knives.

Elijah let them continue until late in the afternoon. Then he built an altar of twelve stones for the twelve tribes of Israel, the descendants of Jacob. Those who were gathered there had to be reminded that the people of the Lord consisted of twelve tribes, and that God's grace was for the people as a whole—not for those who separated themselves from that fellowship.

Elijah then proceeded to prepare the animal for the sacrifice. He had so much water poured over it that even the trenches around the altar were flooded. Now it was humanly impossible to set fire to the offering. That was Elijah's way of showing that the restoration of covenant fellowship could not come from man's side.

Elijah prayed to the Lord to reveal Himself as the God of the patriarchs, the God of the covenant, the God who lives in the midst of Israel and who alone can lay claim to Israel. Elijah wanted God to make it clear that he, as prophet, had spoken in the name of the Lord. Then the people would finally have to admit that the hardening of their hearts had come over them as a judgment of the Lord on account of their sins. In response to this admission the Lord might be pleased to remove the hardening.

Suddenly fire fell from heaven. The fire consumed the burnt offering, the wood, the stones, and the dust. It even licked up the water from the trenches. The awful miracle of grace! The Lord still accepted the offering of His people; He had not rejected them. He still looked upon them in the Christ and wanted to give them His revelation of grace so that they would reject the Baals and bow before Him.

Then all the people fell on their faces and cried out: "The LORD, he is God; The LORD, he is God." There were the people, bowing before the Lord. Were their hearts also bowing before Him, and would they now surrender in faith to the Lord? We can only humble ourselves before the Lord if we also trust in Him. The future would reveal what was going on in their hearts.

Elijah now wanted to push through with the decision and remove the abomination from Israel. Therefore he commanded the people to take the priests of Baal to the brook Kishon and kill them. The people did as he commanded. Thus the Lord's grace once again gained the victory among the people.

During this time of the worst apostasy among the ten tribes, the Lord had been struggling to win the hearts of the people. Because they had broken completely with the house of David, they went from bad to worse. Still, the Lord did not let go of them.

The revelation in the rain. After the slaughter of the priests, Elijah told Ahab to eat quickly at one of the high places on Mount Carmel, for in the spirit he already heard the rushing of an abundant rain. Ahab complied and proceeded to eat, while Elijah approached the Lord.

Elijah bowed down before the Lord and bent over with his face between his knees, completely humbled and broken before the Lord. He was searching his own heart and thinking of the sins of the people. There he confessed all the unrighteousness and prayed for the Lord's grace in the form of rain. Thus he was an intercessor for the people, just as the Christ is the Intercessor who Himself bore the sins of His people.

Is it really so strange that Elijah prayed for the rain which he had already announced, the rain he could virtually hear in the spirit? In our prayer we have to claim that which God in His grace has decided to give us. And we may expect God to hear us, since the Mediator has atoned for our sins.

Elijah prayed seven times. Each time he sent his servant to look out over the sea for any sign of clouds. Elijah did not stop praying until he saw an answer to his prayer.

When his servant brought back a positive answer the seventh time, Elijah sent word to Ahab to drive quickly to his summer palace in Jezreel, or else he would get caught in the storm. The clouds gathered, and there was a very heavy rainstorm. Did Ahab and the people receive this rain as a gift of the Lord's grace in His covenant? Would there now be a return to the Lord and to His grace in the covenant?

The revelation in Elijah's service. The Spirit of the Lord came over Elijah and gave him extraordinary strength, strength to run ahead of the horses of Ahab's chariot all the way to Jezreel. Could the people be given any clearer revelation that the rain came by the Word of grace, the Word of which Elijah was the bearer? Through this same act, Ahab was shown that the prophet of the Lord did not reject him as king but was his herald to the people. If only the king, in fellowship with the prophet, both of them in subjection to the Word of the Lord, would lead the people in accordance with the law!

God in His mercy was still seeking Ahab. For His people's sake, He had been especially concerned with this king. He wanted to use His grace to break the resistance of this rebellious man. What a crime it would be if Ahab rejected Him now!

32: Stillness with God

Is there anyone qualified to tell this story? Every story in which God reveals Himself is beyond our grasp, but this one is particularly far beyond us, since we now have to tell of the stillness there is with God.

However, we must not speculate about this stillness. We are not being told what God is in Himself. What is revealed here is what there is with God for His people in His covenant; we are being told about the stillness of resting in Him. That rest originates with Him, of course. That rest is with Him in the changelessness of His grace and His counsel of redemption. He knows how His grace will finally be victorious in the lives of His people. By faith we learn to understand this and to rest in Him. Then we know His stillness. This revelation of God's stillness, therefore, has nothing in common with mystical speculations about silence.

Is there anyone in a position to reproach Elijah? He did indeed depart from the right way. If we become discouraged and our faith fails us, it is obvious that we have not fought in communion with the Lord and in His strength. We have begun to forsake the faith. Because faith always sees God's cause in the contest, our faith is nourished while it engages in the struggle. If Elijah became discouraged, then it is clear that he foresaw failure. But he could only foresee failure if his eye was fixed on his own struggle.

God's cause never fails! Yet, we always feel so small compared to Elijah. If we had ever experienced the terrible intensity of the struggle as Elijah did, we would have the right to reproach him. Is there anyone among us who has known the enormous strain of total involvement in the struggle, the strain under which Elijah lived?

Struggle and stillness are not mutually exclusive. The revelation of God in the stillness is preceded by violent signs. And immediately after-

257

ward, Elijah is thrown into the middle of the struggle again. He who engages in the struggle must possess the assurance of the victory of God's grace. From that certainty his faith must be fed continually. Only if that happens can he live by the stillness while he is engaged in the struggle.

Only in Christ's case was every comfort, every basis for rest, taken away—by God Himself. "My God, my God, why hast thou forsaken me?" In this cry with which His complaint began, He prophesied that He would once again find that firm foundation, that sure basis. During His suffering, however, He was left entirely alone. By suffering that abandonment, He made it possible for us to experience the stillness.

Main thought: *The Lord reveals the stillness in the struggle.*

Despair. When Ahab told Jezebel what had happened at Mount Carmel, her resistance was not weakened at all. Had Ahab for one moment expected that? This woman would stop at nothing. She even dared to take on the living God in a contest. She sent a message to Elijah in which she swore by her gods that she would kill him the next day, just as he had killed the priests of Baal.

The message took Elijah by surprise. It's not likely that he had hoped to win Jezebel over, but he must have hoped that Ahab would offer her some resistance after the events on Mount Carmel. From this message it was clear to Elijah that Ahab had given in to her and also that this woman would now be in control of Israel. Therefore Elijah got discouraged.

Didn't he know that the cause of God's grace would surely triumph? Apparently he was not able to see it anymore; he could not, in faith, rest in that certainty any longer. He had given himself one hundred percent in the struggle on Mount Carmel. In the process, however, the Lord's cause had become too much his own cause. Now he saw his cause fail. Surely the victory should have been conclusive by now. He forgot that God does not necessarily follow the routes we like to take. That's why he got so discouraged.

He fled from Jezreel. He was not driven by the fear of losing his life, for in that case all he would have had to do was cross the border into Judah's kingdom to find complete safety. He went right through Judah, left his servant behind at the farthest end of Judah's border, and entered the desert.

Elijah was at the end of his rope. How would it go now with the Lord's cause? He no longer saw any future. He wanted to wander around in the desert by himself since there was nothing left for him to do. Perhaps he would die there.

Remembering in the wilderness. Elijah continued into the desert a whole day's journey. Then he lay down under a broom tree and slept. He had no thought of food; he lived from his sorrow.

While he was asleep, an angel of the Lord touched him and told him to get up and eat. Near his head he saw a cake, baked on red-hot stones, and a bottle of water. He ate and drank and fell asleep again. What was there for him to do in life? Even the appearance of an angel left him untouched. The angel woke him a second time and said: "Get up, eat! Otherwise the journey will be too much for you." How fortunate that God does not leave us alone when we are in despair! There is still someone calling for us. This time the angel expressly mentioned the calling by speaking of a road which Elijah was to travel. It is quite something when God calls us anew, even if we do not know what purpose He has in mind.

This time Elijah got up, ate, drank, and went on his way. For 40 days and 40 nights he was sustained by the strength of that food. By a divine miracle, the food provided him with strength for this long period of time. Shouldn't Elijah already have understood from that miracle that faith is fed by a miracle? God's grace for the world in the Christ is a miracle, and by way of miracle it is victorious.

For 40 days Elijah traveled aimlessly through the wilderness. But God had a purpose in all this wandering. During those days Elijah must have come to grips with himself. He must have sensed that he had passed a milestone in the struggle without even being aware of it: he had moved from fighting the Lord's battle to fighting his own. Moreover, he must have recalled Israel's 40-year journey through the wilderness and thought about how the people of Israel first had to find God there before they could enter

Canaan. Now it was Elijah's turn to find the Lord there. This was a preparaton for the further revelation the Lord had in store for him.

The God of the covenant of grace. Elijah's thoughts finally arrived at the point from which Israel's journey through the wilderness had begun, namely, the establishment of the covenant at Mount Sinai. Indeed, it was to that mountain range of Horeb that God brought Elijah at the end of those 40 days. More revelation was waiting for him there, revelation from the God who had made a covenant with Israel.

Elijah spent the night in a cave on the mountain. There the Word of the Lord came to him, saying: "What are you doing here, Elijah?" Elijah answered: "I have been very jealous for the LORD, the God of hosts; for the people of Israel have forsaken thy covenant, thrown down thy altars, and slain thy prophets with the sword; and I, even I only, am left; and they seek my life, to take it away." He addressed the Lord as the God of hosts, the God who fights with the aid of His angels. That's how Elijah viewed the Lord. He lived in that spirit.

In itself this was not wrong. But did he also see that behind that battle of the Lord's was the assurance of the triumph of God's grace? Elijah had forgotten that to some extent. He saw the Lord contending as a human being does, with uncertain prospects for victory. The Lord would have to correct him on this point.

At the Lord's command, Elijah went out of the cave and stood on the mountain. First came a mighty wind which broke off pieces of the mountain and splintered rocks. He saw and heard the force of that howling wind in the mountains, but he noticed that the Lord was not in the wind. The wind only went ahead of the Lord. After the wind came an earthquake, but the Lord was not in the earthquake either. Then came an all-consuming fire. But the Lord was not in the fire either. Then, after all that noise of violence, a deep stillness followed. It was as though Elijah could hear that stillness. There was the Lord!

Elijah took another step forward, wrapped his coat around his face, and enjoyed the stillness. He drank the stillness in. That is how the Lord is! The Lord can be deeply moved and very much disturbed, but behind all of that is the quietness of the assurance that His grace will triumph and save the world. By faith men may rest in that certainty.

How Elijah, the man of fire and struggle, must have enjoyed that stillness! Nobody can endure if he experiences only the battle and does not know that the Kingdom, which here created wind and earthquakes and fire, is ultimately the Kingdom of peace. In this world we cannot get by without all that noise of violence, but we cannot do without the calm that faith brings either.

In that stillness Elijah was again asked what he was doing there. That question was meant to bring Elijah to himself. He had to discover how he had lost the power of faith. On the basis of that discovery, God could comfort him again.

Elijah answered the question with the same words. Those words were not a complaint against God; Elijah was using them to express the depths of his despair. The stillness of the certainty which is with God comforted him even before the Lord said another word.

Would there not be that certainty with God? The Christ was to atone for sin and overcome the world. By now He has done that. God will certainly carry out His counsel of redemption, even though it often seems to us that His cause will fail. By faith we may rest in that assurance. Even in the most troubled times, we experience the stillness with God.

A summons to a further struggle. Immediately the Lord summoned Elijah, who had been strengthened by the stillness, to a further struggle. He was to anoint Hazael to be king over Syria, Jehu to be king over Israel, and Elisha to be prophet in his place. The Lord of the stillness was continuing the struggle; He was going to chastise Israel through Hazael. After that Jehu would execute judgment in Israel. Finally, Elisha's words would be as a judgment in Israel.

Furthermore, the Lord made Elijah feel that he had been too pessimistic in his despair: there were still 7000 in Israel who had not bowed the knee to Baal. There was still a remnant according to the election of grace. For the sake of that remnant, God had not forsaken His people. All the judgments to come would be chastisements directed toward Israel's salvation. What mattered was the Kingdom of peace, which was sure to come.

Hearing the call. From Mount Horeb Elijah went to Abelmeholah. There he found Elisha, who was a rich man. It was the plowing season, and Elisha was busy plowing his fields with twelve yoke of oxen. He himself was leading the twelfth yoke.

Elijah walked up to Elisha and threw his robe on him. Elisha understood what that meant: he was to follow Elijah in the office of prophet, which was now his calling too. He would have to leave his large farm. From then on he would only bring the Word of the Lord to Israel.

What did he have to give up, and what did he get in return? Elisha did not vacillate and count the cost. He heard the call of the Lord and responded at once. It gained the victory over him, and he was prepared to follow. He only asked Elijah for an opportunity to kiss his parents good-by.

By asking Elijah's permission for this, he showed that he was too dependent on Elijah. If Elisha himself heard the call, then he should also be able to distinguish between what he could and could not do. Therefore Elijah answered him: "Go back again, for what have I done to you? I am not the one who is calling you; it is the Lord who claims you."

Elisha prepared a farewell dinner for his house. He killed a couple of oxen, using the wood of their yokes to build a fire on which to cook the meat. By this deed he demonstrated that his task there was finished. Here he already manifested something of the prophetic spirit. After the farewell dinner he departed.

This must have been a comfort for Elijah. The spirit of prophecy would not come to an end with him. The Lord would continue to wrestle with Israel through His Word of grace. Soon even kings would be anointed to chastise God's people— if not by Elijah then by his successor. There would surely come windstorms and earthquakes and fires, but behind it all was the stillness.

Didn't God also reveal Himself to the Christ in the violence of

His judgment? Yet, for Him too there came the stillness of God's eternal fellowship—in His resurrection and ascension. Christ obtained that stillness for all who are His.

Judah with Ephraim

33: Like Sheep without a Shepherd

I Kings 20—22:40

In the first period after the rupture, the two kingdoms stood over against each other as enemies. In the second period, Israel and Judah went out together to battle more than once. In the first period, Ephraim opposed Judah as the northern kings tried to separate their kingdom completely from Judah's house. In the second period, Israel did not return to Judah; what happened was that Judah followed along behind Israel.

For Judah and the house of David, that was a surrender of the grace and honor they had once enjoyed on account of the covenant with David. Jehoshaphat may have sought out the other kingdom in the awareness that the two kingdoms together constituted "Israel," but by his alliance with Ahab he was sanctioning the sin of the kingdom of the ten tribes and surrendering the honor of the Lord's covenant.

In two ways Ahab showed that he was no shepherd or shield for his people. In the first place, he made this clear in his relations with foreign countries. He spared the life of Ben-hadad, who had threatened him and his people, and even made a covenant with him. Sparing Ben-hadad's life should have been out of the question, for Ben-hadad was a mortal enemy of Israel and its king. However, there was more than the security of Israel and its king involved: the Lord's name and His justice in Israel's cause were at stake. Therefore the Lord called Ben-hadad "the man whom I had devoted to destruction" (I Kings 20:42). Ben-hadad was under the divine ban. Because Ahab did not uphold the law of the Lord, he was no shield to his people.

In the second place, Ahab showed that he was no shepherd or shield by his failure to uphold the Lord's justice in internal affairs. He violated that justice in the case of Naboth, for the sake of his own desires. At issue was the specific provision that no one's inheritance was to be

267

alienated. This was a right laid down in the law of Moses. Because Ahab was no shepherd to his people, God had to reject him for the sake of His grace to His people.

The son of the prophets who refused to strike the other son of the prophets was disobedient in his prophetic office. In that command he should have recognized the Word of the Lord; he should have obeyed. He was killed because he took a stand where he could not serve.

It is apparent that Ahab's prophets were not servants of Baal. Yet, they were not true prophets of the Lord either. They were probably connected with the service of the golden calves.

The Lord sent a lying spirit among those prophets. In the lie they uttered, the hand of the Lord was at work. Here, too, the Lord was letting sin run its course; He was punishing sin with sin. Therefore, when the prophets promised success to Ahab, they were not uttering deliberate lies. They were not speaking of success just to win the king's favor. They really believed that the king would be successful in what he proposed to undertake. Zedekiah was earnestly convinced that the Spirit of the Lord spoke through him. That's why he asked how the Spirit could have gone from him to speak through Micaiah.

Main thought: *For the sake of His grace to His people, the Lord rejects the unfaithful shepherd.*

Unfaithful with respect to the foreign enemy. During Ahab's reign, Ben-hadad, the king of Syria, attacked Israel. His soldiers overran the country and finally besieged Samaria. Through messengers Ben-hadad demanded the best of Ahab's belongings and the fairest of his wives and children. Ahab agreed but was told that Ben-hadad wanted more: he wanted to plunder the city.

After conferring with his officers, Ahab refused to surrender the city. When Ben-hadad threatened to burn it down, leaving no more than a heap of ashes, Ahab answered: "Let the one who takes off his armor boast—rather than the one who puts it on." In other words, Ben-hadad should not boast about victory too soon. This was the first manly word from the otherwise weak Ahab.

These words from Ahab reached Ben-hadad during a banquet in his tent. Immediately he gave orders to attack the city. In the meantime, one of the Lord's prophets came to Ahab and told him that the Lord was going to deliver the Syrian army into his hand so that Ahab would acknowledge the Lord's faithfulness to His people. The Lord still wanted to save Israel, for in the Christ He looked upon Israel as His people. There were still 7000 who had not bowed the knee to Baal.

Ahab believed the prophet, but he did not see the miracle of the Lord's grace and faithfulness in the promised deliverance. He did not believe in the Lord, nor did he believe in this word as the Word of His grace. But because he did believe there would be deliverance, he asked just how it would come to pass.

Ahab was told to start the battle with the servants of the governors of the districts. There were 232 of them. Behind them Ahab could muster another 7000 soldiers. That was all there was left of Israel's army, which had taken cover behind Samaria's walls.

When Ben-hadad was drunk in his tent and the Syrian army was unprepared for battle, Ahab attacked in the way the prophet had told him to. In drunken recklessness Ben-hadad issued orders to take alive all who came through the gate, whether they had come for war or for peace. But things did not turn out as he expected. The unprepared army of Ben-hadad was defeated. Ben-hadad barely managed to escape on horseback with some of his horsemen. Yet, the prophet of the Lord warned Ahab that Ben-hadad would come again.

It was clear that this victory was the Lord's doing. Ben-hadad's advisors saw it that way too. They could not deny that there was something special about that Israelite victory. However, they explained the victory in their own way. They were acquainted only with local gods, whose power was limited to specific locales. Thus they assumed that the Israelites worshiped mountain gods, gods who had power on the mountain of Samaria but would not have power on the plains. If Ben-hadad would fight Israel on the plains the next time, he would win an easy victory. And he should remove the kings of the cities, who served under him, replacing them with governors who could instil more unity in the army. Moreover, Ben-hadad would have to rebuild his army.

The following year Ben-hadad marched out again and camped in the plain of Jezreel, near Aphek. Israel's army, which was opposite the Syrians, looked like two little flocks of goats which had gotten separated from the main herd.

Again the prophet came to Ahab and told him that the Lord

would deliver this great multitude into his hand. The reason, again, was that God wanted Israel to acknowledge the Lord's faithfulness to His covenant.

After seven days the battle began. The Syrians were defeated: 100,000 of their men fell. Another 27,000 men were crushed by the collapsing wall of Aphek, behind which they had sought refuge.

Ben-hadad fled to an inner chamber in Aphek. His servants decided to humble themselves before Ahab and beg for Ben-hadad's life, knowing that Israel's kings were known as merciful kings. It was indeed true that Israel's kings, who lived by the grace of the Lord, were not driven by a heathen thirst for revenge. Many times they had shown mercy to their enemies.

Ben-hadad's servants were right about the reputation of Israel's kings. However, those kings did have the duty of avenging the Lord's rights when they were violated. Shouldn't revenge be taken on Ben-hadad, who had wanted to destroy Israel? The Lord still spared the Israelites despite their sins. Because of His grace to His people, He Himself delivered Ben-hadad into Ahab's hand.

When Ben-hadad's servants came to Ahab clothed in sack-cloth, with ropes around their necks, Ahab called Ben-hadad his brother, spared his life, invited him into his chariot with him, and made a covenant with him. Under the terms of the covenant, Ben-hadad would restore only the cities which his father had taken away from Israel.

Ahab was flattered at the thought that a mighty king like Ben-hadad had pleaded with him and had made his servants subservient to him. Because of this flattery, Ahab made the mistake of surrendering the Lord's sovereign claim and honor over against this enemy of His people. Again Ahab showed that he did not live for the Lord's people and could not be a shield for them.

On his way home Ahab met a wounded man with a bandaged head. This man was a prophet of the Lord, but because he looked like a wounded soldier, Ahab did not recognize him. The prophet had asked a fellow student at the school of the prophets to strike him. Because the other man refused to do so, he was killed by a lion. A prophet must be able to recognize the Word of the Lord and must be obedient.

Another man had then struck him. Now he stood before Ahab. He told the king a fabricated story about the cause of his wounds in order to trap him in his own words. When Ahab tripped himself up, the man revealed his identity and prophesied that the Lord would put Ahab's life and Israel's in the place of the lives of Ben-hadad and the Syrians. The Lord had delivered Ben-hadad into Ahab's hand so that divine judgment could be executed on him, but Ahab had let him go.

This prophecy spoiled Ahab's mood. He arrived in Samaria feeling sullen. His eyes had not been opened to his unfaithfulness toward the Lord's people. A return to the grace of the Lord was out of the question for him.

Unfaithful with respect to his own people. Ahab was a weak man without a strong will of his own. Too weak-hearted to oppose Jezebel's evil and too cowardly to go through with the wrong he himself desired to do, he let his wife lead him in everything.

As a lover of luxury, Ahab had an eye for beauty. He built an ivory palace in Samaria and had a pleasure garden laid out near his summer palace in the plain of Jezreel.

One day while he was walking in this garden, he hit upon the idea of adding the adjacent vineyard to his property, to make it one large, beautiful whole. He asked the owner, a man named Naboth, to sell him the vineyard. Ahab was prepared to give him another vineyard in return. But Naboth was not at liberty to give in to the king's desire, for that vineyard was his inheritance. According to the law of the Lord, he was not permitted to surrender it.

Here Ahab did not submit to the law of the Lord and did not show that the Lord's justice was sacred to him above all. He threw himself on his couch with his face to the wall and refused to eat. In this childish way the king showed his displeasure, now that the Lord's justice stood in the way of his desire. There was in Ahab nothing that was holy, no sense of devotion to the justice that protected the people of the Lord and their inheritance. Shouldn't Ahab have shown appreciation to Naboth for holding on to what the Lord had allotted him?

When Jezebel learned the reason for Ahab's bad humor, she sneered that he was a fine specimen of a king. In her opinion a king was not bound by any law; a king could do as he pleased.

Therefore she took care of the matter for Ahab. She wrote letters with the king's seal to the city officials of the town in which Naboth lived, ordering them to proclaim a fast in their city as if some great crime had been committed. Then, at the gathering of the people, they were to put Naboth on trial, using the testimony of two scoundrels, men without any conscience. Naboth was to be accused of slandering the king, a crime tantamount to blaspheming the Lord, in whose name the king ruled. After Naboth was condemned and stoned, the king would be able to take the vineyard for himself.

Like slaves and lackeys, the city fathers did as the queen had ordered. They trampled the Lord's justice underfoot and committed the murder. As soon as Jezebel received the news of Naboth's death, she told Ahab that he could now take possession of the coveted vineyard. Ahab did indeed take it as his own. By doing so, he made his wife's crime his own responsibility. The one who should have acted as Israel's shepherd was responsible for the shedding of innocent blood. And the inheritance of the children of Israel, which was protected by the law of the Lord, he took for himself. In Ahab there was nothing of the Christ. Ahab was rather an antitype of the One who shed His own blood to obtain an everlasting inheritance for His people.

In the Lord's name, Elijah came to meet Ahab in the stolen vineyard. He told him that the dogs would lick his blood in the place where they had licked up Naboth's blood. There would be blood for blood.

Ahab tried to make it appear that Elijah opposed him time and again out of personal enmity. Therefore he said: "Have you found me, O my enemy?" With these words Ahab tried to remove the impression of the Lord's judgment. But Elijah came right to the point and announced that the king and his house would suffer the fate of Jeroboam's house. Ahab's house, too, would be eliminated from Israel; there would be nothing left of it. For the sake of the Lord's covenant with His people, this false shepherd, who sought his own interests and let himself be guided by his wife rather than by the Word of the Lord, would also have to be removed. The dogs would eat Jezebel by the wall of Jezreel.

Ahab was deeply shocked by this announcement of the judgment awaiting him. He tore his clothes, fasted, and walked about slowly as a sign of deep mourning. He must have had to endure Jezebel's mockery, but this time he persisted. He was convinced that the judgment would come. He knew too much about Israel's history to brush Elijah's words aside. Yet, he did not see that this judgment was a judgment of God's grace toward Israel. That's why he did not return to the Lord in his heart, even though he was afraid.

All the same, the Lord took note of this repentance. Because Ahab had humbled himself before Him, the Lord would not carry out this evil during his lifetime. There is no tool the Lord will not use to teach us the true road of peace. By recognizing Ahab's self-humiliation, the Lord was pressing him to genuine repentance for his sins. True repentance is only to be found in the belief that with God there is grace for Christ's sake.

The judgment of the Lord's grace. After the war between Israel and Syria, there was peace for three years. However, Ahab thought that an injustice had been done him. At the time the two kings made their covenant, Ben-hadad promised to return all the cities which had formerly belonged to Israel. In Ahab's opinion, Ramoth-gilead was one of them, but Ben-hadad had not returned it. Ahab, who had become too bold as a result of his victories, was now thinking of taking Ramoth-gilead by force.

In those days Jehoshaphat, the king of Judah, paid Ahab a visit. When Ahab asked him to go out to battle with him, he promised to do so. But before they set out, Jehoshaphat wanted to inquire about the Lord's Word. Ahab agreed and had 400 prophets brought together for that purpose—not prophets of Baal, but not true prophets of the Lord either. These prophets were connected with the idol worship in Israel.

When Ahab asked them whether he should go to battle to capture Ramoth-gilead, they all prophesied that he would be the victor. But Jehoshaphat was not satisfied, for he had seen that they were not prophets of the Lord. Therefore he asked whether it would be possible to consult some other prophet. Ahab said that there was one more prophet, namely, Micaiah, adding that he hated him because Micaiah prophesied nothing but evil concerning him.

Ahab had never heard the Word of the Lord in the Word of His prophets. He had a completely heathen understanding of prophecy. He thought that the prophets with their words brought either a blessing or a curse. If that were so, the roles would be reversed and the Lord would be ruled by the prophets. That's why Ahab was afraid to hear the word of Micaiah. Micaiah had been put in prison because he could do no harm there—so Ahab thought. Apparently Ahab believed that he could bind the power of the Lord!

At the insistence of Jehoshaphat. Micaiah was summoned. In the meantime, the 400 prophets continued to prophesy victory. Zedekiah did so symbolically, using two iron horns.

The messenger who went to get Micaiah urged him to join the others in prophesying something favorable about Ahab. Here was that same foolish notion, the notion that a prophet could say whatever he wanted to. Micaiah declared that he could do nothing but speak the Word of the Lord. How heavily heathendom had influenced Israel that even this had to be spelled out!

At first Micaiah repeated the words of the other prophets, but the king saw that he was ridiculing them. Ahab had to be shown that Micaiah himself had no choice about what he prophesied. When Ahab insisted that Micaiah speak nothing but the truth in the name of the Lord, the prophet said that in a vision he had seen all Israel scattered upon a mountain like sheep without a shepherd. He added that the Lord had said that the Israelites should all return to their homes, for their commander was missing. With these words Micaiah foretold Ahab's death.

Bitterly Ahab said to Jehoshaphat: "Didn't I tell you that Micaiah always prophesies evil concerning me?" But Micaiah went on speaking and explained the harmony among the 400 prophets. He had seen in a vision how the Lord had sent a lying spirit among those prophets. The prophets were not lying intentionally; the Lord governed their minds to such an extent that they themselves saw the lie as the truth. The Lord clouded their minds as a way of punishing them and Ahab as well. Their blindness would send Ahab to his destruction.

What a severe warning this was for Ahab! But he and his prophets were so caught up in their sins that the web of lies could no longer be torn to pieces by God's truth. Zedekiah struck

Micaiah on the cheek. Convinced that he himself was speaking the Word of God, he asked Micaiah how the Lord's Spirit could have left him (Zedekiah) to speak through Micaiah.

The king gave orders to have Micaiah taken back to prison, where he was to be treated especially harshly until such time as the king returned from the battle safely. In this way Ahab hoped to compel Micaiah to think other thoughts about the king and to speak other words. Micaiah answered that if the king did return safely, it would be clear that the Lord had not spoken through him. And he called all the people to be witnesses to the truth of his words.

In spite of Micaiah's words, the two kings went ahead with their plans for the campaign. Apparently Jehoshaphat did not dare go back on his word. Yet, Ahab was afraid, in part because he realized that the Syrians would be aiming at him in particular. In his fear he disguised himself as an ordinary soldier in a chariot.

Ben-hadad ordered the chariot division to make straight for the king of Israel. Mistaking Jehoshaphat for Ahab, the Syrians pressed him into a corner. But when Jehoshaphat called out to his men, the Syrians realized that they had caught the wrong man and let him go.

Ahab, however, did not escape his judgment: a Syrian shot an arrow at random and hit him in the abdomen. Seriously wounded, Ahab commanded the chariot driver to withdraw from the battle. As the battle got more intense, he kept himself propped up in the chariot until evening. Then he died. His blood lay in the chariot.

At the end of the day, the battle was still undecided, but a cry went up throughout the army that every man should return to his home since Ahab, who had planned the battle, was dead. Thus Micaiah's prophecy that Israel would be scattered upon the mountain like sheep without a shepherd was literally fulfilled.

Later the Lord Jesus Christ also used this expression in reference to His people. How often the people are like sheep without a shepherd! Sometimes this is because of the sins of the people themselves, who are punished in their shepherd. However, we have a Shepherd who never puts us to shame, a Shepherd who gave His life for His sheep.

Ahab's chariot was washed at the pool of Samaria, where the dogs licked his blood. Elijah's prophecy about Ahab was also fulfilled. Ahab's life ended in dishonor because he had despised the Lord's justice and had not been a safe shield to the people.

34: Joy in the Lord

I Kings 22:41-51
II Chronicles 17—18:3; 19-20

After the period of estrangement in Judah under Rehoboam, Abijam and Asa, there was a return to the Lord under Jehoshaphat. During his reign, a high point was reached again. This is expressed in a curious way in II Chronicles 17:6: "His heart was courageous in the ways of the LORD." Jehoshaphat was swept along by his joy in the service of the Lord.

This joy in the Lord was typical of Jehoshaphat. Under his leadership, Judah went out singing and playing to see what God would do to the army of its allied enemies.

What remains strange about Jehoshaphat is the way he cast about for an alliance with the kings of Israel (Ahab and Jehoram), even to the point that Ahab's daughter became the wife of Jehoshaphat's son. Political reasons probably induced him to take these steps. No doubt he feared the prospect of civil war and wanted to put a stop to the exhausting war situation which had existed prior to his reign. The fact that he dealt with Israel made him overlook the sins of Ahab's house. He was repeatedly admonished for this.

Main thought: *Joy in the Lord by faith is the people's strength.*

Joy in the Lord's service. Under Rehoboam and Abijam, Judah had become estranged from the Lord. Under Asa the old situation had not been restored; it was bronze instead of gold in Judah. In Asa's son Jehoshaphat, the Lord gave Judah a king who led the people back to their former ways. Under him the kingdom increased in favor with God.

Jehoshaphat began to strengthen his kingdom because Israel's hostility continued to be a threat. He placed garrisons in all the fortified cities of Judah, even in the cities his father had taken from Israel. Although he weighed various means of bringing the conflict with Israel to an end, for the time being he could do nothing else than prepare for defense.

The Lord blessed Jehoshaphat in his work because he sought the Lord. Jehoshaphat experienced God's favor—and Judah with him. Thus, life prospered in all of Judah. There was a bond between the people and the king, who received gifts from his subjects. The people themselves became closely knit. As a result, the kingdom grew in riches and honor. We see in Jehoshaphat, as in an image, something of what has been given to us in the Christ, in whom we enjoy the fullness of God's favor.

Jehoshaphat was happy in the Lord's service. If we truly know the Lord, His service is a joy to us. Through His afflictions, the Christ obtained that joy for us. In his happiness, Jehoshaphat continued the reformation of Judah. Wherever he could, he wiped out the idolatrous cultic practices on the high places.

Jehoshaphat also saw how ignorant the people were of the law of the Lord. Therefore he sent a mission of princes, Levites and priests throughout Judah to teach the people the law of the Lord. This was one way of protecting them from the dangers of involvement in the cultic exercises on the high places.

During the first years of his reign, the Lord preserved him from wars. The fear of the Lord fell upon all the people around Judah. Philistines and Arabians brought him presents. Still, Jehoshaphat continued to strengthen the cities and the army. He was able to mobilize a huge army.

Joy in keeping the law. Finally Jehoshaphat thought it was time to bring an end to the hostility between Israel and Judah. He made an alliance with Ahab. He forged such a close link that his son Jehoram married Athaliah, Ahab's daughter. He also visited Ahab in Samaria and joined him in the expedition to capture Ramoth-gilead.

We have already heard how unfortunately this battle ended for Ahab. After the danger which threatened Jehoshaphat in the battle, Judah's king was able to return to Jerusalem in peace. The Lord had spared his life. Yet the prophet Jehu, the son of Hanani, whom Asa had put in prison, came to meet him. Jehu told Jehoshaphat that the Lord was angry with him because of the alliance he had made with godless Ahab. Israel was indeed Judah's brother nation and was one with Judah, but that did not give Jehoshaphat the right to overlook the sins of Ahab's house, by which Israel was led astray.

All the same, Jehoshaphat sought the Lord in his heart. Therefore Jehu told him that the Lord would not withdraw His favor from him.

In the joy of the confidence that he enjoyed God's favor, Jehoshaphat wanted to press on with the reformation of Judah. Not only in matters of worship were the people to abide by the law of the Lord; in every area of life they were to act in accordance with God's law. To bring this about, the king himself went through the entire land to appoint judges in all the cities, binding it upon their hearts that they were to judge justly, that is, according to the law. After all, they pronounced justice in the name of the Lord. In Jerusalem he established a higher court. When it came to matters of worship, the high priest Amariah had the final authority, while in civil affairs the final authority rested with Zebadiah, the governor of the house of Judah.

Under the leadership of the king, then, Judah was confirmed in the fear of the Lord. The people saw in him something of the promised Messiah.

Joy through faith. In the second half of Jehoshaphat's reign, Judah was suddenly threatened by the Moabites, the Ammonites and some other tribes. The enemy approached carrying huge quantities of goods. Apparently these people had decided to settle in Judah for good, attracted, perhaps, by Judah's prosperity. They came from the southeast, around the southern end of the Dead Sea.

Because they appeared so suddenly and in such great numbers, Jehoshaphat did not feel strong enough to resist them. He sought refuge with the Lord. He summoned all of Judah to Jerusalem. Standing before the people, he prayed to the Lord, the God of their fathers, who had given them this land from which they might now be driven. Would the Lord execute judgment and keep the inheritance safe for them now that they were unable to defend it themselves?

All of Judah, including the women and children, stood there before the Lord. It was a matter between the Lord and the entire people. While the people were together, the Spirit of the Lord came upon Jahaziel, who prophesied that they were to go out to meet the enemy the next day and see the salvation of the Lord. They would not have to fight, for these armies had come up against the Lord. The Lord Himself was going to decide the battle for them.

When Jehoshaphat heard this prophecy, he bowed before the Lord, and all the people bowed with him. In faith they bowed down before they had seen the victory.

The Levites started the hymn of praise. That, too, was joy *before* the victory. Faith can give us such joy because the Lord's promise is so certain to those who believe that it's just as though it has already been fulfilled. This joy through faith in the Lord's promise can be ours too, since the Christ, through His suffering, has obtained these promises and their fulfillment for us. Judah was safe because the Lord, for Christ's sake, took up His people's cause and defended Judah's possession of the inheritance.

Early the next morning, the people left Jerusalem. At the gate the king told the people to be sure to believe the promise. Then they would be established. After consulting with the people, he decided to have them manifest their faith by making singers march before the army and sing of the holy majesty of the Lord. This would fortify the people in their faith. Rarely has an army met its enemy in this way, singing: "Glorify the Lord, for His steadfast love endures forever!" It looked as though Judah had already won the victory!

At the very same time that the people were marching forth and singing, the Lord caused a band to attack the hostile armies. This gave rise to suspicion among the allies, who then began to attack one another. The one group helped destroy the other. All of this happened while the people of Judah went forth singing. This destruction of Judah's enemies was the Lord's answer to the joy of faith He found among His people. If only we would always live in that joy, our lives would be very different today!

Joy in thankfulness. When the people of Judah came to a mountain range from which they could look out over the wilderness, they saw piles of dead bodies ahead of them. The goods and the costly equipment had also been left behind.

It took the people three days to gather up the spoil. A treasure had fallen into their laps, and they had not even lifted a finger for it! The enemies who wanted to push the Lord's people out of their inheritance were destroyed, and the people received a treasure for which they had not worked. Thus the Lord was near His people for Christ's sake, giving them His favor.

On the fourth day the people came together in a valley to praise the Lord in their thankfulness. They called that valley the *Valley of Beracah*, that is, *valley of praise*. Then they returned to Jerusalem, with Jehoshaphat leading the way.

The people came to Jerusalem with joy and entered singing and playing. Everything was happiness. How close the Lord and Judah were in their joyous relationship before and after the march together! It was gold again in Judah—the gold of fellowship with God.

Because of the destruction of Judah's enemies, the fear of God fell upon all the surrounding kingdoms. Therefore Jehoshaphat and Judah had peace. They were secure in their communion with the Lord.

This joy was disturbed by new disobedience on the part of Jehoshaphat. Despite the fact that the Lord had been angry with him earlier because of his alliance with Ahab, Jehoshaphat sought renewed association with Ahab's house. He joined Ahab's godless son Ahaziah in building and equipping ships to haul gold from the land of Ophir. It can happen that a believer has to do business with an unbeliever, but Jehoshaphat was king of the Lord's people. As such he was a type of the Christ. There is no association between the Christ and sin. That would also have to be clear from the reign of the king of God's people. The Lord had already told him that.

Hence, there came a prophet of the Lord to warn Jehoshaphat that the project would not be allowed to go ahead unimpeded. In time all their ships were wrecked.

Fortunately, Jehoshaphat learned obedience from his experiences. When Ahaziah came to him a second time with a proposal about building ships, Jehoshaphat refused to go along with it. His bond with the Lord took precedence over everything else in his life.

Jehoshaphat died in the favor of his God. He had reigned over Jerusalem for 25 years.

35: The Prophet of Penitence

I Kings 22:52—II Kings 1

In the passage of Scripture to which we now turn our attention, we seem to read only of judgment and horror. We read of fire from heaven and an unrelenting judgment of death. When we first go through this passage, there seems to be no light at all.

Yet, we must pay careful attention to the fact that the Angel of the Lord appears here again. It is clear that what is meant in this passage is not a created angel but the Christ, the eternal Word, the Mediator of the covenant. Ever since the time of the judges, He had not revealed Himself directly. He was revealed by way of shadows and types, but never directly. Now, in the climax of the crisis, He appears once more. The Mediator of grace seeks His people.

The judgment upon Ahaziah, then, is the judgment of God's grace upon His people. Ahaziah had to be removed from their midst so that the Lord could show His grace to His people. If we look at our passage in this way, it radiates light.

We cannot help but connect this passage with Luke 9:51-6, where we are told that the Samaritans did not receive Jesus. James and John said: "Lord, do you want us to bid fire come down from heaven and consume them, just as Elijah did?" But the Lord answered: "You do not know what manner of spirit you are of: for the Son of man came not to destroy men's lives but to save them."

We must be careful not to draw a false contrast here between Elijah and the Lord Jesus, as though the one represents law while the other represents gospel. There is no opposition between law and grace in Scripture. The purpose of Elijah's struggle is nothing more or less than to reveal God's grace to His people. Elijah knew the stillness of God. If we could ever say of a human being that he was full of grace, we would say it of Elijah. We say that the Christ is full of grace, but Elijah was a type of the Christ.

283

On the other hand, let's not forget that from the Christ comes judgment. The announcement of Ahaziah's death and the fire from heaven are from the Christ. The New Testament book of Revelation tells us how the Christ judges and will judge. The error of the disciples in Samaria was their failure to realize that judgment is always a judgment of grace, that it is always meant to glorify the grace of God. One day the final judgment will usher in the triumph of grace.

Moreover, the calling of the Lord Jesus here on earth was different than Elijah's calling. The Christ came to suffer for His people in order to reveal God's grace in new glory. For this reason He did not bring judgment at that time. And the circumstances in Elijah's day were different too. The glory of the Word of grace had been fully revealed in Elijah, whereas the Lord Jesus had not yet been recognized by the Samaritans.

When we compare II Kings 1:17 with other available data, we see that Jehoshaphat probably appointed his son Jehoram to be co-regent about eight years before his death, perhaps at the time of his campaign with Ahab. About two years before he died, he must have abdicated in favor of his son. We do not know the reason. The statistics about the reigns of the kings of Israel and Judah during this period are not all calculated from the same point of view. In this way, at any rate, the various data can be harmonized.

Main thought: *The judgment of grace is revealed so that the people will believe.*

Avoiding the Word of grace. Ahab was succeeded by his son Ahaziah, who walked in the ways of his father. The Baal worship at Samaria was maintained as well as the idol worship connected with the golden calves. It was just as though the Lord had not said or done anything through Elijah and the other prophets. Consequently, the Lord turned against Ahaziah in everything and made his life and his reign futile.

After Ahab's death, Moab rebelled against Israel. Moab had paid tribute to Israel since David's days. When David and Solomon reigned in the name of the Lord and were types of the Christ in their reign, the kings of the surrounding nations were made subject to them as a sign that all the nations will one day be subject to Christ's rule of grace. However, now that the reign of grace was rejected in Israel and the kings no longer reflected the image of the Christ, the nations rose up against Israel in their own strength. In this turn of events, the Lord was quarreling with Israel.

From the very beginning, Ahaziah must have had plans to subdue Moab again. But he was prevented from carrying out those plans when he fell through a window and became seriously ill. There he lay, tied down and powerless. And there was no improvement in his condition. It was as though he lay before a wall over which he could not look—much less climb.

In this illness the Lord was confronting him. Would Ahaziah now subject himself to God's providential rule and acknowledge that the Lord in His grace was seeking him in this illness? Would he subject himself to the Lord's grace toward His people and also surrender to this grace personally? Would he submit and confess his sins?

Ahaziah could have asked for the Word of the Lord through the prophet Elijah. He knew where Elijah lived, as we see from later developments. But Ahaziah did not want to humble himself before the Lord. He could not and would not subject himself to anyone. That he was neither willing nor able to submit was the fruit of mankind's sin, the sin of his father's house, and his own sin.

Yet, he could not and would not stay in bed this way. He had to know one way or the other what the future had in store for him. Therefore he sent messengers to Baal-zebub,* the god of flies, the god of Ekron, the god who was supposed to be able to unveil the future. Baal-zebub would be able to tell him whether he would recover from his illness!

Note that Ahaziah did not ask this Baal for healing. Ahaziah could not ask a favor from anybody. Faith that is willing to submit can plead for healing, as Hezekiah did later. Ahaziah only wanted to know what would happen to him. And in this knowing he still wanted to have events within his control.

---

*The original name of this god was *Baal-zebul* (Lord Prince). A Canaanite title for *Baal* was *Zebul*. The change from *Zebul* (Prince) to *Zebub* (flies) may be due to the ridicule of scribes. In the New Testament we meet the name *Beelzebul* or *Beelzebub*, where it means *the prince of demons.*—TRANS.

We must not just point the finger at Ahaziah. All of us are just as unwilling and unable to subject ourselves to God's grace and surrender to it as he was. It is pure grace if it is given to us to do so, if we are able to surrender to grace each day of our lives and in all of life's circumstances.

The answer of the Angel of the Lord. The Lord confronted Ahaziah when he sent the messengers to Ekron. Ahaziah could not do anything without having the Lord thwart his plans. However, it was the grace of the Lord that was confronting him. If only Ahaziah had recognized this!

It was the Angel of the Lord who commanded Elijah to meet the messengers and give them orders to bring the king the Lord's answer, even though the king did not want to ask anything of the Lord. Here the Angel of the Lord, that is, the Christ, the Mediator of the covenant, appears again. This Angel was the One who had spoken to the patriarchs and led Israel in the wilderness; He was the One who is God Himself and who bestows communion with God upon His people. This Angel, the Revealer of God's grace, confronted Ahaziah so that Ahaziah would submit to God's grace.

"Is it because there is no God in Israel that you are going to inquire of Baal-zebub?" This is what Elijah was to ask the messengers. Not only was there a God, that God lived *in Israel* and was bound to Israel by His covenant. He lived in the midst of His people, and later, when the Word became flesh, He would become one of us. Thus He took our sorrows and sins upon Himself and bore our griefs. And He could also take Ahaziah's illness upon Himself; He could comfort him in that illness and cause the illness to work toward Ahaziah's salvation. When we fail to submit to the Lord's grace daily in all things, when we pass the Lord by, we are rejecting the great salvation given to us in the incarnation of the Word.

At the same time, Elijah was to tell the messengers to inform the king that he would not recover. He would not arise from his sick bed; he would surely die. The Lord wanted to put an end to Ahaziah's fruitless life. He made sure that Ahaziah knew the end was coming, so that he could still repent and submit to the Lord's grace. Then his life could still become fruitful for eternity. Would Ahaziah submit?

A consuming fire. Elijah had not told the messengers who he was, but from the description Ahaziah knew that it was Elijah who had spoken to them. They described the prophet as a man with a hairy robe and a leather belt around his waist.

Elijah was a prophet of penitence. By his manner of dress, he witnessed to Israel that all luxury and all possessions in life were forfeited by sin. In time the Lord Jesus would obtain them again for us by His blood, but we must admit that we have forfeited them. That's why John the Baptist came dressed in the same manner as Elijah.

In those words of his messengers, Ahaziah was again confronted with the demand for penitence, the demand which proceeded from the Word of grace. It was exactly this demand, the demand that he humble himself, that Ahaziah wanted to avoid.

Elijah would have to be eliminated, for Ahaziah could not endure having such a figure in his kingdom. Elijah lived on a mountain in the midst of Israel as a witness to the Lord, calling upon Israel and its king to confess their sins. The king sent a captain with 50 men to get Elijah. Now the king would use his authority to silence the Word of God! The Word of grace had to be removed from Israel!

Those men were apparently of one mind with their king, for their captain called out to Elijah: "You man of God, the king says, 'Come down.' " Presumably the man of God was expected to submit to the word of the king. In that case the captain must have been mocking Elijah when he called him a "man of God": there was no room for a true man of God in Ahaziah's kingdom.

Elijah answered: "If I am a man of God, as you say, let fire come down from heaven and consume you and your 50 men." Fire did come down from heaven and consume them. That was a terrible event. But let's make sure that we understand the situation correctly: the Lord's grace had to be victorious in Israel. That's why this blasphemy had to be removed from among the people. Scripture says that our God is a consuming fire—*our* God. He wants to be the God of His people, and therefore all unrighteousness must be wiped out. Indeed, the judgment was a judgment of grace.

Ahaziah sent a second band of soldiers after Elijah. Apparently their captain thought he could intimidate the Word of the Lord with a show of authority, for he said: "Come down quickly!" He and his 50 men were also destroyed. The third captain finally yielded to the Word of the Lord in Elijah, and he and his band were spared.

One day the Christ will cause all the unrighteous to perish. Then the Lord's grace will triumph, and the sovereign rule of grace will be confirmed forever.

The judgment of death. The Angel of the Lord said to Elijah that he was to go with the third captain and not be afraid. How awful these events must have been for Elijah since he still loved his people in spite of their sins! It must have been a great comfort to him that the Angel of the Lord accompanied him and talked with him. Everything Elijah did was done in the name of that Angel.

Thus the background of these events was still grace and compassion. The Church must be aware of this background when it announces a judgment of death to the world. In this regard the Church must follow its Lord.

At the command of the Angel, Elijah stood before the king. Now he could tell the king to his face that he would die. Evidently he was no longer appealing to the king to surrender to grace.

Ahaziah heard the judgment—his rejection. The chaff would have to be burned. Ahaziah had to be removed from among God's people so that God could be merciful to them and see to it that a remnant was saved.

Ahaziah reigned over Israel for only two years. Because he had no son, another son of Ahab became king in his place—Jehoram.

36: Ascension

II Kings 2

We must not regard Elijah's ascension into heaven primarily as an exaltation and comfort for him personally. Never was anyone so fully united with the Word of God as Elijah. It was the Word of God, then, that was exalted in his ascension.

That ascension also had the purpose of strengthening those who remained behind caught up in the struggle. That's why the news of Elijah's imminent departure was revealed beforehand not only to Elisha but also to the sons of the prophets.

Because Elijah was so fully united with the Word of God, he could be a type of the One who *is* the Word of God. His ascension, accordingly, was a prophecy pointing ahead to Christ's ascension. In Elijah's ascension we see the triumph of God's Word over His enemies. That's why Elijah ascended into heaven in a chariot of fire with horses of fire. According to Elisha, Elijah himself was the chariot of Israel and its horsemen. He fought against Israel's enemies—not just foreign enemies but especially the sins of Israel and its kings. In that struggle, the angels served the Word of God. Now these hosts of angels carried Elijah up into heaven.

In a whirlwind Elijah was taken up by the Lord, who was still revealing Himself in this sinful world in a majestic way. Elijah was safe in heaven. Through the Christ he was able to look upon the holy God.

The children of Bethel were the children of the place where the calf worship went on. They must have known Elisha as Elijah's disciple. Their mockery revealed Bethel's contempt and hatred for the Lord's prophet. The children were punished not for showing contempt for an adult but for sneering at the Word of the Lord. In their death, Bethel was punished. Here false worship was confronted by true worship according to the Word of the Lord.

Main thought: *The Lord exalts the bearer of the Word of God.*

The prophecy of the exaltation. The end of Elijah's labors on earth had come: the Lord was about to take him away. But Elijah was not going to die like any other human being. Because he was the bearer of God's Word and because he had initiated the spiritual struggle in Israel, the Lord decided to exalt His servant Elijah and thereby show that the Word of God will triumph.

But how would Israel fare once Elijah was removed from the scene? Would the Word and the Spirit of the Lord then depart from Israel completely? Elisha and the students in the schools of the prophets must have asked themselves this question. The Lord had revealed not only to Elijah but also to Elisha and the sons of the prophets that Elijah was going to be taken away. He wanted them to occupy themselves with this question and look ahead to what the Lord would do.

Elijah did not know that the Lord had also revealed his coming exaltation to Elisha and the other prophets. That's why he told Elisha to remain at Gilgal, explaining that the Lord had sent him to Bethel. At Bethel there was a school of the prophets. Elijah felt that he should admonish the sons of the prophets once more to be faithful to the Word of the Lord. He did not want Elisha to come along because he was not sure whether anyone was permitted to witness his ascension. But Elisha swore that he would not leave Elijah. From this Elijah must have understood that Elisha had some idea of what was about to happen. Elijah decided to await developments.

They went on to Bethel together. There the sons of the prophets came to meet them and said to Elisha: "Do you know that the Lord is going to take your master away from you today?" Elisha answered: "Yes, I know. Just don't talk about it!" Elisha did not want to discuss it; it was still too much for him to comprehend. Besides, he could see that Elijah did not want to talk about it either. They all had to wrestle with the question of Elijah's departure and wait on the Lord. Would the Spirit of the Lord remain with them?

At Bethel Elijah told Elisha to wait, explaining that the Lord had sent him to Jericho. There was another school of the prophets at Jericho. Again Elisha refused. At Jericho the same thing happened as at Bethel.

In Jericho Elijah again urged Elisha to stay behind, for the Lord had sent him to the Jordan River. Elisha again refused, this time with an oath. Then Elijah must have understood that the Lord had revealed everything to Elisha. He acquiesced in Elisha's desire to accompany his master to the end. The Lord would surely make it clear how it was all to come to pass.

A chariot of fire and horses of fire. From Jericho Elijah and Elisha went on to the Jordan. Fifty of the sons of the prophets followed at a distance. The Jordan was full of water; it was too deep to cross. Elijah took his robe, folded it together, and struck the water. The water parted, and the two men crossed on dry ground. When the river closed behind them, they were separated from the sons of the prophets, but Elijah was also separated from his labors in Israel, which now lay behind him. The Spirit, who had miraculously prepared a path through the Jordan River, had also prepared the way for him to God's throne.

Once they had crossed the river, Elijah asked Elisha what he desired from him before they parted. At that point the deepest motivation in Elisha's life came to clear expression: he asked for a double share of the Spirit that was in Elijah—the portion of an oldest son. (An oldest son received two shares of his father's inheritance.)* Indeed, Elijah was Elisha's spiritual father.

Elijah found this a difficult request. The Lord's Spirit was not his to give to Elisha. He would have to leave that decision to the Lord. If Elisha should see Elijah when he was taken away, that would be the sign that the Lord had chosen him to share in Elijah's victory. Then his request would surely be granted.

Suddenly there was a powerful whirlwind and fire from heaven. This was the terror of the Lord on earth. Elisha saw in

---

*See Deuteronomy 21:17. Elisha was not asking to be *greater* than Elijah; he wanted to be a *worthy successor* to him.—TRANS.

that fire a chariot of fire and horses of fire, which separated him from Elijah. Soon Elijah was borne up to heaven.

There was no terror for Elijah in that heavenly wind and fire. Elijah's sins were covered, for they would be reconciled one day through the blood of the Christ. Moreover, Elijah was sanctified through the Spirit. Thus he was placed before the throne of God, to behold the God in whose name he had spoken and fought on earth. It was God's good pleasure to spare Elijah from death; Elijah was glorified bodily and taken up into heaven.

However, that was not just a great comfort and honor for Elijah. The Word of God, of which he was called to be the bearer, was glorified in this event, which revealed that the Word would surely be victorious, regardless of the opposition in Israel. That Word was the Word of grace, which would be fulfilled in the Christ, who Himself is called the Word of God. Elijah's ascension, accordingly, is a prophecy pointing ahead to the ascension of the Christ. Christ is the conqueror. The angels serve Him in His Kingdom, just as the angels served Elijah in his ascension.

The abiding Spirit. At the moment of Elijah's ascension, Elisha called out: "My father, my father! The chariots of Israel and its horsemen!" His heart was with Elijah. He saw in God's Word in Elijah the power which had fought for Israel against all enemies—especially unbelief and sin. Had the Word and Spirit now been taken away from Israel? Elisha tore his clothes in two.

At his ascension, Elijah's robe had fallen from him. Elisha picked it up. He had seen Elijah at his exaltation. Now Elijah's promise would surely be fulfilled. In faith he picked up the robe as a sign that the promise had indeed been fulfilled.

Returning to the Jordan, he took the robe, struck the water with it, and said: "Where is the LORD, the God of Elijah?" He said this in faith, expecting that the Lord would now show that the Spirit was in him also. And he saw the miracle happen: the waters parted.

Didn't the same thing happen at Christ's ascension? True, Elijah did not have the Spirit at his disposal, but the Christ did. And He did not leave us alone but sent us the Spirit from heaven. Since that time, His Spirit has not left His Church.

Walking between the divided waters, Elisha returned to the sons of the prophets and to his work in Israel. For a moment the heavens had been opened before him so that he could behold the triumph of the Word of God. Now he was again faced with the battle.

The sons of the prophets suggested the possibility that Elijah had not ascended bodily into heaven. Perhaps the Spirit had thrown his body here or there upon the earth. They wanted to go and look for it so that they could bury Elijah.

This was foolishness to Elisha. He had seen Elijah's total victory. That total victory is not complete until we are also glorified in our bodies. But because of their insistent urging, he finally let them go. They returned empty-handed. Together with Elisha, they would have to struggle on in the faith that the victory is due to the Word of the Lord.

The life-giving Spirit. While Elisha was in Jericho, the men of that town came to him and pointed out that their town was indeed a good place to live but that the water was bad. As a result, the land was not fertile. Elisha asked for salt in a new bowl. He threw the salt in the spring of water and said: "Thus says the LORD: I have made this water wholesome."

By faith Elisha understood that the Lord now wanted to show that the Spirit of the Lord gives life and fertility on earth. The people were to turn to the Spirit and to the Word of the Lord. The salt was only a sign of the preservative power of the Spirit, and the new bowl was a sign of the newness which the Spirit works. At Elisha's word, the water became wholesome.

Thus the Lord's Spirit not only gives us renewed hearts but also sends His blessing upon the earth and upon our lives on earth. That life will not be fruitless.

The judgment of the Spirit. From Jericho Elisha went to Bethel. As he was nearing his destination, some boys from the city came toward him and mocked him, saying: "Go up, you baldhead! Go up, you baldhead!" These were boys from the city in which Jeroboam had established the worship of the golden calf.

The attitude of this city was hostile towards the Lord's prophet, who was recognized by the boys.

The mockery of the boys expressed the hatred of the people of Bethel for the Word and Spirit of the Lord. That's why Elisha cursed them. Immediately two bears came out of the woods and tore 42 of the children to pieces.

Terrible was the Lord's judgment on these children and—through their death—on the city of Bethel. Because the children walked in the ways of their fathers, the children and their parents were punished together.

God wished to bring the people under the terror of the Word of the Lord so that they would fear Him and believe in Him. When would Israel finally submit to His Word? Those who reject the Word of the Lord today are not punished in the same way as the children of Bethel, but the judgment *is* coming. The Word of God's grace will also be victorious in that judgment.

37: The Whole Earth Is Mine

II Kings 3

The greatest difficulty in II Kings 3 lies in the words: "And there came great wrath upon Israel" (vs. 27). This cannot mean that Israel became angry about the human sacrifice made by Moab's king, for why would the Israelites then withdraw from Mesha and his capital instead of destroying Moab for such an abomination? The text must mean that *the Lord* became very angry with Israel. Israel was not without guilt in this human sacrifice. By their systematic destruction of Moab, the Israelites pushed Mesha to this extreme step.

This shows us how sinful Israel's destruction of Moab was. It is true that Israel was acting on Elisha's advice. In verse 16 and again in verse 17 we read: "Thus says the LORD." In those texts, which promise a remedy for the lack of water, God spoke. Elisha then concluded on his own—and his conclusion was correct—that the Lord was also going to deliver the Moabites into the hands of the Israelites.

But when Elisha went on to advise Israel to destroy the land of Moab totally, he was speaking contrary to the Lord's intention. Only the Canaanites were to be utterly wiped out, and even *their* land was not destroyed; Israel lived on it. After all, the whole earth is the Lord's and may not be destroyed needlessly. Israel was called to be a *blessing* to the earth. When the Lord adopted Israel from among all the peoples as His special possession, He said expressly: "All the earth is mine" (Ex. 19:5).

Moreover, Elisha's advice contradicted the commandment in the law of Moses to the effect that fruit trees were to be spared (Deut. 20:19-20). There is a parallel between this futile destruction of land by Israel and Mesha's act of sacrificing his son to an idol; both are devoid of meaning.

The question arises here how Elisha could give such advice contrary to the Lord's intention. Had he not received a double portion of the

Spirit which was on Elijah? To find an answer to this question, we must look at two more details in the story. How did it happen that Elisha was marching with the army, seemingly without divine orders? Didn't his need for a minstrel point to a lack of readiness on his part to receive God's revelation?

Apparently a wave of nationalism had swept over Israel and had its effect on Elisha. He considered this nationalism to be in line with his prophetic calling—and in a certain sense it was, for it was part of his calling to see to it that Israel was elevated in the face of its foreign enemies. That elevation was to take place in God's name. But how easily such national elevation becomes profane! Then it is not a question of the Lord but of the nation itself.

Something of this spirit must have taken hold of Elisha as well. That's why he marched along with the army, and that's why he needed the minstrel. Caught up in this spirit, he gave advice that was nationalistic in the bad sense of the word.

Elisha was only at the beginning of his career as prophet, and there was much for him to learn from the way the campaign ended. It appeared that the anger of the Lord manifested itself in the death toll in the allied armies. Through these events, Elisha was purified as prophet.

Jehoshaphat had been admonished earlier by the prophet for his alliance with Ahab. He was also punished for his alliance with Ahaziah (see II Chron. 19:2; 20:35-7). But here the case is somewhat different. In a certain sense, this alliance was not a matter of an arbitrary choice on his part; it was necessary to protect the interests of Judah. If Moab could maintain its independence from Israel, how easy it would be for Edom to declare its independence from Judah! From all sides, enemies were threatening to liberate themselves and make war.

It is possible that Jehoshaphat inquired into the Lord's will before embarking on this campaign. This may be what Jehoram was referring to when he said: "Alas! The LORD has called these three kings to give them into the hand of Moab." In any case, the Lord's favor rested on this campaign at first, as the deliverance from distress makes clear.

Main thought: *The Lord gives His grace to His people in order to bless the entire earth.*

National pride. After his short reign, Ahab's son Ahaziah was succeeded by his brother Jehoram. During Jehoram's reign there came an upsurge of national feeling. Jehoram did not permit the worship of Baal, which had been borrowed from other nations, to continue. Israel had its own national god, namely, Yahweh, and

He was worshiped in national fashion via the golden calves at Dan and Bethel. Thus, Jehoram did rid the land of the Baal images, but the Lord was just a national god to him, like the gods the other nations worshiped. The abomination of the image worship (the golden calves) remained.

The Moabites had already declared their independence from Israel after the death of King Ahab, and Ahaziah was not able to punish them for it. When the tribute of 100,000 lambs and the wool of 100,000 rams was not forthcoming, Jehoram decided to make war against Mesha, Moab's king. He mobilized his army outside Samaria. Apparently the people were enthusiastic about this campaign. They were going to restore Israel's honor! It was *Israel's* honor—not the Lord's—that concerned them.

Jehoram sent messengers to Jehoshaphat, the king of Judah, to ask him to take the field with Israel. Jehoshaphat soon agreed, figuring that if Moab could rebel against Israel with impunity, Edom could very well declare its independence of Judah someday.

When Jehoshaphat asked which route they should follow to Moab, Jehoram advised going along the south shore of the Dead Sea. It was also possible to go north of the Dead Sea, which would be shorter. But in the north Moab had strong fortifications and would be on the lookout for the enemy. The southern route required a march of several days through the desert, but it was thought that at that time of year (late spring) there would still be water in the brooks. And in the south Moab lay wide open.

Israel and Judah marched out to war together and made the king of Edom and his army take the field with them. Even though he was not a trustworthy ally, they could at least keep an eye on him so that he would not attack them unexpectedly from the rear.

For David's sake. For seven days they marched together through the desert. When they did not find any water at Moab's border, they were filled with fear. The armies were parched with thirst. If the Moabites attacked them now, they would be defenseless.

Jehoram, who had planned the campaign, was the first one to become desperate. He complained that the Lord had called the three armies together to deliver them into the hands of the

Moabites. Thus he reproached the Lord for their plight, forgetting that the summons to battle had been issued not by the Lord but by him. Jehoshaphat's cooperation had probably convinced him that this campaign was in accordance with the Lord's will. How little he knew the Lord or was able to find strength in Him in time of need!

Jehoshaphat asked whether there was a prophet of the Lord accompanying the armies. A prophet could ask the Lord what to do. There was a prophet with the army—Elisha.

How did Elisha come to be there? Apparently he had attached himself to the army of his own accord. After all, it was Israel's cause that was at stake. Elisha, too, was influenced by national enthusiasm and pride. But did he see clearly enough that he was permitted to give himself to Israel's cause only for the Lord's sake? It is clear from the rest of the story that Elisha no longer saw this point clearly.

Under the leadership of Jehoshaphat, the three kings went to Elisha. They did not send for the prophet; they honored the Word of the Lord, which was with him, by going to him.

Elisha first turned to Jehoram and told him that he had better go to the Baal prophets. But Jehoram dismissed that suggestion. The fact was that he had done away with the Baals and believed that he stood in the Lord's favor. But why had the Lord now brought him here to deliver him and his allies into the hands of the Moabites? Because there was so much misunderstanding and deceit involved, Elisha turned away from Jehoram and swore by the Lord that he would consider their request to ask the Lord's will only for Jehoshaphat's sake.

Apparently Elisha was not in the proper frame of mind to receive the Word of the Lord. Therefore he asked for a minstrel, a harp player, whose music would put his mind to rest. This request was granted, and Elisha was able to proclaim the Word of the Lord. In the Lord's name, he ordered that many ditches be dug in the valley. He prophesied that those ditches would be filled with water, even though the armies would see neither wind nor rain. From the promise of this miracle of grace, Elisha rightly drew the conclusion that the Lord would also deliver the Moabites into their hands.

Very early the next morning, at the time when the morning sacrifice was being made in the temple, water came from the direction of Edom and filled the ditches. Apparently the Lord had caused rain to fall on Edom's mountains during the night. The water streamed toward the valley and filled the ditches. Thus the thirst of men and beasts was quenched.

That same morning the Moabites marched against the allied enemies. From the heights they looked down into the valley in the distance. Just then the rising sun was shining on the water, making it look red. The armies in the valley apparently kept themselves well concealed. This led the Moabites to think that the three kings and their armies had quarreled and started killing each other. They assumed that the red pools were pools of blood, for they were hoping that Edom would rebel against Judah. Thus they thought that the loot was lying there for the taking. Unsuspecting, they went down into the valley. Then the Israelites rallied and killed them.

The Lord showed His people this favor especially for the sake of Judah and Jehoshaphat, the son of David—and ultimately for the sake of His covenant with David, that is, for the sake of the Christ. His grace was upon His people again.

The whole earth is Mine. Elisha advised the kings to destroy all the cities, to cut down the fruit trees, to stop up the wells, and to ruin the fields with stones. He told them to turn all of Moab into a wasteland.

How could Elisha have urged the kings on to such senseless destruction? The land of Moab belonged to the Lord, just as the whole earth is the Lord's. When Elisha gave that advice, he was no longer the Lord's prophet. Swept along by nationalistic passion, he wanted Israel to vent its wrath on Moab. That wrath was not the wrath of the Lord.

The allied armies did as Elisha advised. Before long, most of the country was destroyed. Only the capital city, Kir-hareseth, was still intact, and it was surrounded. From the high points around the city, soldiers with slings hurled stones into the city. Mesha tried to break through the armies of Israel and Judah to the army of Edom, in the hope that Edom would throw in its lot with him, but he was beaten back.

Driven into a corner, he took his oldest son, who was no

longer a child, and sacrificed him upon the wall as a burnt offering to his idol Chemosh. Surely this god would now provide deliverance! The wall itself had been turned into an altar, Mesha reasoned, and therefore nothing could happen to it. At that moment the wrath of God broke out in Israel's army. Many died, and the armies had to withdraw.

Didn't Israel share the blame for this abominable human sacrifice? Shouldn't the Israelites have been satisfied when the Moabites were defeated and were once again made subject to them? At that point the goal of their campaign was reached.

This useless destruction aroused the Lord's anger. After all, it was *His* earth! The treasures that were destroyed belonged to Him! Was Israel any better than the heathen king who sacrificed his son in vain?

Israel had to learn that the earth is the Lord's. Elisha, the Lord's prophet, also had to learn this lesson. The grace which God shows His people for Christ's sake does not have destruction as its aim; its purpose is the blessing and salvation of the entire earth.

38: The Word of Life

II Kings 4

In general, Elijah's prophetic actions were somewhat different than Elisha's. Elijah's ministry was in many respects a revelation of anger and judgment. But Elisha's deeds—with some exceptions—revealed God's compassion for life. This statement does not conflict with what we read in I Kings 19:17. The refusal to accept the mercy that was revealed through Elisha made the judgment more severe for many. In II Kings 4, the life-giving power of the Word of the Lord is revealed.

In the first story, it is made clear that we receive to the extent that our hearts are opened by the Word of the Lord. How much we receive depends on how much faith we place in that Word. The woman received as much oil as the vessels she had collected could hold.

In the second story, we are shown that when people are gripped by the Word of the Lord, they may also claim that Word for victory. Gehazi was not gripped by the Word of the Lord and thus did not take hold of it in faith, no matter how much Elisha compelled him to concentrate by forbidding him to greet anyone on the way. Therefore nothing happened when Gehazi laid the staff on the child's face.

In the last two stories, the Word of the Lord preserves life in a time of famine.

Main thought: *The Word of the Lord is the Word of life.*

According to her faith. In those days the widow of one of the students of a school of the prophets came to Elisha. She was in financial difficulties. Her creditor threatened to take away both her sons as slaves to cover her debt. That was not in accordance with the law of Moses, but this harsh practice was apparently being followed among the people of the Lord.

Elisha understood that it was the Father's will that the liberating power of the Word of His grace be manifested in the face of this harshness. When he asked the widow what she still had in the house, he learned that she had nothing left but a little jar of oil. God's strange and wondrous grace would make use of that oil. The little we have received can become an extended blessing if the Lord sees fit.

Elisha told her to collect as many vessels as she could. Then she was to lock the door behind her. Together with her sons, she was to fill the vessels with oil from the little jar.

Surely that was nonsense. But to someone who believed, it was not nonsense at all! That widow was being tested to see whether she really believed the Word of the Lord, which promised her a miracle.

She did as Elisha commanded and collected many vessels. Then she shut the door so that she would not be disturbed while she was expecting the Lord's miracle in faith. By the miracle of God's grace, she was able to fill all the vessels. When the last vessel was finally full, the oil stopped flowing.

In great gratitude of faith, she went to Elisha to tell him what had happened. He ordered her to sell the oil, pay her creditor, and live with her sons from the rest of the money. Thus the lives and freedom of this woman and her sons were saved by a divine miracle.

By the miracle of God's grace in the Christ, God will also deliver us. Because of the curse of sin, the harshness of life threatens to rob us of our freedom and enslave us all. Through Christ, however, we are freed from the bonds of slavery. And we receive from the Lord as much as we have learned to expect by believing in His Word.

Gripped by the Word of the Lord. One day when Elisha was passing through the little town of Shunem, a wealthy woman invited him to her house for a meal. From then on, it became a habit for Elisha to eat at her house whenever he passed through

Shunem. This was the woman's desire, for she recognized that the Lord's Word of grace for His people was in Elisha.

Later, after consulting with her husband, she had an upstairs room built on the flat roof, a room enclosed by a brick wall. This room she carefully furnished. She had said to her husband that this man of God was different from the other sons of the prophets; he had a special relationship with the Lord. In a particular way, he was holy to the Lord. The sublimity of God's grace was revealed in him.

When Elisha was their guest again, he understood that it was the Lord's will that this house receive the blessing of His Word. But Elisha did not know in what way this blessing was to be given. Therefore he had Gehazi ask the woman what Elisha could do for her. She answered that she did not need anything; the Lord had given her a blessed place among her people. Then Elisha asked Gehazi what he thought. Gehazi had seen better than the prophet what was missing in her life—something of which she could not and would not speak.

When the Lord urged Elisha to give the woman something, He left him unaware of what that gift should be. Gehazi drew Elisha's attention to the fact that the woman had no child. Then Elisha understood what the Lord wanted to give her. Prophetically enlightened, he prophesied that she would have a son within a year.

Not out of unbelief but because this gift was too overwhelming for her, the woman said that the prophet should not raise her hopes in vain. She had already tried to overcome her longing for a child. But at Elisha's word, she did believe. And in faith she received her child. The Christ fulfills the desires and expectations of our lives in surprising ways.

However, when the boy was a few years old, he died rather suddenly in his mother's lap from a sunstroke. Though the woman's faith was not shattered by this turn of events, she did have a struggle on her hands. She knew of only one thing to do—go to the prophet.

She laid the boy on the bed in the guest room reserved for Elisha, for she and the boy would have to be close to the prophet. Without even telling her husband that the child had died, she rode to Elisha that hot afternoon—a trip of more than 20 kilometers.

Elisha, who was then on Mount Carmel, saw her coming and sent Gehazi to meet her and find out what was wrong. But to Gehazi she said nothing. When she came up to Elisha, she took hold of his feet. Gehazi, who had not seen how deeply troubled she was, wanted to push her away, but Elisha said, "Let her be." He was surprised that something very strange had happened without the Lord revealing it to him. What could the Lord's intention be?

Then the woman revealed what had so deeply shocked her. She complained that she would rather not have had a son at all. How she was being destroyed in her struggle to keep believing!

Elisha didn't know what to say; he had to think things over. It was inconceivable that the Lord had given her a son only to take him away from her now. Her seed would remain alive.

Since it wasn't necessary for Elisha himself to go to Shunem, he gave Gehazi his staff and sent him in his place. Gehazi was to allow nothing to distract his attention. He was to greet no one along the way but was to think of the grace of the Lord, which could raise this boy from the dead. When he got there, he was to lay the staff on the boy's face.

The mother, however, did not want to leave Elisha. She had confidence in God's Word only as borne by the prophet. Where could she find refuge if not with the prophet, with the Word of the Lord? Therefore Elisha went with her after all.

Gehazi, who was already on his way, was not gripped by the Word of the Lord and therefore could not lay claim to it in faith. When he laid the staff on the boy's face, it did not help at all. Not by some magical power but by the Word of the Lord as received in faith would this child be enabled to rise. It is the favor of God that gives life.

As Elisha was approaching Shunem, Gehazi came to meet him and told him that the boy had not revived. Then Elisha himself went into the room where the boy was lying. He shut the door so that he would not be disturbed and could concentrate on the Word of the Lord. He stretched himself upon the boy so that the boy's body would become warm. It was as though he wanted to share his own life, which was so completely tied to the Word of the Lord, with the boy. Then he got up and walked once up and down the room.

Elisha had been gripped by the Word of the Lord, but he had

to lay hold of it in a severe struggle of faith. Then, for the second time, he stretched himself upon the boy. The boy sneezed and finally opened his eyes. Life had returned—not through any power Elisha possessed but by the power of the Word of grace.

Through God's favor, the Christ later arose from the dead. That power of His resurrection was already displayed here. By that power, Christ holds fast those who are His, so that they are alive even if they have died. One day they will also be raised by that power.

When the mother saw her boy alive again, she fell before Elisha's feet and bowed down in adoration of the Lord, in whose favor she had placed her hope even in this severe struggle. Is there anything we may not expect from the Lord if we trust the Word of His grace?

The bread of life. Elisha, like Elijah, repeatedly visited the schools of the prophets. Once, when there was hunger in the land, he was in Gilgal. He noticed that the sons of the prophets had suffered from hunger. Because he wanted to treat them well, he had his servant put on the largest pot and boil soup for them.

One of the sons of the prophets, wanted to be helpful, collected wild gourds* in the field and cut them up for the soup. That made the soup bitter and inedible. Apparently they were not familiar with this fruit. The first ones to taste the soup thought it was poisoned and cried out: "Man of God, there is death in the pot!" Then Elisha added some meal to the soup, making it edible.

It was probably while Elisha was still in Gilgal that someone from the neighborhood came to bring him the first fruits of the new harvest—20 loaves of barley together with some fresh grain. With Elisha at the time were not just the sons of the prophets but also some others—about 100 men altogether.

Elisha told them to put the food before the people. The loaves of bread were the small kind common in those days. What did 20 of them amount to when there were 100 men to be fed? So thought Elisha's servant. But Elisha repeated his command, saying that all

*Probably colocynths or, as they are called, bitter apples.—TRANS.

of them were to eat. There would be food left over, he added. It turned out that Elisha had spoken the truth, for he had spoken in accordance with the Word of the Lord.

Time and again, the Word of the Lord provided for people in their need. One day the Christ will come to provide for all our needs. In Him the favor of the Lord is bestowed upon us. What can we possibly lack if we possess the Lord's favor?

39: Accepted as a Gift

II Kings 5—6:7

We know that Naaman was cured by faith, but we do not know whether his faith was a true faith. We have no evidence that it was any more than a faith in magical powers. He did say: "Now I know that there is no God in all the world except in Israel!" These words certainly make it sound as though his faith was a true faith, but they are not conclusive. Even if it were only a faith in magical powers, it would still be a pattern for genuine faith.

We cannot call it superstition that Naaman wanted to take a load of Israel's black dirt back with him. In those days the Lord was indeed linked with that earth in a special way.

Although Elisha said to Naaman, "Go in peace," we are not to conclude that he sanctioned Naaman's bowing down in the house of Rimmon. It is unthinkable that Elisha was simply brushing this matter aside. He blessed Naaman by wishing him the peace of God. If only that blessing would be accepted in faith!

Certainly Naaman came to Israel expecting to be cured by some magical power. Through Elisha's words, he had to learn what faith is. Afterward he still wanted to repay the prophet somehow, thereby repaying the Lord for healing him. At that point he had to learn that what the Lord gives is a gift that cannot be repaid, a gift that must be cherished purely as a gift. In the same way, we have to learn to subject ourselves to grace.

When the son of the prophets lost his ax head, what he said of the ax was that he had gotten it when he asked for it, not that he had borrowed it. Thus the ax was a present from someone. And that, apparently, is why it was so valuable to him. Through the ax head's miraculous recovery, he learned to possess the ax as a gift from the Lord, along with the whole house being built.

Main thought: *What the Lord gives us can only be accepted as a gift.*

Seeking a magical power. In those days the commander-in-chief of Syria's army was a man named Naaman. He was highly esteemed by the king, but he was a leper. In Syria, apparently, lepers were not banned from society as they were in Israel. Although Naaman was stricken with a deadly disease, he was able to serve in a high position in the government.

On one of their raids into Israel, a band of Syrians had captured a young girl who later became a slave in Naaman's house. This slave felt sorry for her master. Therefore she said to her mistress: "If only my master were in Israel, I know the prophet would heal him." Thus the girl was spreading the message of the power of the grace there was in Israel. Whether she fully understood it herself we do not know, but in any case she spoke of the grace which, for Christ's sake, was upon Israel.

When Naaman told the king about his desire to visit Israel to find healing there, his master was happy to let him go and gave him a letter introducing him to the king of Israel. Naaman arrived in Samaria laden with treasure. Obviously, Naaman and the king of Syria looked upon the prophet's power as magical power. Surely Israel's king would have authority over that magician!

When the king of Israel read the letter with the request for Naaman's healing, he tore his garments. He did not realize that the king of Syria was alluding to Elisha's magical powers. He thought Syria was looking for an excuse to start a war.

Elisha found out what was going on and asked Jehoram to send Naaman to him. No magician was sought, as in heathen countries; Naaman had to go to the prophet of the Lord.

Naaman came to Elisha's door with his chariots and horses and gifts. Now he was going to see the magician at last! That magician would probably call on the name of his god, pronounce some magic formulas, and stroke the diseased spots with his hands. Then Naaman would be healed.

Things didn't go quite the way Naaman expected. One of Elisha's servants came outside and told Naaman to bathe seven times in the Jordan River, promising that he would then be cured.

Angrily Naaman turned to go back to his own country. If Naaman wanted to bathe, he would do so in the rivers of Syria, which were a lot cleaner than the muddy waters of the Jordan!

What a difference there is between faith in the Word of the Lord and the expectations of pagans! And how difficult it is for us to submit in faith to that Word and to silence our unbelieving, rationalizing minds!

A gift for Naaman. At this critical juncture, Naaman's servants spoke to their master: "My father, if the prophet had asked you to do something difficult, you would have done it. Why not do what he asks if it is something simple?" No doubt these servants had also expected a magical cure. But they thought the matter over and concluded that there's no harm in trying.

It's almost as though Naaman's servants were instructing us about faith. We have to be taught this lesson again and again. If there was a great deal we had to do for our salvation, we would certainly be willing to do it. Then the honor for our salvation would be ours. But all the Lord asks of us is belief in His Word.

Naaman had probably heard of Israel's God and His prophet from the young slave-girl. Now he allowed himself to be persuaded by his servants. Their words put him to shame. In faith he expected healing from the God of Israel. He bathed seven times in the Jordan and was cleansed from his leprosy; his flesh, wasted by the disease, became like the flesh of a young child. Thus God will cleanse our lives through faith. For the sake of the Christ, this miraculous power was in Israel.

Full of joy, Naaman returned to Elisha and confessed: "Now I know that there is no God in all the world except in Israel!" He acknowledged the Lord as the only true God, the God to whom he owed his recovery.

That was faith on Naaman's part. Yet, he wanted to repay the Lord through the prophet. But the prophet, calling on the name of the Lord, turned down the gifts Naaman offered him. Naaman had to learn to accept what God gave him purely as a gift, a gift that could never be repaid. And he was to treasure it only as a gift. He had to learn to see the free grace of God.

Did Naaman come to see it entirely in that light? He said that he no longer wanted to serve any other god, and he asked permission to take along some of the soil of Israel. Wasn't the Lord bound to that earth in a special way in His covenant?

Naaman also asked that it not be reckoned to him as sin when, in the service of his master, he bowed down in the house of the god Rimmon. All Elisha said in response was: "Go in peace." The Lord's peace was to rest on Naaman! And that peace would indeed be with him if he accepted it in faith, if he accepted whatever the Lord gave him as a divine gift.

Not a time for accepting gifts. Gehazi, Elisha's servant, had witnessed this discussion. His greed had been aroused by the gifts Naaman offered. He went after the chariot, told Naaman a lie, and received from him two talents of silver and two festive garments. Before returning to the city, Gehazi sent away the boys who were carrying the gifts and hid the loot in his house.

He returned to Elisha and acted as if nothing had happened. But the Lord had revealed everything to the prophet. When Elisha asked Gehazi where he had been, Gehazi gave him a devious answer. Then Elisha reproached him, asking: "Was this a time for accepting gifts?" The Lord had wanted to teach Naaman to accept His gift purely as a gift. Naaman had to learn to live by faith in God's free grace.

Gehazi had stood in the way of the work of God's grace in Naaman, whereas he should have been the servant of the prophet and, as such, the servant of the Lord's grace. For that reason, the leprosy would now cling to him. He left Elisha's presence as a leper, white as snow. What will become of us if we stand in the way of the Lord's grace and reject it in unbelief?

The gift to the prophets' sons. At a certain place where some sons of the prophets lived, the house had become too small. These men lived very soberly, sometimes in poverty, depending on what the people were inclined to give them. They asked Elisha for permission to build a new house at the Jordan. They themselves would cut the timber needed for the house. At their request, Elisha went with them.

While one of the men was busy cutting timber, the head of his ax flew from the handle and fell into the water. The man then poured out his troubles to Elisha. It was a double shame that the ax was gone, for it had been a present. This man valued a gift.

Elisha then threw a piece of wood in the water, and the ax head came floating to the surface, where one of the sons of the prophets could grab it. The forces of nature do not work apart from God—not even the force of gravity which had made the ax head sink. The forces of nature work as the Lord intends them to work, and He makes them all subservient to His grace for His people. Here we are shown how God's grace in the Christ governs all things. For the sake of the Christ, all things will be for our good.

After this event, the man who lost his ax head must have possessed his ax in a different spirit. It must have been still more precious to him as a gift of the Lord's grace, as proof of His favor. This applied not just to the ax but also to the new house. All those sons of the prophets learned to see their new house, their prophetic calling, and their lives as a whole in the light of the lesson they learned from the story of the ax head. Thus, in everything we must learn to see and possess the miracle of God's grace in the Christ. What is there that we may not accept as a gift of that marvelous grace?

40: Unsolicited Grace

II Kings 6:8—8:6

In this passage of Scripture, Israel's relation to its foreign enemies is considered. Elisha concerned himself with this matter far more than Elijah had done. In all his actions, even when they involved Israel's conflict with those enemies, Elisha revealed how God seeks His people in His mercy.

That was unsolicited grace, grace that Israel had not asked for. Israel's king Jehoram certainly did not ask for it. All the same, the Lord told him each time where the Syrians would attack. Nor did Jehoram repent during the siege of Samaria. When he tore his clothes, it became apparent that he was wearing sackcloth underneath. It seems that he had put on this penitential garment at Elisha's word. But it was completely covered up; he was wearing it under his usual clothing.

The whole nation was not called to repentance by the king's example. Apparently Jehoram was ashamed of his penitence. Under these circumstances, his penitential act had the same ultimate meaning as any other supposedly meritorious act. Jehoram expected God to grant Israel deliverance on account of this meritorious act—and not because of His mercy to His people for Christ's sake.

That the king viewed his act of penitence in this light is evident from the fact that when the deliverance did not come quickly and he was shown the curse resting upon Israel, he swore an oath that he would have Elisha put to death. There was no question of true submission to the Word of the Lord. In spite of this, there followed immediately the prophecy of Samaria's deliverance on the following day. Here the Lord was ahead of the people and their king, trying to lure them to repentance.

How can we speak of "grace" when neither the people nor the king came to repentance? This is only possible because we are talking about the Lord's relationship to His people for the sake of the Christ. Among that people there was still a remnant according to election. But for Jehoram himself this was not grace; it was not eternal favor in the Christ.

The blinding of the Syrians must not be taken to mean that they could no longer see anything; otherwise Elisha would not have been able to lead them to Samaria behind him. All it means is that they were no longer able to form a clear picture of what they saw.

Main thought: *The Lord shows His people unsolicited grace in order to bring them to repentance.*

Safety. In Elisha's days the traditional enemies of the Israelites were no longer the Philistines, as in former times, but the Syrians. The Lord had placed Elisha in the midst of Israel to reveal His lovingkindness on all sides. This would also come out in Israel's struggles with her foreign enemies. In this way, too, the Lord desired to show His people His goodness, for which they had not asked, in order to put them to shame and bring them back to Himself.

In those days Syria's king was conducting his campaigns not by mobilizing a large army and risking a decisive battle but by sending bands on marauding expeditions. Yet, every time the king of Syria undertook such action, the Lord revealed to Elisha where the invasion was to occur. Elisha, in turn, warned the king of Israel. Then the king of Israel would send an army there and surprise the band of Syrians.

Jehoram had not asked the Lord for such protection. Nevertheless, the Lord granted it, for in Christ He loves His people. Shouldn't this have put Jehoram to shame and brought him to repentance? And doesn't the Lord do this repeatedly? Over and over again, He is the one who takes the initiative. "Before they call, I will answer," He says. We may and must believe in the grace He gives us even *before* we ask for it. But Jehoram did not do so. He did send an army each time at Elisha's word, but he did not submit to the Lord's grace.

Leading enemies into captivity. That the raids were being anticipated was so obvious that the king of Syria could not help but think that Israel's king was being warned in advance. This meant one thing to the king of Syria—treason on the part of one of his government officials! Angrily he discussed the question with them.

One of his servants, however, knew better. He declared that the prophet of the Lord was informing the king of Israel of what the king of Syria said in his bedchamber. Apparently these heathen people had become aware of what the Word of the Lord in Israel could do.

When he learned that the prophet was in Dothan, Syria's king sent a mighty army of horses and chariots there—a mighty army to capture one man! By now these pagans had some idea of the power of the Word of the Lord. They did not yet know just how great that power is, nor did they realize that no military force on earth can overcome it. This they would soon find out for themselves.

Dothan was situated on a mountain. Surrounding the city were more mountains and hills. The Syrians, who had come by night, camped on those surrounding hills. The next morning Elisha and his servant went out. When Elisha saw the Syrians opposite him, he knew he was their target, and his servant realized this too. That's why the servant, full of fear, asked: "My lord, what shall we do?" Had he still not understood that the Word of the Lord never fails and that we are safe under the shield of that Word? Elisha told him: "Don't be afraid, for those who are with us are more than those who are with them."

This the young man was to see for himself. At Elisha's prayer, the Lord opened his eyes to the fiery chariots and horses all around Elisha. The mountain on which Dothan was built and on which they stood was full of them. Elisha and his servant were surrounded by hosts of angels, all of them subject to the Word of the Lord. Thus Elisha was safe, just as all believers are safe.

The eyes of Elisha's servant had to be opened to see this; he saw the angels in a vision. Only then was he able to see what men do not ordinarily see. Today we do not get such visions. Yet, our eyes have to be opened in faith; otherwise this security enjoyed by believers remains hidden from us. God has to reveal it to us somehow.

When the Syrians came down from the hills to capture Elisha, he prayed to the Lord to strike them with blindness so that they would no longer be able to correctly distinguish what they saw.

The Lord answered his prayer, and Elisha could do whatever he wanted with his enemies. He told them that this was not the city they were looking for and promised to bring them to the man they sought. Elisha outwitted them. That was a strategem of war. Yet, it was also true that the force of arms should have been directed not against the prophet but against the king.

There went the Syrians, to be delivered up to their enemy without knowing where they were going. Do unbelievers ever know where they are going? Aren't all of us struck with such blindness on account of our sin? Those who walk in the light of the Word of the Lord walk securely.

In Samaria the eyes of the Syrian soldiers were opened, in answer to Elisha's prayer. There they saw themselves surrounded by their enemies. Jehoram was there too. What must he have thought! There was the enemy he feared, delivered into his hands by one man—the prophet of the Lord. Shouldn't he then have confessed that he was safe from all enemies if he surrendered to the Word of the Lord?

Yet, it appears that Jehoram was not all that deeply impressed by the humiliation of his enemies, for he wanted to kill them. He thought of these enemy soldiers as *his* prisoners—rather than as prisoners taken by the Word of the Lord.

It is true that Jehoram called the prophet his father in his excitement over the spoils. It seemed as though he was placing himself under the prophet's guidance, but the fact of the matter was that his heart still refused obedience to the Word of God. Therefore Elisha rejected his suggestion. Even if Jehoram himself had captured the prisoners, they were not to be killed. Those prisoners were in the Lord's power.

There was another factor to consider. At this time Israel was not at all suited to serving as the sword of vengeance in the Lord's hand. Israel itself was put to shame by the Word of the Lord, and now it had to put the Lord's enemies to shame. At Elisha's command, a meal was placed before the prisoners. After they had eaten, they were allowed to return to their own country. From that time on, the king of Syria did not send bands of raiders into Israel. The Word of grace which the Lord had pronounced upon Israel for Christ's sake conquered Israel's enemies and put them to shame.

A prophecy of deliverance. Ben-hadad, Syria's king, did invade Israel again, this time with a large army to fight the decisive battle. Syria had taken steps to strengthen its position since the previous encounter.

The Lord delivered Israel into Syria's hands. The country was quickly subdued, and Ben-hadad was able to lay siege to Samaria. Now the Lord chastened His people, but only to put them to shame in a surprising way.

Many in the land had taken refuge within the protective walls of Samaria. Hence the city was soon struck with famine. A donkey's head was sold for 80 pieces of silver, and a quarter of a kab of dove's manure for five pieces of silver. There was nothing the people in the city would not eat.

One day the king was walking on the wall, inwardly torn. Elisha was in the city. He had always preached that the Lord would be merciful if the king and the people would humble themselves. And now the king had humbled himself—or so he thought. Hadn't he put on sackcloth underneath his usual clothing?

Was the king really humbling himself? He was not wearing the penitential garment openly to call the whole nation to acts of penitence. Outwardly he kept his royal dignity. Was he inwardly broken before God? He thought that because of his penitence, he deserved speedy deliverance from the Lord.

Surely this was not true humility! He was trusting in his own merit rather than in the Lord's grace! That way he could not help but blame Elisha and the Lord that there was no deliverance yet.

While he was walking on the wall in this frame of mind, a woman called out to him: "Help me, my lord the king!" His rebellious mood was obvious from the answer he gave this woman: "The Lord isn't helping you! How am I supposed to be able to help you with bread and wine?" With these words he put the blame on the Lord.

When he asked the woman what she wanted from him, she told him a gruesome story about mothers eating their own children. Then the king recognized what had happened: Samaria was being struck by the curse which the Lord had already spoken through Moses (see Lev. 26:27-9). He tore his clothes in horror and vexation, allowing the people to see the sackcloth he was wearing underneath. But even in the face of the horrible fulfillment of the Word of the Lord, he blamed the Lord and His prophet. He swore an oath that he would have Elisha killed that same day. Immediately he dispatched a messenger to see that his oath was fulfilled. Now he wanted to break completely with the Word of the Lord.

Elisha was sitting in his house with the elders of the people, who apparently still sought enlightenment and comfort from him. Even before the messenger arrived, the Lord revealed to Elisha what the king had sworn. He also let Elisha know that the king would quickly repent of his vow and hasten to prevent it from being carried out. Therefore Elisha told the elders to keep the messenger outside. While he was still speaking, the messenger arrived, but the king himself followed immediately behind him. Apparently he did not dare go through with this complete break with the Word of the Lord. He was continually torn between two opinions.

In his obstinate mood, the king called out to Elisha: "This trouble is from the Lord! Why should I wait for the Lord any longer? Your word is nothing but a bunch of lies!"

Then something amazing and unexpected happened. Even though neither the king nor the people really humbled themselves before the Lord or cried out for mercy, the Lord prophesied through Elisha that there would be amazing grace for His people. At the gate of Samaria the very next day, a measure of flour would be sold for a shekel, and two measures of barley for a shekel.

How could the Lord promise such deliverance while His people persisted in their sinful attitude? He did so only because He looked upon His people in the Christ and loved them in the Christ. Even in those days, there were still people in Israel who earnestly inquired after the Lord. Thus the Lord wishes to be ahead of us in His grace, bestowing unsolicited grace upon us so that we will truly be shattered by it.

But who could believe such a thing? Who could believe this marvelous promise of grace? The king kept silent, but the captain on whom the king was leaning expressed his unbelief and mocked the prophecy. "Even if the Lord should make windows in heaven to pour grain from them, it would still be impossible," he declared. When we persist stubbornly in our unbelief, we cannot believe God's amazing grace until His Word takes hold of us and overcomes us. For this mockery the captain received this answer from Elisha: "You shall see it with your own eyes, but you shall not eat of it."

A surprise for desperate people. Outside the city gate were four lepers. They reasoned: "If we stay where we are, we will die of hunger. If we go into the city, we will also die of hunger. If we go to the Syrians, they may kill us, but at least we will have a chance of surviving." Even in these poor suffering lepers we find a calculating spirit; they did not take hold of the Word of grace in the expectation of faith.

In the evening, at dusk, they went to the Syrian camp. To their amazement, they found the tents deserted. What had happened? The Lord had made the Syrians hear the sound of a great army approaching. This made the Syrians think that Israel's king had made an alliance with the Hittites in the north and the Egyptians in the south, and that these combined armies were now bursting in on them.

In terror the Syrians fled helter-skelter. They were like fools fleeing from something that does not exist. Without faith in the Word of grace, we, too, are like fools time and again. Yet, this fear was from the Lord, who filled them with terror. The four lepers were amazed that the tents were deserted, but they did not yet know that there was reason to be amazed at the miracle of God's grace in His deliverance of the city.

The lepers feasted on the food they found in the tents. Driven by greed, they hid the treasures in the earth. They actually found time for this! They did not immediately inform the city of what they had found. No, they took the time to line their own pockets first. If grace does not win the victory over us, we, too, live for ourselves. Then we have little time or concern for the Lord's people and His cause.

Finally, in the midst of their nocturnal looting, their consciences began to bother them. Even then they were driven more by fear of the judgment that morning would bring than by any love of their own people. Even in these poor sufferers, we do not find the living faith for which God's cause and His people are more precious than anything else.

Windows in heaven. When the lepers brought the news to the city, the king got up, even though it was still night. He feared a military trick by the Syrians. Finally he was persuaded to send out two horsemen to scout around. Those who advised this move were thinking along the same desperate lines as the four lepers: if the horsemen remained in the city, they would die together with the rest of the city's inhabitants, and if they went out and fell into the hands of the Syrians, they would suffer the same fate as the others who had been murdered or killed in action. In the king's advisors there was not a single gleam of hope or trace of faith.

The scouts found evidence of headlong flight by the Syrians. When this news reached the city, the people—as many as were still able—poured out of the gate to plunder the Syrian camp. Very quickly some returned to the city gate to sell the food they had found. Elisha's prophecy was literally fulfilled: two measures of barley were sold for a shekel, and a measure of flour for a shekel. In a surprising way the Lord had provided relief. This deliverance, too, occurred because the Christ would one day bring complete redemption. That complete deliverance, however, must be accepted in faith.

The Lord will one day judge those who have rejected the Word of deliverance in unbelief. This the Lord showed through the captain who had mocked Elisha's prophecy. The king had commanded him to direct affairs at the gate. Because of the rush to the Syrian camp, he was trampled underfoot and killed. Thus, what Elisha had prophesied came to pass. Likewise, God will one day judge all those who have turned their back on His Word of grace.

Living witnesses. One day the king was asking Gehazi about all the great things Elisha had done. (This happened before Gehazi became a leper.) Apparently the Word of the Lord gave the king no peace. One of the things Gehazi told him was how Elisha had restored the dead son of the Shunammite woman to life. Just as he was telling this story, that same woman came in with her son and appealed to the king for help.

What had happened? At the time of the famine, Elisha had told her it would last seven years. He advised her to leave the country. She had taken his advice and gone to the land of the Philistines. Upon her return, she found that others had taken possession of her house and land. That's why she was now appealing to the king for help.

When Gehazi saw her, he said to the king: "Here are the woman and the boy I was telling you about." Deeply moved, the king asked the woman about the story. In a startling way, the Lord was confronting him with living witnesses of the deeds He had done through His prophet. Something the king had not expected at all actually happened.

Here again we see the grace that comes to us even before we ask for it. Wasn't this the Lord's way of speaking to the king? Would the king look and listen?

Impressed by what had happened, the king saw to it that the woman not only got back her house and her land but also received payment for everything produced on her land during the time it was not in her possession. However, the king's heart was not overcome by the Word of grace. Jehoram went the way of his father Ahab.

41: Divine Persecution

II Kings 8:7-29
II Chronicles 21—22:9

In these stories Elijah again plays a role. The task of anointing Hazael king of Syria, which Elijah had not been able to carry out, is now performed by Elisha. Jehoram receives a letter from Elijah, who has already been taken up into heaven. Ahaziah is put to death by Jehu, whom Elijah had also been commissioned to anoint.

The Lord persecutes Ahab's house in both Israel and Judah. He spreads a net around that house until it is wiped out by Jehu.

Some years after Elijah's ascension, the king of Judah received a letter written by Elijah. Evidently God had revealed to Elijah beforehand how Jehoshaphat's son Jehoram would reign and how his reign would end. That there was bound to be trouble was clear even in Elijah's time: Jehoram married Athaliah, Ahab's daughter, and Elijah was the great opponent of the spirit of Ahab and his house. Elijah probably instructed Elisha to see to it that the letter reached Jehoram at the proper time.

In II Chronicles 22:2 we read that Ahaziah was 42 years old when he became king. This is apparently a copyist's error, for his father was only 40 years old when he died. In II Kings 8:26 we read that Ahaziah was 22 years old when he became king. Thus, at the age of eighteen Jehoram became the father of this son born to Athaliah.

Main thought: *The Lord persecutes the iniquity of His people in order to wipe out that iniquity.*

The enemy anointed by God. Elisha also went beyond Israel's borders—to Syria, the land of the enemy. The Lord had given

Elijah a task he had not been able to carry out, namely, to anoint Hazael to be king of Syria. Israel was to be chastised by this Hazael.

Driven by the Spirit, Elisha went to Damascus, Syria's capital, to carry out this mission. Ben-hadad, Syria's king, was very sick at the time. When he heard that Elisha had come to Damascus, he sent Hazael, one of his officials, to ask the prophet whether he would recover from his illness. Hazael came to Elisha with a large gift, and Elisha told him that the Lord had revealed that Ben-hadad would die.

After giving Hazael this answer, Elisha looked him straight in the eye for a long time. Hazael felt embarrassed, and Elisha began to weep. When Hazael asked him why he was crying, Elisha replied that he knew what horrible atrocities Hazael was going to commit against the children of Israel. Hazael declared that he did not know what Elisha was talking about. After all, he, Hazael, was only a subordinate in Syria. Then Elisha told him that the Lord had shown him that Hazael was to be king over Syria. Elisha must have anointed him at this time.

Here the Lord was having an enemy of His people anointed! It was as if the Lord had forsaken His people and was on the side of their enemies. Apparently the Lord had changed into an enemy of His people. At the same time He loved them in the Christ. What grieved Him most was that He had to chastise them so severely. It was this divine sorrow that was revealed in Elisha's weeping.

Hazael was indeed called to be an instrument in the Lord's hand for the chastising of His people, but Hazael himself did not see his role as chastising. On the contrary, he rejoiced at the misery he would bring upon Israel. Therefore Hazael's way of acting was still sin before God. It is a terrible thing to have to serve as such an instrument in the Lord's hand.

That Hazael had not the slightest inclination to walk in the Lord's ways was clear from the start. When he returned to His master, he lied to him: he declared that Elisha had said that Ben-hadad would certainly get well again. The next day he smothered Ben-hadad with a woolen blanket dipped in water. Later we will learn what harm Hazael did to the children of Israel as king of Syria.

For a while we lost sight of the tribe of Judah. Now we

must pay attention to Judah again, for Ahab's house began to exercise its influence even in Judah. We have already learned that Jehoshaphat's son Jehoram married Athaliah, the daughter of Ahab and Jezebel. This Athaliah was a disaster for David's house.

Two years before his death, Jehoshaphat made his son Jehoram king. Jehoram let himself be guided completely by Athaliah, his wife. His father had given many treasures to his other sons and appointed them to rule over different cities in Judah. But as soon as Jehoram felt established in his reign after his father's death, he had all his brothers and a few other princes murdered. What disgrace that brought upon David's house! Instead of a blessing to the people, David's house became a curse.

Shouldn't the Lord now visit that house with judgment because of this sin? Still, He did not want to wipe it out utterly as He would do with Ahab's house. The house of David would certainly have to be cleansed of the influence of Ahab's house, but for the sake of the covenant with David, a lamp would always be preserved for that house in the form of a descendant on the throne.

Judgment began its work immediately: Edom revolted against Judah's rule. Jehoram gathered his army together and marched against Edom. But he and his army were surrounded by the Edomites. During the night he was able to break through the enemy lines, but his army was in flight and the independence of the Edomites was established. The authority of David's house over its enemies was broken because that house had forsaken the Lord. The king was no longer a type of the Christ.

Jehoram set a bad example by serving idols, and he urged the people on in their idol worship. Then a letter from the prophet Elijah reached him. Because Elijah had already ascended into heaven some years before, the letter, which Elijah must have written several years previously, should have made a very strong impression on Jehoram. In the letter he read that the Lord would visit him with plagues on his people, on his children, on his wives, on all that he possessed, and on himself.

Soon afterward the plague came. The Philistines and the westernmost Arabians invaded Judah. The king went out to meet them with his army. His wives and children went with him, except for Athaliah and his youngest son Ahaziah, also called Jehoahaz. The army was defeated. All the king's wives and children were taken from him by force, and all his possessions outside Jerusalem were looted.

It was after this that Jehoram was struck down by an incurable disease of the bowel, which lasted for two years. At the end of those two years, his intestines came out and he died in great agony. He had reigned for only eight years. During two of those years, his father was still alive.

Jehoram was not mourned when he left this life. He was buried in the city of David, but not in the tombs of the kings. The people did not make a bonfire for him as a sign of mourning. It was as if the Lord had scornfully cast him aside. His name was not given a place of honor in the list of the kings of David's house.

Divine trampling underfoot. Ahaziah, the youngest son of Athaliah and Jehoram of Judah, was made king by the people. He reigned for only one year because his advisors were his mother and his relatives from Ahab's house. Those advisors brought about his downfall.

Ahaziah joined Jehoram of Israel, Ahab's son, in a campaign against Syria's king Hazael. At Ramoth-gilead, Jehoram of Israel was defeated by the Syrians. Jehoram himself was wounded in the battle and went to his pleasure castle in Jezreel to recover. Ahaziah went to visit his uncle there. Just at that point, judgment descended upon Ahab's house through the hand of Jehu, as we shall see in the next Chapter. Ahaziah barely escaped by fleeing to Samaria and hiding there. Later he was found and killed while trying to flee from Samaria.

Because Ahaziah was a grandson of Jehoshaphat, Jehu permitted him a funeral. His servants brought him to Jerusalem, and he was buried with his fathers in the city of David. The Lord had trampled Ahaziah underfoot because the spirit of his grandfather Ahab had been in him more than the spirit of his grandfather Jehoshaphat. For David's sake, however, an honorable funeral was permitted for this son of David's house.

42: Flame and Stubble

II Kings 9-10

Once more the Lord cleanses the kingdom of Israel, this time by means of Jehu. We must remember that behind all the bloodshed is the Lord's grace seeking out His people. However, neither root nor branch is left of the house of Ahab.

Jehu is to be the Lord's instrument in all of this. As the one who is called, he is to be of service to the grace of God in faith. From the moment of his calling, he is in a position of crisis. The son of the prophets who anoints him flees immediately after the anointing. Then Jehu has to come to grips with himself. Will he put himself at the disposal of God's grace by asking for the Word of the Lord and waiting for directions from God, or will his sinful nature fling itself upon that calling? Jehu chooses the latter path.

That decision also determines his future actions. No matter how well he executes the Lord's assignment outwardly, he is inwardly driven by motives other than the obedience of faith. In the cleansing of Israel, he is a type of the Christ on the one hand and an antitype on the other.

Main thought: *God cleanses His people by consuming the godless like stubble.*

Called to be the Lord's instrument. There was one mission given by the Lord to Elijah on Mount Horeb that still awaited completion. Elisha realized that the time had now come to take care of it.

The Lord had shown particular mercy to Ahab's son Jehoram. Again and again He called him to believe. But Jehoram had hardened himself. Now God's patience had come to an end. He would consume Jehoram and the house of Ahab like stubble. That house was going to be destroyed root and branch.

Jehoram was in Jezreel recovering from wounds he had sustained in the wars with Hazael and the Syrians near Ramoth in Gilead. Ramoth itself was still in the hands of the Israelites. The soldiers and their commanders were encamped there. Elisha sent one of the sons of the prophets to Ramoth secretly to anoint Jehu to be king over Israel. He was to return without delay.

This son of the prophets found Jehu sitting among the officers. He called him aside, anointed him, and told him that the Lord had chosen him to be king over Israel with the specific purpose of exercising divine wrath upon Ahab's house. Immediately afterward the son of the prophets left. Jehu did not have an opportunity to ask him anything about his calling.

There Jehu stood. He had just been called by the Lord. Because the son of the prophets had left so suddenly, Jehu was immediately put to the test. Would he have the patience to wait for further instructions from the Lord, or would he immediately set himself up as king and go his own way? God's calling always puts us to the test.

Still undecided, Jehu returned to his companions. They asked him what the crazy man had wanted of him. That's what the commanders of Israel's army called a son of the prophets! How much respect for the Word of the Lord was there left?

At first Jehu kept his calling to himself. He wanted to think things over before saying anything. He just shrugged his shoulders and said: "What could such a madman want?" But his fellow officers noticed that there was something on his mind and kept asking questions. Because they kept after him, Jehu finally told them what had happened.

The commanders immediately declared themselves in favor of Jehu as king. Jehu was a man who normally made up his mind quickly and saw the consequences of actions and decisions. Thus they expected something special of him as king. Lacking a throne, the officers took off their military uniforms, spread them over the bare steps, placed Jehu on their makeshift throne, blew the trumpets, and cried out: "Jehu has become king!" And Jehu let it all happen.

Thus the commanders made the decision for Jehu. Jehu let himself be led, even though he was otherwise a man of quick decisions. He let himself be led this time because he was very eager to be king.

Now that Jehu had chosen his own way, he was not the servant of God's grace to His people. Jehu's sinful nature had thrown itself upon his calling. He would make the most of his calling for his own sake. The Lord would indeed destroy Ahab's house and cleanse His people by the hand of Jehu, but Jehu would not be inwardly devoted to the Lord's cause in faith as he carried out his task. One day the Lord Jesus Christ will also exercise God's wrath, but He will do so in complete submission to the Father, in order that grace may be triumphant.

The cleansing of Jezreel. Although Jehu hesitated for a moment in making a decision that determined the course of his entire life, he was resolute as soon as his mind was made up. He had the city surrounded so that no news of what had happened would get out. Then he went to Jezreel. He raced along in the manner characteristic of him. The watchman in Jezreel could see that it was Jehu approaching from the speed of his chariot. Two messengers were sent to him by King Jehoram, but he added them to his ranks when they chose in favor of him.

Finally Jehoram of Israel came to meet him, accompanied by Ahaziah, king of Judah. Jehu refused peace because of the idolatry and sorcery imported into Israel by Jezebel. He shot an arrow into Jehoram's back as he fled. The arrow pierced Jehoram's heart, and Jehu had the corpse thrown out of the chariot. This happened in the part of the king's garden which had earlier been the vineyard of Naboth. At that instant Jehu remembered Elijah's words to Ahab, which he himself had heard when he walked behind Ahab as his servant.

Ahaziah managed to get away. But Jehu pursued him, and later his men mortally wounded Ahaziah. Ahaziah died as he tried to make his way to Jerusalem. His servants transported his body to Jerusalem, where he was buried. On his mother's side, Ahaziah was a member of Ahab's house. The judgment included him because he walked in the sinful ways of that house.

In the meantime, Jezebel, Jehoram's mother, heard what had happened. She put on her makeup, for she wished to die like a queen. Jezebel had had enough. She had lived for herself, and she also wanted to die that way. How horrible!

When Jehu returned, she looked out the window and called out to him: "Is it peace, O Zimri, murderer of your master?" She called him *Zimri* because Zimri, too, had revolted against his master.

Jehu did not judge her worthy of an answer. He had her thrown out the window, and then trampled on her with his chariot and horses. After he took time to eat and drink, he had someone attend to her. By then most of her body had been torn apart by the dogs in the street. The Word of judgment pronounced on Jezebel by Elijah was fulfilled. One could no longer say, "This is Jezebel." Her name would perish with her forever.

The cleansing of Samaria. Seventy sons and grandsons of Ahab lived in Samaria. Jehu gave the commanders of Samaria the choice of being for him or against him. They chose for him and sent him the heads of those 70 descendants of Ahab in baskets. Jehu had the heads put in two heaps at the entrance of the gate. The next morning he addressed the people from that spot. "I killed Jehoram, but who killed these?" Obviously it was a divine judgment. What he did not mention was that he was the one who had demanded this slaughter. This was his way of showing that God was on his side. Through such tactics he hoped to enlist the people's support.

Convinced that he now had enough power, Jehu killed all who remained of the house of Ahab together with their acquaintances and their priests in Jezreel. Then he went to Samaria again. On the way he killed any brothers and nephews of Ahaziah, king of Judah, whom he happened to meet. They, too, were descendants of Ahab, through his daughter Athaliah.

Farther along the road he met Jehonadab, a Kenite and thus a descendant of Moses' father-in-law. Because of his righteousness and the high standards by which his people lived, this Kenite was highly esteemed by the people of Israel. He chose Jehu's side, and Jehu invited him into his chariot. This strengthened Jehu's position. After all, this righteous man was on his side. This meant that it was Jehu's calling to judge righteously and in obedience to the Lord. Did Jehu live up to that calling?

In Samaria he killed all the remaining members of Ahab's family. By means of a trick he managed to wipe out all the Baal priests throughout the country. The slaying of the Baal priests was in accordance with the Lord's will, but for Jehu himself, the political consideration that those Baal priests were loyal to Ahab's house was uppermost. Then the temple of Baal and the idols in Samaria were destroyed.

In this judgment upon Ahab's house, Jehu was not the faithful servant of the Lord's grace. Later this would become even more clear. All the same, in the love in which He is constantly seeking His people, the Lord used Jehu to cleanse Israel of idolatry and the idolatrous royal house.

Israel got another chance. Would it now surrender to the Lord's grace with a perfect heart, or would the king and the people continue to turn away in willful rebellion? Everyone in Israel who truly feared the Lord must have awaited the results of this cleansing in suspense. Something of the Spirit of the Christ was still alive in Israel. What would the outcome be?

Continuing in sin. Because Jehu had exercised the Lord's vengeance upon the house of Ahab, the Lord promised him that his descendants would occupy the throne of Israel for four generations. This was certainly not a reward Jehu merited. In the destruction he had wrought, his heart had not been upright with the Lord.

In this blessing upon Jehu's house, the Lord was setting the seal of His approval on the extermination of Ahab's house. How much the Lord hated that house for the sake of His people was clearly evident in this blessing upon Jehu.

Jehu had removed much idolatry from Israel, but he promoted the idol worship in Bethel and Dan. The king and the people still did not turn to the Lord and the obligations of His covenant. That's why the Lord chastised Israel.

Hazael, Syria's king, captured all of Tansjordan. The word which Elisha had spoken to Hazael at the time of his anointing was already being fulfilled. Misery came upon Israel. Where was the honor and security of the Lord's people?

While Israel was groaning in distress, Jehu died. He had not been able to deliver the country. The hope entertained by the people when he took over as king had not been fulfilled. In his heart he had not listened to the calling of the Lord.

In contrast to the life of Jehu shines the glory of the Christ, who was faithful to God in all things. One day He will be a flame consuming the godless like stubble. The Christ will execute the judgment of God's grace. And those who belong to Him will judge along with Him.

This was not the situation with Jehu and the people in those days. Still, the Lord continued to seek Israel for a long time.

Ephraim against Judah Again

43: The Struggle of the Spirit

II Kings 11-12

Athaliah kills her own grandsons. She is hostile toward her own flesh and blood because those grandchildren are also of David's line. What we see in Athaliah is not just a desire for power; she has inherited from Jezebel, her mother, a hatred of the Word and service of the Lord, a hatred of the covenant of the living God, a hatred of the Christ.

As Athaliah wipes out the royal seed, she is a tool in the Lord's hand by which the house of David is cleansed from its tie with the house of Ahab. During this period David's house is being cut off at the root, as it were, so that it may grow again in godliness. The effects of the cleansing are not fully realized until generations later.

Even Joash does not choose independently for the Lord's covenant. The murder of Zechariah, the son of his protector and benefactor, is committed with his authorization!

How intimately David's kingship had been bound up with the priesthood! Because David chose for the service of the Lord with all his heart, he was the leader in that union. In Joash's days, the priest Jehoiada is temporarily the leader, giving David's house an opportunity to choose independently for the Lord once again. But such a choice is not made. Jehoiada's son Zechariah is murdered. Then judgment has to strike David's house again. In history the Lord's Spirit continually wrestles to bring forth the form and type of the Christ in that house.

In spite of his unfaithfulness, Joash is a shoot from the stump of Jesse and a branch from his roots (Is. 11:1). Thus he is a type of the Christ.

Main thought: *The Spirit struggles to bring forth the type of the Christ.*

333

The shoot from Jesse's stump. Athaliah learned that her son Ahaziah, king of Judah, had been killed. She took note of this event and considered it a blow to David's house. As a daughter of Jezebel, she hated that house. Now she saw her opportunity to seize power and bring the house of David to ruin. Therefore she ordered that all her grandsons be killed. This woman hated her own flesh and blood because she viewed those grandsons as descendants of David, with whom the Lord had established His covenant. That's how far hatred of the Christ can go.

Without knowing it, Athaliah was a tool in the Lord's hand to execute judgment on David's house. How that house had surrendered to sin as a result of its tie with the house of Ahab! The idolatrous people of Judah were also being punished in this humiliation of David's house.

Still, the Lord could not and would not break His covenant with David. There had to be salvation for that house! Ahaziah's sister Jehosheba was married to Jehoiada, the high priest. She hid Joash, her youngest nephew, in the room where the bed linens were kept. Later she secretly reared him in her own house near the temple. The Lord was going to exalt him and restore the house of David in him.

Because of its sin, David's house had been cut off at the root, as it were. Yet the Lord preserved one shoot of that house. Didn't the same thing happen later when the house of David had come to total ruin? The Lord caused the Christ to be born of that house. In spite of the people's sin, God was faithful to the promise He made to David.

The exaltation. When Joash was seven years old, Jehoiada judged that the time had come to make him king. He made an agreement with the captains of the royal bodyguard, who then swore allegiance to Joash. Then these captains, following up on what Jehoiada had commanded, used their influence with the priests and the Levites in the land and also with the heads of households. They all came to Jerusalem.

On the appointed day, the day on which the priests and Levites in charge would be coming off duty, Jehoiada had the captains of the bodyguard come to the forecourt. In order not to arouse suspicion, they arrived unarmed. Jehoiada gave them the weapons that were still in the temple from David's time. He put these captains at the head of the priests and the Levites, who were also provided with weapons. The group which was being relieved of duty after serving in the temple was divided into three companies assigned to guard the exits of the forecourt. The group that was coming on duty was divided into two companies and was to serve as a guard around the young king.

Then Joash was brought outside. The royal crown was placed on his head, and the law of the Lord was put in his hand. The high priest and his sons anointed him. All the people gathered in the forecourt shouted for joy and cried: "Long live the king!" The trumpets were blown.

In the royal palace Athaliah heard the noise and came outside to see what was going on. When she saw the young king, she tore her clothes and cried, "Treason!" At Jehoiada's command she was led away and put to death.

No civil war resulted from this act. On the contrary, the people rejoiced at the restoration of David's house. And Jehoiada made a covenant between the Lord on the one hand and the people with their king on the other, as well as a covenant between the king and the people. Together they would serve the Lord. As a sign of their resolve, they destroyed the temple of Baal and killed the chief priest.

Under the guardianship of the priesthood. Joash grew up under Jehoiada's guardianship. Under his guidance Joash learned about the service of the Lord. It looked as though his heart was inclined to fear the Lord.

Because of the godlessness of his predecessors, the house of the Lord had been neglected. A thorough restoration was necessary, and Joash resolved to have the repair work done. The Levites collected money throughout the land. Part of the regular income from the services was to be used for this purpose as well. But after 23 years, nothing had been done about repairing the temple. It appeared that all the money that came in was used for the regular services, which had been reinstated. Therefore, at the king's urging, Jehoiada made a large offering box with a hole in the lid. This box was for contributions intended for the restoration of the temple only.

The Lord made the people willing. A great deal of money came in, and the temple was repaired. The people worked on this project with great faithfulness, and therefore it was not necessary for them to give an accounting. The money that was left was used to replace the utensils of the temple. With great joy the people celebrated the service of the Lord in His house.

Not only had the house of David been restored, the house of the Lord was restored as well. It seemed that Judah was entering a new period of growth in the Lord's favor. There was only one cloud on the horizon: Joash had chosen this direction under the guidance of the high priest. It still had to be proved that he chose for the Lord's covenant in his heart. Time would tell whether Joash, like his forefather David, would be able to lead the people and the priesthood in the ways of the Lord.

The murder of Zechariah. Jehoiada died at the ripe old age of 130. He was buried with great honors where the kings were buried in the city of David, for he had done a great deal for the people by leading them back to God and His service.

Now it would become clear whether Joash was truly a leader in the fear of the Lord. After Jehoiada's death, the princes of Judah, prominent men who began to feel their own importance, came to Joash. They flattered him and probably congratulated him on being relieved of the guidance of that old man. Now Joash would have to show that he was independent—by allowing freedom of religion in Judah! And Joash let himself be persuaded. He thought he was acting independently, but he was actually being led by his nobles. We only become independent in the fear of the Lord when we choose for Him with our whole heart.

Thus, idol worship arose again in Judah. For that reason, the wrath of the Lord was kindled. The Lord sent prophets to witness against the king and the people, but they would not listen to them. The Lord's Spirit came upon Zechariah, Jehoiada's son, with exceptional power. Publicly he witnessed to the people against their sin and warned that the Lord's blessing would depart from them.

Soon conspirators were plotting against Zechariah. With the

authorization of Joash, he was stoned in the outer court. He died saying: "The Lord will see it and avenge it." That's how far Joash was willing to go. Not only had he demonstrated his gross ingratitude toward his benefactor, he had also shown that he wanted to break with the Word of the Lord. What awful things we wind up doing when the Word of the Lord becomes a burden to us!

The house of David still was not sufficiently cleansed; it was still not independent in the service of the Lord. Once again the Lord used Hazael, Syria's king, against Judah. Although the Syrian army was much smaller than Judah's army, Judah was defeated. The Lord had forsaken Judah. It looked as though there would be a siege of Jerusalem. But Joash headed this off by handing over to Hazael all the treasures he found in the house of the Lord. Everything that had formerly been devoted to the Lord and was not even used when the temple was restored was now surrendered in this shameful payoff. Did Joash think that the Lord would approve of such commerce?

That's why the wrath of the Lord continued to exert pressure. Joash, who had been wounded in the battle, was attacked by his servants and killed. Because of Judah's humiliation, the people revolted against their king. He was buried without honors. They did bury him in the city of David, but not in the tombs of the kings. His name was not among Judah's honored.

What would happen if God was not faithful to the house of David? One day the Christ would come, and He would reconcile the unrighteousness of Judah and of the entire people of God, together with the unrighteousness of their leaders. In Him God's people would find protection. Yet, throughout history the Spirit of the Lord searched for a king who would be a better type of the Christ than Joash.

44: Extreme Long-suffering

II Kings 13; 14:23-29

For the sake of His covenant with Abraham, Isaac and Jacob, the Lord was extremely long-suffering even toward the kingdom of the ten tribes. That kingdom threatened to fall, but the Lord still postponed that event. Soon that kingdom would be abandoned, although a few individual believers would be saved. After the captivity, a few from that kingdom would return with the two tribes. In those elect few, the ten tribes would be saved after all.

The expression *strike the ground with them* in II Kings 13:18 means *shoot them to the earth.*

Main thought: *For the sake of His covenant, the Lord is extremely long-suffering with His people.*

Still answered. Israel's King Jehu was succeeded by his son Jehoahaz. Jehoahaz was a true son of his father; like him, he walked in the sin of Jeroboam, the son of Nebat, that is, the sin of idol worship. There was still no bowing down before the Lord as the high and exalted One; rather, the Lord was pulled down to the level of earthly life—by being represented in the form of a calf. Although the people spoke the name of the Lord, He was not really served. The people served the forces of nature instead. For Jehoahaz, the Lord was the God of Israel, just as each of the other nations had a god of its own. In this way men tried to prevail over the Lord.

338

Of course the Lord became incensed at such attitudes. During Jehu's time, the Syrians had already occupied the entire area of Transjordan. Now they pressed across the Jordan River and occupied part of the land there too. Jehoahaz was powerless to resist them or drive them back. It got so bad that he finally had nothing left but 50 horsemen, ten chariots, and 10,000 infantrymen. Syria's King Hazael rendered the soldiers of Israel so powerless that they were as the dust of the earth to be trampled underfoot.

In his anxiety Jehoahaz called solemnly upon the Lord. How could he possibly do this when he did not really turn to the Lord in his heart? It certainly was no prayer of faith on his part. He was appealing to the Lord because he saw no other way out. To some extent he sensed the just judgment in his defeats. It is a terrible thing to understand something of that judgment and still not bow before the justice of God's eternal judgment in an effort to find eternal salvation.

The king's prayer was not one of faith, but the Lord answered it anyway. He looked upon the Christ, who is the true Intercessor for His people. His heart was moved by the oppression which His people, whom He still loved for the sake of the Christ, suffered at the hands of the Syrians. Among the people there were still some who truly feared the Lord. In them He was bound to that people.

The Lord heard the prayer of Jehoahaz and did not forsake His people. But the deliverance did not come until the reigns of his son and grandson.

Still not rejected. Jehoahaz was succeeded by his son Joash. During his reign the Lord began to deliver Israel from the Syrians. Syria's King Hazael, of whom Elisha prophesied that he would bring distress upon Israel, died. His son Ben-hadad became king in his place. Joash was able to stand up to Ben-hadad. The judgment foretold by Elisha had come, and now deliverance would come again.

Elisha was still permitted to prophesy about that deliverance on his deathbed. As he lay dying, he was visited by Joash. Weeping, Joash bent over him and lamented: "My father, my father! Israel's chariot and its horsemen!" What he meant was that Elisha was the strength of Israel. Here Joash still called Elisha his father, his spiritual mentor. He acknowledged that in the prophet, that is, in the Word of God borne by the prophet, the strength for Israel's battles was to be found.

Although Joash worshiped idols too, he apparently did not dare to break with God's Word completely. And because the tie to the Word had not been altogether broken, the Lord showed mercy and did not yet reject the people. He remembered His covenant with Abraham, Isaac and Jacob, and He looked upon this last tie to His Word as fruit of that covenant. For this reason Elisha was permitted to prophesy that there would be deliverance.

Elisha told the king to take a bow and arrow and to draw the bow. Then Elisha laid his hands on the king's hands and ordered him to shoot an arrow eastward through the open window. Elisha said that this was an arrow of the Lord's deliverance from the power of the Syrians. Elisha had laid his hands on the hands of the king in the name of the Lord. The deliverance would come from the Lord; He would turn His weapons against the Syrians.

Now Joash accepted that promise in faith. Therefore Elisha told the king to shoot more arrows toward the ground. The king shot three times. Then he stopped. If he knew that those arrows were a sign of the delivering power of the Lord against the Syrians, why didn't he shoot the entire bundle? Did Joash really believe the promise of deliverance? And did he really appreciate this sign? Faith always values the sign and seizes hold of the certainty of God's promise in the sign. In the same way, believers today use the sacraments, which are a sign and a seal.

Joash did not act out of faith. Elisha became very angry because the king had shot only three times, and he told the king that now he would defeat the Syrians only three times. If he had shot five or six times, he would have defeated the Syrians completely.

After this Elisha died and was buried. But the promise lived on—the whole promise of the Word of God as well as the promise of deliverance from the Syrians. This the Lord revealed by way of a peculiar sign.

In those days bands of Moabites repeatedly invaded the land. One day, just as a man was about to be buried in the same burial vault in which Elisha was buried, one of these bands of Moabites appeared. Because the corpse was shoved into the grave chamber hastily, it touched the bones of Elisha. Immediately the dead man came to life again. Elisha had died, but the power of the Word of life which he had borne had not died. Israel was to live by the power of the Word of the Lord.

Joash experienced this. He defeated the Syrians three times and drove them from the land west of the Jordan, although the Syrians still continued to occupy Transjordan. This deliverance was a sign that Israel would live, that God's people would live eternally for Christ's sake. This kingdom would be destroyed before long, but a remnant would be saved.

Still not sentenced. Joash was succeeded by his son Jeroboam (usually called Jeroboam II). It was Jeroboam I, the son of Nebat, who had introduced image worship into Israel. Jeroboam II walked in the ways of his namesake.

Although the image worship was an abomination, the power of the promise, spoken by a prophet named Jonah, was not broken by this sin. The Word of life was going to be victorious. The Lord would answer the prayer of Jehoahaz even further. Jeroboam II succeeded in driving the Syrians out of Transjordan and was then able to restore the ancient borders of the kingdom. In the battle against the kingdoms of Damascus and Hamath, he triumphed over the Syrians in the north and defeated the Moabites in the south, with the result that Israel once more extended from the road to Hamath all the way to the Dead Sea.

The Lord had looked upon Israel's bitter distress with compassion and mercy. Who would help this people if He did not do it? This people and this kingdom, after all, were still His. The Lord had not yet said that He would wipe them out from under the heavens. Although Israel was becoming ripe for judgment, the sentence had not yet been pronounced. On the contrary, the Lord had His servant, the prophet Jonah, prophesy that the kingdom would be restored once more. Would Israel learn from the compassion the Lord continued to show?

45: Sanctified and Made a Blessing

Jonah 1-4

Jonah, the son of Amittai, was the prophet who was sent to Nineveh. He was also the prophet who told Jeroboam that the kingdom of Israel would be restored to its ancient borders (II Kings 14:25).

Jonah's refusal to preach in Nineveh, the capital of Assyria, stemmed not so much from a fear that the Assyrian kingdom would become a threat to Israel as from a reluctance to see God extend His mercy to the heathen. Israel's continuous struggle with the nations had contributed to this begrudging attitude, which meant hatred where the heathen were concerned. But this attitude was rooted *mainly* in Israel's pride in the salvation it had received, in its status as God's chosen people. If Israel was not living by grace alone, aware of its own unworthiness, surely it could not understand the grace of God, which aims at the salvation of all peoples. Israel refused to be a blessing to the nations.

The flesh in Israel (the old nature) would have to die. Jonah's descent into the depths of the sea is a sign of that dying. Such a dying in and to the flesh was accomplished by the Christ. Thus He can become a blessing to the nations.

It was because of the Christ that Jonah's preaching in Nineveh could bear so much fruit, despite the fact that Jonah himself had not been cured of his disobedience. Jonah persisted in his disobedience even after preaching in Nineveh. To the very end he was a type of stubborn Israel.

God spared the great city of Nineveh. The basis of this mercy was His grace toward His people in the Christ. We are not to say that God was still bound to the world after the fall by a tie of paternal love simply because it was *His* creation. Sin broke that tie completely. In the Christ God restored that tie with His people in the covenant of grace. In His people He is now bound to the world also—including Nineveh, which He guides. He guides the entire world, to open it up to the glory which is in the Christ.

Main thought: *The one who was sent becomes a blessing after he is sanctified.*

Going under in disobedience. The prophet Jonah was commissioned to tell King Jeroboam II that God would allow him to restore the ancient borders of the kingdom. But Jonah received another assignment as well. In those days a world kingdom was springing up to the east—Assyria, with its capital city of Nineveh. That world power eventually subjected many nations, but it was guilty of a terrible sin: it plundered the world and used the treasures it had stolen to beautify Nineveh.

The world was being impoverished and destroyed—this world to which God was bound. Therefore God could no longer tolerate this behavior on Nineveh's part. Moreover, Nineveh reveled in her passion. Jonah had to preach against this sin of Nineveh; he had to deliver the warning that God would destroy the city.

When Jonah received this message, his jealousy as a Jew, as a son of the chosen race, was stirred up. Had God not given His grace to Israel only and should He not deal with Israel only? Those heathen people were not worthy to have God deal with them or send a prophet to them!

What arrogance! Did Jonah suppose that God had chosen Israel because it was any better than the other peoples? Didn't Israel, too, have to live by grace, by undeserved favor? Wasn't Israel called to carry the good news of that grace to all peoples and thereby become a blessing to the world? But Israel no longer lived by grace alone and therefore did not want to become a blessing to the other nations. The spirit of Israel as a whole was also the spirit that lived within Jonah.

Jonah fled in disobedience. When he refused to go to Nineveh, he could no longer bear to live in the land where God revealed His countenance and grace. Therefore he went to Joppa and boarded a ship heading for the Atlantic Ocean. He wanted to get as far away as possible—as if there were a place where he could hide from the Lord! We act just as foolishly as Jonah when we try to close our hearts to God.

The Lord hurled a great wind at the ship. When the prayers of the sailors to their gods were of no avail, Jonah was awakened so that he could pray to his god too.

Jonah had been sleeping all this time. He was at the end of his rope. Although he was fleeing, he felt there were no options in life for him anymore. His despondency made him sleep so soundly that not even the storm awakened him.

The sailors were convinced that there was divine revelation in this storm. Those men did not ascribe everything to lifeless forces of nature, as people do today. Unfortunately, they thought of the forces of nature as divine in themselves.

However, it was the living God, the God who shows grace to His people, who was at work in this storm. God controlled the forces of nature and revealed Himself in them, just as He still controls them today and reveals Himself in them. Thus the sailors were talking about divine wrath.

They also believed that the gods would point out the object of their wrath by means of the lot. In those days the living God still revealed Himself in special ways. One of those ways was by the casting of the lot. When the lot was cast, the sailors discovered that the Lord's anger was being revealed against Jonah in this storm.

The sailors questioned Jonah, and he told them that he served the living God who controls heaven and earth in His grace to His people. He admitted his disobedience and said that he knew this storm had come upon them because of him. By their disobedience, believing people can sometimes be a curse to the world.

Jonah also said that the storm would subside if the sailors threw him into the sea. The sailors were afraid; they had heard of the living God and dreaded delivering His prophet up to death. But their efforts to row to shore were in vain; the storm grew in intensity. Finally they picked Jonah up and threw him overboard. Immediately the storm died down. This was a sign that they had done the right thing.

Jonah had surrendered himself to death. He was the guilty one. He delivered himself up to God's righteous judgment. When he was cast into the depths, was he surrendering to the eternal wrath of God? What a terrible fate that would be! Imagine how Jonah must have felt as he sank into the depths of the sea. Thanks be to God, there was another who descended into the depths of God's wrath, namely, the Christ. And He, through His suffering in obedience, ascended out of the depths. Through His work there is reconciliation and salvation for those who are His, those who really ought to perish under God's justice.

Likewise, there was deliverance for Jonah. God arranged for a big fish to swallow him. By means of a miracle He kept Jonah alive inside that fish. Is that possible? Of course! Why shouldn't the God who brings people from spiritual death to new life be able to keep a man alive inside a fish?

Worshiping the God of grace. The Lord still had His intentions with Jonah. Jonah had been a type of disobedient, proud Israel, but now he would have to become a type of sanctified Israel, which humbled itself, lived by the grace of God, and in that way became a blessing to the nations. The old Jonah, the disobedient Jonah, would have to die, and another Jonah would have to arise. By God's strength in us this can happen. It can happen in us because the Christ died for us and rose again. God causes us to share in the death and resurrection of the Christ.

This happened to Jonah when he went down into the depths of the sea and when he was inside the fish. While he was in the depths, he surrendered to God's sovereignty, but he also cried out for grace. When he found himself alive within the fish, he understood that his prayer had been heard, that God was going to return him to His people, that he would see God's temple again. But he also realized that he had been saved purely by grace. How small Jonah must have felt before God!

In the fish he prayed to the God of grace. He confessed that he was lost, that there was no hope left for him, that he had been saved only by God's grace, that God in His grace had answered his prayer, and that he would be restored again. In this new state of mind, Jonah could go and preach to the heathen citizens of Nineveh. If he himself lived by grace and no longer boasted of anything in himself, it would be a joy for him to preach God's grace to the heathen.

For three days and three nights Jonah was in the fish. At the Word of the Lord, that is, at the Word of grace which extends over all things, the fish spit Jonah up on dry ground. Having passed through the depths, Jonah returned to life. In this he was a type of the Christ, who passed through death and arose to life.

The blessing of the preaching. Now the Lord again ordered Jonah to go and preach in Nineveh. This time Jonah went. Whether he was fully obedient and would continue to live in the same spirit as when he was inside the fish would soon become evident. In any case, he went to Nineveh. There he preached the Word of the Lord, declaring that the city would be destroyed in 40 days.

Nineveh was a big city. To crisscross the city and cover all of it would have taken three days. But Jonah preached only one day and then left the city again. Doesn't this make it clear that the old Jonah had surfaced again, and that he begrudged these unbelievers the mercy God chose to show them?

How unwillingly Jonah must have preached that one day! If it had depended on Jonah, the preaching would have remained fruitless. Yet, great blessing resulted from it. Nineveh's king heard about Jonah's preaching. Apparently the one told the other. Jonah's words had an immediate effect. Even the king submitted. He put on his penitential garment and ordered a fast for man and beast. The animals would scream from hunger and thirst, and the sound of their voices would be passed on by men to God as a plea for mercy.

What made Jonah's preaching so fruitful? It was fruitful not because of Jonah but for the sake of the Christ, who was obedient unto death and who, after He had been sanctified, became a cause of eternal blessedness to all who obey Him. The Christ earned God's grace for His own, but because of that grace, He also gives the Word of God power to bring about a temporary repentance and restraint of sin in unbelievers. Nineveh did not turn to the living God in its heart, but it did turn away temporarily from its worst sins. What moved the city was not belief in the eternal grace of God but fear of temporal punishment.

Yet, God looked upon that temporary repentance as fruit of His Word and of the Christ. Therefore He did not destroy Nineveh. How merciful God is! Will He not be gracious, then, to those whose hearts hope in Him?

Hardening in disobedience. How disobedient Jonah was and how much the old spirit had arisen in him again became clearly evident: he sat down opposite Nineveh to witness the destruction of the city. How he would rejoice in that destruction!

The repentance of Nineveh grieved him, for it showed him that God was being merciful to Nineveh. That much he saw. But in rebellion he reproached God for being long-suffering. Jonah had been right when he fled! Now he wanted God to take his life so that he would not have to witness the salvation of the heathen!

How could Jonah be so hardened after appealing to God's grace out of the depths inside the fish? When God leaves us to ourselves, we no longer live by His grace. We become proud of what we think is ours, and we begrudge others His compassion. In Jonah it is revealed to us that we are only able to live for the Lord through the Spirit of the Christ.

The Word of grace, which directs all things, made a castor oil plant grow up quickly, and Jonah rejoiced in the shade it provided. But that same Word of grace prepared a worm that made the plant wither. The Word of grace also caused Jonah to pant for breath because of the sun's heat. God had something to teach Jonah.

When Jonah insisted that he was right to be embittered at the withering of the plant, God put Jonah's sin clearly before him. He was embittered because a plant had withered. Yet Jonah had contributed nothing to the growth of that plant, which existed by the Word of the Lord. Why shouldn't God have compassion on a city that depended for its existence on the Word of grace, a city in which there were so many children, so many young lives that could still be opened up to everything? God wanted to preserve the generations of the heathen until the time of the proclamation of the Word of grace to all people.

Jonah did indeed fall back into disobedience. And Israel was not sanctified. But the Christ in His suffering was wholly sanctified to God. By His Spirit, the power of His obedience will go forth continuously so that His people may be sanctified to the service of God.

46: Self-complacency

II Kings 14:1-22; 15:1-7
II Chronicles 25-26

We find self-exaltation in both Amaziah and Uzziah. They become strong because of the Lord's good pleasure in them for David's sake. But then they exalt themselves. This self-exaltation is born of a certain self-complacency. Over against this self-complacency stands the good pleasure of the Lord for David's sake and for the sake of the Christ. Belief in that good pleasure of the Lord makes for humility.

Yet this self-complacency of Amaziah and Uzziah keeps assuming different forms. Amaziah is pleased with himself as the brave conqueror of the Edomites. Therefore he includes the gods of the Edomites in his worship services. The greater the variety of gods, the greater the king. The heathen idea here prevails that the gods are subject to the kings, that their help is at the kings' disposal as long as the kings honor them.

In the case of Uzziah, there was no serving of foreign gods. Uzziah exalted himself and took pleasure in himself as God's favorite. Since he thought everything and anything was permitted him, he overstepped his bounds and acted as priest himself. From that moment on, he carried the sign of the Lord's scorn on his forehead.

Neither of these kings was completely rejected, however. Amaziah lived fifteen years beyond the death of his conqueror, Joash. And Uzziah had a son who was able to serve as regent and lead the people in the fear of the Lord.

Main thought: *The Lord's good pleasure for David's sake overcomes the self-complacency of the kings of David's house.*

348

Amaziah's exaltation. After Judah's King Joash was killed, his son Amaziah became king. In him lived the same spirit as in his father Joash. He did serve the Lord, but not with a perfect heart. He had his own interests at heart.

First he established himself in his kingdom and brought judgment upon those who had killed his father. In that judgment he acted entirely in accordance with the law of the Lord and did not let himself be led by any desire for revenge: he killed only the murderers—not their children.

Amaziah then mobilized Judah's army—300,000 men. He also hired 100,000 men from Israel, for he intended to fight against the Edomites, who had revolted. A prophet of the Lord warned him, however, that he should let the men of Israel go. The Lord was not with Israel, and therefore those soldiers would bring God's wrath upon him. When Uzziah asked what should be done with the hundred talents of silver promised to the men of Israel in payment, the prophet answered: "The LORD is able to give you much more than this." When we are obedient to the Lord, we can forget about money and suffer losses as we turn back from the wrong way. Our losses must not keep us from doing what is right. Amaziah bowed before the Word of the Lord and discharged his hired troops.

Then he led his own army against the Edomites. The Lord was with him, and he won the victory. But pride, self-assuredness, and a thirst for revenge immediately took possession of Amaziah; he had 10,000 Edomite prisoners thrown to their death from the top of a rock.

Returning from his campaign, he received a warning from the Lord; the 100,000 men of Israel whom he had sent home were embittered about being discharged and retaliated by conducting a marauding expedition in Judah during his absence. Many people were killed, and the land was plundered.

But Amaziah did not heed the warning. He had brought back with him the gods of the Edomites, and he set them up for worship. He wanted to assure himself of the help of those gods. The more gods, the stronger the king. Didn't he realize that the service of those gods was inimical to the grace of the Lord, by which alone we are exalted?

Only the good pleasure of the Lord for the sake of David, that is, for the sake of the Christ, would exalt Judah and the house of David. When a man believes that, he becomes humble and dependent on the Lord. Then he rejects everything else as an abomination. But Amaziah had exalted himself. The Lord's good pleasure toward the house of David would break him.

Amaziah's humiliation. A prophet of the Lord admonished Amaziah. Had the grace of the Lord not proved to be stronger than all the power in which the Edomites trusted? Haughtily the king turned the prophet away. Who had assigned him to be the king's counselor? The prophet did go away, but not before he made one more comment: "From the fact that you do not listen to me, I see that the Lord has decided to destroy you." But Amaziah did not listen to this last warning either.

In his bold recklessness he dared Joash, the king of Israel, to go to war against him. He wanted to restore the power of David's house over the ten tribes. Joash answered him with a scornful parable and warned Amaziah about the dangers of the proud self-assurance he had developed as a result of his victory over the Edomites. Although those words came from Joash, they should have impressed Amaziah, for they were to the point. But Amaziah's heart was closed; he did not hear the voice of the Lord in those words of Joash.

When it came to a confrontation, Judah was defeated, Amaziah was taken prisoner, Jerusalem was captured, and part of the wall was torn down. Amaziah received his freedom only when he agreed to hand over hostages and a large treasure. The Lord had humiliated him.

The Lord's good pleasure to the house of David did not tolerate Amaziah's self-exaltation. In this humiliation God was being gracious to the house of David and to Judah for the sake of the Christ. He remembered His covenant.

Even for Amaziah there was still mercy. He regained his freedom and outlived Joash by fifteen years. Yet the people were restless. Ever since Amaziah turned away from the Lord, treason had been brewing. Finally an agreement was reached. Amaziah fled to Lachish. There his enemies caught up with him and killed him. On a royal wagon he was brought back to Jerusalem and buried with his fathers. Although he had been removed from God and from the midst of His people, there was still mercy for him in his burial.

Uzziah's exaltation. Uzziah, a young son of Amaziah, was made king in his place. Although he was only sixteen years old, the people apparently had high expectations of him. He did not disappoint them. He did what was right in the eyes of the Lord and was blessed beyond most of the kings of Judah. Uzziah reigned for 52 years. Zechariah, a prophet of the Lord, was his advisor.

The Lord made Uzziah very prosperous. One of the first things he did was to go to war against the Edomites, who had seceded from Judah again toward the end of his father's reign. He subjected them and also subjected the Philistines and the Arabians. The Ammonites were forced to pay him tribute. He expanded his kingdom to the Egyptian border.

Uzziah fortified Jerusalem's wall, built towers in the wilderness, and dug many wells there for his numerous flocks. He also applied himself to agriculture and reorganized the army. During his reign, his work supervisors invented clever instruments with which to shoot arrows and large stones. Uzziah's fame spread abroad, for the Lord was with him in a marvelous way. The good pleasure of the Lord rested upon him for the sake of His covenant with David. Uzziah was God's favorite.

Uzziah's humiliation. Uzziah was well aware that he was God's favorite. This awareness was dangerous, for in his own mind he began to exalt himself on account of it. If he was God's favorite, more was permitted him than others—or so he thought.

One day he overstepped the bounds which had been set for him: he went into the sanctuary to burn incense on the altar—something only the priests were allowed to do. How foolish and presumptuous! He rejected the limits set by God and thereby became a god unto himself.

Azariah, the high priest, went after the king with 80 priests to keep him from committing this sin, telling him that he was not permitted to enter the sanctuary to burn incense. Azariah did not address him by his royal title but simply called him *Uzziah*. The king had forfeited his royal honor by reaching for an honor that was not rightfully his.

Uzziah became angry about this resistance to his wishes and rejected the warning of the Lord. As anger arose in him, so did leprosy; it broke out on his forehead. The Lord covered Uzziah with scorn because in his proud self-assuredness he had assaulted what God made holy.

The priests were astonished and thrust Uzziah out of the sanctuary. When he understood what had befallen him, he fled from the place. Evidently he bowed under the scorn which the Lord had laid upon him. He now realized what an abomination he had committed.

He viewed this abomination in the light of the favor which the Lord had bestowed on him. Yet he must have hoped that there would be grace for him in spite of his sin. For the rest of his life, to be sure, he was banned from society; he could no longer enter the house of the Lord or attend to matters of government. But the Lord gave him a wise regent in his son Jotham, who led the people in the ways of the Lord.

The Lord's good pleasure for the sake of the Christ also conquered this self-exaltation in the house of David. The covenant was not broken. When Uzziah died, he could not be buried in the kings' graves because of his leprosy. He was buried in the field next to those graves.

47: Wayward Children

II Kings 15:32—16:20
II Chronicles 27-28

The main character here is King Ahaz of Judah, who goes as far as he can in rejecting the Lord. When he has a new altar built, patterned after the one in Damascus, he pushes the altar of the Lord into a corner. He even dares to say: "The brass altar will be mine to investigate." In other words, Ahaz will think the matter over and decide what to do with the Lord's altar. Later he cuts the vessels of God's house into pieces and locks the doors. The house of the Lord meant here is the actual temple building, not the front court in which Ahaz carried on his sinful cult. At least he was consistent.

Yet, even during this period we see the Lord seeking Judah. Very moving is His concern for the prisoners who were carried away from Judah to be made slaves in Israel. In Isaiah 7 we read how the Lord urged Judah to accept His favor in the battle against Rezin and Pekah, "these two smoldering stumps of firebrands" (vs. 4). It was in those days that the Immanuel sign was given. In all of this the Lord was calling: "Return to Me, you wayward children!"

Main thought: *Because of His covenant, the Lord calls His wayward children.*

Life before the face of God. Uzziah was succeeded by his son Jotham. Jotham was a child of his father's faith. He knew he was God's favorite, but he did not exalt himself because of it.

God's favor manifested itself in blessings on him and on Judah. He succeeded in beautifying the house of the Lord and fortifying Jerusalem. He also built forts and towers in the wooded hill country. He fought against the Ammonites, who had apparently risen up in revolt, and made them pay tribute.

Jotham led the people in the fear of the Lord and ordered his ways before the Lord his God. This is not to say that all the people of Judah behaved as the Lord's children. The cultic services on the high places remained. That was a self-willed form of worship; the Lord wanted His people to worship Him only in the temple in Jerusalem. The link with the temple, where God revealed Himself, symbolized the tie to the Christ, in whom God reveals His favor. That self-willed form of worship, which was free of this tie, was itself idolatry. That's why the people were so easily persuaded to worship other gods as well on the high places of Judah.

During the reign of Jotham, two kings made an alliance and began to invade Judah—Rezin of Syria and Pekah of Israel. In this way the Lord chastised His children, the people of Judah.

Punished with godlessness. Under Jotham the people had not returned to the Lord. Therefore the Lord punished them by giving them the kind of king they really wanted. Jotham's son Ahaz was in full agreement with the spirit of idolatry that reigned among the people. He walked in the ways of Israel's kings; that is to say, he worshiped images. He also served the Baals—and in the most abominable way. He even sacrificed his sons to idols. The entire country was filled with high places for idol worship.

Now Judah looked like the land of Canaan in the old days of the Canaanites. It was as though the Lord had not driven out those Canaanites, as though He had not devoted the land of Canaan to the service of His name. It appeared that there was nothing left of the fear of the Lord. In spite of all this, the Lord did not want to break with Judah. Because of His covenant, the power of His Word of grace had to triumph. He continued to call the people to love Him.

Love's mercy. The Lord caused King Rezin of Syria and King

Pekah of Israel to mobilize their forces against Judah. Rezin marched from Damascus through Transjordan. Ahaz went out to meet him, but he was defeated. Then Rezin moved on to the region south of Judah and subjected the Edomites, who had long been subject to Judah. At the same time, Pekah invaded Judah from the north and decisively defeated Ahaz; 120,000 men were killed in that battle. One of the king's relatives and even his prime minister fell by the hand of Zichri, a mighty man of Ephraim.

Ephraim dominated Judah completely. Some 200,000 men, women and children were carried away captive to become slaves in Israel. Moreover, the land was plundered. The Philistines and some of the Edomites seized this opportunity to occupy parts of Judah. Finally Rezin and Pekah besieged Jerusalem. That seemed to signal the end for Judah.

During this troubled time the Lord still gave a sign to show that He had not rejected Judah. When Israel's soldiers returned to Samaria with prisoners from Judah after the first victory, they were met by a prophet of the Lord named Oded. This prophet said: "The Lord, in His wrath against Judah, has delivered this people into our hands. We served as an instrument of chastisement in the hand of the Lord, who is also the God of our fathers. However, you did not want to be an instrument in the Lord's hand; you vented your own lust for revenge on Judah. Would you now make these people of Judah your slaves and add this further guilt to the sins you have already committed? Send the captives back, for the fierce wrath of the Lord is also upon you!" Some men of Ephraim who are mentioned by name were gripped by these words. They, too, confronted the army in Samaria. Then they clothed and fed the prisoners and brought them back to Jericho, some on donkeys.

The consciousness of unity still spoke for just a moment in this time of intense hatred. This was possible only because of the working of the Word and Spirit of the Lord. This Word of the Lord was like a shield over the lives of many in Judah. What moving proof of the Lord's love for His wayward children! The Lord had not forsaken life in Judah. In the Christ, the covenant remained eternally sure.

Immanuel rejected. At the time of the attacks by Rezin and Pekah, the Lord sent the prophet Isaiah to Ahaz to tell him not to be afraid of those two powers but to trust in the Lord, who would deliver him. The Lord even invited the king to ask for a sign to confirm His promise, but Ahaz had no desire to hear the Word of the Lord and did not bother asking for a sign. He did not want the Lord or His help.

The Lord was determined to fulfill His promise anyway. Therefore He gave a sign that He was with Judah in this time of distress. It was at this point that the Lord unveiled the name *Immanuel,* which is a name for the Christ, in whom God is with us. How sure God's covenant is that this could be said in such a time!

Ahaz, however, did not want the help of the Lord. Instead he looked for help from Assyria, the world power on the rise in those days. Judah did get temporary relief with the help of Assyria, but Ahaz and Judah did not see the Lord's hand in this. That's why this world power later turned against Judah. The king and the people of Judah themselves had asked for this scourge.

Ahaz robbed his own house and the house of the Lord in order to send a present to Assyria's king, Tiglath-pileser, and thereby win his favor. The Assyrian king did march against Damascus and conquer it. He also invaded the land of Pekah. This gave Judah some relief. Ahaz went to Damascus to pay his respects to Tiglath-pileser.

While he was there, he saw an altar that looked far more beautiful to him than the Lord's altar in Jerusalem. To the eye of the flesh, its luxuriousness and magnificence must have made it seem much more beautiful than the Lord's altar with its straight lines. The service with which *we* wish to honor God always seems more beautiful than the straight lines of life lived according to the laws of God's covenant.

From Damascus Ahaz sent orders to Uriah, the high priest in Jerusalem. He was to make an exact replica of the altar in Damascus. The high priest, who was supposed to be a type of the Christ as the Mediator of the covenant, actually lent himself to this desecration!

When Ahaz returned to Jerusalem, he found that the new altar had been constructed in accordance with his wishes. He himself burned sacrifices on it, and he ordered the priest to do the same. The Lord's altar was pushed aside. Later the king would have to think about the question what should be done with it. Evidently he did not yet dare do away with it completely.

Hardening under the chastisement. In the meantime, Ahaz's friendship with the king of Assyria did not turn out to be as advantageous as he had hoped. He had to plunder the temple again to hold on to that friendship. It seemed that Tiglath-pileser threatened him with an invasion of Jerusalem. Therefore Ahaz hid anything and everything that might remind the Assyrians of the service of the Lord. He himself had chosen for the Syrian gods; at the time he thought they had proven to be more powerful than the Lord. Now he was ashamed of the service of the Lord. Judah was not to look any different from the heathen countries. Worship of the Lord might arouse the anger of the king of Assyria.

Even in his fear of the king of Assyria, a power he himself had summoned onto the scene, Ahaz did not turn to the Lord. On the contrary, the more he was oppressed, the more he turned his back on the service of the Lord. Finally he locked the doors of the Lord's house. Judah was finished with the Lord. Immanuel, the Christ of God, was now completely rejected.

Yet, Isaiah had not only prophesied that God had rejected Rezin and Pekah, he had also declared that in due time God would judge the world power of Assyria. God kept on calling: "Return to Me, you wayward children!"

48: A Return to the Lord

II Kings 18:1-8
II Chronicles 29-31

Scripture sometimes characterizes people in peculiar ways. Of Hezekiah we read: "He trusted in the LORD the God of Israel; so that there was none like him among all the kings of Judah after him, nor among those who were before him." Above all else, Hezekiah was a man of faith. By his faith he pressed on with the reformation of Judah. In this regard he was a type of the Mediator, who is the Pioneer and Perfecter of our faith (Heb. 12:2). Through the Mediator, that power of faith was present in Hezekiah. Later, by that same faith, he prayed for the people in the war against Sennacherib.

The question of the music by which the Lord was praised comes up repeatedly in connection with the reformation under Hezekiah. This matter is raised in II Chronicles 29 and especially in II Chronicles 30:21, where we read about the priests and Levites singing to the Lord with loud instruments (literally: with instruments of the Lord's power, that is to say, with instruments used to praise the power of the Lord's grace). In glorifying the power of the grace that was theirs because of the Mediator, the hearts of the people had to open up to faith.

It is noteworthy that in a time when confession of sin clearly belonged in the foreground, music is emphasized heavily. There is no confession of sin if we do not see the power of grace and embrace it in faith. In other words, we must worship the Lord in the power of grace if we are to confess our sins.

Main thought: *The mediator leads the people to return to the Lord.*

The restoration of the service of the Lord. Ahaz was succeeded by his son Hezekiah. Whereas God had punished the
people of Judah by giving them godless Ahaz as their king, He
now turned His favor toward His people again by giving them a
king who feared the Lord—Hezekiah. Hezekiah was like his father
David in that he was upright before the Lord. In his actions he
looked to David as his example.

One of Hezekiah's first public acts was to open and repair the
doors of the Lord's house, which Ahaz had locked up. As a sign of
his reverence, Hezekiah had them overlaid with gold. Whereas
Ahaz had said that Judah was done with the Lord, Hezekiah wanted to seek the Lord again—for and with his people. Would the
Lord, who had been rejected for so long, be willing to give Himself
to His people again? The fact that the Lord had put it in
Hezekiah's heart to seek Him was intended as a sign that the
relationship between the Lord and Judah was *not* finished.

Hezekiah understood that since he was the mediator between
God and the people, he had to lead the people back to the Lord
again. That's just what he did, with a strength of faith that no king
of Judah before or after him ever showed. How had such strong
faith come into his life? By faith our Mediator obtained deliverance for His people. He wants to lead them back to God again and
again, even after they fall away. Through this Mediator, that
strength was in Hezekiah.

He called the priests and Levites together in the forecourt. After he drew their attention to the sins Judah had committed and
the disasters which had come over the people as a result, he said
that he wanted to renew the covenant with the Lord on behalf of
the people. He called on the priests and Levites for support in this
effort. After all, *they* had been called to the special service of the
Lord. He ordered them to sanctify themselves and the house of the
Lord so that a service could be held there.

The Levites took these words of the king more seriously than
the priests. The priests had grown too accustomed to idol worship. They hesitated. What did the service of the Lord really
mean? How could they worship a God they could not see, a God

they could only serve by faith? The king was indeed making a beginning, but would he be able to follow through on his intentions? How strange it seems to the flesh to live by faith!

Nevertheless, many priests were also moved by the king's words. They cleansed the temple of all traces of idolatry. The Levites took everything the priests had removed and carried it outside the front court to the brook Kidron. Then they cleansed the front court. The utensils of the temple were also repaired. After sixteen days they went to the king to tell him that everything was ready.

Then the king called the officials of Jerusalem together in the front court. There the covenant with the Lord was to be renewed. Would the Lord hear and relent?

An offering of seven bulls, seven rams, seven lambs, and seven male goats was prepared. This would be a burnt offering through which the people could devote themselves anew to the Lord. In part it would also serve as a sin offering, an offering intended to seek reconciliation for the sins of the kingdom, of the sanctuary, of Judah. Because it was a sin offering, the people laid their hands on the goats. This act symbolized that the goats took the place of the people and that the sins of the people were laid on them. The goats were then sacrificed as a type of the sacrifice of Christ on the cross. In the same way we may lay our hands on the Lord Jesus Christ and find reconciliation.

While these sacrifices were being made, Hezekiah had the Levites sing and play music. Would the Lord turn to His people? This could not happen without faith that the Lord was gracious. Through the music and singing, Hezekiah had the people praise the grace of the Lord in order that the people would believe.

The people bowed before the Lord together with their king to humble themselves in a confession of sins and a demonstration of their dependence. That was their way of saying that in faith they wanted to accept the Lord's grace. They praised the Lord for such a long time that joy broke through in their hearts at last. They had found their Lord again. He wanted to give Himself to them as He had done before.

After this the king declared that the people were to bring the Lord their freewill offerings. Hadn't the communion with the Lord been restored? The people brought so many offerings that the priests could not keep up with the work. The Levites had to help them. There they were, bringing burnt offerings and thank offerings to the Lord and serving Him with gladness.

The Passover for all Israel. All of this happened in the first month of the year, the month in which the Passover was supposed to be celebrated. But the covenant renewal was not completed in time to celebrate the Passover. Therefore Hezekiah decided that the Passover, which had not been celebrated for a long time anyway, would be celebrated in the second month instead. This was allowed in the Lord's law as an exception. The king did not want to wait another whole year.

He also remembered the ten tribes that had been torn away from his house. He did not propose to bring them back under his rule, but he did want them to join Judah in celebrating the Passover. The Spirit of the Mediator was at work in Hezekiah; he was disturbed about the apostasy from the Lord among the ten tribes.

Not only did Hezekiah call Judah to the Passover, he also sent messengers with letters throughout all Israel. Some of the people of the ten tribes had already been carried away captive by the king of Assyria. In his letters Hezekiah made an appeal to the people of the northern kingdom to return to the Lord in faith. Then the Lord would certainly show them mercy, extend His favor to them, and bring the captives back.

Apparently the king reigning over the ten tribes of the northern kingdom permitted this. But the messengers were received everywhere with scornful laughter and ridicule. The people in the northern kingdom had become completely estranged from the service of the Lord in the temple. The service of idols in connection with the worship of the calves—that was something. But the services in the temple, where the Lord's grace was acknowledged in faith and His Word obeyed—that was nothing! Only a small number of people from a few tribes humbled themselves before the Lord and came to Jerusalem. Yet, in Judah the power of grace broke through; the people came as one man.

The city was cleansed of idolatry, for the Passover would

have to be celebrated in a sanctified city. For lack of time, however, many had not been sanctified according to the law of Moses. Therefore they did not slaughter the Passover lambs themselves; the Levites did it for them. Hezekiah also prayed that the Lord would look upon these people in His grace in spite of this. The Lord heard Hezekiah's petition and made the people one in His service.

For seven days the people celebrated the feast of unleavened bread. At this feast, too, there was a mighty sound of singing and of music to praise the greatness of the power of grace. The words of Hezekiah, in which the faith of the one who served as mediator between God and the people came to expression, gripped the hearts of the Levites, who then taught the people and led them in the ways of the Lord.

The feast was extended for seven more days. The inhabitants of Judah rejoiced together with those from other tribes who had come to live in the land of Judah and also with people from the other tribes who had come to Jerusalem specifically for this feast. Such a feast had not been celebrated since the days of David and Solomon. At the end the priests stood up and blessed the people. This was possible only because the Lord had heard their prayer. God's favor rested on His people once again.

Deeply affected by this feast, the people went through the entire land of Judah rooting out all traces of idolatry. They also went through parts of the kingdom of Israel to sanctify the people there. Evidently the king of Israel and the people there permitted this. For a little while Israel was not able to withstand the power of grace. But these efforts did not lead to a reformation of the northern kingdom. Afterward everyone returned to his own place.

Love for the service of the Lord. The king regulated the services of the priests and the Levites in accordance with the instructions David had laid down. He also appealed to the people to bring regular offerings to the Lord and to give the priests and Levites the first fruits and the tithes.

The king himself set the example, and his words reached the hearts of the people. The Spirit of the Lord Jesus Christ moved them through the words of the king. The people gave so much out of their love for the service of the Lord that the gifts had to be stored temporarily in rooms which the king made available for this express purpose.

Thus the Lord's grace had gained the victory over the people once again. Faith had burst out among them. This happened under the leadership of King Hezekiah, whom the Lord had given to the people as a type of the Mediator.

49: No Longer a People

II Kings 15:8-31; 17:1-41

God rejected the northern kingdom of Israel, which had become a symbol for apostate people. In the course of time, things had degenerated to the point that Israel was God's people in appearance only.

When God rejected the northern kingdom, He was not breaking His covenant with His people. What He refused to do was reveal Himself any longer to His people within the kingdom of the ten tribes. Later a few were sifted out. They returned along with captives from the kingdom of Judah. Together with these returning captives from Judah, they made up the restored twelve tribes. The rest of the people of the ten tribes either became absorbed into the various nations or intermarried with those who were imported to live in the land Israel had once occupied. From this intermarriage the Samaritans were born as a people.

In the description of the causes of Israel's apostasy, we read that the Lord "tore Israel from the house of David." What the break with David's house—and thereby with the promise given to that house—involved in principle was the rejection of the Lord's grace. Israel preferred its own flesh, its desire for sinful independence, to the grace of the Lord.

In II Kings 17:34, the people of Israel are referred to as the children of Jacob, "whom he named Israel." This reminds us how Jacob wrestled to win God's grace. Such wrestling is always necessary, even though God in His grace gives Himself in His covenant. The people of the northern kingdom had not wrestled to win this grace. On the contrary!

The Lord sent lions among the people who had been imported into the land of Israel by Assyria's king. Then a priest arrived to teach them the ways of the god of that land—a priest of the calf worship. Before long a new cult developed, a mixture of calf worship and other idolatry. This cult was in harmony neither with the law of the Lord nor with the calf worship introduced by Jeroboam.

Of course the Lord could not possibly be satisfied with this situation. It was not out of any feeling of satisfaction that He put an end to the plague of the lions. His purpose in ending the plague was to keep His name from being completely forgotten in that land. The fact that His name was still mentioned there was a sign that He had not let go of the people. He wanted to restore the knowledge of His name. The Samaritan people, who had come into being through intermarriage, rejected idol worship in the course of time and embraced the law of Moses. Later the Christ came to them and talked with the Samaritan woman and the people of Sychar (see John 4:5). Still later, Philip preached the gospel there with great blessing (Acts 8).

Main thought: *In His faithfulness to His covenant, the Lord rejects those who are His people in appearance only.*

Anarchy. After the death of Jeroboam II, the kingdom of the ten tribes fell apart completely. Over a short period of time, several kings succeeded each other; most of them got to the throne by murdering the king before. They did not serve the Lord when they reigned as kings over His people; instead they desired the power for themselves. They played with the throne. And this among the people who were supposed to be the Lord's! On several occasions there was no reigning king at all. Whenever a king succeeded in establishing himself on the throne, he continued in the sin of Jeroboam, the son of Nebat, by serving idols.

Zechariah, the son of Jeroboam II, reigned for only six months. His successor Shallum, who killed him, reigned for only one month. Shallum was killed by Menahem, who reigned in Samaria for ten years. During Menahem's reign, Pul, the Assyrian king, already marched against the land. This Assyrian action may have been provoked by a punitive expedition which Menahem had undertaken against Tiphsah (Tappuah). Menahem had taken atrocious revenge on this city (II Kings 15:16). However, he was able to buy the Assyrians off and keep them from subjecting his kingdom completely.

The most important king in those days was Pekah, who had murdered Menahem's son Pekahiah. In alliance with King Rezin of Syria, Pekah oppressed the kingdom of Judah under Ahaz. But

Tiglath-pileser, whom Ahaz had summoned to help him, invaded the kingdom of Israel, captured the northern part of it, and carried the inhabitants away to Assyria.

Deportation. Pekah was killed and succeeded by Hoshea, who reigned for nine years. Hoshea continued in the sin of worshiping images. However, he was not as hostile to the Lord and the house of David as his predecessors had been. Most likely he allowed the inhabitants of his kingdom to go to Jerusalem to worship the Lord in His temple. Yet, it was under Hoshea that the end came. Sin finally bore fruit in judgment.

Shalmaneser, the king of Assyria, marched against him. The first time Hoshea was still able to buy off a complete surrender by paying him tribute. But the Assyrians discovered that Hoshea had entered into negotiations with Egypt, Assyria's enemy. Then the Assyrian king marched against Hoshea once more. He conquered the entire land, captured Samaria after a three-year siege, imprisoned Hoshea, and carried the people away into captivity. They were scattered over various parts of his empire.

At that point the kingdom of Israel ceased to exist. Never would this kingdom be restored. The great mass of the captives mixed with the peoples among whom they were living. A few did return later on. They, together with others who were preserved from the kingdom of Judah, constituted the restored twelve tribes. The Lord did not break His covenant with His people, but He did abandon the kingdom of the ten tribes. He rejected the people of that kingdom because they were His people in appearance only. The Lord's long-suffering is great, but judgment finally strikes.

The Lord's rejection of the kingdom of Israel was a prophecy pointing to the rejection of the people who have not believed in Him. Yet, those peoples are saved in the chosen remnant. God does not set aside His covenant with the nations.

The cause of the rejection. At the same time, this kingdom of Israel belonged to the people the Lord had chosen. He had adopted the Israelites as His people, delivered them from Egypt, and given them His covenant as well as a land from which He drove out the former owners. In that land His people were to serve Him alone. But the people had continued to serve idols in that land, just as the peoples who lived there before them had done. The people of Israel rejected the claims of the Lord's covenant. If they still mentioned the name and service of the Lord, they interpreted that service as they themselves saw fit, and tied it in with the worship of the golden calves.

Another cause of misery was the break that the kingdom of the ten tribes had made with the house of David. That separation had indeed come from the Lord as a judgment on David's house, but the ten tribes, under the leadership of Jeroboam, accepted the break all too eagerly. They wanted to be on their own and go their own way. They did not want to live by the light of the promise given to David's house, that is, by the light of the Christ and of the grace of God in Him. They were children of Jacob, but they did not behave as such. Jacob had wrestled for grace, which was why God called him *Israel*. But his descendants in the ten tribes did not wrestle to obtain grace; instead they rejected it over and over.

It is because the Lord wishes to give us His full favor that He becomes so angry when it is rejected. Such rejection touches the Lord very deeply. His rejection of the ten tribes was a rejection in anger. The Lord is also moved to anger today when the peoples reject His grace. How He will show His anger on the last day!

Remembering the Lord's name. For some time the land of Israel was largely uninhabited. During that time wild beasts multiplied there. Later the king of Assyria transported many people from his kingdom into the vacant territory. There they suffered from a plague of lions, which they ascribed to the fact that they did not know the god of that land and had no idea how he wished to be worshiped. At their request, a priest of the former calf worship came and settled at Bethel. He taught them to call on the name of the Lord in connection with that image worship. But they continued their idolatry at the same time. Their worship services became a mixture of image worship and idolatry.

With their pagan notions they thought of the Lord as a god who belonged to that land alone. Yet, they were right in assuming that their ordeal with the lions had something to do with the Lord.

It did not satisfy the Lord that they were making a show of calling upon His name again. All the same, the plague apparently ceased. The Lord did not want people to stop mentioning His name in the land He had once sanctified in a special way. By removing the plague, He gave a sign that the service of His name in that land had not come to a complete end. He was going to restore that service there again.

In time this came to pass. The Jews who had stayed behind in the land intermarried with the peoples who were brought in. From this intermarriage the Samaritans were born as a people. Later these Samaritans rejected idolatry and accepted the law of Moses. Still later, the Lord Jesus Christ revealed Himself to them, even though He did not reveal Himself to any full-blooded heathen nation. In that action there was an acknowledgment of the significance of the earlier history. After the ascension of Christ, the apostles and evangelists proclaimed the gospel there, and many Samaritans accepted the grace which their Jewish forefathers had rejected.

Judah

50: The Intercession of the Mediator

II Kings 18:9—19:37
II Chronicles 32:1-23

That Hezekiah is a man of faith (see Chapter 48 above) is also evident from this portion of Biblical history. In faith he is the intercessor for his people and thus a type of the Christ. At first there were moments of wavering on Hezekiah's part. The Christ is the only one who never wavered.

Hezekiah prayed to God and asked Him to take the side of His people. When the Assyrians boasted that they had not marched on Jerusalem without the Lord, they were telling the truth. Later the Lord Himself confirmed this.

God was against Judah. This was also the meaning of Hezekiah's words to Isaiah: "This day is a day of distress, of rebuke, and of disgrace; children have come to the birth, and there is no strength to bring them forth" (II Kings 19:3). The children were dying during birth; that is to say, Judah was succumbing in the face of the oppression. Judah could not survive, for God was on the side of her enemies.

Hezekiah proceeded from the conviction that God was surely on Judah's side eternally for the sake of His covenant. In the Christ, God can be on the side of His people and yet, at the same time, be against the way they reveal themselves in the flesh. Now Hezekiah prayed that God in His mercy would turn toward His people again.

The Lord did indeed choose Judah's side again. He did so for the sake of His servant David (II Kings 19:34), that is, for Christ's sake. He chose against Sennacherib because of his haughty words and his blasphemy. This heathen king did not want to be God's whip; he wanted to exalt himself against the Lord. Therefore the Lord would put a hook in his nose and a bridle in his mouth and make him turn back on the road by which he had come. That God had chosen the side of Judah once again is evident from the names He used to address His people—"the virgin daughter of Zion, the daughter of Jerusalem."

Main thought: *The Lord hears the mediator when he inter-*
cedes for the deliverance of His people.

The day of distress. The Lord had abandoned the kingdom of
the ten tribes. Its downfall came when the Assyrian king overran
the land. Now only the kingdom of Judah was left, with Hezekiah
as its king.

Hezekiah was a king who feared the Lord. He reinstated the
service of the Lord and rooted out the services on the high places.
When Samaria was destroyed, the Lord had spared Judah.

Yet, eight years later the king of Assyria was on the march
again, invading Judah. Hezekiah took counsel with his princes and
his men of valor. He made the people stop up the wells, and he
diverted the water under the ground toward Jerusalem so that the
Assyrian army would not have any water if it laid siege to
Jerusalem. The king also fortified Jerusalem's wall. Standing fast
in faith, he told his soldiers not to fear the Assyrian king and his
hordes: "There is one greater with us than with him. With him is
an arm of flesh; but with us is the LORD our God." How firm
Hezekiah stood in his faith! The people were awakened to faith by
these words of the king.

Without much opposition, Sennacherib captured most of
Judah. Stronghold after stronghold fell, and the Assyrians
swarmed over Judah. (Isaiah 10:28-32 gives us a vivid account of
the Assyrian advance upon Jerusalem.) At that point Hezekiah
wavered and offered to pay the Assyrian king whatever tribute he
wanted. He said he was sorry for his earlier refusal to pay the
tribute which the king of Assyria had imposed upon him.

That refusal to pay tribute had been an act of faith, but now
Hezekiah was wavering. There is only One who never wavered in
the hour of trial—the Lord Jesus Christ. All we can do is look to
Him. Yet, Hezekiah was a type of the Christ, and His Spirit was in
him. Hezekiah's faith would revive again. Sennacherib's breach
of promise served to bring him back to faith.

Sennacherib demanded a huge settlement from Judah. In order to pay it, Hezekiah had to take the gold with which he had
paneled the doors of the Lord's house. But once Sennacherib
received the payment, he broke his word and advanced farther into

Judah. He also sent a great army to Jerusalem under the command of his field officers.

The Rabshakeh,* who was the king's spokesman, stood at the foot of the wall and called out to the representatives whom Hezekiah had sent to the wall for this consultation: "Do not put your trust in Egypt, for Egypt will let you down every time. Nor can you trust in the Lord, for Hezekiah has taken away His high places." Apparently this fool interpreted the removal of the high places as a cutback in serving the Lord! "Neither can you trust in your own strength," said the Assyrian general, "for if I gave you 2000 horses, you would not even be able to put horsemen upon them."

Then the Rabshakeh touched on a sore spot. He said: "You cannot trust in the Lord, for I have not come up against this place without Him." This hit the people hard. Could the Lord really be with the king of Assyria and against Judah? Would the kingdom of Judah be destroyed just as the kingdom of Israel had been? The people's faith in the Lord's grace was given a severe blow. Hezekiah's officers called to the Rabshakeh that there was no need for him to speak in Hebrew, for they could understand Aramaic.

The general understood why they wanted him to switch to Aramaic, but he went on shouting to the people on the wall in a still louder voice not to be deceived by Hezekiah, who wanted them to trust in the Lord. Evidently Hezekiah's faith had revived once more: he had addressed the people again. Rumors about his words had even penetrated the army of the Assyrian king. Attacks are always made on the faith of the Lord's people, for it is through faith that they receive strength from God.

Then the Rabshakeh tried to win the people over to the king of Assyria with a tempting offer, but he went on to blaspheme the Lord: "The Lord will not be able to deliver Jerusalem out of my hand any more than the gods of the other nations were able to deliver their peoples." At the command of Hezekiah, the people on the wall kept their silence. Yet the Rabshakeh's words must have hit home. Could the Lord really be on the side of their enemies?

---

*This is a title that was given to certain Assyrian officers. *Rab* means *head* or *chief*.—TRANS.

The light of God's Word in the darkness. Hezekiah's officers told him what the Assyrian general had said. When he heard their message, he tore his clothes, put on sackcloth, and went into the temple to pray. Hezekiah's reviving faith was on trial here. It was possible that the Lord was on the side of Judah's enemies. Would the Lord not be faithful to His covenant and to His Word to David? Or would He maintain His faithfulness by taking Judah along the road of deep humiliation through the fall of Jerusalem? Wouldn't the Lord be moved with compassion for Judah and take Judah's side?

Hezekiah sent messengers to the prophet Isaiah, who was then in Jerusalem. He complained that Judah might well go under in this perilous situation. Would the Lord not take note of the words of the Rabshakeh, which were so full of pride and blasphemy, and for that reason choose the side of Judah once again?

The messengers returned with an answer: the Lord had indeed heard the blasphemies uttered by the Rabshakeh. The Lord would frighten the king of Assyria off by a rumor. He would cause him to return to his own land, where he would be killed by the sword.

When this Word of the Lord came to Hezekiah via the prophet Isaiah, light broke through the darkness again. Hezekiah's faith and the faith of the people rose once more. In a struggle of faith, the king had thrown himself into the breach for the people. The Rabshakeh received a negative answer and took it to Sennacherib, who had penetrated as far as Lachish by then and was besieging it.

The Lord's response to Hezekiah's prayer. At Lachish Sennacherib heard that the king of Ethiopia was coming to wage war against him. That rumor represented the beginning of the fulfillment of Isaiah's prophecy. If the Ethiopians were really marching against Sennacherib, he could not allow Jerusalem to stand as a threat in his rear. Therefore it was essential to persuade Jerusalem to surrender quickly. To attempt this Sennacherib sent messengers to Jerusalem with letters for Hezekiah.

In those letters the blasphemy was complete. The letters told Hezekiah that he should not let himself be fooled by his God. After all, not one of the gods of the other nations had been able to deliver his people from the hands of the Assyrians.

Hezekiah took the letters to the temple and spread them out before the Lord. By this action he meant to say: "Will You, O Lord, not take note of this blasphemy and therefore choose the side of Your people?" Hezekiah also prayed: "You are Israel's God. Here in this temple, You show us Your favor in Your covenant. And You rule over all the kingdoms of the earth. Look now upon this blasphemy which Sennacherib has written. It is indeed true that all the peoples have been defeated because their gods were not real gods. Will You not show that You alone are God—by delivering Your people?"

Hezekiah made an appeal to the honor of the Lord in His grace toward His people. He wrestled in faith, and his prayer came before the Lord's throne. He was the intercessor for his people. As such he was a type of the Christ, who is always interceding on behalf of His people. Through the Christ, this spirit of prayer was in Hezekiah, and for the sake of the Christ, the Lord heard.

In answer to his prayer, the Lord sent Hezekiah a message by way of Isaiah: "The Lord says this about Sennacherib: 'The virgin daughter of Zion despises you.' " Here the Lord spoke of His people by a name of honor again, a name in which He expressed His favor toward Judah. The Lord had chosen Judah's side once again and would now fight against Judah's enemies.

In this answer the Lord also said this about Sennacherib: "You said, 'I have climbed the mountains of Lebanon with my chariots; I have drunk from strange waters; and I have dammed up rivers.' You have not borne in mind that you were able to do this because of My will, which made the hands of the nations limp before you. You have elevated yourself in pride against Me. Therefore I will put My hook in your nose and My bridle in your mouth, and I will lead you back to your own country as a tamed beast."

To Hezekiah the Lord promised a sign that deliverance would have to come through God's favor; in the third year after Sennacherib's invasion, he would be able to sow and reap again in peace just as if Sennacherib had never been there. Sennacherib would not even come up to besiege Jerusalem. The Lord would bring this about for David's sake, that is, because of the covenant

in which David walked with the Lord. And the deliverance of all
the people of God would begin with Jerusalem.

The deliverance. That same night an angel of death went
through the Assyrian army and killed 185,000 men. When Sennacherib found so many Assyrian soldiers dead in the morning, his
strength was broken. He returned to his country, to the capital city
of Nineveh. Later two of his sons killed him in the temple of his
idol. Another son became king in his place. With this the
deterioration in the house of Sennacherib, in Nineveh, in Assyria
had begun.

Has the promise of the Lord been completely fulfilled? Did
the deliverance of all the people of God begin at Jerusalem? At
that time Judah was indeed freed completely. But weren't Judah
and Jerusalem later subjected by the world power of the time?
Though the people were restored to their land, they were never
restored to their former glory.

What we must learn to see is that Jerusalem and the temple
received their fulfillment in the Christ, in whom God gives Himself
to His people. From Him proceeds the deliverance of the entire
people of the Lord. Even though God's people will experience
days of distress, the Lord will choose the side of His people again
and again for the sake of the Christ, who intercedes for them.

51: The Need for a True Mediator

II Kings 20
II Chronicles 32:24-33

"In those days" must be understood to mean at the time of the Assyrian invasion. In the light of the promise recorded in II Kings 20:6, Hezekiah's illness should be placed at the beginning of this invasion. Then we can better understand his passionate prayer for recovery. Hezekiah wanted to save his people. This desire showed that the Spirit of the Mediator was in him. As a result of his sickness and recovery, his dependence upon the Lord was strengthened so that he would truly be able to serve as his people's deliverer.

The statement that the shadow went back ten steps does not necessarily mean that the sun went backward in its course. This phenomenon could have been caused by a peculiar refraction of the sun's rays. This strange phenomenon caused by God would be a sign for Hezekiah either way.

Difficult to understand is what we read in II Chronicles 32:31; when the ambassadors of Babylon's rulers were visiting Hezekiah, "God left him to himself, in order to try him and to know all that was in his heart." The first difficulty lies in the fact that God left him. He did not leave him completely—in the sense that Hezekiah's heart would no longer be bound to the Lord in faith. The Lord withdrew His favor from Hezekiah as regards his life in the flesh—to the extent that He withheld from Hezekiah the presence by which He protected him, warded off attacks against him, and provided for his support.

This episode must be placed in a wider perspective. We must remember that Adam was called to live by God's favor. He had every advantage, and that favor was displayed to him in all kinds of ways. To reconcile and cover what Adam did wrong, the Christ had to hold onto that favor while everything went against Him and God forsook Him.

Here, in Hezekiah's case, the test was already being made. By faith

Hezekiah acted as head and mediator. But Hezekiah faltered, despite the fact that his faith had been strengthened beforehand by his recovery and his deliverance from the hands of the Assyrians. All flesh yields to temptation. From this we learn that only the Christ is able to stand firm in a time of severe trial. Hezekiah's failure cries out for the Christ.

The other difficulties are to be resolved in the same way. God puts Hezekiah on trial; that is to say, He "tempts" him to faith. He looks for faith and steadfastness in Hezekiah so that when the entire people falter, the Lord may deliver them for Hezekiah's sake and raise them up out of the depths.

The same thought lies behind the words "to know all that was in his heart." To know, in this case, is to see it. If Hezekiah would show evidence of faithfulness, God would return Judah to His fellowship.

Hezekiah's actions seemed so full of promise. God now brings out into the open what there was in Hezekiah's heart, so as to take it into account in the continuation of history. When Hezekiah fails, it is made clear that the old covenant with its form of shadows and shadowy mediators is not sufficient for salvation. The end of the old covenant begins to show up here, in the time of believing Hezekiah, just as the impotent reformation under God-fearing Josiah testifies emphatically that the end is near. By yielding, Hezekiah cries out for another Mediator, the Mediator who became our surety of a much better covenant.

Hezekiah's sin is self-elevation, that is, a resting in the honor he had received in the world because of his deliverance from the hands of the Assyrians. From his life during this period (especially his politics), we see that he no longer lives solely out of faith. He regards his own power as a political factor alongside other such factors. That's why he can contemplate allying himself as an equal with Babylon against Assyria and placing his confidence in that alliance.

Read his appraisal of life as it comes to expression in his song of praise, which is recorded in Isaiah 38:9-20. What we find there is not just an appreciation of life by someone with an Old Testament perspective, someone who does not yet have a clear picture of life after death. Those who have the light of the New Testament must join Hezekiah in his affirmation of life. We, too, must say: "The living, the living, he thanks you, as I do this day; the father makes known to the children your faithfulness."

Main thought: *Hezekiah's failure as mediator cries out for the true Mediator.*

A revelation of special favor. At the beginning of the Assyrian invasion, Hezekiah became deathly ill because of a severe growth (swelling). The Lord sent the prophet Isaiah to tell him that he was going to die. Therefore he was to put his house in order.

Hezekiah thought of the danger in which His people found themselves. He had reinstated the service of the Lord in Judah, and he hoped the Lord would use him to bring deliverance to His people and lead them to walk in His ways again. It was Hezekiah's sincere desire to be the deliverer of His people. But now everything was being cut off. What would become of His people? Wouldn't God take his desire to serve into account?

Hezekiah turned his face to the wall so that he could concentrate on the Lord alone. In his prayer he reminded the Lord about what he had done and what he still hoped for. This was not boasting on Hezekiah's part; the Spirit of the Mediator Jesus Christ was in him.

The Lord heard Hezekiah's prayer. Isaiah had not gotten very far away from the palace when the Lord sent him back to tell Hezekiah that he would recover and would already go up to the temple after two days. The Lord would add fifteen years to his life and would deliver Judah from the hands of the Assyrians. Hezekiah's wish had been granted. He was allowed to be the Lord's instrument in delivering His people.

The Lord was not arbitrarily going back on His Word. The Lord acknowledged Hezekiah's special calling and gave him an extra fifteen years to carry out that calling. From everything that happened, Hezekiah was to see that the Lord acknowledged this special calling, that it was not just something that had sprung up in Hezekiah's heart but was truly from the Lord. In all of this, his incentive must have been the opportunity to serve as deliverer of his people—in dependence upon the Lord.

Hezekiah had asked for a sign to confirm his faith that he would recover. The sign would also assure him that he could consider his recovery as proof of God's special favor and as an acknowledgment of his calling. The Lord gave him such a sign. At his wish, the shadow moved back ten steps. This natural phenomenon convinced Hezekiah all the more of God's special care.

But Hezekiah's faith, which was further strengthened by this sign, did not exclude the use of proper means. At Isaiah's command, a cluster of figs was put on the growth on the king's body.

Then Hezekiah recovered from his illness.

There is no point in arguing that his recovery was due to the means employed. The recovery was of the Lord—but the Lord chose to work through means in this case. Yet, it is noteworthy that at a time when trust in the Lord was so necessary, the Lord did choose to work through such means.

After his recovery, Hezekiah sang a song to the Lord in which he spoke of his sorrow at the prospect of death and his happiness at being allowed to go on living. How strongly Hezekiah clung to life! He did this because he valued life as a gift of God and because he desired to serve the Lord. We must cling to this life in the same way.

Yielding in a time of trial. After Hezekiah's recovery, the Lord granted Judah deliverance from the Assyrians. In this regard, too, Hezekiah was allowed to fulfill his calling as the people's deliverer. How dependent on the Lord he had shown himself to be all that time! Would he now also be able to bring about lasting deliverance for Judah?

Because Sennacherib had been forced to stop short of Jerusalem, Hezekiah came to be highly esteemed among the nations. They hoped that Judah's good fortune would signal the beginning of their own deliverance from the power of the Assyrians. Hezekiah received honors and gifts from all over. Thus his treasury, which had been depleted by one settlement he had made with Sennacherib, was replenished again. But the honors being heaped upon him posed definite dangers. Would Hezekiah go on looking to the Lord only?

One day some ambassadors came to him from Babylon. Like so many other nations, Babylon groaned under the Assyrian yoke. These emissaries came to congratulate Hezekiah on his recovery and to hear about the amazing sign of the shadow. Yet, this stated purpose was intended to cover up the real object of their visit: they wanted to talk with Hezekiah about an alliance against Assyria.

Hezekiah showed the emissaries all the treasures of his house and all the means at his disposal. Thus he seemed to be giving serious consideration to the idea of an alliance. He no longer put his trust in the Lord alone; he trusted in his own power, and now he wanted to strengthen that power through an agreement with Babylon. Had he forgotten that the Lord had delivered Judah by a miracle? Shouldn't faith in the Lord be like a miraculous sign at a time when a world power was coming up and threatening the nations more and more? Why, then, this alliance with Babylon?

Hezekiah's willingness to consider an alliance made it clear that however much he had been blessed by the Lord and strengthened in his faith, he could not be the perfect deliverer of Judah. Moreover, Judah's existence was coming to an end. The old covenant, in which God adopted only the people of Israel as His people and taught them by way of shadows and gave them shadowy mediators, was coming to an end. The failure of Hezekiah cried out for a better Mediator, a Mediator who would obtain an eternal salvation and bring the covenant in a new form.

At the Lord's command, Isaiah told Hezekiah that one day all those treasures and his people as well would be carried away captive to Babylon, the nation with which he had just made an alliance. When Hezekiah asked in sorrow whether he himself would live to see that misery, the Lord promised him that the judgment would not come during his lifetime.

Hezekiah humbled himself under the judgment. He believed that there would yet be deliverance for his people—in God's time and in God's way. One day, through the Mediator who was to come, the Lord would triumph over the sins committed by His people, including Hezekiah. In that faith Hezekiah was able to bow under the judgment. And because he humbled himself, the Lord promised that the judgment would not strike during his lifetime. It would be postponed. This made Hezekiah happy. He had not lived in vain after all.

52: The Power of Grace
in a Time of Judgment

II Kings 21
II Chronicles 33

We are not just to tell of Manasseh's conversion using a matter-of-fact framework—misery, salvation, thankfulness.* If we did, we would be forgetting that the main issue is not the relationship of God to Manasseh but the relationship of God to His people.

In the book of Kings we are told of Manasseh's godlessness—but not of his conversion. What this book wants to get across to us, apparently, is that Judah became ripe for judgment because of Manasseh's sin. The later change in Manasseh was not enough to avert the judgment. Not even the great reformation under Josiah could turn the tide. We must also keep this thought in mind as we tell the story of Amon.

Manasseh's conversion then takes on a special meaning for us. Judah's judgment is indeed certain, but grace remains stronger than sin. Through Manasseh, this is demonstrated to all the believers among the people. In this way Scripture's intention with regard to Manasseh's sin becomes clear. Roaring rebellion characterized him until he was subdued by grace as a proof of the power of that grace.

The triumph of grace over Manasseh in a time of judgment is a prophecy pointing ahead to the triumph of grace through the cross and resurrection of the Christ. After all, the route Manasseh took (imprisonment followed by deliverance from captivity) mirrors the route that the Lord Jesus Christ was to take.

Main thought: *Manasseh is subjected to the power of grace in a time of judgment.*

---

*This is the basic scheme of the Heidelberg Catechism, one of the outstanding catechetical products of the Reformation.—Trans.

In utter rebellion. Manasseh was twelve years old when he became king of Judah. Apparently one of Hezekiah's younger sons was chosen to succeed his father. Perhaps the people saw something special in him. But when the Lord gave Manasseh to Judah as king, He did so in judgment.

The boy became king too early. He was not able to withstand the temptations arising from the luxury that surrounded him because he was king. He wanted the freedom to do as he pleased. He was not at all interested in considering himself as called by God in the bond of the covenant to be a shield for his people.

That meant that Manasseh would have to oppose the work of his father, Hezekiah. And that's just what he did—intentionally. He began by rebuilding the high places which Hezekiah had destroyed. And he offered sacrifices on them—but not to the Lord. Instead he taught the people to worship the Baals there. Thus Manasseh deliberately desecrated his father's work of faith and trampled it underfoot.

He proceeded systematically in his rebellion against the Lord. In the house of the Lord he erected altars for the Baals. In addition, he imported the worship of the sun, moon and stars from Babylon and Assyria. The heavenly bodies became gods to him. In those days that was the highest form of idolatry. By means of that idolatry, Manasseh wanted to withstand the service of the Lord. For this cult, too, he built altars in the front courts of the Lord's house.

The Lord had given Israel the sacrifice for purposes of reconciliation. The sacrifice was a prophecy pointing to the remission of sin through the Lord Jesus Christ. But Manasseh made his sons go through the fire. He even wanted to subject the divine power to himself by means of magic and fortune-telling.

Manasseh provoked the Lord to His face, in order to free himself from Him completely. How could the Lord tolerate such behavior? Wasn't His tolerance an indication that He was beginning to forsake His people? He was leaving the people of Judah to their own sins. The judgment upon Judah was ripe. Thus it became clear what sin does to people.

But to show that grace is always more powerful than sin—even though God was now forsaking Judah—the Lord interfered in Manasseh's life and in the life of Judah. To be sure, this interference would do nothing to avert the judgment upon Judah; all it would do was show the power of grace. It would serve as a prophecy pointing to the triumph of grace which was to come through the Christ.

The turnaround. When Manasseh sealed his rebellion against the Lord with the spilling of much innocent blood in Jerusalem, the Lord intervened. Manasseh's aversion to the Lord had driven him to rule in a completely highhanded way. Instead of being a shield for his people, he was a constant threat.

The Lord brought the commanders of the army of the Assyrian king upon him. Jerusalem was an almost impregnable fortress, but the Assyrian army evidently took the city without much difficulty. Jerusalem's strength lay completely in the Lord's protection. Manasseh was bound with bronze chains and led away captive to Babylon.

When Manasseh was still king, the Lord had often sent prophets to him and to the people, but they paid no attention to the Lord's voice. Manasseh had wanted his freedom. Now the one who wanted to be free was in chains. Likewise, all who want to free themselves from the Lord are bound in that they are under sentence. It's a good thing we know that even the Lord Jesus Christ was bound for our sins once, in order to set us free.

In Babylon Manasseh was distressed by his bonds. The original text reads that *the Lord* distressed him. Apparently Manasseh did not just sigh in captivity; the Lord made him see that he was imprisoned under divine judgment. That broke Manasseh. He prayed earnestly to the Lord, who was seeking him in this distress and still wanted to be his God. He humbled himself before the God of his fathers. He acknowledged what God had been to his father and—through his father—to Judah.

The Lord heard his prayers. Then came something Manasseh could scarcely have hoped for; he was restored to his throne in Jerusalem. This may have come about in connection with a change in ruler in Assyria, but it was the Lord's doing. In this restoration of Manasseh, the Lord displayed the power of His grace to overcome sin.

Having returned to Jerusalem, Manasseh experienced that the

Lord is God. He could not yet submit completely to the Lord in his distress; only after God's grace had revealed itself to him could he do so. Then he saw that the Lord's grace was stronger than he was and he understood the intention of that grace for him and for Judah.

The restoration of the Lord's claims. Having turned back to the Lord, Manasseh was able to reign again. He became a monarch who ruled over himself as well as over his people. He fortified Jerusalem, and in all the established cities of Judah he put armed forces, so that he could offer resistance to any future invasion by Assyria. In faith he dared to take up the battle with Assyria.

Of course Manasseh now tried to root out the idolatry. He took the idol he had erected in the house of the Lord and removed it from Jerusalem, along with the altars. He also restored the altar of the Lord and sacrificed thank offerings and peace offerings on it. In those days the heavens were opened over Judah again.

But the people still sacrificed on the high places. Although they sacrificed to the Lord there, they were not sacrificing in accordance with the law of the Lord in the Lord's house. Therefore the sacrifices on the high places were sinful; they posed a great danger that the people would start wandering away from the Lord again. Manasseh was not able to push through a complete reformation of Judah.

When Manasseh died, he died in faith. The Lord's grace had become too strong for him. But the main thing is not that we die saved. The greater part of Manasseh's life had been a disgrace. And that part of his life—not his later turnaround—was decisive for Judah. The early years of his reign had made Judah ripe for judgment. Important for us, too, is *how* we have lived.

The abiding sentence upon Judah. It became clear immediately after Manasseh's death that judgment was not averted from Judah: he was succeeded by his son Amon, who did what was evil in the Lord's eyes. Amon ruled entirely in the spirit of his father's early years on the throne. Judah had once followed

Manasseh in his sins. Now the Lord punished Judah anew with the godlessness of Amon.

Amon reigned in Jerusalem for only two years. His servants killed him and were killed in turn by the people. Thus, disintegration began to drag Judah down. The judgment slowly worked its way through all of Judah's life. This judgment could be arrested for a while by a turnaround on Judah's part, but it could not be averted anymore.

Manasseh's sin was decisive for Judah, then. Grace, it is true, was triumphant over Manasseh, but the people remained under judgment. This situation cried out all the more for Christ's victory over God's judgment. The Christ triumphed by suffering the judgment for us. Just as Judah lay bound under the judgment, we are bound under judgment if we remain outside of the Christ—all of us.

53: The Need for Reformation by the Spirit

II Kings 22-23
II Chronicles 34-35

Josiah is the great reformer of Judah. In this respect he is even greater than Hezekiah. In II Kings 23:25 he is characterized as follows: "Before him there was no king like him, who turned to the LORD with all his heart and with all his soul and with all his might, according to all the law of Moses; nor did any like him arise after him."

Yet, the reformation under Josiah was not able to save Judah. God's judgment was fully decided. No matter what transformation overcame the people, it would not be enough to save them from destruction. That was the situation from God's side. When we look at the situation from man's side, we see that sin was so deeply rooted in Judah that even the reformation under Josiah could not turn the people back and bring about a conversion of the heart.

Because of Manasseh's sin and the innocent blood he had spilled in Jerusalem, the Lord had fully decided upon judgment. Again, we will not do justice to this segment of Biblical history if we focus mainly on pious Josiah and his serious intentions. If we were to adopt such a perspective, we would have to say that his life was a failure. What this story reveals to us is that the old covenant was powerless to save the people as a people. In its decline, the old covenant cries out for the new.

In the new covenant comes another reformation—the reformation of the heart through the indwelling of the Spirit, the reformation by which the law is being written on our hearts. Although the prayers of Josiah could no longer penetrate to the grace of God for His people, the Christ has opened the way to that grace through His blood. Thus Josiah's work cries out for the Christ, and his impotent reformation cries out for a reformation by the Spirit.

We may not conclude from this that the old covenant was not a form of the same covenant of grace in which we live today. However, in the old covenant the spirit of servanthood unto fear dominated. The

387

Church was in its childhood and was therefore placed under guardians and supporters, that is, under the law. In its Old Testament dispensation, the covenant still gave prominence to external legal forms. There the law had meaning especially as an external restraining force. But the human race cannot be saved by such means; it will be saved only by the indwelling of the Spirit, who renews us according to the demands of the law.

Although Josiah knew that preservation was no longer possible for Judah as a people, he proceeded vigorously with his reformation. In such circumstances conversion has both the right motive and the right purpose. The main issue with regard to conversion is not our salvation but the restoration of the Lord's claim on us.

Still, we might ask whether Josiah really continued in that spirit to the very end of his reign. His action against Pharaoh Neco points to something different. Apparently he thought that he would still be able to raise Judah once more to the important status which the Lord's people had enjoyed under David and Solomon. His action may have been occasioned by his distrust of Neco's words. Yet, since he knew that Judah's role had been played out, he was biting off more than he could chew when he took the field against the Egyptian king.

In a certain sense, therefore, we may view these times as the end of Judah and the beginning of the end of the old covenant. Although it is true that Judah was restored after the captivity, it was never restored completely. Judah remained in subjection to the world power of the time. Hence the theocracy could not be restored.

Main thought: *Josiah's reformation cries out for a reformation by the Spirit.*

The impotence of the old covenant. Manasseh had filled Jerusalem with his sins. For that reason God had decided on judgment for Judah. Judah was ripe for that judgment. Manasseh had returned to the Lord, to be sure, but his conversion could not avert the judgment. This became clear when Amon succeeded Manasseh as king. Amon again did what was evil in the eyes of the Lord.

Yet, after Amon the Lord gave Judah another king who feared Him—Josiah. Josiah came to the throne as a boy of eight. In a certain sense he was fortunate that his father had died when he was still so young; as a result, he was raised by believers—his mother and her counselors.

When Josiah was still very young, he chose definitely to serve the Lord, and he began to root out the idolatry in his immediate surroundings. Sometimes boys and girls stay in line only because of pressure from their parents, but they do not have to wait until they are 20 or older to make a definite choice for the Lord. They can make such a choice when they are very young, as Josiah did.

When Josiah got older, he began with the restoration of the temple, which was in disrepair. The money for this restoration came from freewill contributions by the people in the offering box and the contributions of the king. There was not much supervision of the management of the money, for the men assigned to that task were trustworthy.

In the eighteenth year of Josiah's reign, when he was 26 years old, he sent his secretary Shaphan to the high priest Hilkiah to count and store the money which had been offered by the people. Then Hilkiah informed Shaphan that he had found Moses' Book of the Law.

The Lord had decreed that His law was to be read to the people at each of the great feasts. Obviously this had not been done for a long time. The Book of the Law had been put away in a forgotten place. Believing parents still told their children what they knew about the covenant and the service of the Lord, and the prophets still tried to keep the knowledge of the Lord alive among the people, but the Book of the Covenant had been forgotten. That was an abomination. Now Hilkiah had found it and had rescued it from under the dust.

The Lord was behind this event, of course. Now the people would read in that book about the judgment with which the Lord had earlier threatened them as punishment for apostasy. Now they would realize that the end had come for Judah.

Shaphan brought the Book of the Law to the king and read it to him. Josiah tore his clothes, for he understood that Judah had made itself doubly worthy of judgment. Immediately he sent messengers to Huldah, the prophetess, who lived in Jerusalem, to ask her for the Word of the Lord. She sent them back to Josiah with the message that nothing could avert the judgment upon Judah. It was too late. Yet, because Josiah had torn his clothes and had humbled himself before the Lord, the Lord would postpone the judgment so that it would not come during his lifetime.

Apparently the Lord did not allow Josiah to penetrate to God's grace for His people in his prayers. Judah would be destroyed, and Jerusalem would be taken. The covenant in which Israel lived with the Lord was the old covenant; it was temporary. It had to pass over into a new covenant, the covenant in which God's people live with the Lord today. Accordingly, in that old covenant Josiah could not find God's grace for the people of Judah anymore. The Lord Jesus Christ, however, would open the entrance to the eternal grace of God for His people through His blood. Therefore the new covenant is far more wonderful than the old. The old covenant was a prophecy pointing ahead to the new.

Josiah's reformation. Josiah knew that the judgment upon Judah was sure to come, but he wanted to press ahead with the reformation of Judah anyway. In this he showed a diligence unmatched by any king before or after him. He did not declare that there was no point in reformation since it could not save Judah anyway. He wanted to go ahead with the reformation solely for the sake of the honor and righteousness of the Lord. The Lord has a right to be served, even if our service does not bring about our salvation.

Josiah called together the elders of the people and also the priests and the prophets. As much as possible, he wanted the entire people, from the highest to the lowest, in the front court of the temple. When they had assembled, he had the law read to them. There the king stood, as a humble servant of his God, listening with all the others to the Word of the Lord and its judgments.

Yet, the people did not want to humble themselves in dust and ashes. They only shouted that they wanted to accept the covenant with the Lord again. The people didn't know what they were saying.

Josiah got the consent of the people to press on with the reformation. And that he did—systematically. He cleansed Jerusalem of all traces of idolatry and sun worship. He smashed the altars and images of his grandfather Manasseh to pieces and burned them outside Jerusalem. He threw away the altars for sun worship which Ahaz, one of his forefathers, had erected on the roof of one of the annex buildings of the temple. Even altars that Solomon had allowed his wives to erect were destroyed. He defiled the Valley of Hinnom, near Jerusalem, where children had been sacrificed.

Josiah also pressed on with the reformation outside Jerusalem, throughout all of Judah. He defiled all the high places, where sacrifices had been offered not just to the Lord but also to the Baals. All the priests and Levites who had served on the high places were brought together in Jerusalem under the supervision of the high priest and under the teaching of the law. He did not permit them to serve at the altar in the temple.

Josiah wanted to restore the Lord's rights in Judah. He was able to push the reformation through, but the hearts of the people did not return to the Lord.

Josiah was a type of the Christ, who would manifest the righteousness of the Lord to all peoples. But the Christ was able to do what Josiah could not do, namely, change the hearts of people. The Christ would send His Spirit, who would bring about the reformation of the heart in the new covenant.

The avenger from David's house. Josiah also went beyond Judah's borders, to Bethel, the seat of the idol worship instituted by Jeroboam I. He had the bones of the priests of that cult, who were buried there, dug up. Then he burned those bones on the altar. He also smashed the altar to pieces and burned the symbol of Astarte. Only one grave was left undisturbed—the grave of the prophet who had come from Judah in Jeroboam's time to predict this judgment (see I Kings 13:1-10).

Thus, what the Lord had threatened was literally fulfilled. The son of David's house had come as an avenger of the Lord's rights, which had been violated. One day David's great Son will also bring judgment. Then the claims of the Lord's covenant will be wholly restored.

Josiah exercised judgment not only in Bethel but also in the cities of Samaria. He killed all the priests of the high places on the altars, burned human bones on the altars, and destroyed all the temples on those high places.

A Passover without a passing over. After Josiah's return, in the eighteenth year of his reign, a great Passover feast was held in Jerusalem. Nothing quite like this feast had ever been held before. The princes and government officials contributed much to this Passover feast.

The Passover was intended as a memorial of Israel's deliverance out of Egypt and of the night when the angel of death passed over the houses whose doorposts had been smeared with blood. Would this Passover in Josiah's time perhaps mean that the judgment would pass Judah by? Or had the Lord fully decided upon judgment? Soon the answer would become clear in a terrible way.

Out of that same Egypt, Pharaoh Neco now came marching up. Although he said that he had no intentions with regard to Judah but only wanted to help Assyria, Josiah took the field against him. In a battle near Megiddo, Judah was defeated and Josiah was killed in action.

The people were deeply shocked by this defeat. Even when a king like Josiah was leading the people, the Lord was not with them in battle! The name *Megiddo* lived on in their memory as a name for disaster.

For the next few years, Egypt ruled over Judah. Josiah's son Jehoahaz, whom the people had made king, was removed from the throne by Pharaoh Neco. Jehoiakim, the brother of Jehoahaz, was made king instead, and Jehoahaz himself was carried off to Egypt.

The same land of Egypt from which the people had once been delivered now ruled over them again. It was as if the people had been sent back to the house of bondage. The Passover they had just celebrated did not preserve them from disaster. Neither did the blood of lambs cleanse Judah from sin. The old covenant was coming to an end. It's a good thing we know that our Passover lamb was slain for us—the Lord Jesus Christ, who is *the* Lamb. His blood cleanses us from all sin.

54: Fading Light

II Kings 24-25

The temple and the reign of David's house had been given as a light for Israel and for the whole world. When David's house was carried away and the temple was destroyed, the light in Jerusalem was extinguished. After that God's revelation still came to the people by means of prophecy in Babylon and through Jeremiah for those who remained in Judah. But the old covenant, which had been bound to Jerusalem in a special way since the time of David and Solomon, slowly disappeared.

The Son of David who is not bound to Jerusalem would have to appear. The elevation of Jehoiachin from imprisonment in Babylon was a prophecy pointing ahead to this exaltation of the house of David.

Main thought: *The light in Jerusalem fades in order that it may appear anew in the Christ.*

The first deportation. Pharaoh Neco had conquered Josiah, dethroned Jehoahaz, and placed Jehoiakim on the throne in Jerusalem. But this Egyptian monarch was defeated by Nebuchadnezzar, the king of Babylon. Nebuchadnezzar also laid siege to Jerusalem and captured it. He bound Jehoiakim with bronze chains, with the intention of carrying him away to Babylon. But he changed his mind and left him on the throne, in exchange for hostages and an immense amount of treasure.

For three years Jehoiakim remained subject to the king of Babylon. Then he rebelled. Nebuchadnezzar was too busy in his

393

own country to take action against Jerusalem. All he did was to send bands of marauders to plunder Judah. These bands were made up of Babylonians and men from the subject nations as well.

It was really the Lord who was sending these raiders. The Lord was fulfilling the Word of His prophet. Jeremiah, in particular, was given the task of telling the king and the people continually that they were to subject themselves to the king of Babylon. Then there would still be mercy for the people.

The glory of David's house and the grace which God showed the people in that glory had ended. The old covenant was coming to an end. Especially through Manasseh's sin, the house of David had so completely forfeited the Lord's favor that it could not be restored to its former condition. Neither the people nor their king listened to Jeremiah. Now Judah was being plundered as a result.

Jehoiakim died, and his son Jehoiachin became king in his place. Jehoiachin lived and ruled like his father—in disobedience to the Word of the Lord and in rebellion against the king of Babylon. This time Nebuchadnezzar himself marched against Jerusalem. When Jehoiachin saw that he could not defend the city, he surrendered and went out to meet the king of Babylon. That was the second time Nebuchadnezzar marched into Jerusalem. He carried away the king and the princes and all the craftsmen and smiths. All of them were sent to Babylon. He also took along the treasures from the Lord's house and the king's palace. This darkened the honor of David's house and of the house of the Lord. The light began to fade in Jerusalem. One day it would shine again far more gloriously in the Christ. The light in Jerusalem was being taken away.

The second deportation. The king of Babylon made Zedekiah, Jehoiachin's uncle, king in Jerusalem. Zedekiah was the third son of Josiah to occupy the throne. (The other two were Jehoahaz and Jehoiakim.) Would the house of David now listen to the prophetic Word? Zedekiah ruled in the same manner as his predecessors and also rebelled against the king of Babylon.

Again Nebuchadnezzar marched against Jerusalem and laid siege to the city. The seige lasted about a year and a half. When the hunger in the city became intolerable, the Babylonians captured the lower city. Not long afterward, the king fled secretly with his army during the night. This humiliating retreat was another disgrace to the house of David.

The Babylonians pursued Zedekiah and caught him, deserted by all his troops, in the plain of Jericho. They took him bound to Riblah, where Nebuchadnezzar had retreated. There his sons were killed before his eyes. Then Zedekiah's eyes were gouged out, and he was carried away in bonds to Babylon.

Nebuchadnezzar's patience with Jerusalem had run out. The temple, the palace of the king, and the houses of the rich and powerful were burned. The walls of the city were broken down. The house of the Lord and the palace of the king went up in flames, as the king himself was carted away to Babylon in disgrace.

Where, now, was the Lord's favor toward His people, the favor of which He had given a sign in the temple and in David's sovereign rule? The crown of Jerusalem was gone for good. The Lord did not intend to break the promise He had given to the house of David; He would fulfill that promise in a completely different way in the Christ.

All the prominent people in the entire land of Judah were exiled to Babylon. All the gold and silver and bronze from the temple went to Babylon too. Many of the prominent people of Judah were put to death. Only the poorest of the people were left behind. The glorious history of Judah was past. The old covenant was fading away. The new covenant would come in its stead.

The destruction of the people in Judah. The king of Babylon appointed Gedaliah as governor over the people who had remained in Judah. After the Babylonians were gone, the soldiers of Judah who had fled over the borders returned with their captains. Gedaliah swore to them that if they subjected themselves to his authority, they would have nothing to fear from the Babylonians. Under Gedaliah's leadership, the people seemed to be attaining a new prosperity. But judgment pursued even these people who had been left behind.

The king of Ammon was jealous of Judah's restoration. Therefore he incited Ishmael, one of the captains of Judah's army, to kill Gedaliah. Although Gedaliah had been warned (see Jer.

40:13—41:3), he allowed himself to be caught off guard and was killed. Then the Jews were afraid that the king of Babylon would take revenge. They requested Jeremiah to inquire of the Lord for them (Jer. 42-44). In the name of the Lord, Jeremiah told them that they should stay in Judah. Then no harm would befall them.

In spite of this advice, they fled to Egypt and even took Jeremiah with them by force. Therefore Jeremiah had to prophesy to them that the revenge of Babylonia's king, which they thought they could escape by fleeing, would come upon them in Egypt, where they sought refuge. This happened just as Jeremiah said it would.

New hope. It appeared that the last had been heard of Judah. There did not seem to be any ground for hope left. Yet, in those darkest of times, God gave a sign that He had not forgotten the house of David but was mindful of His promise.

In Babylon a new king succeeded to the throne. In the thirty-seventh year after Jehoiachin had been taken captive, this new king (Evil-merodach) took him from prison and elevated him above all the kings who were imprisoned and even allowed him to sit at his table in the palace. Jehoiachin was also awarded a yearly cash allowance.

Why this elevation of Judah's king? The hand of the Lord was at work in this event. Believers could look upon it as a prophecy that the house of David would be lifted up again one day.

The exaltation came in the new covenant in the Christ. To this Son born of David's house God has given all power in heaven and on earth. His sovereignty is no longer bound to Jerusalem. And through the Spirit, whom David's Son would send, the whole earth was again to become a temple of God.

Captivity

55: A Kingdom Not of This World

Daniel 1-2

Jerusalem and the temple had fallen. The house of David was humbled, and the people of Judah were in exile. The light shining in Jerusalem had been snuffed out.

In this dark hour, God tripled the light of His Word in prophecy. During the exile, three great prophets appeared on the scene—Jeremiah, who lived among those left behind in Judah, Ezekiel, who lived among the captives, and Daniel, who lived at the Babylonian court. Again the Lord's light shone through in the life of the peoples.

The prophecy of the Kingdom of the Christ came particularly to Babylon. Over against the kingdom of Babylon, which is of this world, stands the Kingdom of Christ, which is not of this world.

In Nebuchadnezzar's life we notice a peculiar shift. After the confirmation of his reign, he is busy wondering what will happen in the future (Dan. 2:29). Then he sees that his throne certainly will not stand forever. The vision of the statue in his dream is the Lord's response to those thoughts. Later he wants to compel the entire world to worship Babylon's power. This power is symbolized by the statue erected by Nebuchadnezzar in the Plain of Dura. And in his old age Nebuchadnezzar falls prey to self-glorification, as we see from his words: "Isn't this the great Babylon I have built?" (Dan. 4:30). Without the power of grace, we do not improve as we get older. Pride is the sin of old age in particular.

Main thought: *Babylon receives a prophecy about a Kingdom that is not of this world.*

The preparation of the prophet. Among the hostages whom Nebuchadnezzar had carried off to Babylon after the first conquest of Jerusalem at the time of Jehoiakim were many young men from the nobility of Judah. These young men were given an opportunity to become pages at the court. Nebuchadnezzar ordered the superintendent of his palace to select the most handsome and intelligent of them to be trained for that position in all the wisdom of the Babylonians. The trainees were to be fed with food from the royal table.

Among those who were selected were Daniel and his three friends Shadrach, Meshach and Abednego. With Daniel as their spokesman, the four asked to be excused from eating the king's food and drinking his wine. That food and drink was devoted to idols and was not prepared in accordance with the law of the Lord. Even in captivity these four young men were faithful to the obligations of the Lord's covenant. These four were faithful in the Lord's strength.

When objections were raised by the superintendent, the four asked for a ten-day trial period. At their request they were given nothing but bread and vegetables to eat and water to drink. The Lord moved the heart of the superintendent to comply with their wishes. After the trial period they looked healthier than all the others. In faith they had ventured to request this test. Because they were faithful, they were not put to shame.

Besides, God gave these four young men more insight into the wisdom of the Babylonians than the other trainees. This insight was also the fruit of faith. By their knowledge of the Lord in His grace through faith, they saw through the wisdom of the Babylonians and gained mastery over that wisdom. The Lord also gave Daniel the gift of prophecy. Daniel was permitted to receive the light of divine revelation in Babylon.

Once the three-year period of preparation was over, the king talked with each one of the trainees. Daniel and his friends excelled in this examination. The Lord had blessed them so much that their wisdom went far beyond the wisdom of the wise men of Babylon. As a result, they were in the king's presence daily. The Lord had prepared a place for them at the court. Through them He wished to reveal Himself to Babylon and to the nations. For this purpose He had made them faithful to His covenant.

Babylon's wise men put to shame. Near the beginning of his reign, Nebuchadnezzar had a disturbing dream. When he awoke, the dream still bothered him, even though he did not remember just what he had dreamed. He called in all the wise men to learn from them what it was that he had dreamed. They asked the king to tell them the dream; then they would give him the interpretation. The king said that he did not remember the dream and threatened to kill them all and destroy their houses if they did not comply with his wishes. But if they succeeded in making known the dream and its interpretation, they would be honored in royal style.

Again the wise men asked to hear the dream first. The king reproached them for being unable to tell him the dream. If he himself told them the dream, they could easily tell him any interpretation that came into their minds. Now he did not trust their wisdom anymore. Therefore he was determined to have them put to death.

Although the wise men protested that there was no one who could possibly do what the king asked, that no monarch had ever asked such a thing of his wise men, and that only the gods were able to comply with such a demand, the king issued an order that the wise men were to be put to death. By saying that only the gods were able to do what the king asked, the wise men were admitting that they were not really in contact with the gods after all, despite their pretense. All the wisdom of those wise men proved to be futile. Heathendom with its wisdom had disappointed the king.

The wise men were being rounded up to be put to death. Even Daniel and his friends were to be killed. As foreigners they did not really belong to the caste of wise men, but they were counted among them anyway.

Daniel first found out what had happened when the soldiers came to arrest him. He asked the king for a short delay, promising that he would tell the king the dream and its interpretation. He did so in the belief that the Lord wished to make His light shine over Babylon by way of this dream.

If the Lord did indeed intend to use Daniel and his friends for that purpose, this would be an act of mercy on His part. Therefore Daniel and his friends prayed all night for God's mercy. The Lord heard their prayer and caused Daniel to see in a vision what

Nebuchadnezzar had dreamed. He also gave him an understanding of the meaning of the dream.

Daniel thanked and praised God, who has the kingdoms in His hand and who alone is able to give light and wisdom on earth. That light is in the Christ, the Promised One, who was awaited by Israel.

The next morning Daniel asked to be admitted to the king's presence. When the king asked him if he was able to tell him the dream and its interpretation, he answered that no one on earth could do that—not even the wise men. However, the God in heaven whom Daniel knew, the God who was worshiped in Israel, did reveal mysteries. For Christ's sake, that God still concerned Himself with His people. Thus the treasure of the revelation received by God's people became known in Babylon.

Kingdoms and the Kingdom of God. Daniel said that Nebuchadnezzar had seen a statue in his dream. Its head was made of gold, its chest and arms of silver, its belly and thighs of brass, its legs of iron, and its feet of iron mixed with damp clay. This statue portrayed successive world empires. The golden head was Nebuchadnezzar's kingdom. The statue was excellent and exceedingly bright, Daniel declared, adding that its appearance was frightening.

Any world power is both impressive and frightening if it does not proceed out of faith. This applies to the entire development of the world. The glory of the development of culture is dazzling, but its appearance is frightening if it is turned against the sovereign rule of the Christ. This would also be true of the world powers that would succeed one another.

Nebuchadnezzar had seen something else as well. A stone cut by no human hand crushed the statue. There was nothing left of it but dust, which was blown away by the wind. That stone became bigger and bigger until it filled the entire earth.

That stone is the Kingdom of the Christ, who has been given to us not by man but by God Himself. His Kingdom shall conquer the kingdoms that are of this world and shall one day fill the earth. Christ's Kingdom is not *of* this world, but it is indeed *for* the world of men. It is to govern the life of men now, even though it will not come into its full glory until the return of the Christ.

Daniel ended his interpretation by saying: "The great God has made known to the king what will happen in the future." The king in his heart had been preoccupied with the future. Would his kingdom last forever? This dream was the Lord's answer to the question that was troubling him. There is only one kingdom that will stand forever—the Kingdom of the Christ.

Acknowledging the sovereignty of Israel's God. Nebuchadnezzar realized immediately that Daniel's interpretation of his dream was correct. Gripped by that interpretation, he fell down before Daniel and worshiped him because of the light that was in him. The king bowed before the light of prophecy. He saw Daniel as an ambassador of Israel's God and ordered that an offering be made to this God in honor of Daniel. However, Nebuchadnezzar did not confess the God of Israel to be the only true God. He acknowledged Him only as the highest God. Yet, he did acknowledge that all authority and all light is with the Lord. Thus, something of the Kingdom which God would erect on earth through the Christ was revealed in Babylon, as well as something of the special glory of that Kingdom.

The king showered gifts on Daniel and appointed him to be ruler over the whole province of Babylon. Through Daniel's influence, Shadrach, Meshach and Abednego were also entrusted with government functions in Babylon. Thus the four came into prominence. For them this was a great honor, an honor they received for God's sake. Yet, they were being put in a difficult position in Babylon. In the midst of a heathen environment, they were to reveal what life in the fear of the Lord is like.

56: The Power of Grace in Babylon

Daniel 3

The statue which Nebuchadnezzar erected in the Plain of Dura was not an idol but a symbol of the glorious power of Babylon. However, men were asked to worship that statue. At that point the power of Babylon became an idol. Moreover, Nebuchadnezzar asked his subjects to acknowledge the gods of Babylon, who had given him the victory. The gods of the defeated nations were not as great as Babylon's gods. That Babylon's glorious power is central here is also evident from the pompous string of governors and other officials and from the pompous enumeration of musical instruments.

Over against this idolatry, the Lord revealed the power of grace in the deliverance of the three men in the burning fiery furnace. Notice what these men were saying: "God is mighty to deliver us, and He will deliver us. But if not, we still will not worship your statue." They were not entirely certain that God would deliver them. If their deliverance served to reveal His name, He would certainly deliver them. But if their deliverance was not necessary for that purpose, they would perish and God would glorify Himself in some other way.

We may not conclude from this story that God will always deliver His children in the way He delivered those three men. God does not always grant us such dramatic deliverance. He will reveal His name! Eternal salvation is certain; the deliverance from the fiery furnace was only a sign of that salvation.

We may be inclined to think of the Christ as the fourth man in the burning fiery furnace. This cannot be established conclusively on the basis of the Scriptural data. But even if the fourth man was a created angel, his presence was still a revelation of God's communion in the Christ with our life and suffering. Thus there is a prophecy here of the incarnation of the Word. Because of their communion with the Christ, the three men in the flaming furnace were not in distress. In "The Prayer of Azariah [Abednego] and the Song of the Three Young Men," which is recorded in the Apocrypha, we read that it felt as if a cool wind from a dew-covered morning was blowing around them.

Main thought: *The power of grace is revealed in Babylon*

Self-glorification. Nebuchadnezzar had undertaken a journey through a large part of the world and had established a world empire. When he returned, he worshiped the power he had acquired. At the beginning of his reign, he had been impressed with the instability of all things. Now he worshiped power.

A thought came to him: he would erect a huge statue in the Plain of Dura as a sign of Babylon's power. Then the representatives and governors of the subject nations would be made to come and worship the statue. In doing so they would acknowledge Babylon's power as divine. Moreover, they would be honoring Babylon's gods as stronger than the gods of the other nations.

There stood the statue, almost 28 meters high and three meters across, entirely overlaid with gold. It sparkled in the sun. All the ruling officials in the world empire of Nebuchadnezzar had gathered in front of it. At a given sign, when the music started to play, the whole crowd fell prostrate before the statue. All nations were being enslaved: Babylon alone was god. Babylon stood by its own power. It was true that the gods had helped, but Babylon was not dependent on the grace of the Lord.

This event represented a dare and a challenge to the Lord, whose name Nebuchadnezzar had already heard. Would the Lord now reveal Himself here and demonstrate that the power of His grace was greater than Babylon's power?

Confessing the power of grace. Nebuchadnezzar thought that he himself had originated this plan, of course, but he was really being directed by the Lord. In the glorification of Babylon, Nebuchadnezzar was going to encounter the power of grace. God also leads us when we sin. He punishes sin with sin and caused sin to culminate in the sharpest contrast with grace.

Immediately Nebuchadnezzar encountered opposition. Three men named Shadrach, Meshach and Abednego (the three friends of Daniel) had not prostrated themselves before the statue. (Apparently Daniel himself was not present.) These three men, who remained upright in the midst of all those kneeling people, must have been visible right away. The whole crowd was on its knees worshiping the greatness of one man. Whenever anyone dares to adopt a contrary attitude by kneeling before God and refusing to kneel before human glory, he immediately makes himself conspicuous. This applies to our time too.

In the assembled throng there were men who envied the three friends of Daniel. Nebuchadnezzar had put the three in positions of honor as governors of the province of Babylon. Their envious enemies now brought accusation against them to the king.

At first Nebuchadnezzar's attitude was sympathetic: he simply invited the three to show that they really meant to pay the required honor to the statue. But if they refused, they would be subject to the punishment he had decreed: they would be thrown into the burning fiery furnace. "What god could possibly deliver you out of my hand?" the king asked in threatening tones, challenging the power of the Lord's grace.

The three men answered that there was no need for them to make excuses to the king; there was nothing for which to apologize. Consciously, for the Lord's sake, they had refused to join in the worship of Babylon's power. They worshiped only the God of grace, the God of Israel. That God was able to deliver them by His grace. And He would certainly do so if it was necessary for the revelation and honor of His grace in Babylon. But if it was not necessary, they would perish. Then God would reveal His name in some other way. In any case, the three men refused to bow down before the statue. They put their fate in the hands of the living God.

The three men knew that the Lord would grant them deliverance if it was necessary for the honor of His name. In the same way, the Lord will deliver us if it serves His honor. We can be sure that He will give us eternal salvation through faith in Him. But we must surrender ourselves into the hands of the Lord.

Will we be able to do this as well as the three men who faced death in the fiery furnace? We must not be dazzled by the strength of faith displayed by these three. The God who gave them grace to be faithful will give it to us, too, if we look to Him and not to our own strength.

Communion with the Christ. The refusal of the three men made Nebuchadnezzar furious. Precisely because he had been so sympathetic to them, he was now twice as angry. He commanded that the furnace be heated up seven times hotter than usual. Then strong men from the king's army bound Shadrach, Meshach and Abednego fully clothed. Their clothes would immediately catch fire in the furnace.

Nebuchadnezzar's anger was actually rebellion against the living God. The king was heading for a collision with the power of grace. That collision took place at once: when the soldiers carried the three condemned men to the opening at the top of the flaming furnace and threw them down into the furnace, the soldiers' clothes caught fire from the sparks. The screams of the soldiers as they were burned to death must already have said something to Nebuchadnezzar about the Lord, against whom he was now fighting.

Through the openings at the bottom of the furnace, where the fire was fed, Nebuchadnezzar watched to see how the three condemned men would perish. But he jumped up horrified, for he saw them walking around in the fire unharmed! And there was a fourth man with them, a man who looked like a son of the gods! Nebuchadnezzar called to his counselors to come closer, to check on what he was seeing.

We do not know for sure who that fourth man was. Perhaps it was the Angel of the Lord, that is, the Lord Jesus Christ. Otherwise it must have been an ordinary angel. In any case, the Lord let it be known by this marvelous occurence that in the Christ He is in the midst of His own. He was with His own in the fiery furnace in Babylon.

The three men were not harmed by the fire. After all, it is the Word of grace that governs all things, even the strength of the fire. Because God was there in the Christ with those men, their plight in that fiery furnace caused them no distress. On the contrary, the Lord's presence was a joy to them! Here we see something of the

Kingdom of God's grace, in which He preserves His own.

At Nebuchadnezzar's command, the three men came out of the furnace. The king and his counselors could see for themselves that their hair was unsinged and their clothes unscorched. Indeed, their clothes didn't even smell of smoke!

Then Nebuchadnezzar had to acknowledge the power of the God of grace. His own kingdom would not be able to stand over against the Kingdom of grace which the Christ was going to establish on earth. Over against the sign of the power of Babylon (the statue) stood this sign of the power of the Lord's grace.

Nebuchadnezzar's public acknowledgment. The king praised the God of Shadrach, Meshach and Abednego for this miraculous deliverance by which He had responded to the faithful profession of His name. Nebuchadnezzar had a decree sent throughout his kingdom to the effect that no one was to blaspheme this God. Anyone who dared to blaspheme Him would be torn limb from limb and his house would be destroyed. "There is no other god who can give deliverance in such a way," proclaimed the king. We should note that Nebuchadnezzar did not acknowledge the Lord as the only true God; he said only that the Lord is superior to all the other gods.

Yet, in accordance with God's counsel, this acknowledgment served a purpose. The world left completely to itself would not yet succumb to sin. The world was being *preserved* so that the gospel of deliverance through the Christ would be preached there one day.

57: The Sovereignty of Israel's God

Daniel 4

Even though there is a transition from the first person to the third person in Daniel 4, the entire chapter is a proclamation by Nebuchadnezzar. The king's acknowledgment of the most high God is not to be viewed as the fruit of a true conversion. Yet, when he spoke of God's eternal kingdom, Nebuchadnezzar certainly was not thinking only of what we call the Kingdom of God's power. We must not forget that this acknowledgment was a result of the Word-revelation which came to him by way of his dream and the interpretation of that dream by Daniel. After the fall, this Word-revelation is always connected with the Christ. We must remember this as we read Daniel 4.

Daniel admonished Nebuchadnezzar to break with his sins by practicing righteousness and to do away with injustice by showing mercy to the oppressed. As long as his reign bore some resemblance to Christ's reign of grace, his peace would be extended. Christ's kingship is the norm for any and every kingship on earth.

What was revealed to Nebuchadnezzar about Christ's Kingdom through his earlier dream must have played a role in his thoughts throughout his life. It is noteworthy that he first referred to Daniel by his Hebrew name and then added: "he who was named Belteshazzar after the name of my god." Here we have an acknowledgment of the Jews as the people among whom the special revelation of God was to be found.

This revelation to Nebuchadnezzar is connected with Christ's coming in the flesh. By this penetration of God's Word, the world was to be preserved so that it would later be able to receive the gospel.

Over against Nebuchadnezzar's self-exaltation, in which he liberated himself from the living God, stands his acknowledgment that sovereign authority only comes by bowing down before the God who, in the Christ, concerns Himself with His people and with the world.

409

Nebuchadnezzar's brand of insanity is connected with self-exaltation.
When someone imagines himself to be an animal, all his authority is
gone.

Main thought: *All authority on earth depends on God's reign*
of grace through the Christ.

A warning in a dream. In the last days of his reign,
Nebuchadnezzar had a dream that filled him with fear. He saw a
tree whose top reached into the heavens. This tree, which could be
seen over the whole earth, was thick with leaves and fruit. The
beasts of the field found shade under it, and the birds of the air
found shelter in its branches.

Then a supernatural being appeared out of heaven and
shouted in a strong voice that the tree was to be cut down. Only the
stump was to be left in the ground. This messenger from heaven
apparently thought of a human being when he saw this tree, for he
said that he was to be chained with an iron and bronze band in the
grass, that he was to sleep under the bare sky, and that his lot would
be with the beasts in the grass of the earth. The messenger literally
said that the mind of that person would become so confused that
he would imagine himself to be an animal.

As Nebuchadnezzar later told it, the messenger also said that
this was sure to happen because it was a decision of the holy ones.
Daniel spoke of a decision of the Most High, but for Nebuchadnezzar's Babylonian consciousness it was a decision of the council
of the gods. The insanity would last seven periods of time, until
this person acknowledged that the Most High has sovereignty over
the kingdoms of men.

Nebuchadnezzar suspected that this dream was a revelation
given to him by the God who had already revealed Himself to him
several times. And he sensed that the dream concerned him. That's
why it filled him with fear. The God who revealed Himself in Israel
was often so close to Nebuchadnezzar! It is characteristic of that
God that Nebuchadnezzar was warned before the judgment struck.

The interpretation by the Spirit of prophecy. The king asked all the Babylonian wise men for the interpretation of his dream. Not one of them could provide it. The fear of this prophecy of judgment closed their minds. Not one of them could catch the light of revelation. How futile the fortune-telling of unbelievers is when contrasted with the revelation of the living God! Then the king called for Daniel, who was the head of the wise men. As a foreigner, however, Daniel had never become a regular member of their group.

When the king told him the dream, Daniel saw its interpretation by the Spirit of the Lord. At first he was beside himself at the horror of the judgment. How terrible is God, who yet gives Himself to His people in His grace!

Brought to his senses by a word from the king, Daniel said that he wished the judgment in the dream on the king's enemies. Unfortunately, that judgment concerned Nebuchadnezzar himself. Nebuchadnezzar was the tree. Insanity would overtake him and he would be driven out from among men. This would come over him on account of his self-exaltation, and it would last until he humbled himself before God.

As God's prophet, Daniel pleaded with the king to break with his self-exaltation and show his humility by being merciful to the oppressed. If only Nebuchadnezzar's reign showed some resemblance to Christ's reign of mercy, God would lengthen his peace. But if he chose to free himself completely from God, judgment was sure to come.

In this warning Nebuchadnezzar was allowed to hear something of what the reign of Christ would be like. Because Christ would be truly subject to God, He would be sovereign over all things. He would be merciful to the poor. All earthly kings are to conform to that kingship of the Christ.

The coming of judgment. At first Nebuchadnezzar was impressed by the revelation he had received. But such feelings are only temporary if they do not lead us to return in our hearts to the God of grace. Gradually the king freed himself from the impression this episode had made on him.

One day about a year later, he was standing on the flat roof of his palace overlooking the city he had adorned with many buildings. Pride swelled up in his heart and he spoke some words by which he liberated himself from the God of heaven and earth: "This is the great Babylon I have built as a royal residence by the strength of my power and in honor of my glory!" Immediately he heard a voice from heaven telling him that his authority had been taken away and that the judgment would now come.

At once a peculiar insanity came over Nebuchadnezzar, an insanity that made him feel and act like an animal. He was driven out of human society. He lived like an animal. His hair and his nails grew, and everything human in him degenerated.

People are given authority; every person has it. Now the one who had boasted of his authority had lost all his authority. What he lost first of all was his authority over his own mind. The remnant of the image of God which is still present in every human being for Christ's sake was completely desecrated and perverted in Nebuchadnezzar. This shows us how far God sometimes goes in judging and punishing people—even though He remains a God of grace. Yet, for Christ's sake there was mercy even in this judgment, for it served to call Nebuchadnezzar back.

Learning a certain justice. After the designated seven periods of time, Nebuchadnezzar's senses were restored. (We do not know just how long these periods of time lasted.) The first thought that entered his mind was that he should acknowledge the God who had revealed Himself to him as the God to whom all sovereignty belongs. That God was the God of Israel.

However, Nebuchadnezzar did not acknowledge this God as the only true God; he saw Him only as the highest God. Even so, he again humbled himself before God's majesty. And for Christ's sake God was merciful toward this heathen king. Nebuchadnezzar was accepted by the people again, and he regained his authority. His counselors and lords acknowledged him, and his kingship took on even greater splendor than before.

Some time afterward, Nebuchadnezzar sent out a proclamation to all corners of his kingdom in which he explained what had happened. He humbled himself to such an extent that he did not try to conceal the humiliating experience he had gone through.

And he acknowledged that all sovereignty belongs to the God who had revealed Himself to the king by way of Daniel, who was one of the Jews. In this way some knowledge of the living God was kept alive in the world. God was safeguarding the world until the gospel of the Christ who was to come could go forth to the nations and His Kingdom could be established among all peoples.

58: Like a Potter's Vessel

Daniel 5

The history that forms the background of Daniel 5 can perhaps be reconstructed as follows. Nabonidus was the last king of Babylon. But he was gone for a considerable length of time. While he was away, his son Belshazzar was the actual ruler. Returning to his throne, Nabonidus fled before the advancing Persians, who conquered Babylon without any opposition and took him prisoner. However, his son Belshazzar maintained a foothold in a part of the city. Several months after most of the city had been conquered, Cyrus arrived on the scene. Seven days later the remainder of the city was captured by surprise, and Belshazzar was killed while defending it. This surprise attack was launched during the night of the feast of which Daniel 5 tells us.

We should not tell this story as a personal judgment upon Belshazzar. If we were to use such an approach, we could indeed attach quite a few warnings to the story. (Ministers of the gospel have often preached about this story in exactly that way.) We would then be forgetting that Belshazzar was the king, the representative of the Babylonian kingdom that was to be broken into pieces.

When Belshazzar profaned the vessels of the temple, it became obvious that the Babylonian kingdom no longer left any room for expectations regarding the Kingdom of God. Although this rising world power had long been in opposition to the will of God, God had seen fit to use it for the safekeeping of the world until the coming of the Christ. But now the Babylonian world empire could no longer serve that purpose.

We must remember that judgment came upon Belshazzar because he profaned the vessels of the temple. The God who showed grace to His people Israel maintained His honor. Thus, even though we must tell of judgment, we are to speak first of all of God's grace and faithfulness as He upholds the covenant. The Christ maintains His glory in the destruction of His enemies.

414

Main thought: *God maintains His grace in the destruction of His enemies.*

Blaspheming the God of the covenant. There were several more kings of Babylon after Nebuchadnezzar. The last of them was Belshazzar. He was the son of a man who had seized the throne of Babylon by force. Perhaps his mother was of Nebuchadnezzar's line, which would mean that he could still be counted as one of Nebuchadnezzar's sons.

The Persians had already conquered much of Babylon. In one part of the city, Belshazzar held out stubbornly. It was during this period that he gave a great dinner party to which he invited his government officials and his wives. By giving that party, he displayed a reckless and flippant attitude. In his wantonness he ordered that the vessels from Jerusalem's temple be brought in so that his guests could drink from them while honoring the gods of Babylon. Those vessels were the ones Nebuchadnezzar had carried away to Babylon, the ones the Israelites had used in Jerusalem to honor the Lord, the God of the covenant. In this act, the Lord's grace for His people was scorned and the name of the Lord was profaned.

The Lord condemned this world power in which the greatness of man was worshiped. Yet, He chose to use it to preserve the nations until the day of Christ's coming. If they had been left to themselves, the nations would have torn each other to pieces.

But the Lord would not allow the kingdom of Babylon to fall into the sin of blaspheming Israel's God. If that were permitted, Babylon would bring the nations destruction rather than preservation. Therefore, when Belshazzar began blaspheming, the judgment of the Babylonian kingdom was sealed. The Lord would soon make this clear to Belshazzar.

Fear of the unknown God. Suddenly there appeared a hand above the king's throne, a hand that wrote a few words on the plaster of the wall. When the king saw it, he wanted to jump up, but he was paralyzed with fear. His knees were knocking. The God who shows grace to His people had pronounced judgment on

Babylon. Now He was writing the sentence on the wall! But Belshazzar did not know this God, nor did he want to know Him. It is precisely the fear of the unknown that brings such great feelings of horror over us.

Belshazzar immediately summoned his wise men to read and interpret the mysterious words on the wall. He would greatly reward the man who succeeded. The hope of an interpretation apparently reduced the king's consternation somewhat. But he found that not one of his wise men could decipher the words. Then the fear of the unknown overpowered him anew. Even the lords of the realm were beside themselves.

Here we see the feeling of horror that will overtake all who do not know the God of the covenant. Without the grace that is ours in the covenant, He remains a stranger to us, filling us with dread.

Revelation through the Lord's prophet. During the disturbance caused by all this consternation, the queen mother came into the room. She reminded the king that there was another wise man he could turn to—Daniel, in whom, as she said, was the spirit of the gods. Evidently Daniel had been all but forgotten by Nebuchadnezzar's successors. The queen mother, however, who may have been a daughter of Nebuchadnezzar, remembered very clearly what Daniel had done.

When Daniel was brought in, he refused the king's gifts. Because he served the true God, he did not prophesy for wages. But he was willing to read the writing and interpret it. He reminded the king how Nebuchadnezzar had exalted himself and been brought low until he honored the God who made Himself known in His covenant with Israel. Belshazzar knew these things. Yet he had defied the God of grace, the God who also held his life in His hands. Hence Belshazzar's judgment and the judgment of his kingdom were revealed in those mysterious words on the wall.

On the wall was written: *Mene, Mene, Tekel,* and *Parsin,* which means: *numbered, numbered, weighed,* and *divided.* The days of Belshazzar and of the Babylonian kingdom were numbered. The Lord had weighed that kingdom and found it wanting. There was not one single blessing for God's Kingdom left in

Belshazzar or in his reign. He and his power would therefore be cut to pieces. His kingdom would be given to the Medes and the Persians.

Even though Daniel had announced Belshazzar's end and the end of his kingdom, he was honored royally. Most likely Belshazzar's feeling of horror subsided once he had learned the meaning of the words on the wall.

The judgment of God's grace. That same night the Persians made a surprise attack. In the defense of what remained of the city, Belshazzar was killed. The end of the Babylonian kingdom had come.

The God of grace will judge all who free themselves from Him and do not want to serve Him in His grace. He will cut off all life in which He finds nothing left of His Spirit, all life He finds wanting. The sovereignty and the victory will belong eternally to His grace, that is, to the Christ.

59: Worshiping the Name of the Lord

Daniel 6

Jerusalem had been captured and the temple destroyed. The divinely established place of worship had been profaned. Would the worship of God's name now cease completely? That was the main issue in this struggle in Babylon—not the safety of Daniel or his power over the kingdom.

Imagine what would have happened if Daniel's enemies had been victorious, if prayers to God had really ceased for 30 days. The existence of the world would then have become impossible, for the world can only exist by this bond of prayer between heaven and earth.

The Christ is immediately revealed to us in this story. Jesus prayed in the night and in the hour of darkness when no one could pray anymore. In the same way, He prayed on the cross. There the Christ continued the worship of the Lord's name. In His strength, Daniel, too, was able to pray in opposition to the king's prohibition.

We may not tell only of Daniel and his faithfulness and ultimate reward as we present this story to the children. This is also clear from the following consideration: we cannot possibly say that God will save all believers from all temporal danger and distress just as He saved Daniel. It could have been God's will to let Daniel die. Think of all who have died for their faith! Because it had to be revealed that the world cannot exist without the bond of prayer, the Lord decided to save Daniel. That was His only reason for saving Daniel. If it serves the honor of His name, He will save us in our hour of peril.

It is true, of course, that God loves His children, but He loves them for His own sake. In His grace He often connects the honor of His name with the safekeeping of His own in the world. Daniel in his exaltation is a type of the Christ in His exaltation.

For the heathen it was no problem that prayers were to be addressed

418

to no one but the king for 30 days. As a descendant of the gods, the king was the representative of divinity. When the people stopped praying to their national gods for a while, the absolute dominion of the Persian empire was confirmed.

The king was obviously a weakling who let himself be led by his lords. Apparently he spent his life's strength in carousing and drunkenness. For just one night he abstained.

The unbreakable law of the Medes and Persians was clearly the pride of this kingdom, but it was also its poverty. From this story, too, it is evident that the laws enacted in that kingdom often oppressed men's lives. The rule in effect there was: justice must be done, even though the world should perish. Through the cross of the Christ we learn: let justice be done so that the world may be saved. Christ has fulfilled the demand of the law so that righteousness may again be the spirit by which we live.

Main thought: *The worship of the Lord's name on earth is maintained.*

The plot. Jerusalem had indeed been captured and the temple destroyed. The divinely established place of worship had been profaned. But the believers prayed to the Lord also in their captivity. The bond of prayer between heaven and earth had not been broken. But that was just what the enemy wanted to do—break that bond.

When the transition from Babylonian rule to the world empire of the Medes and Persians was made, the king reorganized the kingdom: 120 governors (satraps) were placed over the kingdom, and three presidents were placed over the governors. Daniel was one of those three presidents. Daniel had been richly endowed by the Spirit of the Lord—not only with faith and the gift of prophecy but also with great wisdom. Therefore he excelled and soon eclipsed the other two presidents. The king was even considering placing Daniel at the head of the entire kingdom. Then the king would be relieved of all responsibility and could live entirely for his own lusts.

At this point the other presidents and the governors became very jealous. But it was not just jealousy that motivated them. There was also their enmity against the Jews, that strange people who alone enjoyed the privilege of being included in God's covenant. This enmity against the Jews was in fact enmity against their God. Because of this enmity, these leaders did not want Daniel holding the top position in the kingdom.

They kept an eye on Daniel and conferred regularly, but they could not find any cause for accusation in his conduct. They decided that the only way they could get rid of Daniel was to bring the laws of the kingdom into conflict with the laws of his God. In that case he would be faithful to his God.

An occasion for such a conflict was easily found. Together the two presidents and the governors went to the king and proposed that he enact a law that for 30 days no prayers were to be made except to the king. (In that culture, the king was the representative of the divinity.) This unity in prayer would serve to consolidate the kingdom.

This decision was to be enacted as a law of the Medes and the Persians, a law which could not be broken. Thus the schemers wanted to use the laws of that world kingdom to do Daniel the greatest injustice. Those laws often served to ruin life. The law of the Kingdom of God, however, preserves life.

Suppose that the law had been obeyed. Suppose that for 30 days nobody prayed to the Lord. Then the people of God and the whole world would not have been able to exist any longer. God's people live by prayer, and it is because of prayer that the whole world finds its safety. Thus it was essential that this plot on the part of the enemies of God's people not be allowed to succeed. What if prayer on earth really did cease? Fortunately, the world cannot be silent about God's name, no matter how hard people try—even today.

Daniel's prayer. Daniel heard about the king's decree: anyone who transgressed the king's command would be thrown into the lions' den. Yet, he understood that it was not just his life that was at stake. If Daniel had thought that there was nothing more than his life at stake, that would have been weakness on his part. The real issue was the name of God and the worship of that name. In faith Daniel submitted to God. That submission gave him the strength to withstand the king's command.

At the set hours, three times a day, Daniel prayed as he always did in his upper room, which looked out toward Jerusalem. By facing Jerusalem, he wanted to convey that he was continuing the prayers that had earlier taken place in Jerusalem. Today there is no longer a set place for worship. Because of this, Daniel's "looking toward Jerusalem" means for us "looking to the Christ."

Daniel's enemies found him praying in his upper room and brought him to the king. The king was sad, for he leaned on Daniel for the running of the kingdom. He had also seen something special in Daniel's faith in Israel's God. That God was a strange God, and His people were a strange people. Would the king oppose the God of Israel in this matter?

The king postponed his decision until evening and looked for a way to rescue Daniel. But toward evening the governors pressed him with a reminder that the law Daniel broke was a law of the Medes and Persians. The kingdom would become powerless and would break up if such a transgression went unpunished. Here Daniel's enemies used the so-called highest law to do the highest injustice. How people sometimes misuse the law! What God's law aims at is to protect people.

The king finally had to give Daniel up. His last words to him were: "May your God, whom you serve continually, deliver you." Apparently he did remember the strange power of this God.

Thus Daniel was faithful to the name of the Lord even unto death. He prayed. He was able to remain faithful only in the strength of the Christ. The Christ is the One who prayed when hell had broken loose and nobody could pray anymore. If the Christ had not prayed then, the world would have perished. In that prayer in the midst of His suffering lies the victory and our reconciliation.

Because the Christ was victorious, those who believe in Him will win the victory by faith. We need not worry beforehand whether we will be strong enough. The Lord will give us the strength we need for the conquest.

The Lord's response. After Daniel was thrown into the lions' den, the door was sealed so that no one could attempt a rescue. The king did not spend that night in his usual fashion. He neither ate nor drank. And he must have wondered whether God would now make His justice prevail over the king's justice.

Was God going to deliver Daniel? Does God always deliver His own from temporal danger and distress? If we believe, He will save our lives and see to it that our lives are not lived in vain. But whether He delivers us from a particular temporal danger depends on whether the honor of His name would be exalted by our deliverance. For His own sake He delivered Daniel. And for His own sake He will also deliver those who believe in Him. He connects His honor with the protection of His people.

Daniel submitted to the Lord's will. Yet, he must have cried out to God from the lions' den. God may have decided to save Daniel, but Daniel had to receive God's grace through faith in prayer. In answer to prayer, God shut the lions' mouths. Daniel acknowledged that he was worthy of death, but he asked God to deliver him for the honor of His name in Babylon. Daniel was praying as the Christ prayed. His prayer was heard in the midst of his fear.

The next morning the king found Daniel alive. Daniel acknowledged that God had delivered him because he was innocent before God in this matter; he would not have been able to act any differently. He also insisted that he had not committed any crime against the king. The transgression of the king's command was no injustice because the command itself was an injustice.

After Daniel was pulled up out of the lions' den, those who had set the trap for him were thrown into it with their wives and children. The lions tore them apart. Not only was the king exercising human revenge, the Lord was avenging His justice on those who had despised the worship of His name, those who made themselves enemies of His people, those who wanted to make the world's existence an impossibility. That's how God rewards those who hate Him.

The royal decree. Then the king published a decree addressed to all people. In this decree he declared that everyone was to tremble before the God of Israel. The king confessed that the Lord is the living God and true King, that He is the Deliverer, the God who performs wonders of deliverance on earth.

Of course we are not to regard this deed as proof of a true

conversion on the part of the king. Neither were the nations in his empire converted to the living God by the decree. Yet, the name of the Lord was honored throughout the empire. And because of this tie to the name of the Lord, the world could be preserved until the coming of the Lord Jesus Christ in the flesh. How this revelation of the Lord to the entire world must have fostered the later hope of the gospel!

Daniel was honored in the kingdom. In this exaltation he was a type of the Christ, who was obedient to God in all things. In His exaltation to God's right hand, the Christ received all power in heaven and on earth.

Daniel's deliverance was also a prophecy pointing ahead to the deliverance of Israel from Babylonian captivity. If only Israel's worship remained intact, the people of the covenant would not and could not perish. Daniel had prayed daily for this deliverance when he "made confession before his God," that is, when he confessed the sins of the people and expressed his faith that God would be merciful.

After the Exile

60: The Temporary Restoration of the Lord's House

Ezra 1-6

The Jews who returned from exile were mainly households from the former kingdom of Judah. Still, some members of the other tribes were among them. Thus the people of Israel were re-established in Canaan as the twelve tribes.

However, this was only a partial, temporary restoration. Although the temple was rebuilt, the glory of God's grace did not fill it as it had filled the first temple. And the ark was not rebuilt. Neither did God reveal Himself anymore by means of the Urim and Thummim.

Moreover, David's house was not restored to its former sovereign rule; the people of Israel remained dependent on the world power of that time. The situation cannot be compared to Solomon's time, when the king's palace stood in the shadow of the beautiful temple. The glory of the Kingdom of God, in which God's dwelling will be with men and the Son of David's house will exercise sovereign power, was only faintly foreshadowed in those days.

This imperfection in the restoration was the result of Israel's sin. Yet, these events, too, happened under God's direction. The people had to be led more and more away from the shadow to the reality. They had to be slowly set free of the old covenant, that is, of the old form of the covenant of grace, and made ready to receive the new covenant.

It was at this time that Haggai spoke some words that gave light: "I am with you, says the Lord of hosts, with the Word in which I made a covenant with you when you came out of Egypt, and with My Spirit abiding in your midst. Fear not" (Hag. 2:4-5). Now it was a matter of hoping for the Word, which became only partly visible in the sign. The fulfillment of that Word was all but ready to come in the Christ.

We are to view Ezra 4:6-23 as an insertion. It shows us how the

427

Samaritans hindered and thwarted the work not only when the temple was being built but also later, when the walls of the city were rising. Thus, verse 24 should be read as directly following verse 5.

> **Main thought:** *The Lord's house is temporarily restored as a prophecy pointing to God's indwelling in the Christ.*

The return brought about by the Word of the Lord. Almost 70 years had passed since the first Jews had been carried away into captivity. Now the time was sure to come when Israel would return to its land, when the service of the Lord would be restored in Canaan.

The Babylonian empire had just been replaced by that of the Medes and Persians. The first ruler of the new empire was Cyrus. Would such a world ruler ever allow the Lord's people to go back home? Would he give them permission to re-establish themselves in Canaan? That could only happen by a miracle of God's grace.

Long before this, the prophet Isaiah had said that one day a certain king would come to the throne of a world power. The Lord would command that king to let His people go. As a servant of the Lord, he would obey. Cyrus had probably heard of that prophecy. That Word overpowered him; he did not dare back out of it. The Lord was too strong for him.

Cyrus sent a proclamation throughout all of his kingdom to the effect that the Lord had charged him to build a house for Him at Jerusalem. In the proclamation he acknowledged that the Lord, the God of heaven, had given him all the kingdoms of the earth. All who belonged to the people of the Lord should go up to Jerusalem to build that house. The people among whom the Jews had been living were to give a freewill offering of gold or silver or of other costly things or of animals for the temple of the Lord. Just as they once did when they went out of Egypt, the Jews were to depart with the treasures of the people among whom they had been living as strangers.

Events unfolded in accordance with the king's command. The people gave as they were able for the service of the Lord at

Jerusalem. King Cyrus also returned the vessels of gold and silver which Nebuchadnezzar had once carried away from Jerusalem. By the grace of the Lord, these vessels were restored to their original service. The king turned them over to Shesh-bazzar or Zerubbabel, a son of Jehoiachin and thus a descendant of the house of David. This Zerubbabel became the leader of the expedition and was recognized as its head.

Unfortunately, not all the exiles chose to return. Many had come to feel quite at home in the land of their exile and had prospered there. The wish to serve the Lord in the temple was not an all-absorbing desire in their lives. By remaining behind, they disavowed the covenant and the grace of the Lord.

For the most part, the Jews who returned were members of the tribes of Judah and Benjamin—in other words, families of the former kingdom of Judah. Still, a few Jews from the other tribes went with them. Thus the people were re-established in Canaan as the twelve tribes of Israel. The Word and Spirit of the Lord moved those who went. Here, too, it became evident that Israel was God's people only by the power of grace.

Many priests and Levites went along. Among them were some who were not certain about their lineage. Zerubbabel decided that they would be considered priests as far as their support was concerned but that for the time being they would not serve in the sanctuary. Once the people had a high priest, he could ask for a decision from the Lord by means of the Urim and Thummim.

Thus Zerubbabel hoped for such a complete restoration of the communion between God and His people that they could ask for the Lord's will. That complete restoration did not come about. The old covenant was not restored in its full glory. The people would have to learn to hope for the new covenant, in which we may enjoy full communion with God through the Christ and through His Spirit.

The beginning of the restoration of the Lord's service. In the seventh month, shortly after their arrival, the people gathered as one man in Jerusalem. This national assembly was led by Zerubbabel, who was the actual head, and Jeshua, the high priest. The first thing they did was to rebuild the altar of burnt offering on its old site so that they could offer sacrifices to the Lord. They were afraid of the people who lived in the land itself and all around it, and they sought communion with the Lord at the altar in order to be strengthened in their faith. In this seventh month they also celebrated the Feast of Tabernacles.

But these were still temporary measures. They had not yet begun with the building of the Lord's temple. Quickly they took the necessary steps. They had cedar wood imported from Lebanon. In the second year after their arrival, the foundations of the temple were laid.

When this was done, the priests and Levites praised the Lord so that the people, in faith, would meet the Lord in worship. Then all the people shouted for joy and praised the Lord.

But there were some older people who had seen the temple of Solomon before it was destroyed. They did not shout for joy but wept aloud. Although the foundations of the new temple were spacious, just as Cyrus had commanded, where were the riches and the power of Solomon's day? Would this new temple ever become anything?

That was unbelief on the part of those elderly people, for what really counts is not the means but the grace of the Lord. Yet, there was something proper about those misgivings, for the restoration would not bring back the former splendor. The people would have to put their hope in the glory which would be revealed in the Christ.

The shouts of the younger generation drowned out the weeping of the elderly. But the younger people did not understand the meaning of the history of those days—the meaning of the temporary character of this restoration.

Faltering in a time of temptation. In the former kingdom of the ten tribes, the Samaritans had emerged as a people. They were born of intermarriage between the Jews who had remained in the land and the peoples brought into the land to settle there. When these Samaritans heard that the returned exiles had begun to restore the temple in Jerusalem, they asked for permission to help with the building. They said that they, too, had been offering sacrifices to the Lord ever since they were introduced to His worship.

But the worship in which they engaged was the false cult of the golden calves, a service according to the will of men and not in accordance with the covenant of the Lord. Furthermore, these people originated from intermarriage of Jews with other peoples, which was something the Lord had forbidden. These people did not keep the Lord's covenant. Therefore Zerubbabel, Jeshua and the heads of the households refused to allow them to help with the building. From that time on, the Samaritans were bitter enemies of the exiles who had returned to their land.

In this request of the Samaritans there had been a temptation for the people. Would they keep the covenant of the Lord in a pure form? They did not yield to the temptation. But did they really overcome the temptation by faith, or was their refusal also motivated by national pride? If they had all acted out of faith, they would have been able to withstand the opposition and trouble the Samaritans gave them from that time on. Because they had not acted out of faith, they were not able to cope with the resistance of the Samaritans.

The Samaritans bribed the counselors of Cyrus, with the result that he withdrew his favor and cooperation. The work of restoration was no longer patronized from all sides. As a result of the opposition, the people became disheartened. Their hands became slack, and the work of restoration was suspended. Faith had not won the victory; the people had faltered in the face of temptation.

The Samaritans opposed the work not only then but also much later, under the kings Ahasuerus and Artaxerxes. By then the building of the temple had long been completed and the people were busily engaged in rebuilding the walls of Jerusalem. By sending the king of Persia a letter in which the former rebelliousness of Jerusalem was pointed out, the Samaritans even managed to have a prohibition issued against completing the rebuilding of the city. However, all the Samaritans achieved in the period now under discussion was a suspension of the rebuilding of the temple. In a time of temptation, faith did not emerge victorious.

The rebuilding of the temple. Work on the temple stood still for about fourteen years. The people did go to Jerusalem for the feasts during that time, and the services at the restored altar did continue, but zeal for the house of the Lord was in short supply. The rich built splendid homes for themselves, but the people claimed that the times were not favorable for rebuilding the Lord's house.

Then the Lord sent the prophet Haggai. In the name of the Lord he reproached the people for their slackness. If only they would start working on the house of the Lord in love, they would see how much the Lord blessed them. Now they were experiencing nothing but adversity because the Lord was not first in their lives. This prophetic message made an impression on the people, and they set to work immediately.

At the same time Haggai spoke a word of comfort to the people. The means and manpower at their disposal fell far short of what Solomon had had at his command. All the same, the Lord was with them with the Word of His covenant and with His Spirit. If only they believed that, they would see a splendor much greater than that of Solomon's temple. This restoration was only temporary. To this temple the Christ would come. He would again make the whole earth a temple of God. The prophet Zechariah, too, strengthened the hands of Zerubbabel and Jeshua to do the work.

The people really needed this strengthening, for the governor appointed by the Persian king authorized an investigation when he heard that the restoration work had begun again. He even had the names of the foremen written down. He was told that the temple had been destroyed by Nebuchadnezzar as a result of the people's sin. Cyrus had then given an order that it should be rebuilt, but opposition had brought the work to a halt.

The governor sent off a report to Darius, the king of Persia. In this report he informed the king of what he had been told and requested that a search be made to find out whether all these things were true. Sure enough, in the archives a document was found which told of the decree of Cyrus. Darius then ordered his governor to assist the rebuilding with all possible means. Anyone who did not obey this decree was to die by hanging.

Darius even wrote: "May the God who has caused His name to dwell there overthrow any king or people that shall put forth a hand to alter this or to destroy this house of God which is in

Jerusalem." With these words Darius acknowledged the God of Israel. He also asked for the intercession of the priests at Jerusalem on behalf of himself and his children. Israel again received the honor of being a nation of priests that prayed for the well-being of the world.

Because the Lord favored His people, it was possible to complete the rebuilding of the temple. In the sixth year of the reign of Darius, the temple was dedicated with appropriate sacrifices. Later, at the appointed time, the people celebrated the Passover with great joy. They rejoiced in the Lord. If only they would not just trust in the temple and in their own service of the Lord! If only they would continue to look forward to the coming of the One in whom all the foreshadowing would be fulfilled, the One in whom God would give His full favor to His people!

61: The Law Reinstated

Ezra 7-10

Ezra was a scribe, but not in the later, unfavorable sense of the term. He was skilled in the law of Moses, and he was the compiler of the books of the Old Testament.

The time of Ezra was a time of transition. Before going into captivity, the people were repeatedly guilty of acts of idolatry—but not after the exile. Now the law would prevail in Israel. This change was due especially to the work of Ezra. After that, unfortunately, the people fell into another sin—seeking their righteousness in keeping the law.

Apparently Ezra came from Babylon to Jerusalem to see to it that the law was reinstated in the life of the returned exiles. Thus it would appear that the first group of exiles, who returned from Babylon under the leadership of Zerubbabel and Jeshua, were motivated mainly by a craving for freedom.

Through Ezra, the people were made subject to the righteousness of the Lord. In this way Ezra is a type of the Christ, who frees us from the law—provided that in this context we think of the law only as a power that controls and restrains us from without. Christ does that by putting His Spirit in us and writing the law on our hearts. However, in so doing He reinstates the righteousness of the law in us.

Ezra is still more a type of the Christ when he identifies himself with the sin of the people and makes confession just as though their sin was his own sin. The confession of guilt in Ezra 9 arises to God from the innermost depths. Ezra is appalled, just as Christ was filled with a sense of horror and deep distress in Gethsemane (Mark 14:33).

Ezra proceeds to cleanse Israel of foreign wives. As a type of the Christ, he clears his threshing floor (see Matt. 3:12; Luke 3:17) and acts with a zeal that spares nothing. Of him, too, it is true: "The zeal of God's house has consumed me."

The foreign wives were sent away together with their children. In the New Testament we read that "the unbelieving husband is consecrated through his wife, and the unbelieving wife is consecrated through her husband; otherwise your children would be unclean, but as it is they are holy" (I Cor. 7:14). However, in the Old Testament the people had to be Levitically, ceremonially consecrated—as a shadow of the holiness of God's people. The sword that strikes Israel here is a prophecy pointing to the sword that would strike the Christ. Indeed, it strikes Israel's own flesh and blood via the children.

Main thought: *The righteousness of the law is reinstated.*

Going up to Jerusalem. When the king of Persia gave God's people permission to return to their own land, many did so, under the leadership of Zerubbabel and Jeshua. But there were many others who had prospered in Babylon and chose to remain behind. Many priests and Levites, in particular, stayed on in the land of captivity. The members of the first expedition were apparently more concerned about gaining their freedom from captivity than about reinstating God's righteousness and law in the life of His people.

Therefore God caused another spirit to arise among those who remained behind. The Lord did this especially by means of the priest Ezra. Ezra was filled with zeal for the law of the Lord and wanted to see that law reinstated in the life of God's people in Judah.

Apparently he regarded it as a disgrace that so many priests had remained behind in Babylon. Thus he wanted to rouse particularly the priests, the Levites and the temple servants. These he hoped to bring with him to Jerusalem.

In advance he informed Artaxerxes, the king of Persia, of his plans. God put it in the heart of the king to give these Jews his complete support. The king himself sent Ezra an important gift of gold and silver as well as some gold and silver plates and bowls from the royal treasury. Ezra was even allowed to take up a collection among the inhabitants of the land. He could also call upon the Jews who still remained behind to offer their gifts for the restoration of the Lord's house at Jerusalem. In that way he collected a great treasure.

The king also offered Ezra a band of soldiers and horsemen for the journey through the desolate regions. But the purpose of Ezra's trip was the reinstatement of the Lord's righteousness. That righteousness would serve him as a shield of protection. Therefore he declined the royal escort.

In the first month, Ezra gathered all who intended to go with him. It soon became apparent that although there were many priests, there were few Levites. Once more Ezra issued an appeal for Levites. This time God gripped their hearts, and many came.

Ezra saw to it that a precise count was made of the treasure he had received. He placed the treasure in the hands of twelve priests he set aside for this purpose. They would bear the responsibility for protecting it. It was not Ezra's personal treasure but the Lord's. Then they began their journey.

On that journey of many weeks, the Lord kept them safe. With all their possessions, they arrived in Jerusalem. The treasure was counted and weighed; nothing seemed to be missing. Ezra had also brought with him a letter from the king to the governors, ordering them to provide whatever help Ezra needed in all he undertook. A great offering of dedication and thanksgiving was sacrificed to the Lord at Jerusalem.

The Lord gave Ezra the goodwill of the people who lived in Jerusalem. They did not ask why this man from a foreign country should come to tell them what the law is; they simply subjected themselves to him as someone sent by God.

The Lord Jesus Christ likewise came to us to reinstate God's claims on our lives. Shall we now reject Him as a stranger, or shall we acknowledge Him as the One sent by God?

A confession of guilt. Some time later several officials came to Ezra and told him that many of the Jews were married to daughters of heathen families living in the land. By this inter-marriage the people had again rejected the law and had denied the special character they possessed as God's people.

When Ezra heard this, he tore his clothes and pulled hair from his head and his beard. He was appalled and filled with a sense of horror as he thought of the power of sin and of the judgment that would have to come because of the sin.

Ezra saw that sin not just as the sin of the people; it was also *his* sin. He took that sin completely upon himself, for he belonged to that people and was one of them. The Lord Jesus, too, became one with us. He took our sins upon Himself and was appalled, particularly when He came into the garden of Gethsemane and began to be filled with a feeling of horror and deep distress. On the cross He suffered the horror of our sins when God forsook Him.

Ezra sat in stunned horror until the time of the evening sacrifice. Though the officials spoke to him, he heard no one. He suffered on the people's behalf in the depths of his heart.

Finally he arose, kneeled down before the Lord, spread out his hands to heaven, and prayed: "O my God, I hardly dare appear in Your presence, for our iniquities have risen higher than our heads, and our guilt has mounted up to the heavens. Formerly our fathers sinned, and You sent us off into captivity. Now You have again given us some light and a start at restoration. But we have forsaken Your commandments again. Will You now hold back the anger that threatens to consume us, so that there is no remnant left or any escape? There is no one who can stand before You."

Ezra humbled himself because he identified himself with the sins of the people. The Christ also humbled Himself to the deepest contempt and agony of hell. When Ezra prayed that prayer, he was submitting to the judgment of God.

Clearing the threshing floor. This confession of guilt worked infectiously on the people, and many joined Ezra in a confession of sin. Through his confession of guilt, they saw a ray of hope. They sensed that this man, by being utterly shattered, had touched the depths of God's mercy. This was indeed so, and it was possible because the Spirit of the Christ was in Ezra, the Spirit of the One who alone could open up the depths of God's mercy for us by being shattered on the cross.

The people also said that they were ready to break with their sins. At this Ezra was seized with an uncompromising zeal. This, too, shows how the Spirit of the Christ was in him, the Spirit of the One who was consumed by zeal for God's house. We have to confess our sins and then forsake them. Hence Ezra sent a proclamation throughout all Judah that every man was to appear in Jerusalem within three days.

In three days' time, there they were. That it was winter and the rainy season did not hold Ezra back. There they stood before him in the pouring rain—all of them. Ezra addressed them. They shook from the cold and the rain, but they also trembled before the power of the Word of the Lord that came to them through Ezra.

Very few resisted; the people were overcome by this power. However, they did argue that the cleansing of the people could not take place in one day. They asked Ezra to appoint a commission before which all who were married to foreign wives would appear.

This was done. The foreign wives were sent away with their children. Then there was weeping in Israel because families were broken up. This misery befell those wives and children because of the sin of the people, who had rejected the law. The righteousness of the law had to be reinstated in Israel so that Israel could again be a holy people, a consecrated people.

God's covenant was still limited to Israel. The other nations still could not share in that covenant. All the same, the situation called for the coming of the Christ, through whom the dividing wall between Israel and the nations would fall away so that the other nations, too, would be able to share in God's covenant.

The separation put into effect by Ezra at this time was a sign of the separation there must be between us and sin—and also a sign of the triumph over sin in the Christ, who identified Himself with our sin. A sword went through His soul, just as a sword went through Israel here. Through the power of His suffering, we must be cleansed of our sins.

Let us be thankful that the Christ was sent to us from God for just this purpose. We must learn to put our faith in Him. Then He will awaken His power also in us.

62: A Witness

Esther 1-10

The book of Esther (Hadassah) is really the book of Mordecai. In the last chapter of the book we read that Mordecai "was great among the Jews and popular with the multitude of his brethren, for he sought the welfare of his people and spoke peace to all his people." All of Mordecai's acts, from the beginning of the book of Esther to the end, are to be viewed in this light. He picks up news at the court and seeks to have as much contact with the court as possible. He does all this for the sake of the welfare of his people, who are constantly on his mind. In this regard he is a type of the Christ.

The events described in the book of Esther most likely took place after many of the exiles had returned to their own land. That return is described in the book of Ezra. Thus the story of Esther and Mordecai is probably to be placed between the book of Ezra and the events discussed in the book of Nehemiah.

Many of the exiles had apparently made a comfortable life for themselves in the land of exile and chose to remain there when the others left for Jerusalem. Thus they were living in disobedience. In spite of this, the Lord remembered them and gave them a deliverer in Mordecai.

Many of those who stayed behind were later absorbed into the various nations. But now these Jews were placed among the nations one more time to be a witness. The Jews were still the Lord's special people, and it was for His name's sake that their lives were threatened. That special significance of the Jews came to an end after Christ's work on earth. Later pogroms against the Jews are not to be regarded as attacks on the Lord's people and are not to be identified with Haman and his motives. Persecution of the Jews in the twentieth century is driven by other motives.

Main thought: *The Lord's people are placed among the nations as a witness for His name's sake.*

The first link with the court. Not all of the exiled people of the Lord had taken advantage of the opportunity to return to their own land. Evidently they were well off in the land of their captivity. Although they did not completely forget the covenant and the promise and the law of the Lord, the covenant obviously did not govern their whole life. They were not driven by an all-consuming longing for the revelation of the Lord's grace in His temple. Thus they were living in disobedience. In spite of this, the Lord remembered them; He had not broken His covenant with His disobedient children.

In those days Ahasuerus (Xerxes) was king of the Medo-Persian empire. Once he had acquired great power, he thought about undertaking a major expedition against the Greeks. In that connection he called all the great and powerful of the realm together in the captial—Susa. For 180 days he debated his plans with them. At the end he was so satisfied with the way things had gone that he gave a banquet for all the people in Susa, a banquet that lasted for seven days. In royal splendor he sat with his subjects, both great and small, at the banquet table. Queen Vashti had dinner with the ladies.

On the last day of the feast, when dinner was finished, the king wanted the queen to make an appearance and show her beauty to everyone there. That was contrary to custom. Sometimes the ladies did share dinner with the men, but when dinner was finished and the heavy drinking began, the ladies who had been honored would withdraw. Now the king, who was drunk, wanted to have the queen brought in at the conclusion of the dinner. Because Vashti was a woman of character, she refused, probably hoping that the king would back down when confronted by her firm attitude.

But the king felt insulted. Were all these glorious days now to end in this defeat at the hands of a woman? He sought the advice of his counselors. After they talked it over, their spokesman answered that Vashti had done wrong not only to the king but also to the princes and all the peoples of the kingdom. If the queen could be disobedient and not suffer punishment, all the wives would rebel against their husbands and the empire would fall apart.

These counselors were flattering the king; they did not dare stand up to him for the wrong he had done. They proposed that the queen be removed from her royal position. All of this should be done by royal decree, as a law of the Medes and Persians which could not be revoked. They feared that the king would later change his mind about Vashti and that they would then have the wrath of Vashti to contend with. The king followed their advice, and Vashti was permanently removed from her royal position.

It was probably after these events that Ahasuerus made his planned expedition against the Greeks, which lasted for three years and ended in failure. On his return home, Ahasuerus tried to forget his disgrace and defeat. Then he thought of Vashti and expressed his grief that events had taken such a course. His servants advised him to have a search made throughout his vast empire for many beautiful virgins. These virgins would be brought to the harem in Susa, where the king would choose the most beautiful one and make her his queen.

In those days there was a certain Jew named Mordecai who could be found daily in the vicinity of the palace. Mordecai was very much concerned about the well-being of his people and constantly tried to find out what was going on at the court. He wanted to do whatever he could to benefit them.

This Mordecai had adopted his cousin, the daughter of his uncle, as his own daughter. She was much younger than he was, and he saw to it that she was included among the maidens who were to be presented to the king. (Her Persian name was *Esther*, which means *star*; her Hebrew name was *Hadassah*.) If she were to become part of the court and if she received the honor of being chosen as queen, Mordecai would be in a strong position to act through her on behalf of his people.

The desire to be of help to his people was the motive behind Mordecai's action. The welfare of God's people—that was the concern of his heart. This desire was of the Holy Spirit, but the way in which Mordecai tried to fulfill his desire was not of God. How did he dare surrender Esther to such a heathen way of life?

That he was pursuing a wrong course was already apparent from his command to Esther not to tell anyone that she belonged to the Jews. After all, the Jews were a hated people. That also meant that Esther could not tell anyone that she was Mordecai's cousin. But God governs even the sinful deliberations of men and uses them to carry out His counsel. Esther was elevated to the position of queen, and Mordecai hoped that he would be able to have influence through her.

At about the same time, Mordecai discovered that two of the king's attendants had treasonable plans. The two were planning to kill the king. Mordecai made these plans known to Esther, who told the king in Mordecai's name. Mordecai must have hoped in this way to obtain a certain position at the court, but he was disappointed in this hope. No one paid the slightest attention to him. The Lord can sometimes allow us to wait, even when we have the good of His name in mind. By waiting, Mordecai was being purified.

The threat. Ahasuerus made Haman his prime minister, second only to the king in the whole empire, and decreed that he was to be shown the same honor as the king himself. Whenever Haman entered or left the royal palace, everyone bowed down before him. Mordecai was the only one who did not bow down. This Jew, who bowed down before the Lord and was liberated in faith by the grace of the Lord, rejected such a servile attitude toward any man. When the king's court attendants asked him why he transgressed the king's command, he admitted that as a Jew who feared the Lord, he rejected such servility. By this point, then, Mordecai was further along than when he forbade Esther to say that she belonged to the Jews. Now there was more believing submission to the Lord to be seen in his actions.

The court attendants drew Haman's attention to Mordecai, to see whether Mordecai would be able to prevail against Haman. They took delight in this conflict, which was a life-and-death struggle. Haman might have ignored Mordecai, but he took offense at his resistance because Mordecai was a Jew and belonged to that special but hated people. Haman sought revenge by looking for ways to destroy all the Jews.

Soon he had his plans ready. He wanted to lay them before the king, but he was aware that he was beginning a deadly struggle with that people and also with the strange God of that people. Therefore he had lots (*purim*) cast in his house with his wife and his advisors, to see what date the gods would indicate as favorable for carrying out his plans. Without such an indication from the gods, he did not dare take the first step. The lot was cast in the first month of the year, but the last month was indicated as the favorable time.

Haman did not delay in laying his plans before the king. His hatred moved him to action. He spoke to the king about a peculiar people scattered over many lands, a people with laws of its own, the laws of its God, which were in conflict with the laws of the kingdom. He proposed that a decree be issued to all the provinces that on the thirteenth day of the last month, all Jews were to be destroyed. The loss that would be suffered as a result of diminished taxes from the victims would be fully covered by the loot that would be seized. Haman guaranteed that a large share of this loot would wind up in the king's treasury.

The king, who may well have sensed a thirst for personal revenge behind this plan, said he would allow his favorite to attack the Jews and seize their treasure. He gave him his signet ring to seal the requested decree. Letters were sent by courier to all the king's provinces.

Again, for the sake of His name, the Lord's people were in danger. Would the Lord forsake them now? For the sake of His name and His covenant, He had placed them in the world as a wondrous witness.

Mordecai's intervention. Wherever the king's edict was heard, it caused great commotion, particularly among the Jews. The people in Susa were especially perplexed. Mordecai put on sackcloth and ashes and went to the entrance of the king's gate. Since no one was allowed to enter the king's gate in mourning clothes, Esther sent him other clothes when she heard what he was doing, but he refused them. Then she had the king's eunuch, who had been appointed to wait on her, go and ask Mordecai why he was mourning. In reply Mordecai informed her of the king's edict and had a copy of the decree delivered to Esther. He even told her the exact sum of money Haman had promised to pay into the king's treasury for the destruction of the Jews. Finally, he charged her to go to the king and plead her people's cause.

Esther shrank from this mission. Was she now to reveal that she belonged to the Jewish people and perhaps fall into disfavor with the king? For 30 days she had not been summoned by him. Were the king's affections for her cooling? Besides, no one could go to the king on his own without risking death.

Esther refused. But Mordecai sent word to her that she was not to imagine that she would be spared because she was the queen. If she refused, the Lord would surely provide deliverance for his people apart from her. The judgment would strike only her. And she should ask herself whether it was perhaps possible that the Lord had placed her at the court for just such a time as this.

At these arguments Esther gave in. She gave herself to the Lord's cause and promised that after two days she would go to the king. In the meantime, all the Jews in Susa were to join Mordecai in humbling themselves before the Lord in fasting and prayer for her. She would do the same with her maidens. Then, if she perished, she would perish. The Lord could allow her to perish and still provide deliverance for His people, perhaps through her death. In any case, she would give herself to the Lord's cause.

In this frame of mind Esther went to the king. When he saw her, he held out his scepter to her as a sign that he was pleased to see her. The king was so pleased with her that he promised to give her whatever she asked, even if it was the half of his kingdom. The idolatrous honors paid to the king did indeed separate him from his people. But through the Lord's favor upon His people, Esther was able to intercede for them with the king.

Esther did not quite dare to come out with her request and thereby reveal that she belonged to the Jewish people. She only asked the king to come with Haman to have dinner with her that evening. They did so. Even at this banquet she did not yet dare raise her request. Instead she asked the king if he and Haman would dine with her again the next evening. Then she would tell him what she really wanted. But her plan was set. She was just waiting for the most opportune moment.

Haman returned home excitedly from the banquet. But in the gate he saw Mordecai, who would not bow before him. Haman restrained himself. When he got home, he boasted to his wife and friends of the distinction that had come to him, but he also aired his frustration about Mordecai's attitude. At the advice of his wife and friends, he had a gallows constructed. There he would have Mordecai hanged. Mordecai would become a particular disgrace among the Jews. Haman's hatred turned against Mordecai especially because Mordecai was the first among his people and was their advocate. In the same way, hatred was directed especially against the Christ.

The elevation of the deliverer. In the night between the first and second banquets with Esther, Ahasuerus could not get to sleep. Therefore he had someone read him the historical records of his kingdom, especially those that concerned his own reign. From these records he learned about the assassination plotted against him by two of the king's eunuchs—the assassination plot exposed by Mordecai. Then the king inquired about the reward Mordecai received for this. When he heard that no reward had been given, the king decided that one would still be granted.

In the morning Haman was asked for his advice on this matter. Haman assumed that he was the one to be honored. Hence he proposed that the man whom the king was pleased to honor be publicly honored in the city square while wearing the royal robe and sitting on the king's throne. This honor then fell to Mordecai. Haman himself was ordered to lead Mordecai through the city streets shouting: "Thus shall it be done to the man whom the king delights to honor!"

Sad and utterly humiliated, Haman returned home and told his wife and his friends what had happened to him. Then they all became frightened and said to him: "If Mordecai, before whom you have begun to fall, is of the Jewish people, you will not prevail against him but will surely fall before him." Here they were acknowledging that there was something special about God's people and their leader. In the same way, the exaltation of the Mediator Christ will one day become a horror to His enemies.

While Haman was still talking with them, the king's attendants arrived to take Haman to Esther's banquet. At dinner the king asked Esther what her request was and promised that he would grant it even if it was the half of his kingdom. Obviously the king was especially pleased with her. Strengthened by his attitude, in which she saw an answer to prayer, she now dared to come forward with her request. She begged for her life and thereby revealed that she belonged to the Jewish people. At the same time she begged for the lives of her people. She said that she would not have brought this matter up if it had merely been the intention to make slaves of the Jews. When the king did not immediately understand what she meant, she pointed to Haman as the one who was threatening her life. Haman grew pale with fright, for he realized that the mood of the capricious king would now turn against him. The king would hate him for his wicked intentions.

In his anger the king arose and went into the palace garden. When he returned, he found Haman upon Esther's couch begging for his life. This was such a violation of good manners that it made the king even more angry. At once he sentenced Haman to death. When the king was told that Haman had had a gallows built for Mordecai, he ordered that Haman himself be hanged on it. Thus the fear of Haman's wife and friends was realized; he had fallen before Mordecai.

In his place the king appointed Mordecai prime minister; Esther had made it known how he was related to her. Haman's estate, which the king had given to Esther, was turned over to Mordecai so that he would have a palace befitting his station. The end of history, which is in God's hands, will bring the exaltation of the Mediator.

The deliverance. Esther then begged the king to revoke Haman's order. How would she be able to endure seeing her people destroyed? Again the king was pleased to hold out his golden scepter to her, but he could not revoke a law of the Medes and Persians. However, he left it to Mordecai to do whatever could be done.

Mordecai found a solution: a royal decree would be proclaimed throughout all 127 provinces of the empire to the effect that the Jews would have permission to unite and defend themselves and kill all those who attacked them. They would also be allowed to appropriate the possessions of their attackers. That decree made it clear to the entire kingdom that the king's favor had turned around, that he was now protecting the Jews. The news about Haman's fall and Mordecai's elevation confirmed this. Mordecai went in and out of the palace with the same ceremony as Haman had when he was prime minister.

The city of Susa shouted for joy. Apparently Haman's administration had been filled with arbitrariness and terror. The Jews in Susa and throughout the entire kingdom were filled with joy. Again the light of God's grace broke through to them. Many from the heathen peoples joined hands with Israel; they were afraid of what the Jews might do to them, and they sought safety in joining them. If only the Jews had seen this deliverance as evidence of God's favor toward His people!

On the thirteenth day of the last month, the day which had been designated for their destruction, the Jews mobilized and defeated their enemies. Nobody dared to offer resistance. And in all the provinces the Jews were promoted for Mordecai's sake. In Susa 500 enemies of the Jews were killed, including the ten sons of Haman. Even though personal revenge played a role in this slaughter, the Jews were exercising the Lord's judgment on those who hated Him. That they were not killing for personal gain is apparent from the fact that they did not take the possessions of the dead, even though they had been given the right to do so.

The very next day, the Jews celebrated their deliverance throughout the entire kingdom. But the revenge continued in Susa that day, at Esther's request. Another 300 men were killed, and the bodies of the ten sons of Haman were hanged on a gallows. The crime of persecuting the Jews had to be wiped out so that the Jews could live in freedom. In Susa the Jews celebrated on the fifteenth day of that month.

Mordecai described this history. Ever since then, at the express command of Mordecai and Esther, the Jews have held a celebration every year on the fourteenth and fifteenth day of the last month to remember this deliverance. That celebration, called the Feast of Purim, is still held today. Even to His disobedient people God had shown His grace, His favor which forgives sins.

Mordecai served the king as his prime minister. In his exaltation he did not forget his people. With strong ties he remained bound to his people and his people to him. His whole administration was geared to the well-being of his people, and he continually pleaded their cause with the king.

This makes us think of our Mediator, who in His exaltation continuously remembers His people. He, too, has the power over all things in His hands. In His sovereign rule, He continually has the best interests of His people in mind. Of that Mediator Mordecai was no more than a type. For the sake of that Mediator, God showed His grace to His people in the days of Mordecai. If only the Jews would come to understand that when they celebrated the Feast of Purim! Let us look to our Mediator, who always remembers His people.

63: The Temporary Restoration of the City of God

Nehemiah 1-13

Zerubbabel and Jeshua brought about the restoration of the temple, and Ezra saw to it that the authority of the law was reinstated. Now Nehemiah worked to restore the city and regulate the social and political life of the Jews. The walls of Jerusalem were rebuilt, and the city was made safe. It also became inhabited. Social injustices, such as the oppression of the poor by the rich, were removed by the power of the Lord's Word.

Yet, even this restoration was only temporary, as we see from the complaint of Nehemiah and his co-workers that they were slaves of foreign kings (Neh. 9:36). This temporary restoration called for the complete redemption of life through the Christ, by whom life in all its relationships is saved. The measures taken by Nehemiah were a prophecy pointing to the righteousness that would be found in the Kingdom of God.

This shows us clearly that Nehemiah is a type of the Christ. He pushes the restoration through in spite of opposition.

It is understandable that Nehemiah repeatedly points to his righteousness. What he means by that is not a pleading on the basis of a law-righteousness. When he prays, "Remember me according to my righteousness," he does not include a reward for himself for all he has done for the people. In the words "Remember me," we hear a prayer for a blessing upon the people in this sense: "God, please see how he does not have himself in mind but gives himself for the well-being of his people. May God hear him for that reason." In all of this, the heart of the mediator speaks in Nehemiah. In him lives the Spirit of the Christ, in whom alone was perfect righteousness. The Christ is the one who gave Himself for the people.

449

Main thought: *The city of God is restored temporarily as a prophecy pointing to the Kingdom of God.*

The coming of the builder. After the reformation under Ezra, the people in Judah and Jerusalem again had to suffer much opposition because of the hatred from the side of the Samaritans. They had started to rebuild Jerusalem's walls, but an order came from King Artaxerxes that the building was to be stopped. Apparently Ezra retreated from public life. He was a scribe, and he occupied himself with the collection and examination of the books making up the Old Testament.

In those days a Jew named Nehemiah was the cupbearer at the court of Artaxerxes. He was a believer who held fast to the Word of the Lord. This Nehemiah received a communication from someone who had come from Jerusalem concerning the miserable condition of the people and the city. Deeply shocked, he resolved to intercede with the king in favor of Jerusalem.

He waited a few months as he prepared himself in prayer, basing his constant plea on the promises the Lord had given His people. Had the Lord not promised that He would bring His people back from the dispersion and again grant them glory in Jerusalem? He also prayed that the Lord would put it into the king's heart to be merciful to him. After all, even the king was a man whose heart the Lord could lead.

One day when Nehemiah went about his duties as cupbearer, the king asked him why he was so sad. The king was not accustomed to seeing him look sad. Now Nehemiah had to say what depressed him so. Trembling with fear, he managed to tell the king that it was the situation of the city in which his ancestors were buried that made him sad. When the king then asked what it was he wanted, Nehemiah answered, with his heart crying out to God for help, that he would like the king to send him to Jerusalem to rebuild the city. How hazardous that request was! It was Artaxerxes himself who had given the order to stop the building!

Evidently the king contemplated the request while the queen was sitting next to him. Her presence probably helped the cupbearer get a favorable response. How tensely Nehemiah must have waited! But God touched the king's heart, and he agreed to the request after Nehemiah set a certain time limit on his absence.

Nehemiah arrived in Jerusalem with an escort of horsemen. He was armed with letters of recommendation in which it was stipulated that the governors were to be helpful with everything Nehemiah needed for the building program. The one who was to restore Jerusalem in the name of the Lord had arrived! He was given by God Himself. In the same way, the Christ was given to us for the restoration of our life.

The building of the city. Nehemiah had not let the city officials and the nobles know the reason for his coming. First he wanted to make an investigation on his own. After a few days' rest, he went out of the gate by night accompanied by just a few men to investigate the condition of the walls. Evidently it was a night bright with the light of the moon. He found destruction everywhere. At a certain place there was so much rubble that the horse on which he was riding could not get through.

When he returned, he called the city officials and the nobles together and pointed out the deplorable state of the wall. Now he told them the purpose of his coming. He also told them how God had touched the king's heart in his favor. These words of Nehemiah gripped the hearts of the people. The Spirit of the Lord gave power to his words. The people saw that God's grace was turning to them again. Therefore they were immediately ready to get started on the work.

That Nehemiah had been wise by first acting in secret soon became clear. Rulers from the nations that lived in Canaan and the area around it came to Jerusalem when they heard rumors about the activity. They derided Nehemiah for the work he was doing and accused him of rebellion against the king. In answer Nehemiah only said that the God of heaven would make the work prosper. The Jews would just go on building. Their enemies despised them for this work in which they were engaged because nothing united them with Jerusalem or with the grace which God granted and revealed to that city.

Under Nehemiah's supervision, the work went on. Everybody, high and low, got involved; every family made a section of the wall its own responsibility. Safety would return to Jerusalem, and life there would be restored.

Nehemiah was a type of the Christ, who makes life safe and restores it. In His service, however, we must all work in close communion with one another to restore life, to make it once again a life in which God's righteousness prevails. Then there will be safety.

Only a few leaders refused to become involved. They were too high and mighty to be servants of the grace God bestowed upon His people. What an abomination! Fortunately, there were others who worked twice as hard. Even the women helped with the work.

Progress despite enmity. The hatred of the enemies of the Jews grew. And inside Jerusalem there were traitors who kept those enemies informed of what was going on. This happened because some of the enemies were married to women from Jerusalem.

A plot was hatched to attack Nehemiah and his men, but the plan leaked out. For this reason Nehemiah armed his men. Half of them served as armed guards; the other half served as builders, but they kept their swords in their belts. Those who carried the bricks held a spear in one hand. Nehemiah's men agreed that when they heard the sound of the trumpet, they would all mobilize to defend the city.

Nehemiah was not discouraged by the opposition. His faith stood up under this trial. He also encouraged the people, saying that God would fight for them. His faith was not in vain, for when the enemies learned that their plot had leaked out, they backed off. Nevertheless, it was essential to remain alert.

Nehemiah and his immediate helpers did not get out of their clothes day or night. Nehemiah had completely dedicated himself to his people and his work. Always within him was the Spirit of the Christ, who gave Himself for His people in a much higher sense. In His faithfulness, the Christ withstood all enmity.

The restoration of social justice. Nehemiah had to overcome still other difficulties. Great needs arose among some of the people because so many men had been taken out of the fields. Moreover, agriculture seems to have suffered some setbacks. The people began to complain. The rich oppressed the poor even though all the people, as members of the one people of God, were brothers.

Three categories of people were complaining. Those who had no possessions were forced to sell their sons and daughters into slavery. (This harsh custom was encouraged by the rich.) Then there were those who had to sell their possessions to be able to pay their debts. Finally there were those who, in order to be able to meet the demand for tribute imposed by the king of Persia, had taken out loans on their goods and had to come up with such high interest payments that they had practically nothing left.

This distressed Nehemiah. He called the rich people together and reproached them because the Lord's people were again being defamed among the heathen on their account. It is evident that justice did not prevail among God's people and that life was oppressed in their midst.

Once again Nehemiah's words gripped the hearts of the people, and they promised to act differently. He made them swear an oath to that effect. After they had taken the vow, he took hold of his robe in such a way that it formed a sack. Then he let it fall open. He shook out the bag, as it were, and said: "So shall the Lord shake out every man who does not keep this vow." The whole assembly voiced its amen and praised the Lord. They were all happy about the emancipation of life that was now going to come. And they stuck to their word too.

Nehemiah did not accept any of the compensation to which he was entitled as one of the Persian king's governors. He himself contributed toward the work of building the walls. Moreover, there were some 150 people at his table—Jews who had returned from the dispersion (Neh. 5:17). He prayed: "Remember for my good, O my God, all that I have done for this people" (5:19). He wanted the Lord to notice that in all uprightness he had done everything for the people, that he had not sought his own interests. He wanted God to remember him as the head of the people in the sense that God would bless the measures he took for them.

This makes our thoughts turn to the Christ, who gave Himself for His people and did not seek His own interests. The Christ in His Kingdom also intends to restore social justice.

Renewing the covenant. In the seventh month of the year in which the walls were rebuilt, all the people assembled in Jerusalem to celebrate the Feast of Tabernacles. At this feast Ezra read the law to all the people, and the Levites explained its meaning to them. Here Ezra came to the forefront again, next to Nehemiah.

The reading of the law made a deep impression on the people, and they began to weep and mourn for their sins. Ezra and the Levites admonished the people and told them that they should not cry at the feast but enjoy the Lord's favor. By being happy in the Lord, they would be strengthened. For the first time since the days of Joshua, they celebrated the feast in huts made of branches.

After the fasting was over, they held a day of feasting and prayer, a day on which they confessed their sins before the Lord in humble prayer. Then they renewed their covenant with the Lord, promising to walk in His ways. They would not mingle with the other nations, and they would keep the sabbath. They promised to make contributions for the house of the Lord, and the service of the priests was regulated.

In all of this Nehemiah set an example for them. He was a type of the Christ, who wants to renew the covenant between God and His people again and again. The Israelites of those days were still compelled to lament that they had not come to a position of complete freedom, that they still had to pay tribute to the Persian king. This restoration of Israel, too, was only temporary. The old covenant was coming to an end. The situation of those days cried out for the coming of the Christ, who would bring complete restoration and complete freedom from the power of sin.

The dedication of the wall. It took 52 days to rebuild the wall. Those were days of great tension because of the hatred from the side of the Jews' enemies. The people would not have been able to endure such tension for very long.

During this period the enemies tried more than once to lure Nehemiah outside Jerusalem under the pretext that someone was stirring up trouble for him at the Persian court. Shouldn't they confer together to see what could be done about that? One day someone tried to persuade him to flee into the Holy Place, telling him that his life was in danger. Nehemiah saw through all these ruses and always refused. When he was told to flee to the Holy Place, he answered that he was not afraid for his life and would not sin by going into the Holy Place. Again and again the enemies tried to halt the building of the wall and weaken Nehemiah's authority with the people. But Nehemiah was in a hurry for the sake of the work itself and because of his promise to the king of Persia that he would return.

Jerusalem's walls were now restored to their former condition. Thus Jerusalem was a large city again. But the number of inhabitants was small. Therefore Nehemiah divided the people and made some of them live in Jerusalem. In that way the city became populous again.

Finally the moment had come when the wall could be dedicated. Nehemiah put two choirs of thanksgiving on the west side of the wall, thanking and praising God. They would meet again in the east, near the temple. Also, a great sacrifice of thanksgiving was offered. The entire people rejoiced in the Lord. Now there was safety within the walls of Jerusalem again. This, too, was only a sign. How safe believers are since God Himself, for Christ's sake, is a wall of fire around them!

After that Nehemiah returned to Susa, as he had promised. However, some years later he was back in Jerusalem again. Then, too, he busied himself in the people's interest.

The enemies of the Jews, who had made the work of restoring the walls so difficult, had taken up residence in Jerusalem. Tobiah, who was related to the high priest Eliashib by marriage, had been given a room in the temple, where the law of the Lord was read. The law taught that the Ammonites and the Moabites were never to come into God's congregation because of the evil they had done to Israel. And Tobiah was an Ammonite!

Deeply moved by what the law decreed, Nehemiah put Tobiah out of the room, threw his furniture out, and ordered that the room be cleansed. He also saw to it that the people again gave the tithes they had neglected to give. He argued with those who did business on the sabbath, he had Jerusalem's gates closed during the sabbath, and he did not allow the Tyrian merchants to congregate outside the walls during that time.

Moreover, Nehemiah had to fight against the same evil as Ezra: some of the men had again taken foreign wives. In his zeal

Nehemiah argued with them, cursed them, struck them, and pulled out their hair. He made the people vow that they would not commit these sins again. He drove Jehoiada, the son of the high priest, out of the temple because one of his sons was married to the daughter of Sanballat the Horonite, who had opposed the building of the wall more than anyone else.

Thus Nehemiah maintained the discipline of the Lord among the people. The strongest walls are of no avail if the people within them do not live according to the law of the Lord. The Christ also called for discipline among His people. Only in obedience to the Lord's will is there safety under His protection.